Polis and Praxis

Polis and Praxis

Exercises in Contemporary Political Theory

Fred R. Dallmayr

The MIT Press
Cambridge, Massachusetts
London, England

This book was set in Baskerville
by The MIT Press Computergraphics Department
and printed and bound by The Murray Printing Co.
in the United States of America.

Library of Congress Cataloging in Publication Data

Dallmayr, Fred R. (Fred Reinhard), 1928–
  Polis and praxis.

  Includes bibliographical references and index.
  1. Political science. I.Title
JA71.D285   1984   320′.01′1   84–12252
ISBN 0–262–04078–6

For Dominique and Philip

Ecce haereditas domini filii filiaeque:
merces fructus ventris . . .

Contents

Preface

The present volume assembles a number of essays written during the past three or four years — essays that, following Hannah Arendt's lead, I call "exercises." As used here the term seeks to underscore the exploratory, non-systematic, or "*en route*" character of the individual chapters and the study as a whole. Political theory today, it seems to me, finds itself in a state of deep ferment or tension — a ferment arising from pervasive subterranean dislocations, or what Arendt at one point labeled a "crisis in culture." In this situation, political thought cannot be content with the rehearsal of canonical texts or the cultivation of past theoretical "systems" or doctrines — although, to be sure, there cannot be a direct exit from historical traditions or the history of ideas. As in the case of the much belabored "end of metaphysics," a move beyond traditional political teachings can only take the form of their dissemination and oblique insertion into a renewed assessment of political experience.

The exercises continue some investigations I had begun in an earlier study entitled *Twilight of Subjectivity*, a study that meant to offer building blocks for an emerging "post-individualist" theory of politics (where "post-individualist" is closely akin to what others prefer to call "post-modern"). Basically the focus of the previous volume was on the effects of the eclipse of subjectivity in various topical areas — more specifically: on the repercussions a "decentering" of the *cogito* was prone to have in the domains of intersubjectivity, man-nature relations, social development, and ethics. The present exercises are animated by similar concerns, though slanted toward more overtly political themes. Taken as a whole, the study raises again the question, What happens if the "subject" is dislodged as linchpin of theoretical inquiry? What would be the implications of this change for our understanding of political action or "*praxis*"; for the analysis of such key terms as political "power" and "freedom"; for the construal of political "conversation" and "discourse"; and, finally, for a proper assessment of political theory or philosophy itself? While addressing diverse issues, the assembled chapters are thus linked at least by a common problematic or set of central preoccupations.

The questioning of subjectivity also renders ambivalent the notion of an authorial subject as source of insights. Without in any way implicating them in my failings or shortcomings, the study gives ample room to a few philosophical or intellectual mentors whose works have nurtured my thinking in writing these essays. Foremost among these mentors are Martin Heidegger, Hans-Georg Gadamer, Maurice Merleau-Ponty, Michel Foucault, Michael Oakeshott, and Hannah Arendt. There are a number of other thinkers who, to a lesser degree but by no means marginally, form part of the conversational context giving rise to these chapters. Listing them in random sequence I want to recognize particularly the influence of William Connolly, Richard Bernstein, Hwa Yol Jung, William McBride, Calvin Schrag, Karl-Otto Apel, and Jürgen Habermas.

In mentioning these names together I do not wish to suggest a theoretical consensus among them—which would be patently inaccurate. Even among the group of primary mentors I am far from denying important differences of accent or perspective. Still, I believe these differences are not of the radical nature, and sometimes not of the kind, they are purported to be. Thus, in the case of Gadamer and Heidegger, I cannot at all agree with Habermas's claim, advanced in his *laudatio* for the former, that Gadamer's work involves the "urbanization of Heidegger's provincialism." This claim is disavowed by Gadamer himself who (in his *Heideggers Wege*) praises his teacher's far-flung impact, noting that "in order properly to assess Heidegger's presence one has to move to a global scale." In my view, the difference between the two has to do more with the distinction between prudential judgment and radical philosophical thought; and, as Gadamer would be the first to concur, prudence or moderation is not unequivocally a philosophical virtue.

In acknowledging my debt to particular thinkers, I should add, I do not mean to endorse indiscriminately their entire opus. In the case of Arendt, for example, I am uneasy about the neat segregation of political "action" from "labor" and "work"—although I find her categories useful and challenging for analytical purposes. The same might be said of Oakeshott's bifurcation of "enterprise" and "*civitas*." Concerning Foucault, *Twilight of Subjectivity* voiced reservations regarding the stark displacement or "end of man." His more recent publications, however, have gone a long way toward removing these apprehensions. Thus, I completely share his dislike of the "government of individualization" and his belief (expressed in "The Subject and Power") that the "problem of our days is not to try to liberate the individual from the state, and from the state's institutions, but to liberate us both from the state and from the type of individualization which is linked to the state. We have to promote new forms of subjectivity through the refusal of this kind of individuality which has been imposed on us for several centuries."

The boldness of Foucault's statements, and of many Heideggerian initiatives, is offset in the present volume by a cautious concern for continuity. Occasionally, the balance may be tilted strongly toward caution—as in the discussion of "conversation" (in the final chapter), which may shortchange the diversity of idioms. To a large extent, the balancing effort is motivated by a maieutic or pedagogical impulse: the desire for steadiness of learning through the maintenance of shared assumptions. At this point, I would like to single out a few young people whom I had the good fortune to teach during recent years and who fostered my maieutic sense: Stephen Schneck, whose careful dissertation on Scheler deepened my appreciation of this complex and mercurial thinker; John Burke, whose work on Arendt solidified my admiration and affinity (without removing divergences of detail); and, last but not least, Thomas Hancuch, whose intense mode of listening allowed me to say things in class I did not "know" before.

The manuscript was typed and retyped by Patricia Flanigan, whose efficient and reliable help I gratefully acknowledge. The volume is dedicated to my children, Dominique and Philip. May they be able to chart their own course "between past and future," tradition and innovation—in the direction, it is hoped, of a more peaceful and less exploitative cosmopolis.

May 1984

Polis and Praxis

Introduction

The opening lines of Martin Heidegger's *Letter on Humanism* read, "We are still far from pondering the essence of action (*Handeln*) seriously enough. We view action only as causing an effect; the actuality of the effect is judged by its utility. But the essence of action is accomplishment (*Vollbringen*)."[1] These lines, which date from 1946, were written chiefly in response to developments in French postwar philosophy, especially the rise of existentialism. Seen in its larger implications, however, the passage clearly carries a broader significance—a significance which has not diminished in the intervening decades. Since the time of the *Letter*, the existentialist concern with action has been seconded and amplified by parallel trends in analytical philosophy, trends concentrating on the intentionality of human behavior and on the role of intentions as causes of action and their effects.[2] On a still broader scale, it is possible to discern a subtle shift of attention in contemporary social and political thought: a shift involving a progressive deemphasis of epistemology in favor of pragmatic or "practical" preoccupations. Yet, in the absence of a further clarification of action and practice, the precise contours of this shift are bound to remain hazy or obscure. Basically, the boundaries of epistemology (and of traditional philosophy as such) can scarcely be unsettled by merely internal rearrangements or conceptual modifications—modifications evident, for example, in the substitution of a practical for a cognitive "subject" or the replacement of external causation by the internal-intentional production of effects. In light of the prevalence of such rearrangements Heidegger's statement, it seems to me, retain its relevance and sense of urgency even today.

Actually, the import of the passage is not restricted to recent or contemporary trends; its full significance, I believe, emerges only against the backdrop of a more long-range or epochal transformation—a transformation encapsulated in the label of the "end of metaphysics" and manifest in the decline or disappearance of great "metaphysical systems" since Hegel's time. As can plausibly be argued, virtually all philosophical perspectives or movements emerging since that period have in some fashion espoused a "pragmatic turn," that is, a shift of focus from cognitive-theoretical to practical issues. In the immediate aftermath of the Hegelian opus, a prominent case in point is Marx, whose *Theses on Feuerbach* extolled the role of "sensuous human activity" as a counterpoint to both idealist and materialistic metaphysics. Later in the same century, Nietzsche subordinated theoretical speculation and cognition to volitional endeavor, especially the so-called "will to power." Emphatic versions of the pragmatic turn characterize subsequent orientations in both European and Anglo-American settings (above and beyond the obvious case of "pragmatism"). In the latter context, the turn is prominently displayed in Wittgenstein's move from the empiricism of the *Tractatus* to the linguistic pragmatics of *Philosophical Investigations*, and more generally in the transition from positivism to a more "holistic" outlook stressing the concrete-historical parameters of inquiry. In the context of European phenomenology, Husserl's early accent on transcendental cognition was progressively challenged by more mundane and practical-existential modes of analysis—a change highlighted in Sartre's gradual displacement of "consciousness" in favor of existential and social "praxis."[3] The turn persists in post-existentialist (or "post-structuralist") European thought: thus, Foucault's writings deal not so much with discourses as "discursive practices," and less with substantive features than with the enactment of power or "power-action." Viewed cumulatively, the developments sketched lend historical support to Heidegger's admonition to ponder "seriously enough" the meaning or "essence" of human action.

In his *Letter on Humanism* Heidegger locates the meaning of action in "accomplishment" (*Vollbringen*), that is, an act of "bringing forth" or "bringing to fruition." Attributing an ontological status to the term—and thus differentiating it sharply both from subjective self-enactment and the instrumental production of effects—he writes, "To accomplish means to unfold something into the fullness of its being, to guide it forth into its fullness (*producere*). Therefore, we can really only accomplish what already 'is'; but what 'is' above and before everything is Being." Elsewhere, Heidegger describes genuine action as participation in an ontological event or happening: the disclosure of the "truth" of Being as it occurs in artworks and similarly creative initiatives. "Where 'bringing forth' specifically yields the open disclosure or truth of Being," we read in "The Origin of the Work of Art," "the accomplished result may be called a 'work'; bringing forth in this manner is the core of creative action (*Schaffen*)." According to Heidegger, however, creativity is not merely a causal-intentional act—the deed of a practical "ego"—but carries passive-receptive features as well: in the sense that the emerging "work" simultaneously transforms its agent. For this reason, "bringing forth appears rather as a receiving or borrowing within the arena of disclosure"—an aspect ignored by "modern subjectivism," which misconstrues creativity promptly as "the inspired feat of autonomous agents." In still another context, Heidegger links genuine action with a "poetic" mode of endeavor, using "poetic" in the sense of the Greek "*poiesis*" seen as a creative-ontological event. "Everything depends on our ability," he notes, "to grasp this 'bringing forth' (or *poiesis*) in its full scope and at same time in the spirit of the Greeks." Approached in this light, "bringing forth only comes to pass insofar as something enclosed or concealed unfolds into manifest appearance; this unfolding rests upon, or is involved in, what we call disclosure."[4]

The notion of a "practical ontology" or "ontological praxis" is not restricted to Heideggerian philosophy; traces of it can be found in numerous contemporary thinkers, including Merleau-Ponty and Foucault. In *The Visible and the Invisible* Merleau-Ponty speaks of a distinctive "praxis" which "does not hold before itself the words said and understood as objects of thought or ideas"—a praxis which, dislodged from subjective (ego-centered) moorings, reflects a kind of "neo-teleology": one "which no more permits being supported by a *consciousness of . . .*, nor by an ek-stasy, a constructive project, than does the perceptual teleology." Emphasizing the passive-receptive features of ontological praxis, the same study observes, "Philosophy has never spoken—I do not say of *passivity*: we are not effects—but I would say of the passivity of our activity, as Valéry spoke of a *body of the spirit*: new as our initiatives may be, they come to birth at the heart of being, they are connected onto the time that streams forth in us, supported on the pivots or hinges of our life." Without directly embracing ontological vocabulary Foucault's writings frequently betray a similar outlook.

Thus, in defining "discourses" as "practices" or modes of human praxis, he sharply segregates such praxis from causal-intentional designs. "I shall abandon any attempt," he writes, "to see discourse as a phenomenon of expression—the verbal translation of a previously established synthesis"; properly construed, "discourse is not the majestically unfolding manifestation of a thinking, knowing, speaking subject but, on the contrary, an arena in which the dispersion of the subject and his discontinuity with himself may be determined." Quasi-ontological overtones at least are present in another passage which speaks of "a metaphysics of the incorporeal event (which is irreducible to a physics of the world), a logic of neutral meaning (rather than a phenomenology of subject-based signification), and a thought of the present infinitive (in lieu of a mental derivation of the future from a past essence)."[5]

A decentered praxis—one not tied to a "thinking, knowing, speaking subject"—inevitably undercuts, without abolishing, the traditional distinction between theory and practice or between the active and the contemplative life. In any event, praxis in this sense is not the application of a prior theoretical blueprint, nor does it furnish (in a narrowly inductive vein) a reservoir of cognitive lessons. In his *Letter on Humanism* Heidegger places ontology explicitly at the threshold of the theory-practice dichotomy. Attentiveness to Being, he states, "is neither theoretical nor practical but comes to pass before this distinction." In particular, such attentiveness "transcends all (theoretical) contemplation since it tends to the light or clearing which alone renders possible seeing or contemplating as *theoria*." Simultaneously, the same outlook is "a doing or acting—but a doing which surpasses all (intentional or instrumental) practice"; what it pits against the latter is not the "grandeur of an achievement" nor the "range of its effects" but rather "the modesty of its inconsequential accomplishment." The unsettling impact of decentered praxis reverberates also in more recent philosophical literature. Thus, one of Foucault's books speaks of the possibility of "a new relationship between theory and practice. At one time, practice was considered an application of theory, a consequence; at other times, it had the opposite sense and was thought to inspire theory, to be indispensable for the articulation of new theoretical frameworks. In any event, their relationship was understood in terms of a process of totalization—a process where the two sides together would yield a homogeneous system. At the present juncture, however, the study notes, "the question is seen in a different light. The relationships between theory and practice are far more partial and fragmentary." While theory (in the cognitive sense) is "always local and related to a limited field," practice is simply "a set of relays from one theoretical point to another"—just as theorizing conversely can be considered "a relay from one practice to another."[6]

Discarding the theory-practice dichotomy does not mean abandoning its constitutive terms; but their sense and premises are bound to be seriously affected. Heideggerian ontology clearly does not relinquish philosophical inquiry—although he prefers to replace "philosophy" (and traditional metaphysics) by a more inconspicuous type of reflection which he calls "commemorative" or "recollective" thinking. Ontological reflection, his *Letter* states, "is (insofar as it happens) recollection of Being and nothing else." Such reflection, he elaborates, is essentially a "thinking *of* Being," in the dual sense that it "thinks about" and simultaneously "belongs to" or is claimed by Being—with the result that thinking never completely surveys or grasps its field (which always remains partially concealed). Ontological reflection, against this background, inevitably yields partial and discontinuous insights or glimpses—glimpses unable to coalesce into a full-fledged metaphysical system. In a more polemical vein, Foucault stresses the non-systematic character of theory. Attention to decentered events, he notes at one point, "requires a thought freed from contradiction, from dialectics, from negativity; thought that accepts divergence; affirmative thought whose instrument is disjunction; thought of the multiple." The happening of such events, he continues, "cannot be approached through the logic of the excluded third, because it is a dispersed multiplicity; it cannot be resolved by the clear distinctions of a Cartesian idea, because as an idea it is obscure-distinct; it does not respond to the seriousness of the Hegelian negative, because it is a multiple affirmation; it is not subjected to the contradiction of being and nothingness, since it is being" (with non-being itself inherent in being).[7]

Non-systematic theorizing of this kind is not the exclusive province of philosophers; tentative steps in the same direction have also been undertaken by some contemporary political thinkers. In one of his earliest writings, Michael Oakeshott advocated a subdued, non-totalizing mode of thought which "does not claim for philosophy any special source of knowledge hidden from other forms of experience" or any "immunity" from contingent events—a mode recognizing "neither 'authorities' nor 'established doctrines' which depend upon something extraneous to themselves for their establishment." The implications of this outlook are spelled out in greater detail in his more recent book *On Human Conduct*. Defending his preference for "theorizing" over alternative terms like "theory" or "theorems," Oakeshott notes, "My use of 'theorizing' as a transitive verb is not an inadvertence; it is the recognition of the enterprise as one of learning to understand; that is, as a transitive engagement." Although propelled by an "unconditional" commitment to learning, theorizing in this view does not pretend to systematic-epistemic knowledge, but only to an ongoing clarification of its own limitations or conditions of possibility. "The engagement of understanding," we read, "is not unconditional on account of the absence of conditions, or in virtue of a supposed terminus in an unconditional theorem; what constitutes its unconditionality is the continuous recognition of the conditionality of conditions. And consequently, this engagement to be perpetually *en voyage* may be arrested without being denied." As Oakeshott adds, "The theorist who drops anchor here or there and puts out his equipment of theoretic hooks and nets in order to take the fish of the locality, interrupts but does not betray his calling." In contrast, an investigation denying its conditionality "surrenders its opportunity of achieving its own conditional perfection" and therefore, in the end, "catches no fish."[8]

The notion of a conditional, non-systematic mode of theorizing surfaces also in several of Hannah Arendt's works, including her *Between Past and Future*. In that volume Arendt places theorizing or "thinking" in the "gap of time between past and future"—a gap which is not simply transtemporal but rather the "small non-time-space in the very heart of time." Echoing Heidegger's phrase of the "inconspicuous furrows" of thought (at the end of the *Letter on Humanism*), she describes the "path paved by thinking" as the "small track of non-time which the activity of thought beats within the time-space of mortal men and into which the trains of thought, of remembrance and anticipation, save whatever they touch from the ruin of historical and biographical time." Theorizing from this vantage point clearly is not a self-sufficient or "spectatorial" enterprise, nor can it produce a self-contained epistemic edifice. "My assumption," Arendt adds, "is that thought itself arises out of incidents of living experience and must remain bound to them as the only guideposts by which to take its bearings." The same volume also emphasizes the need of contemporary thought to

move beyond traditional (metaphysical) categories—a need which neither Kierkegaard nor Marx nor even Nietzsche fully managed to live
up to: "The traditional oppositions of *fides* and *intellectus*, and of theory
and practice, took their respective revenges upon Kierkegaard and
Marx, just as the opposition between the transcendent and the sen-
suously given took its revenge upon Nietzsche, not because these oppositions still had roots in valid human experience, but, on the contrary,
because they had become mere concepts, outside of which, however,
no comprehensive thought seemed possible at all."[9]

The dislodging or decentering character of experience affects not
only thinking but human action as well. As one should note, the term
"experience" in the present context is not equivalent to "sense perception" (in the empiricist tradition), but rather signifies a complex
learning and seasoning process—a process transforming agents in the
midst of actions, thus disclosing, in Merleau-Ponty's words, "the passivity of our activity." The contours of this non-empiricist (and non-
idealist) conception are fleshed out at some length in Merleau-Ponty's
Phenomenology of Perception. Commenting upon the genesis of both
cognition and practical initiatives he observes, "It is upon our experience
of the world that all our logical operations concerned with significance
must be based; but the world itself is not a fixed significance common
to all our experiences which we discern in them, some (uniform) idea
which breathes life into the growth of knowledge." Countering the
pretensions of spectatorial formulas, the study insists that the experiencing agent "does not successively occupy different points of view
beneath the gaze of some unlocated consciousness which is reflecting
on them." Unable to obtain a prior synthetic overview of experience,
neither the theorist nor the agent can pursue their respective endeavors
in an unscathed manner: "My voluntary and rational life, therefore,
knows that it merges into another power which stands in the way of
its completion"; given this ongoing challenge or incursion, "what I
understand never quite tallies with my living experience, in short, I
am never quite at one with myself." A similar non-empiricist conception
also surfaces in some of Foucault's arguments, especially when he
opposes "actual experiences" to abstract utopian blueprints. "If scientific socialism emerged from the *Utopias* of the nineteenth century,"
he states at one point, "it is possible that a real socialization will
emerge, in the twentieth century, from *experiences.*"[10]

Transformative experience plays a key role in the political thinkers mentioned—far beyond the range of previously cited passages. Thus, Oakeshott's *Experience and Its Modes* offered a careful analysis of the experiential underpinnings of both cognition and practical behavior. Likewise, his definition of political action as the "pursuit of intimations"—in *Rationalism in Politics*— can be interpreted without difficulty in an experiential vein. The broader, practical-ontological connotations of the term are highlighted most dramatically in one of Arendt's early writings. Portraying the general attitude or disposition of a kindred spirit, Rahel Varnhagen, Arendt observes, "Her whole effort was to expose herself to life so that it could strike her 'like a storm without an umbrella'." Congruent with this effort, "she preferred not to use characteristics or opinions on persons she encountered, on the circumstances and conditions of the world, on life itself, for purposes of shelter. . . . All that remained for her to do was to become a 'mouthpiece' for *experience*, to verbalize whatever happened." Needless to say, to serve as such a mouthpiece was neither comforting nor reassuring, for experiences typically transgress or outstrip customary moorings: "The particular traits one had to have or to marshal within oneself were an unflagging alertness or capacity for pain; one had to remain susceptible and conscious."[11]

What renders experience in this sense vulnerable is its non-isolation or lack of enclosure, that is, its openness to the "world"—which (next to our natural habitat) is chiefly a world of fellow humans. To the extent that it is marked by reciprocal action or interaction, this world takes on the features of a public-political space or a "polis"—which is the central focus of the present volume. Again, Arendt's writings provide crucial guideposts in this terrain, especially her differentiation of "political action" or "praxis" from instrumental fabrication ("work") and causal-mechanical reaction ("labor")—although Oakeshott's distinction between political or "civil associations" and instrumental "enterprise associations" can fruitfully be invoked along similar lines.[12] As used here, the terms "polis" and "praxis" mutually support and explicate each other, in the sense that "polis" is a public space constituted and maintained by praxis, just as genuine "praxis" or political interaction is possible only in a public arena. Seen as an outgrowth of experiential praxis, "polis" is not a synonym for a homogeneous organism or self-contained "system," and even less for a merger of particular designs in a uniform common will (endowed with supreme power or "sovereignty"). For similar reasons, political interaction cannot be equated with habitual or consensual concordance, nor conversely with sheer hostility: since the first would submerge praxis in knowledge (if not in apathy), while the second would replace it by mutual isolation or else by one-sided subjugation. Together with Arendt and Foucault, I view politics basically as an "agonal" undertaking—that is, as a tensional, serious-playful contest revolving around the quality or excellence and ultimately the very "point" of political life. Using slightly different vocabulary, politics can also be described as the cultivation of a particular interhuman "practice": namely, the practice of "friendship"—a term denoting not so much personal intimacy as a public relationship steeped in mutual respect and a willingness to let one another "be."[13]

The view of politics sketched needs to be amplified in several respects. First of all, as indicated, "polis" does not coincide with a uniform epistemic or volitional structure. In the modern setting I consider it particularly important to differentiate polis from the "State," and especially from the so-called "nation-state"—notwithstanding Hegel's portrayal of the State as incarnation of universal reason. Whatever considerations may have justified this portrayal at an earlier juncture, events during the past hundred years have inexorably revealed the State's baser lineage: as an embodiment not of reason but of ethnic emotions and an aggressive chauvinism. The hazards implicit in this lineage are immeasurably heightened in our time by the State's monopoly of force—which, in the case of the "superpowers," means monopoly of nuclear force. "The chief reason warfare is still with us," Arendt observes at one point, "is neither a secret death wish of the human species, nor an irrepressible instinct of aggression, nor, finally and more plausibly, the serious economic and social dangers inherent in disarmament, but the simple fact that no substitute for this final arbiter in international affairs [that is, the state] has yet appeared on the political scene." Nor, she adds, "is a substitute likely to appear so long as national independence, namely, freedom from foreign rule, and the sovereignty of the state, namely, the claim to unchecked and unlimited power in foreign affairs, are identified."[14] Against this background, a cultivation of polis-life today requires a strengthening of political interaction in contexts situated both below and above the level of the State; differently put: only a combination of local or regional politics with the emerging institutions of "cosmopolis"—that is, a linkage of closeness and distance—can curb the arrogance of State-centered force.

The linkage of closeness and distance also has a bearing on the description of politics as a practice of friendship. Joined with the emphasis on local and regional interaction, the description might suggest a one-sided preference for familiar bonds and customary-traditional settings—which runs counter to the internationalism and global interpenetration of cultures characterizing our age. This impression tends to be heightened by accounts which associate the practice with a devotion to "familiarity" or else insist on the segregation of friends from enemies. In my view, however, such accounts ignore important facets of the practice. In cultivating a friendship, I believe, we also become susceptible to a certain uniqueness or unfamiliarity which we do not wish to invade or transgress—a belief congruent with a Heideggerian passage which depicts man basically as a "creature of distance," or rather as a creature whose farness emerges precisely under conditions of nearness or close proximity.[15] Thus, attention to proximate surroundings and local settings is able and likely to generate also a taste for the unfamiliar or for what Eichendorff at one point called "beautiful strangeness" (schöne Fremde), and consequently for those distant lands and cultures which internationalists today rightly pit against narrow modes of ethnocentrism. On the other hand, the stress on familiarity is in one sense not entirely misguided. Only by participating in local and regional affairs, it seems to me, do we learn, and become proficient in, political practice or praxis in general—while the reverse procedure invariably ends in speculative abstractions. From this perspective, local and regional politics emerges as the training ground for global interactions, and the small-scale polis as the laboratory for cosmopolis.

The emphasis on local practices, one should also note, is not meant in a simply static-descriptive sense—which would submerge politics in conventionalism or habitual routines. Given the experiential, open-ended character of praxis, politics on every level exhibits also an innovative or transformative quality, a quality which for some purposes might be called its "normative" dimension. What renders the latter term dubious or suspect is its complicity in traditional antinomies, especially in the empirical-normative or "fact-value" polarities. From the vantage point of this volume, politics is not merely a prevailing mode of conduct, but also—and simultaneously—an undertaking nurtured by memories and future aspirations, especially aspirations for the "good life" (to use classical vocabulary). In view of this intrinsic multidimensionality, I cannot readily subscribe to the polarities mentioned, nor to the rigid opposition between custom and ethical imperatives or between tradition and freedom. For the same reason, I cannot endorse a simple ethical traditionalism—even in the subtle form recently articulated by Alasdair MacIntyre. Although sharing his appreciation of public "virtue" (or "virtues"), I find implausible his vindication of traditional communal ethics against radical innovation, encapsulated in the stark alternative "Nietzsche or Aristotle?"[16] Unless amenable to constant challenge and reexamination, even admirable habits or ways of life degenerate into platitudes or restrictive prejudices, thus undermining the requisites of experiential political praxis. On the other hand, to remain relevant (and avoid paternalism), ethical reform cannot blandly ignore communal bonds. Differently phrased: moral "transvaluation" occurs not simply through an exodus from public life, but rather through its deepening and restructuring—a process for which friendship on its various levels provides again an instructive model.

The ambition of this study is not to offer a close-knit propositional framework, which would run counter to its non-totalizing perspective; shunning systematic ambitions, the volume rather assembles a series of theoretical "exercises"—all of which deal with facets of the polis-praxis correlation. As used here, exercises denote tentative and only partially continuous explorations, that is, a theorizing "en route" venturing—albeit hesitantly—beyond traditional categories and philosophical benchmarks. Both the term and its explorative connotations are actually borrowed from Hannah Arendt, whose *Between Past and Future* staked out a similar path. As Arendt remarked at the time, her book was "an experience in thinking"—which "can be won, like all experience in doing something, only through practice, through exercises." Not aspiring to either inductive or deductive certainty, she added, the inquiries in her book endeavored only "to gain experience in how to think; they do not contain prescriptions on what to think or which truth to hold." Pertinent to my purposes are also her comments on the style of presentation, particularly on the essay format. "The essay as a literary form," she wrote (correctly, I believe), "has a natural affinity to the exercises I have in mind"; what holds them together is "not the unity of a whole but of a sequence of movements which, as in a musical suite, are written in the same or related keys."[17]

The opening essay of the volume reviews in broad lines the situation of "political philosophy today," analyzing the general shift from a more cognitive-epistemic outlook, represented by Leo Strauss, to a practical-ontological perspective as formulated by Heidegger and Merleau-Ponty; the essay portrays politics basically as the inauguration, cultivation, and refashioning of the practice of friendship, paying tribute in this respect to both Arendt and Aristotle. The second chapter explores the notion of political praxis and its relation to "experience," drawing inspiration chiefly from the arguments of Gadamer as well as the writings of Arendt and Oakeshott, while simultaneously differentiating praxis from the Habermasian view of communicative action. The next two chapters pursue the implications of such praxis, concentrating specifically on the effects of experiential decentering or dispossession on the status of "power" and human "freedom." Regarding the former topic, the third essay portrays Foucault's evolving conception of a "nonproprietary" and "capillary" power, paying particular attention to his distinction between power and violence—a distinction loosely akin to Arendt's thoughts in this area. Since, in Foucault's treatment, power is intimately linked with human freedom, the essay prepares the ground for the following chapter, devoted to the discussion of Heidegger's political perspective and especially his "ontology of freedom." Deviating from widespread interpretations, the chapter basically depicts Heidegger as a philosopher of freedom (and solidarity), although freedom in his case signifies less a human capacity or possession than a condition of possibility of action.[17]

The investigation of power and freedom furnishes the backdrop for the two following chapters, dealing with the merits and disadvantages of Habermasian "critical theory." Relying on Foucault's (and Heidegger's) notion of decentered and discontinuous praxis, the fifth chapter raises the question to which extent critical theory may be described as a "humanism," that is, a man-centered outlook treating freedom basically as a personal faculty and emancipation as progressive liberation from power and politics. After recapitulating some historical background of the theory (stretching as far back as Marx), the essay reaches the conclusion that at least the Habermasian version carries strong "humanist" overtones—a conclusion which is not meant to denigrate personal initiative and responsibility, but only to alert to their opaque philosophical premises. The merits of Habermas's posture emerge more strongly in the context of "applied" political inquiry, and especially in the field of "public policy" analysis: countering narrowly technocratic and empiricist tendencies, Habermas's emphasis on critical "discourse" opens policymaking up to broad-scale public deliberation and scrutiny—although, in my view, discourse needs to be reformulated in the sense of a more open-ended conversation, and policymaking subordinated more fully to the non-purposive dimensions of polis-life. The concluding essay provides an overview of diverse modes of communicative interaction, moving beyond Habermasian categories. On the basis of Gadamer's hermeneutics as well as Oakeshott's comments on the various "idioms" of speech, the chapter distinguishes between four main types of exchanges: general conversation, pragmatic or everyday "chatter," epistemological and normative discourse, and poetic-innovative speech; without collapsing praxis into linguistic interaction, an effort is finally made to correlate this scheme with distinct facets of politics. (The appendix explores in detail the topics of "life-world" and "communicative action" as delineated in Habermas's recent work.)

In criticizing humanism as well as introducing novel aspects of power and freedom, the exercises sketched join contemporary forays into "post-metaphysical" terrain—but without impatience or reckless haste. As such the move in this direction is far from whimsical or idiosyncratic: its impulse derives chiefly from the discontinuity of our age, and especially from the rupture of the long-standing tradition of Western thought. The fact of this rupture and its implications for political theory have nowhere been more forcefully expressed than in Arendt's writings. "When the thread of tradition finally broke," she observes at one point, "the gap between past and future ceased to be a condition peculiar only to the activity of thought and restricted as an experience to those few who made thinking their primary business. It became a tangible reality and perplexity for all; that is, it became a fact of political relevance."[18] However, recognition of this perplexity led her not simply to discard traditional concepts, but rather to reassess and rethink their point or status. This is also the general mood prevailing in this volume—a mood reflected in the combination of mentors invoked. Without alleging a bland uniformity, the following essays steer a precarious course between Gadamer and Heidegger, between Merleau-Ponty (in his existentialist leanings) and Foucault, and also between Oakeshott and Arendt. In general theoretical terms, this course tries to strike a balance between continuity and discontinuity, familiarity and unfamiliarity, metaphysics and post-metaphysics. On a concrete political level, the same course involves a blending of local praxis and global interaction, of polis and cosmopolis.

1
Political Philosophy Today

Esurientes . . .

Engaging in "political philosophy," or broaching it as a topic, today requires justification if not an apology. As a label for an intellectual or academic pursuit, the phrase certainly cannot match the compactness of "biochemistry" or "nuclear physics." In the latter cases, irrespective of the talents or shortcomings of individual practitioners, widespread agreement prevails regarding the legitimacy or feasibility of the disciplines as domains of inquiry. Not so with respect to "political philosophy," taken as an ongoing (and not merely retrospective) enterprise. For some time now, at least since the turn of the century, this enterprise has been severely ailing; actually, in the eyes of some, it has not only been moribund but become extinct. A number of postmortems have been written over the past decades, and although in many ways exaggerated or premature, accounts of this nature have been indicative of a widespread uneasiness regarding the intellectual viability or possibility of political reflection.[1] Even where the enterprise continues to be championed, its traditional designation carries overtones of an oxymoron: its constituent elements—politics and philosophy—seem related only through antithesis, after the fashion of "cruel kindness" or "pious scoundrel."

This is a slightly revised version of my inaugural address presented at the University of Notre Dame on 21 March 1980.

Among the factors responsible for this state of affairs, positivism
has frequently been singled out as the chief culprit or causal influence.
This assessment is not entirely unwarranted, given positivism's narrow
focus on empirical-scientific knowledge and its almost complete disregard of practical-human issues, a disregard predicated on the presumed unsuitability of these issues for philosophical or scientific
investigation. Yet, positivists have not been alone in this neglect. At
least during the first part of this century, almost all the leading thinkers—including Wittgenstein, Whitehead, and Husserl—were united in
their abstinence from political topics or in their reticence to deal with
them as philosophers. Most of them would probably have agreed with
Wittgenstein's statements which appear toward the close of his *Tractatus*,
published in 1921: "We perceive that even if *all possible* scientific questions should be answered, our life problems are not yet even touched
upon. But, of course, there is then no more problem; and this is
precisely the answer. The correct method of philosophy would really
be this: to say nothing but what can actually be said, that is, only
propositions of natural science—something which has nothing to do
with philosophy."[2]

To be sure, the precarious condition of political philosophy has at
no time been indicative of an actual or imminent demise of either
philosophy or politics per se. In the philosophical arena, our century
from its inception has witnessed momentous advances in logical rigor
and analytical precision. Both inside and outside the positivist camp,
philosophers made bold strides toward uncovering the ultimate foundations of pure scientific or theoretical knowledge, foundations completely untarnished by mundane contingencies. While Russell and
Whitehead, in the *Principia Mathematica*, resumed and implemented
the Leibnizian project of a "mathesis universalis," Wittgenstein's *Tractatus* sought to pinpoint the logical structure of a fully transparent,
universal language which would replicate the structure of the real
world. Similar aspirations were present also in other philosophical
camps. While neo-Kantian thinkers tried to regain access to Platonic
"ideas" by probing the transcendental-logical dimension of consciousness, Husserl's phenomenology aimed at capturing "essences" or the
essential features of phenomena by "bracketing" contingent details
as well as naively held opinions characteristic of the "natural (or non-
reflective) attitude." All of these efforts have to be seen as silhouetted
against the stark backdrop of successive political cataclysms and con-

vulsions, a sequence including two world wars, the collapse of empires, worldwide economic depression, and the rise of fascism and totalitarian regimes. Clearly, politics has not been dormant during our era. Apart from repeated catastrophies our century, deviating from liberal models of the past, has spawned the emergence of centralized bureaucracies, vast mass movements, and fervently held ideological creeds—trends which were incompatible with, and even diametrically opposed to, the philosophical ambitions sketched. Commenting on the *Tractatus* and its aftermath during the interbellum period, the historian Stuart Hughes has pointed to the absence of a serious "philosophy that could speak to the ordinary citizen about problems close to his most pressing concerns." Once the gulf between thought and practice had become irremediable, he added, the outcome was predictable: "The meticulous scientists of words and symbols and the 'terrible simplifiers' of Jacob Burckhardt's nineteenth-century nightmare, in their mutually incompatible endeavors, would have the field all to themselves."[3]

It is probably fair to observe that today we are no longer quite in the same predicament highlighted by Hughes in the interbellum years. A number of farsighted and perceptive thinkers in the meantime have focused their attention on the political domain, thus narrowing somewhat the gulf separating thought and practice. However, it seems equally fair to say that the basic quandary has not been significantly lessened and, more important, that the possibility of linking reflection and politics, and thus the intellectual viability of "political philosophy," has by no means been fully shown or clarified. One promising strategy to make headway in this dilemma may be to concentrate initially on the meaning or meanings of "philosophy" as viewed in contemporary thought (or some versions of contemporary thought), in the hope of gathering clues for the clarification of our theme. This is the strategy I intend to follow in the present chapter.

What I propose to do is, first of all, to probe in somewhat greater detail the distinctive character or significance of "philosophy" in our age, with the goal of drawing subsequently some inferences or lessons for our topic, the meaning of "political philosophy today." Regarding the first task or probe, I would like to take my cues primarily from two prominent thinkers of our century—thinkers whose arguments, in my view, reveal with particular poignancy the undercurrents and subterranean transformations in contemporary thought and who, I might add, have been for me a source of intellectual nourishment and inspiration for many years: Martin Heidegger and Maurice Merleau-Ponty. Instead of ranging broadly over their writings, I shall concentrate mainly (though not exclusively) on two relatively succinct essays or accounts. As it happens, both accounts were written roughly at the same time, about a decade after World War II and articulated in a French context: the first is Heidegger's essay on *What Is Philosophy?* (Qu'est-ce que la philosophie?), presented as opening statement at a colloquium held in 1955 in Cerisy-la-Salle in Normandy; the second is Merleau-Ponty's address *In Praise of Philosophy* (Éloge de la philosophie), delivered as his inaugural lecture at the Collège de France in 1953. Having delineated the major thrust of these writings, I shall shift attention from philosophy to political philosophy. At this point, in order to gain my bearings in that domain, I intend to focus briefly on a justly celebrated and well-known formulation of our theme, perhaps the most well-known formulation in the postwar period: Leo Strauss's study entitled *What Is Political Philosophy?*, whose lead essay bearing the same title was written and first presented at about the same time as Heidegger's address. After offering an assessment of Strauss's formulation, I shall, by way of conclusion, sketch some of my own concerns and preoccupations and some central issues which, in my judgment, political philosophy faces today.

I

The question raised in Heidegger's essay *What Is Philosophy?* does not merely aim at the clarification of a school doctrine or particular philosophical standpoint; the issue is not merely to define the meaning of "analytical philosophy," or "linguistic philosophy," or even of "phenomenology," or "existential phenomenology" (although, as is well-known, Heidegger's outlook is strongly indebted to the latter orientation). Nor is the concern simply to gain a general overview of the various conceptions of philosophy advanced in different epochs of history and then, through a process of distillation and abstraction, to arrive at a common denominator or universal definition. As Heidegger notes, such an approach "can indeed be carried out with great erudition and with the help of much accurate information." Proceeding in this way, we may be able to "acquire thorough, differentiated, and even useful knowledge about how philosophy has been presented or treated in the course of its history." However, he adds, "in so doing we do not in the least have to enter into philosophy in such a manner as to reflect upon (and let our thinking be guided by) the nature of philosophy." Thus, "along this path we shall never reach a genuine, that is, a legitimate answer to the question: what is philosophy?"[4]

According to the essay, to be legitimate or appropriate the answer to the question has to be "a philosophizing answer—one which, as a response, philosophizes itself." In order to arrive at such a response, the original question has to be understood not simply as an exhortation to conduct a detached semantic analysis but as an invitation to participate in an ongoing philosophical enterprise or to join in the act of philosophizing. "When we ask: What is philosophy?, we seem to be talking *about* philosophy," Heidegger writes. "By asking in this way we are apparently taking a stand above and, therefore, outside of philosophy. But the aim of our question is to enter *into* philosophy, to tarry in it, to conduct ourselves in its manner, that is, to 'philosophize'." To address ourselves properly to the initial question thus requires abandoning a "spectator's" perspective in favor of a readiness to become embroiled in the question to the extent that we are "moving within philosophy and not outside of it or around it"; such an embroilment in turn presupposes, however, that philosophy is not purely a cerebral exercise but that it affects us and *matters* to us—and matters not only incidentally but in our whole life or in our core. "The path of our discourse," we read, "must therefore be of such a kind and direction that whatever philosophy deals with concerns us directly, that it touches us (*nous touche*) and indeed touches us in our very nature."[5]

In attempting to delineate the meaning of philosophy seen not as a technical-professional specialty but as a central human preoccupation, Heidegger points to its distant historical origins: its beginnings in classical Greek thought. As he insists, only through a recollection of its long-standing antecedents can the term acquire its distinctive significance. "If," he observes, "we use the word 'philosophy' no longer as a worn-out title and, instead, hear it in the context of its source, then it sounds thus: *'he philosophia'*." The term "philosophy" now "speaks to us in Greek" and "as a Greek word indicates a path" or direction signal. The reference to historical origins reflects not only an antiquarian interest; rather, it is prompted by the circumstance that philosophy first began to *matter* seriously in classical Greece and that it first shaped the experiential core of Greek life—an influence which was bequeathed as a legacy and challenge to subsequent Western civilization. In a passage which almost literally harks back to statements of his teacher, Edmund Husserl (in *The Crisis of European Sciences*), Heidegger affirms the basically philosophical character of the "Western mission," a character manifested in the global repercussions of its modes of inquiry: "The statement that philosophy is in its nature Greek says in essence that Europe and the West (and these only) are in the innermost course of their history originally 'philosophical'; this is attested by the rise and dominance of the sciences." To perceive our place in the world, against this background, necessitates attentiveness to the Greek tradition, a tradition which is not a straitjacket but a matrix for continued self-clarification: "The word *philosophia*," he adds, "appears, as it were, on the birth certificate of our own history — even on the birth certificate of the contemporary epoch which is called the atomic age. That is why we can ask the question, What is philosophy? only by entering into dialogue with Greek thought." The impact of Greek thought, moreover, is evident not only in the term "philosophy," but also in the formulation of the question "What is?" (or "*ti estin*") — at least to the extent that the query concerns not merely the identity of particular objects but seeks to grasp the basic meaning or point, that is, the "whatness" or *quidditas*, of everything encountered in the world. Thus, one can say that "both the theme of our question — 'philosophy' — as well as the way in which we ask 'what is that . . . ?' are and remain Greek in origin."[6]

According to Heidegger's account, the antecedents of our theme can be traced back to the pre-Socratics, the time of Heraclitus and Parmenides. During that period, the term "*philosophos*" made its appearance, a term which designated a special kind of "lover": namely, the lover of the "*sophon*" or a sort of wisdom. The wisdom or insight cherished in this case can, in Heidegger's view, be elucidated through the Heraclitean aphorism "*Hen Panta*," meaning "all is one" — where "all" refers to all particular things and "one" to the fabric in which all things cohere or are gathered. The love of the *philosophos* thus concerned the manner in which all things are maintained or sustained in being or, differently phrased, in which "Being" sustains and gathers all particular things or beings. While insight or wisdom of this sort was still immediately available or accessible to the pre-Socratics, subsequent generations had to make a deliberate effort to grasp the *sophon* or to raise it to the level of a question — an effort which became the hallmark of *philosophia*. Once the question was asked, What is any thing or being insofar as it *is*? (or: What is the Being of all particular beings?), Heidegger notes, "thinking turned into 'philosophy' " in the Greek sense; philosophy became a "kind of aptness or competence enabling the inquirer to focus on being (any particular being) in respect to what it is insofar as it has being." Prepared by the Sophists, he adds, "the move or step to 'philosophy' was first undertaken by Socrates and Plato. Then, almost two centuries after Heraclitus, Aristotle characterized the move through the following statement: 'Thus, what is sought (by philosophy) both in previous times as well as now and in all the future and which forever seems to elude it, is encapsulated in the question: What is being (*ti to on*)?'"[7]

Ever since the time of Socrates and Plato—but preeminently in the context of Greek thought—philosophy therefore designated not so much an aimless curiosity but the unsettling quandary of how anything is or can be (or how there is Being). Yet, although the basic thrust of philosophy has remained fairly constant over time, Heidegger argues, the particular manner in which the central question was raised or the way in which it was treated and answered has tended to vary over time. In classical Greek philosophy, the question was on the whole given a substantive-ontological treatment, in the sense that Being was seen as substantive foil or supporting ground or fountainhead of particular beings. Thus, in the previously mentioned passage, Aristotle continued by paraphrasing his statement in these terms: "This question (namely, what is being?) signifies: what is the 'isness' or 'essence' of beings? (*tis he ousia?*)" For classical Greek thought, Heidegger comments, "the Being of beings consists in the 'isness' or essence; the latter, however, is further specified by Plato as 'idea' and by Aristotle as '*energeia*' (or actuality)." The manner in which Aristotle perceived the functioning of Being construed as *ousia* or *energeia* can be gleaned from a sentence in the first book of his *Metaphysics* where he says that "philosophy is '*episteme ton proton archon kai aition theoretike*'," that is, a theoretical grasp of first principles or ultimate foundations or causes.[8]

The crucial issue for Heidegger is the character of philosophy or philosophical inquiry—not so much the nature of particular answers or solutions offered at various times, including the era of classical Greece. The definition offered by Aristotle, he writes, may, with some provisos, be considered as "*one* answer among many others." Although, with the help of Aristotle's formulation, it is feasible to reconstruct and interpret both "the thinking before Plato and Aristotle" and later developments, it can "easily be pointed out that philosophy itself and the manner in which it conceives its own enterprise have changed in many ways during the subsequent two thousand years." Actually, with regard to the emergence of *philosophia*, Heidegger finds a sharp break between the pre-Socratics and later thinkers which renders difficult a reconstruction of the former through classical categories. Even within the history of ancient Greece, we read, the Aristotelian definition "is only one particular interpretation of Greek thought and of the task assigned to it" and "can in no case be transferred back to the thinking of Heraclitus and Parmenides." Regarding later changes or modifications, the essay points especially to the Cartesian quest for certainty or certain knowledge anchored in the *cogito*, a quest which inaugurated "modern" philosophy. "In his *Meditations*," the address states, "Descartes asks not only or not in the first place the question '*ti to on*' — what is being insofar as it *is*? Rather, he queries: what is *that* being which is truly being in the sense of certainty (or *ens certum*)." As a result, "certainty becomes the yardstick for that specification of Being (*ens qua ens*) which derives from the indubitability of the *cogito (ergo) sum* for man's ego. Thereby, the ego emerges as the distinctive *subjectum* and the nature of man enters for the first time the domain of subjectivity in the sense of ego."[9]

Yet, despite the manifold changes and transformations, Heidegger assigns to the classical, and especially Aristotelian, formulation a privileged status in the history of Western philosophy. "We must not overlook the circumstance," he notes, "that, precisely in and through all its changes, philosophy from Aristotle to Nietzsche has remained the same or unified." The nature of this unity is not directly spelled out in the essay discussed; however, Heidegger has repeatedly elaborated on the topic on other occasions, usually under the labels of traditional or Western "metaphysics" and of a possible "end of metaphysics." Thus, in his inaugural lecture of 1929, entitled "What Is Metaphysics?," traditional metaphysics was presented as a speculative ontology in which the central philosophical question (*ti to on*) was phrased as an inquiry into the essence of beings per se or in their totality, a totality which, in turn, was derived from a substantive foundation or "ground" or an underlying "first cause." In view of this reliance on a substantive foundation, Heidegger at later points defined or circumscribed traditional metaphysics as "onto-theology," that is, as an ontology in which the first cause is *"causa sui."* He has also expressed his reservations with regard to this legacy. "The onto-theological character of metaphysics," he noted in an address in 1957, "has become questionable for us, not because of any atheism, but rather because of the experience of a thinking which has perceived in onto-theology the as yet *unreflected* unity of the nature of metaphysics." In the context of the essay discussed here (*What Is Philosophy?*), he addresses a similar reservation with Aristotle, namely, his definition of philosophy in terms of "first principles and causes." "After two-and-a-half thousand years," he observes, "it would seem to be about time to ponder what the Being of being(s) has to do with 'principles' and 'causes'. *In what sense is Being conceived that such things as 'principle' or 'cause' appear qualified to set their seal upon, and take charge of, the Being of beings?*"[10]

Reservations of this kind are not intended as a rejection of traditional philosophy, but only as a safeguard against dogmatic acceptance and repetition. In the context of the essay discussed, criticism of metaphysics is designed mainly to stimulate a rethinking of its premises, a rethinking which requires a willingness to take seriously the basic questions guiding past philosophers and to engage them in discourse in terms of these questions. To embark on the task of philosophizing, Heidegger states, presupposes that "we enter into dialogue with (traditional) philosophers" seen as practitioners of *philosophia*. In dealing with metaphysics or any other mode of thought, "it is one thing to delineate and describe the opinions of philosophers; it is an entirely different thing to discuss and talk through with them what they are saying or about what they are speaking." Given the perennial question of *philosophia* (*ti to on*) and assuming that philosophers have always been preoccupied with articulating or saying "what (any) being is insofar as it *is*," our discourse or dialogue with them "must also be governed by the same concern, namely, with the Being of being(s)." Although averse to doctrinaire repetition, Heidegger emphasizes, philosophical questioning and rethinking thus signifies not actually "a break with the past nor a repudiation of history, but rather an effort of appropriation and transformation." It is precisely this latter effort which is meant by the term "destruction" (as used in *Being and Time*). "Destruction," he notes, "does not designate demolition, but rather a careful dismantling, decomposing, and bracketing—namely, the bracketing of merely historical assertions about the course of philosophy. Destruction means: to open our ears, to emancipate or free ourselves for what speaks to us in traditional thought as the 'Being of being(s)'; by listening to this interpellation we become attentive and attuned to this question."[11]

The essay *What Is Philosophy?* does not indicate directly what a re-thinking of *philosophia* might concretely entail or what might be an appropriate contemporary response to the perennial question (*ti to on*); however, Heidegger has not been entirely silent on that score in other contexts. When addressing himself to the issue, what he seems to find dubious or "questionable" in traditional ontology is chiefly its tendency to effect a "doubling of the world," either by juxtaposing a world of "essences" to the world of "appearances" or by stipulating a substantive foundation or cause of the world—a criticism which does not proceed from a motivation to collapse or curtail the tension implicit in the thrust of *philosophia*. Although dealing with the "Being of being(s)," Heidegger argues, traditional thought has tended to focus on the component terms as distinct realms and on their precarious relationship—but without thinking through the distinction itself. In his view, however, the phrase "Being of being(s)" does not denote separate domains but a duality (*"Zwiefalt"*) and intimate reciprocity: "We conceive Being appropriately only if we think it in its difference from beings and the latter in their difference from Being. In this manner difference itself comes into view." When seen in the light of this difference, the classical phrase acquires a transitive or active connotation: "Being of being(s) means: Being which 'is' being(s)—where the term 'is' operates transitively, in the sense that Being pervades being(s) in the manner of a transition." Such transition, moreover, should not be construed as a bridge or linkage between otherwise independent components; rather, both Being and being(s) are intelligible only in terms of "difference," which, as the "In-Between," both separates and joins them together.[12]

Although reticent to offer concrete direction signals, *What Is Philosophy?* is eloquent in portraying the preconditions or underpinnings required in genuine philosophizing. To embark on this venture, Heidegger emphasizes, our thinking has to respond or correspond properly to the central question (*ti to on*); thus, philosophizing "always and necessarily—and not only accidentally and occasionally—is pitched or attuned; it finds itself in an attunement." This need of attunement was clearly recognized by classical thought in its insistence that philosophizing presupposes an attuned (though non-emotional) "mood" or "pathos." Thus, we read in Plato's *Theaetetus* that "this is very much the distinctive 'pathos' of a philosopher: to wonder (*thaumazein*); for there is no other beginning of '*philosophia*' than this." Similarly, Aristotle's *Metaphysics* affirms that "it is through wondering (*thaumazein*) that men in old times as well as now have begun to philosophize." As Heidegger adds, however, the mood mentioned is not merely the beginning of philosophy in the sense of a temporal starting point or initial cause: "The 'pathos' of wondering does not simply stand at the threshold of philosophy in the same way in which, for example, the surgeon's operation is preceded by the washing of his hands; rather, wondering carries and pervades philosophy." Regarding the term "pathos," incidentally, the essay points to its terminological roots, in an effort to obviate its confusion with emotionalism or subjective sentiment: "We usually translate 'pathos' as passion or ebullient emotion; however, the term is connected with '*paschein*' which means to suffer, to endure, to undergo, to be borne along, to be in some manner shaped or tuned." Regarding the character of the special philosophical "pathos" of wondering, Heidegger stresses its peculiar combination of withdrawal and attraction, of closeness and distance: "In wondering we retreat in a manner: we step back, as it were, from (any given) being—from the fact that it is as it is and not otherwise. However, wondering does not exhaust itself in this retreat; rather, in retreating or withdrawing it is at the same time forcibly drawn toward and, as it were, captured by that from which it retreats. Thus, wondering is the 'pathos' in which the question of Being unfolds."[13]

Both in content and in tone of presentation, Merleau-Ponty's *In Praise of Philosophy* resembles Heidegger's essay. The parallel is particularly evident in his plea for a philosophy which *matters* or in his critique of a purely academic or professional philosophy. "The modern philosopher," Merleau-Ponty observes, "is frequently a functionary, always a writer, and the freedom allowed him in his books admits an opposite view. What he says enters first of all into an academic world where the choices of life are deadened and the occasions for thought are cut off." By and large, philosophers in modern times have tended to be writers of books or designers of doctrines; but "the philosophy placed in books has ceased to challenge or touch men. What is unusual and almost insupportable in it is hidden in the respectable life of the great philosophical systems." As an antidote to the sway of school doctrines and academic respectability, Merleau-Ponty—together with Heidegger—counsels a renewed attentiveness to classical *philosophia*, especially as inaugurated by Socrates. In order to understand the "full task of the philosopher," he writes, we must realize that writers of philosophical texts cannot and have never "ceased to recognize as their patron a man who never wrote, who never taught, at least in any official chair, who talked with anyone he met on the street, and who had certain difficulties with public opinion and with the ruling powers: We must remember Socrates."[14]

Merleau-Ponty's address also corroborates Heidegger's account with regard to the distinctive pitch or attunement pervading philosophy, the "pathos" of wondering, which arises from a combination of a yearning for truth and an awareness of ignorance. "The philosopher," we read, "is marked by the distinguishing trait that he possesses *inseparably* the taste for evidence and the feeling of ambiguity." Even those, he adds, "who have aimed to work out a completely positive philosophy have been philosophers only to the extent that, at the same time, they have refused the right to install themselves in absolute knowledge. They taught not so much this knowledge as its becoming in us, not the absolute but, at most, our *absolute relation* (or attunement) to it, as Kierkegaard said." The "pathos" of philosophy, according to Merleau-Ponty, thus resides neither in the possession of wisdom nor in its rejection or skeptical indifference, but rather in an intrinsic tension or tuning—the tension between retreat and attachment: "One must be able to withdraw and gain distance in order to become truly engaged, which is also, always, an engagement in the truth." Differently phrased: "What makes a philosopher is the movement which leads back without ceasing from knowledge to ignorance, from ignorance to knowledge, and a kind of rest in this movement." We might also recall that, in another context, Merleau-Ponty has described the "pathos" of wondering characterizing philosophy as the readiness "to learn again to see the world," as the aspiration to restore "a power to signify, a birth of meaning, or a wild meaning, an expression of experience by experience."[15]

There is, in my judgment, a further affinity which has to do with the formulation or reformulation of *philosophia* and its central thrust in terms of "difference." This affinity can be seen in Merleau-Ponty's notion of a "limping philosophy" (or of the "limping" character of philosophy). As in the case of Heidegger's reformulation, the notion derives from uneasiness or dissatisfaction with the traditional "doubling of the world." Unable to abscond to a separate world of his own—a "second world" (of essences), so to speak—the philosopher finds himself awkwardly or obliquely inserted in our common world, but without being able to make it completely his home. "A philosophy of this kind," Merleau-Ponty's address observes, "understands its own strangeness, for it is never entirely in the world, and yet never outside the world." Peculiarly mundane, the philosophical enterprise "cannot be a solitary tête-à-tête of the philosopher with truth; it cannot be a judgment given from on high on life, the world, history, as if the philosopher *was not part of it*—nor can it subordinate the internally recognized truth to any exterior instance of it. It must go beyond this alternative." The relationship between internal and external can and should be translated into the connection between the philosopher and society—or between philosophical judgment and everyday opinion. In Merleau-Ponty's words, "Our relationship to truth passes through others; either we go towards truth with them, or it is not towards truth that we are heading. But the real difficulty is that, if truth is not an idol, the others in their turn are not gods; there is no truth without them, but it does not suffice to attain to truth to be with them."[16]

The relationship between the philosopher and society thus is marked by a curious mixture of presence and absence—or, in the words of our text, by a "rebellious gentleness" and "pensive engagement" which "disquiet those who are with him." Nowhere was this mixture more compellingly illustrated, in Merleau-Ponty's view, than in the classical "patron" of philosophy. "The life and death of Socrates," he writes, "are the history of the difficult relations that the philosopher faces— when he is not protected by literary immunity—with the gods of the City, that is to say, with other men and with the fixed creeds whose precepts they extend to him." The trouble here arose neither from conformism nor from a straightforward rebellion which would oppose knowledge to prejudice. Rather, with Socrates it was "something different": "He teaches that religion is true and he offered sacrifices to the gods; he teaches that one ought to obey the City and he obeys it from the very beginning to the end. He is reproached not so much for what he does as for his way of doing it, his motive." According to Merleau-Ponty, everything that Socrates did was "ordered around the secret principle that one is annoyed if one does not comprehend." What was at issue between him and his judges or accusers was not a stark confrontation between belief and disbelief or between knowledge and ignorance, but rather a different manner of seeing and living in the world: "Socrates believes in religion and the City, in spirit and in truth; they believe in them to the letter. He and his judges are not *on the same ground*." What brought the issue to a head was the circumstance that "it is in the world of the philosopher that one saves the gods and the laws by understanding them"—an operation which "is not so innocent." For, "religion interpreted, this is for the others religion suppressed"; also he gave reasons for obeying the laws, but "it is already too much to have reasons for obeying, since over against his reasons other reasons can be opposed, and then respect disappears." He "comes before the judges, yes, but it is to make them comprehend what the City is. As if they did not know! As if they were not the City!"[17]

In the end, Socrates cannot live in the City, which, however, he refuses to leave. His posture is marked by a kind of "irony," revealing "a distant but true relation with others." In light of this example, Merleau-Ponty comments, "it is useless to deny that philosophy limps: It dwells in history and in life, but it wishes to dwell in their center, at the point where they come into being with the birth of meaning." Not being content with "what is already there," philosophizing is rather "the utopia of possession at a distance; hence, it can be tragic, since it has its own contrary within itself." The awkwardness or obliqueness of reflection, from this perspective, is not a defect, but rather a warrant of its internal tension or attunement. "The limping of philosophy is its virtue," we read. "True irony is not an alibi—it is a task; and the very detachment of the philosopher assigns to him a certain kind of action among men." Nor does his hobbling render the philosopher some kind of monster or freak. For, being a part of the City, the philosopher is evidently an ordinary man—but a man "who wakes up and speaks." On the other hand, ordinary man "contains silently within himself the paradoxes of philosophy because to be completely a man, it is necessary to be a little more and a little less than a man."[18]

II

In following Merleau-Ponty's argument, we have already begun to move, at least implicitly, from philosophy toward political philosophy. To make this move explicitly, no statement is more instructive in my view than Leo Strauss's treatise on *What Is Political Philosophy?* The study comprises a number of essays and provides a rich tapestry of substantive concerns and insights—all of which, however, are linked in some manner with the central topic indicated by the title. The lead essay offers comments on the character of philosophy, on the meaning and objective of political philosophy, on the decline or decay of political thought in recent times and some of its reasons, and also longer remarks on a prominent text exemplifying classical political reflection. Although all of Strauss's observations are broadly pertinent and deserving of attention, I shall concentrate here mainly on those passages which directly bear on our own theme.

Before tackling the basic question raised in its title, the lead essay stresses first of all the close ties between political philosophy and philosophical inquiry in general. As a reflective enterprise, Strauss notes, the former necessarily is a part or ingredient of a "larger whole": "Since political philosophy is a branch of philosophy, even the most provisional explanation of what political philosophy is, cannot dispense with an explanation, however provisional, of what philosophy is." In elucidating the latter issue, the essay makes reference (though not *expressis verbis*) to the "pathos" animating genuine reflection: namely, the attitude of wondering prompted by the tension between knowledge and ignorance. "Philosophy is essentially not possession of the truth, but quest for the truth," we read. "The distinctive trait of the philosopher is that 'he knows that he knows nothing,' and that his insight into our ignorance concerning the most important things induces him to strive with all his power for knowledge." While not firmly in possession or control of his target, the philosopher would cease deserving this name by evading inquiry concerning those ultimately decisive matters or by disregarding them because they cannot be completely settled. Although regarding "possible answers," the essay adds, "the stage of discussion or disputation" may never "reach the stage of decision," philosophy does not on this count become futile as long as it retains a "clear grasp of a fundamental question" which, in turn, requires some notion "of the subject matter with which the question is concerned."[19]

Regarding the "fundamental question" or the character of the wisdom sought by philosophical inquiry, Strauss conceives it in terms of the perennial thrust of *philosophia* (*ti to on*), a thrust which he formulates as search for the "isness" or essence or nature of all things *per se* and as they are related to the totality of all beings. "Philosophy as quest

for wisdom," he affirms, "is quest for universal knowledge, for knowledge of the whole." All men, including philosophers, have some vague
views or tentative opinions about the nature of things and their coherence in a larger or total fabric. However, philosophy seeks to scrutinize and transcend such views in the direction of genuine insight or
rigorous cognition ("*episteme*"); its goal is "to replace opinions about
the whole by knowledge of the whole." Instead of "the whole" or
totality, he continues, "philosophers also say 'all things'." Therefore,
"quest for knowledge of 'all things' means quest for knowledge of
God, the world, and man—or rather quest for knowledge of the
natures of all things: the natures in their totality are 'the whole'." As
can be seen, Strauss's definition of philosophy is couched basically in
terms familiar from traditional metaphysics and illustrates by and large
the perspective designated by Heidegger as "onto-theology." Within
the confines of metaphysics, however, it seems fairly clear that his
notion of essence (or *ousia*) leans more in the direction of the Platonic
"idea" than of Aristotle's *energeia*. This circumstance can be gleaned,
for example, from a later statement in the same essay according to
which classical philosophy "viewed man in the light of the unchangeable
ideas, that is, of the fundamental and permanent problems." To be
sure, affinities with Platonism can be gathered from many other passages and have been noted repeatedly by commentators. One might
also point out that, in addition to the classical legacy itself, concern
with "essences" or "ideas" was a trademark of Husserl's phenomenology in the early part of our century and even of some versions of
neo-Kantianism (especially the "Marburg School" where Strauss studied)
which tried to blend Kant's a priori categories with Platonic teachings.[20]

Turning from philosophical reflection in general to its branch or
offshoot, Strauss defines political philosophy basically (or first of all)
as a philosophy *of* politics in the sense of an application of philosophical
inquiry to the political domain; seen in this light, it emerges as "the
conscious, coherent and relentless effort to replace opinions about
political fundamentals by knowledge regarding them," that is, to acquire
genuine knowledge (*episteme*) about the essence or "nature of political
things." In pursuing its goal, political reflection takes its point of departure necessarily from everyday opinions or commonsense assumptions. Relying to some extent on Husserl's notions of the "life-
world" and the "natural attitude," Strauss acknowledges the initial
relevance and legitimacy of pre-scientific or pre-reflective understand-

ing: "At least every sane adult possesses political knowledge to some degree. Everyone knows something of taxes, police, laws, jails, war, peace, armistice." Of course, opinions of this kind need to be reflectively scrutinized to yield essential insight; it is only when assumptions "concerning the nature of political things" are "made the theme of critical and coherent analysis that a philosophic (or scientific) approach to politics emerges." Such a coherent analysis, however, requires a focus on normative standards, due to the intrinsic nexus of the "nature" of human affairs with their "telos." One does not grasp their nature or "understand them as what they are, as political things," Strauss notes, "if one does not take seriously their explicit or implicit claim to be judged in terms of goodness or badness, of justice or injustice, that is, if one does not measure them by some standard of goodness or justice." Development of such a standard or measure again proceeds initially from everyday experience, for "all political action is guided by some thought of better or worse," a guidepost which "implies thought of the good." While thought of this kind is at first simply an unquestioned viewpoint, it shows itself on reflection "to be questionable. The very fact that we can question it, directs us toward such a thought of the good as is no longer questionable—towards a thought which is no longer opinion but knowledge." All political experience, Strauss concludes, "has then in itself a directedness towards knowledge of the good: of the good life, or the good society." As a corollary, political philosophy can be formulated as "the attempt truly to know both the nature of political things and the right, or the good, political order."[21]

Construed as such an endeavor, political reflection in Stauss's view has fallen on evil days in recent times; in fact, the intellectual scene in our century is pictured in the darkest colors. "Today," we read, "political philosophy is in a state of decay and perhaps putrefaction, if it has not vanished altogether. Not only is there complete disagreement regarding its subject matter, its methods, and its function; its very possibility in any form has become questionable." The essay in this context points to the divorce between philosophy and politics, that is, to the pervasive abandonment of politics by serious philosophy. "As regards the philosophers," we are told, "it is sufficient to contrast the work of the four greatest philosophers of the last forty years— Bergson, Whitehead, Husserl, and Heidegger—with the work of Hermann Cohen" (one of Strauss's teachers at Marburg) "in order to see how rapidly and thoroughly political philosophy has become discredited." In light of this divorce and intensified professional compartmentalization, the conclusion imposes itself "that today political philosophy does not exist anymore, except as a matter for burial, that is, for historical research, or else as a theme of weak and unconvincing protestations." Regarding the underlying reasons for this decay, Strauss stresses mainly the claims that political philosophy is "unscientific" or else "unhistorical," claims which are associated respectively with the sway of "positivism" and "historicism." According to the essay, the first perspective amounts to the view that "scientific knowledge, that is, the kind of knowledge possessed or aspired to by modern science, is the highest form of human knowledge," while "value judgments" are eschewed as non-empirical and unverifiable. Despite the damaging effects of positivism, the second perspective, "historicism," is actually portrayed as the more destructive outlook and as the really "serious antagonist of political philosophy"—mainly because "historicism" treats, or is said to treat, all knowledge as transient and all normative yardsticks as outgrowths of contingent historical conditions. (Although he had just been presented as one of the "four greatest philosophers of the last forty years," one may note that Heidegger is also described at this point as "the most radical historicist" of our century.)[22]

As an antidote to the contemporary decay, Strauss counsels a return to classical political philosophy, or what he calls the "classical solution," as inaugurated by Socrates and formulated chiefly by Plato and Aristotle. Among the many virtues of this legacy, he emphasizes especially its "simplicity" and also its pristine freshness. The classical solution, he notes, arose at a time when "there was not yet in existence a tradition of political philosophy. In all later epochs, the philosophers' study of political things was mediated by a tradition of political philosophy which acted like a screen between the philosopher and political things"; it follows from this "that the classical philosophers saw the political things with a freshness and directness which has never been equalled." Among the classics or "ancients," Strauss accords primary attention to Socrates (as presented by Plato and Xenophon) because he was the first to practice political philosophy by endeavoring to know truly the "nature of political things" and the "right, or good, political order." Regarding the "nature of political things," Socrates established clearly the linkage between essence and moral "telos" in application to both man and the "polis," by showing that, just as in human nature soul and reason were superior to body and instinct, so the proper ordering of the "polis" required basically the rule of wisdom or reason over unreason. As Strauss adds, the classical term for ordering the "polis" was "*politeia*" or "regime"—a term which he circumscribes as "the form which gives society its character" or as "the form of life of a society, its style of life, its moral taste, form of state, form of government, spirit of laws." Given the variety of possible and actual regimes, however, classical political thought does not treat them all indifferently, but rather seeks to determine which "is better, and ultimately, which regime is the best regime." The pursuit of this goal is guided not by opinions or conventions but by rational insight which discloses "the best or just order of society which is *by nature* best or just everywhere or always."[23]

The conception of political philosophy discussed so far is marked by strong internal tensions and even, one might say, by ineradicable antinomies. For clearly, the delineation of essences points to a transcendental or a priori dimension, while actual political life, in contrast, seems to operate on a contingent or a posteriori level. Whereas the ideal regime is said to be best "everywhere or always," political regimes as ways of life necessarily exist not everywhere or always but in time and space or in a certain situation. Differently phrased: while ideal "nature" may be amenable to pure cognition (or *episteme*), practical life remains cognitively opaque and elusive. The tension is recognized in Strauss's essay in the distinction between ideal human goodness (or the "meaning of good man") and "good citizenship," two notions which are presented as virtually incompatible. The same antagonism can also be gleaned from the stress placed on Plato's *Laws* rather than the *Republic*—the former being described as "his political work *par excellence*," mainly because of its attentiveness to the requirements of citizenship. Yet, Strauss's account does not entirely ignore the *Republic*, especially the "allegory of the cave." "By leaving the cave one loses sight of the city, of the whole political sphere," he writes. Therefore, "if the philosopher is to give political guidance, he must return to the cave, from the light of the sun to the world of shadows"—which means that "his perception must be dimmed, his mind must undergo an obfuscation" (an obfuscation apparently endured by the Athenian stranger in the *Laws*). Strauss's general treatment of the *Republic*, it seems to me, has a bearing on the antagonism mentioned. At some points, his writings suggest that the *Republic* brings to light not "the best possible regime but rather the nature of political things—the nature of the City"; but given the linkage between "nature" and "telos" (or goodness), this argument is not fully intelligible. At another point he indicates, I think more tellingly, that the *Republic* discloses the limits of (mundane) politics by showing that the ultimate aim of human life, namely, human "goodness," cannot be reached at all through politics but rather through a life devoted to contemplation or pure reflection.[24]

Given its stark, antinomial character, the antagonism affects not only the relationship between man (or philosopher) and citizen, but is bound to penetrate into the definition of "political philosophy" itself. In the previously sketched formulation, the phrase denotes basically a "philosophy of politics," where the term "philosophy" designates the reflective treatment or vantage point, while "politics" indicates the topic or subject matter—a subject matter which, in the end, proves to be peculiarly extrinsic or recalcitrant to reflection. In a later context, *What Is Political Philosophy?* actually offers a second or revised definition of the phrase, a definition which is said to reveal a "deeper meaning" of political philosophy. "From this point of view," we read, "the adjective 'political' in the expression 'political philosophy' designates not so much a subject matter as a manner of treatment." Approached in this sense, " 'political philosophy' means primarily not the philosophic treatment of politics, but the political, or popular, treatment of philosophy, or the political introduction to philosophy—the attempt to lead the qualified citizens, or rather their qualified sons, from the political life to the philosophic life." In light of this revised formulation, the task of political philosophy is not so much to acquaint the philosopher with politics, but rather to guide the citizen from politics toward reflection. While, from the perspective of the first definition, the terms "political" or "political things" enjoyed a relative integrity which made them worthy of at least some philosophical attention, the second definition clearly places politics on a subordinate, purely mundane level. In lieu of the "philosophy of politics" conveyed by the first approach, the second construal basically refers to a "politics of philosophy"—where politics stands for the external threshold or ramparts of reflection.[25]

The need for such a politics or political defense of philosophy, Strauss holds, is due to the latter's precarious condition. Throughout history, philosophy in his view has been endangered or threatened by hostile forces; with greater or lesser urgency, it has been compelled to defend itself against opposition chiefly from two sources: namely, from (mundane) society or actual political communities; and from rival claimants to wisdom or knowledge, rivals including revealed religion and theology. Regarding the relationship with society, Strauss acknowledges the possibility of a partial accommodation in some circumstances, an accommodation which typically takes the form of a "popularization" or popular justification of philosophy in terms of its benefits to society and to the proper ordering of the "polis." Such means, however, are hazardous and never fully reliable because, in the end, the antagonism or gulf cannot be bridged. While society invariably requires a fabric of opinions or customs, philosophy in its quest for knowledge tends to rupture this fabric. More important: in challenging prevailing political opinions as prejudices, philosophy ultimately concludes by challenging politics itself as a prejudice. While the "polis" or political community values public involvement, citizenship, and civic virtue, philosophy in Strauss's view teaches that the "private life" or the life devoted to reflection (or *episteme*) is preferable or supreme. In light of this irremediable strain, special strategies are required to prevent outright collision or contamination. Among these strategies—which are the heart of the "politics of philosophy"—Strauss concentrates chiefly on distinctive modes of writing and teaching, namely, "esoteric" modes, designed to shield reflection from nonphilosophical intrusions. "Philosophy or science, the highest activity of man," he writes, "is the attempt to replace opinions about 'all things' by knowledge of 'all things'; but opinion is the element of society; philosophy or science is therefore the attempt to dissolve the element in which society breathes, and thus it endangers society. Hence philosophy or science must remain the preserve of a small minority." As he adds, philosophers are well advised and should "respect the opinions on which society rests." However, "to respect opinions is something entirely different from accepting them as true. Philosophers or scientists who hold this view are driven to employ a peculiar manner of writing which would enable them to reveal what they regard as true to the few, without endangering the unqualified commitment of the many to the opinions on which society rests. They will thus distinguish between the true teaching as the esoteric teaching and the socially useful teaching as the exoteric teaching; whereas the exoteric teaching is meant to be easily accessible to every reader, the esoteric teaching discloses itself only to the very careful and well-trained readers after long and concentrated study." In Strauss's account, an accurate grasp or exegesis of the history of political thought presupposes an awareness that all or most of the leading political thinkers practiced in some measure "esoterism" or the politics of philosophy.[26]

III

In this concluding section I would like to offer briefly some appraisals of Strauss's arguments, and also indicate some directions in which my own thoughts are tending at this juncture. Strauss's work, in my judgment, deserves much praise and admiration for its fervent and unrelenting dedication to the task of revitalizing and restoring political thought from the infirmity in which it had lingered in past decades. Clearly, as long as cognition and valid argumentation were entirely restricted to empirical investigation or analysis, political reflection could not possibly lay claim to legitimacy or integrity as an intellectual pursuit. By invoking the classical legacy, especially in its Platonic version, Strauss's writings have upheld a lofty vision which present political theorists and subsequent generations can emulate. Let me also single out among his accomplishments his usually simple and jargon-free writing style, a style which seems to be consciously patterned after the "noble simplicity and quiet grandeur" which he fondly attributed to the ancients. These characteristics, of course, are in full harmony with another quality he ascribed to the classics and which is in particularly short supply in our age: the absence of "fanaticism" conjoined with the spirit of "serenity or sublime sobriety."[27]

Despite these and numerous other merits — and limiting myself again strictly to issues relevant to our theme — I cannot refrain from noting certain quandaries or drawbacks besetting his portrayal of "political philosophy." First of all, especially to the extent that the phrase is a synonym for the politics of philosophy, Strauss's account corroborates and reinforces the divorce or gulf between philosophy and politics which I mentioned earlier and which he himself bemoaned in his essay; by portraying politics as an external bulwark shielding private reflection, his treatment (wittingly or unwittingly) raises added doubts regarding the "very possibility" of political thought as a viable philosophical enterprise. More important, particularly when linked with distinctive modes of teaching and writing, the bifurcation tends to be injurious, if not lethal, to both components of the politics of philosophy.

Although sometimes necessary as a defense mechanism in times of persecution, "esoterism" in my view can by no means be transformed into a virtue or a general characteristic of philosophical reflection— for the simple reason that the two notions are antithetical. While there may be esoteric or hermetic cults and perhaps an esoteric religion, there cannot be, I believe, an esoteric philosophy as long as the latter is seen as open-ended discourse and inquiry. Cultivated behind closed doors, philosophical "truths" inevitably degenerate into dogmas or passwords among the initiated, and "knowledge" into the emblem of an intellectual coterie. The effects are equally damaging, however, to the other component. Where philosophers "reveal what they regard as true to the few" while leaving intact the "unqualified commitment of the many to the opinions on which society rests," politics becomes the preserve of the ignorant; robbed of insight or vision, social and political life turns into an uninteresting and ultimately meaningless venture.

Apart from these immediate effects, the notion of a politics of philosophy casts a shadow, I am afraid, on the proposed revival of classical political thought. When seen in connection with esoterism, the proposal seems designed to encourage not so much a rethinking of the questions animating classical *philosophia* as rather the canonization of time-honored doctrines, if not the cultivation of ancient folklore. The impression is strengthened by the description, at one point, of classical political thought as a "solution." I am aware that several other passages in Strauss's writings are at variance with the notion of a doctrinaire "classicism." Thus, *What Is Political Philosophy?* cautions us that "the evidence of all solutions is necessarily smaller than the evidence of the problem," and also that the philosopher ceases to be true to his calling when his certainty of a solution "becomes stronger than his awareness of the problematic character of that solution." In a later text he questions the feasibility of a direct transplantation of the classics into the contemporary setting. "We cannot reasonably expect that a fresh understanding of classical political philosophy will supply us with recipes for today's use," he writes. "For the relative success of modern political philosophy has brought into being a kind of society wholly unknown to the classics, a kind of society to which the classical principles as stated and elaborated by the classics are not immediately applicable. Only we living today can possibly find a so-lution to the problems of today."[28] Although I find these comments plausible and persuasive, I also consider them incompatible with the thesis of an esoteric philosophy.

Still within the confines of classical thought, there is another feature adversely affected by the politics of philosophy: the example of Socrates. Where philosophy is treated as the concern of the few guarded against the many, the Socratic mode of life tends to become unintelligible; given the availability of esoteric modes of writing and teaching, together with other modes of escape, his trial and death turn into an avoidable accident. It is precisely this avoidability which seems to have inspired later philosophers—including Aristotle when he was placed in a similar predicament. As Merleau-Ponty observes, "Aristotle, seventy-five years later, will say, in leaving the city of his own accord, that there is no sense in allowing the Athenians to commit a new crime against philosophy." However, Merleau-Ponty also notes the restrictive effects on both reflection and the city. Socrates, he adds, "works out for himself another idea of philosophy," one which "does not exist as a sort of idol of which he would be the guardian and which he must defend," but which manifests itself "in its living relevance to the Athenians, in its absent presence, in its obedience without respect." Thus, "Socrates has a way of obeying which is a way of resisting, while Aristotle disobeys in seemliness and dignity." In this connection, let me interject that some passages in Eric Voegelin's writings seem to point in a similar direction. Referring to the "parable of the cave" and the Platonic version of the "saving tale," he comments at one point that "the Saving Tale is not a recipe for the abolition of the 'counterpull' ('anthelkein')" tying us to existence but implies "the confirmation of life through death" in the midst of this tension: "The death of Socrates which, just as the death of Jesus, could have been physically avoided, is representative because it authenticates the truth of reality."[29]

Irrespective of these and related repercussions, there are, I think, intrinsic philosophical considerations which militate against the politics of philosophy. As can readily be seen, the latter notion is an application or illustration of the metaphysical "doubling of the world," of the assumption that there is a "second" substantive world providing a haven of retreat—an assumption whose questionable character I have previously noted. These earlier comments can now be amplified or rephrased. Segregated from the domain of politics and the mundane realm in general, reflection is bound to be robbed of its content or concrete sustenance; restricted to the exploration of a priori categories or transcendental "forms," philosophy is in danger of lapsing into vacuity—or at least of being confined to the dissection of purely "analytical" propositions (which, in the end, turn out to be tautological). These observations throw into relief the hazards involved in the traditional bifurcation of "form" and "matter," "essence" and "appearance," or "universals" and "particulars." In this context, I might also voice some reservations regarding the "parable of the cave" as traditionally presented or interpreted. As it seems to me, the shadowy interior and the sunlit exterior of the cave cannot simply be opposed to each other as two separate habitats or modes of existence. Unless, I would tend to argue, the rays of the sun are somehow able to penetrate inside the cave, they are not going to reach us at all. Differently phrased: light, whatever its source, is not light unless it lights up the darkness; but in this case, the cave itself is not simply or unequivocally a place of dark shadows. Perhaps, one way to reformulate the parable might be to say that the cave's interior and exterior are merely the two sides of the "duality" of Being, or the two modalities of (ontological) "difference."

The hazards of esoterism and of the metaphysical bifurcations it presupposes can also be illustrated in another manner: namely, in terms of the relation between thought or "theory" and "practice." By presenting "private life" or a life devoted to pure contemplation (or *episteme*) as the supreme mode and goal of human existence, Strauss adopts an ambivalent if not paradoxical posture toward practice or practical conduct. To the extent that pure reflection is treated as the "highest activity of man," practice curiously collapses into, or merges with, theory; on the other hand, the politics of philosophy also recognizes a mundane social-political activity or involvement on the part of the "many"—an activity which, however, is entirely extrinsic and recalcitrant to philosophical contemplation. Thus, practice appears simultaneously as synonymous with, and antithetical to, theoretical insight. By favoring clearly the contemplative or non-mundane option, Strauss's argument also leans in the direction of a spectator perspective or a "spectator theory of knowledge"—a perspective which is at variance with his own portrayal of classical political thought. The classics, his essay observes, did not "look at political things from the outside, as spectators of political life," but rather spoke "the language of the citizens and statesmen." However, it is hard to conceive or comprehend the notion of an esoteric participation. In these matters I find helpful and cogent Paul Ricoeur's caveat, phrased in these terms: "It is a great illusion to think that one could make oneself a pure spectator, without weight, without memory, without vantage point, and regard everything with equal concern."[30]

Let me finally turn to some of my inclinations or orientations in regard to our topic. First of all, given the antinomies besetting the politics of philosophy—antinomies highlighted especially in the metaphysical "doubling of the world"—I prefer to assume a somewhat closer association between philosophical reflection and mundane or substantive domains of inquiry. This preference extends both to empirical social-scientific investigations and to historical interpretations of social events or phenomena. Bent on repelling the dangers of "positivism" and "historicism" and on salvaging the autonomy of political thought, Strauss's writings have tended to drive a deep wedge between the latter and contemporary modes of empirical research as well as interpretive historiography and hermeneutics. In my view, however, philosophical reflection cannot simply be regarded as a font of wisdom or knowledge, exempt from the need to learn from concrete-scientific explorations; nor is the "positivist" label supple enough to capture the sense of empirical findings. In Merleau-Ponty's words, "How could any philosopher aware of the philosophical tradition seriously propose to forbid philosophy to have anything to do with science?" Being embroiled in the task of thinking about his experience and his world, how could the philosopher "except by decree" be "given the right to forget what science says about this same experience and world?" As Merleau-Ponty adds, in a hopeful tone, "We need neither tear down the behavioral sciences to lay the foundations of philosophy, nor tear down philosophy to lay the foundations of the behavioral sciences"; for "every science secretes an ontology" and "every ontology anticipates a body of knowledge."[31] Similar considerations apply, I believe, to the relationship between reflection and historical exegesis. In this domain, the term "historicism," as used by Strauss, appears to me too massive and inflexible an instrument to grasp the nuances of hermeneutics and especially the distinction between historical determinism, on the one hand, and a concern with temporality, on the other. This latter concern is illustrated, for example, in Voegelin's conception of human existence and consciousness as a temporal experience, and his portrayal of history as a "moving presence" leaving in its wake "a trail of equivalent symbols in time and space." In Heidegger's writings, one may also note, the temporal "disclosure of Being" is not only at variance with, but explicitly opposed to "historicist" categories. If the "history of Being" were construed as a mere historical process or sequence, he states at one point, one would entirely miss its meaning and lapse into the "dominion" and "perplexities of historicism."[32]

Moving beyond these observations affecting the status of philosophy in general, let me proceed to some comments on political philosophy in particular. In light of the quandaries troubling traditional episte-mology (and political thought conceived as theoretical *episteme*), I find it advisable or preferable to treat political reflection more clearly than in Strauss's account as a version of "practical philosophy" (as this term has been used since Aristotle). In adopting this stance, I derive some inspiration from Hannah Arendt's eloquent defense of the *"vita activa"* or of the life devoted to participation in the public realm. However, a great deal depends on the proper interpretation of political "action" or "praxis." In dealing with such action, Strauss presents it as an activity aiming "at either preservation or change" and "guided by some thought of better or worse"—where the "thought" appears as the directing principle or precept, and the action as the implementation of the precept. This approach, in my view, is neither very adequate nor felicitous, mainly because it obscures the distinction between praxis and technical designs or ideological blueprints. In recent and contem-porary political theory, the battle against this confusion has been waged with particular fervor by Michael Oakeshott. In his inaugural lecture entitled "Political Education," delivered at the London School of Eco-nomics in 1951, Oakeshott attacked as deficient two rival conceptions of political action, both backed up by a long pedigree of spokesmen: namely, on the one hand, the "empiricist" or behaviorist view according to which action is a succession of impulses or responses to stimuli; and on the other, the rationalist thesis according to which it is the enactment of axioms or ideas. While the first conception, he observed, reduces politics to a haphazard and ultimately pointless process, the second insists on a "point"—but one divorced from the practice itself. Regarding the second notion, the lecture criticized especially the as-sumption that reasons or political purposes "may be, and should be, gathered in advance" or can be understood "as an independently premeditated beginning for political activity." Opposing both empiricist and rationalist teachings, Oakeshott argued that political action "springs neither from instant desires, nor from general principles, but from the existing traditions of behavior themselves" and that "the form it takes, because it can take no other, is the amendment of existing arrangements by exploring and pursuing what is intimated in them." Since politics, he added, is never "anything more than the pursuit of intimations," it is basically "a conversation, not an argument."[33]

In shifting the accent to praxis and practical philosophy, I do not mean to be misunderstood as advocating the surrender of reflection to political opinion or partisan whims; what is involved is not a surrender, but rather an oblique insertion or envelopment. Both of the philosophers whom I invoked earlier in this chapter seem to give support to such a perspective. Heidegger at one point delineated a special or distinctive mode of thinking, which he designated as "Andenken," that is, as "commemorative" or "recollective thinking." Concerned with the recollection of Being, he noted, such a thinking basically undercuts or precedes the traditional dichotomy of theory and practice; differently phrased: "Andenken" is neither synonymous with, nor simply antithetical to, mundane-human activity. Merleau-Ponty's In Praise of Philosophy juxtaposes the philosopher and the Manichaean man of action (who tends to view everything in black and white); but he also notes a certain artificiality or deficiency in this opposition. "The philosopher of action," we read, "is perhaps the farthest removed from action, for to speak with depth and rigor is to say that one has no desire to act." On the other hand, "the Manichees, who throw themselves into action, understand one another better than they understand the philosopher, for there is a certain complicity among them: each one is the reason for the being of the other." Yet, although agreeing that the "difference exists" and that the philosopher is a "stranger" to this "fraternal melée," Merleau-Ponty also questions whether the distinction really separates the reflective individual from the ordinary or practical man. "It is rather the difference," he says, "in man himself between that which understands and that which chooses, and every man, like the philosopher, is divided in this way." Thus, there is something contrived "in the portrait of the man of action whom we oppose to the philosopher," for "this man of action is himself not all of one piece."[34]

The notion of politics as a practical activity still needs to be fleshed out with regard to the distinctive mode or kind of activity involved. In this respect, much can be learned, I think, from Strauss's focus on *"politeia"* or "regime" and his portrayal of the latter as "a specific manner of life" or the "manner of living of society and in society." Where I hesitate to follow him, however, is in his identification of regime and "form" ("form of society, form of state, form of government") and in his subscription to the (metaphysical) view "that the form is higher in dignity than the matter." Eschewing this dichotomy but preserving the emphasis on a way of life, I would prefer to describe politics as a human practice or as the learning of a practice: namely, as the ongoing initiation into the practice of friendship. In choosing the latter term, I realize that I need to add immediately several caveats or provisos. First of all, I have to recognize that, under normal circumstances, we are not dealing with a particular intimacy or familiarity, but rather (in Aristotle's words) with a "watery kind of friendship"—one which typically exceeds the bounds of consanguinity, family ties, and face-to-face interaction. Nor should the term necessarily be equated with a distinctive team spirit or with the joint endorsement and pursuit of a common principle or goal (a notion which is simply another version of the rationalist construction of action); rather, what is common or shared in society may be simply a mutual respect, including above all a respect for difference. Furthermore, and more important, by adopting the above formula, I do not mean to revive or embrace without qualification the conception that the nature of politics resides in the "friend-foe" distinction—mainly because this conception tends to treat enmity as the corollary and equivalent partner of friendship. In my view, however, friendship and enmity are by no means on an equal footing or deserving of equal attention as human practices. Among the many lessons we have learned from Hegel is the insight that friendship and social peace are typically the outcome of conflict or a struggle for mutual recognition, a struggle in which questions of power are rarely absent. However, we sometimes forget what is also but not uniquely a Hegelian lesson: namely, that conflict is not an end in itself nor a fixed premise rooted in a fictional "state of nature." Thus, although normally reconciliation is achieved only through struggle, conflict obtains meaning only through its anticipation of peace.[35]

In depicting politics in this manner, I note that I am also departing somewhat from Oakeshott's account when he presents friendship as an illustration of what is involved in a "conservative disposition." Describing the latter disposition as the tendency to prefer "the familiar to the unknown," "the tried to the untried," and "the near to the distant," he goes on to claim that this tendency is well exemplified by relations of friendship, relations which spring from familiarity and subsist "in a mutual sharing of personalities." Friends, he writes, "are not concerned with what might be made of one another, but only with the enjoyment of one another; and the condition of this enjoyment is a ready acceptance of what is and the absence of any desire to change or to improve." However, we surely do not want to prevent friends from changing—even in entirely unknown or untried directions—or abandon them when this happens; but changes of this kind are prone to be deeply unsettling on all sides and cannot readily be fitted into a "conservative" outlook. In my view, friendship involves not only enjoyment of the familiar, but also an openness toward the unfamiliar and even a readiness to "risk oneself," at times, in untried relationships. In this sense, I find more plausible Oakeshott's inaugural lecture, where the "pursuit of intimations" is circumscribed also as the exploration of a sympathy, but an exploration which does not simply cultivate the near at the expense of the distant. "The arrangements which constitute a society capable of political activity, whether they are customs or institutions or laws or diplomatic decisions," he affirms, "are at once coherent and incoherent; they compose a pattern and at the same time they intimate a sympathy for what does not fully appear. Political activity is the exploration of that sympathy; and consequently, relevant political reasoning will be the convincing exposure of a sympathy, present but not yet followed up, and the convincing demonstration that now is the appropriate moment for recognizing it."[36]

There is another aspect where I am not entirely at one with Oakeshott: namely, in his portrayal of politics as "a conversation, not an argument"—to the extent that the phrase excludes serious preoccupation with, or discussion of, questions relating to the "good life." The notion of a "conversation," incidentally, is also used emphatically by Richard Rorty in his recent book, *Philosophy and the Mirror of Nature*, again with an edge against critical-normative discourse. As it seems to me, however, ethics is not necessarily tied to traditional epistemology; on the contrary, precisely when the accent is placed on praxis or practical political participation—and away from the "spectator" role—do moral questions begin to *matter* or to acquire concrete significance. Differently phrased: unless tied to moral and broader philosophical concerns, "conversation" is in danger of succumbing to ritual. This is the peril which Richard Bernstein highlights poignantly when, in reviewing Rorty's study, he accuses him of endorsing inadvertently the "myth of the given" or of slipping into a spectator stance. "If we accept Rorty's claim," he writes, "that all justification, whether of knowledge or moral choices, cannot hope to escape from history and only makes sense with reference to social practices, we are still faced with the critical task of determining which social practices are relevant, which ones ought to prevail, be modified or abandoned. 'Hammering this out' is not a matter of 'mere' rhetoric or 'arbitrary' decision, but requires argumentation." To be sure, there remains the question how such argumentation can or should meaningfully proceed—a question which I cannot hope to settle in this context (but postpone to the final chapter). Relying on Heidegger's and also Voegelin's notion of *"anamnesis"* or *"Andenken,"* I have tried at another place to sketch the contours of a "recollective ethics," deviating from both inductive and rationalist approaches. However, the same point could also be made under the rubric of friendship. In his *Nicomachean Ethics*, Aristotle delineates three kinds of friendship—utilitarian, hedonistic, and qualitative-moral—adding the argument that the last of these both embraces and is superior to the other two. "It is only between those who are good and resemble one another in their goodness," he says, "that friendship is perfect. Such friends are both good in themselves and, by the same token, desire the good of one another. But it is those who desire the good of friends for their friends' sake who are most completely friends, since each loves the other for what the other is in himself and not for something extrinsic which he need not have."[37]

Perhaps I should mention one last issue at this point, although "last" not in the order of importance: the issue of the relation between Athens and Jerusalem. On this score, Heidegger and Strauss are at least in partial agreement, since both argue that philosophy, originating in Athens, can at best only lead to the threshold of faith, but is incompetent to portray the image—and even less to design the architecture—of the Holy City. Curiously, while insisting strongly on the separation of philosophy and theology, Strauss—in pleading the case of classical thought—also vindicates what Heidegger has described as the legacy of "onto-theology." On the other hand, Heidegger—in seeking to transcend this legacy—does not thereby erect a barrier to faith but only corroborates more fully the previously mentioned incompetence.[38] In presenting political praxis as the initiation into friendship, I have implicitly already intimated a linkage, perhaps an underground tunnel, between the two cities—if indeed the Maundy antiphon is right in saying *"ubi caritas et amor, Deus ibi est."* But the difficulty consists in grasping the character of the linkage. As it seems to me, the two cities are by no means located on a single plane, in the sense that the "heavenly" city would somehow be a territorial annex or a temporal extension of the earthly one. Nor are they founded on two coequal planes, with the effect that Jerusalem could enjoy extraterritoriality from all places or locations—a situation which would make her an abode of the elect while degrading Athens into a city of untouchables. Despite their radical difference, the two cities, I feel, have been implicated with each other for some time, their walls having been breached long ago; in a sense, in the midst of Athens or her interstices, Jerusalem has always been lying in wait—not as a historical destiny, nor as a mission to be implemented, but as a hidden sense. This is why, despite an internal distance or exile and despite the "prohibition of the name," philosophers have never ceased to speak obliquely and in a roundabout way also about Jerusalem. This is also why, in the midst of the conflicts and agonies of the day, political thinkers through the ages, latter-day Athenians one and all, have continued searching for the linkage or tunnel—never quite knowing the direction, stumbling badly all along the way, tapping like blind men with a cane the rocks and curbsides for the sounds or echoes of a noiseless promise: the promised city of peace.

2

Praxis and Experience

Patiendo non agendo beamur

Political philosophy—in accord with an old tradition going back to Aristotle—is frequently defined as a "practical" mode of thinking, and politics as a type of "praxis" or "action." As part of conventional wisdom, these descriptions are easy to repeat—and hard to understand. For, how can thinking or philosophy be "practical," and in which sense is politics an outgrowth of "praxis" or "action" (whatever these terms may mean individually)? Questions of this kind have gained particular urgency in our age, mainly due the obsolescence of many traditional forms of theorizing or the (so-called) "end of metaphysics"— a demise sometimes viewed as harbinger of purely practical pursuits. Marx's celebrated dictum, in his *Theses on Feuerbach*, that hitherto "philosophers have only interpreted the world in various ways, but the point is to change it" has often been invoked in this context, but rarely explained—especially as regards the sense and origin of the "change" postulated. What commonly renders invocations of this type opaque is the half-hearted character of the announced break with metaphysics: evident in the simple substitution of an "acting subject" for the thinking ego (the former being construed either in the singular or the plural). In the present century, Max Weber's formulations in this domain— his differentiation of purposive-intentional "action" from merely re-active, causally induced "behavior"—have achieved virtually canonical or normative status; in line with his teachings, contemporary parlance tends to speak of social or political "action" when and "insofar as the acting individual attaches a subjective meaning to his behavior" and "insofar as its subjective meaning takes account of the behavior of others and is thereby oriented in its course."[1]

Weber's distinction between action and reaction—or between activity and passivity—reverberates widely through recent philosophical and social-theoretical discussions, notwithstanding the great diversity of frameworks and initiatives. These discussions have been reviewed from various angles; the most trenchant and reliable analysis, however, is still Richard Bernstein's *Praxis and Action: Contemporary Philosophies of Human Activity* (published in 1971). Sweeping in scope, the study examined the status of "praxis" and "action" in four major intellectual settings: Marxism, existentialism, pragmatism, and (post-Wittgensteinian) analytical philosophy. Apart from admiring the range of scholarship, I find inspiration particularly in two aspects of Bernstein's work. The first aspect is his attentiveness to the Hegelian legacy: each intellectual trend is carefully silhouetted against the backdrop of Hegel's thought, especially as found in the *Phenomenology of Mind*. The second aspect is the definition of "praxis" taken over from Aristotle—which I intend to borrow for present purposes. In the more restricted sense, Bernstein wrote, praxis "signifies the disciplines and activities predominant in man's ethical and political life"; given that "for Aristotle, individual activity is properly a part of the study of political activity— activity in the '*polis*', we can say that '*praxis*' signifies the free activity (and the disciplines concerned with this activity) in the '*polis*'." Regarding general conclusions, however, the study's findings did not depart significantly from Weber's formulations. On the whole, praxis or action was shown to be construed as either collective purposive activity (styled "revolutionary praxis") in Marxism or a purely inward "decision" or "project" of consciousness in existentialism; the closest parallel to the dualism mentioned was found in analytical philosophy, in the juxtaposition of intentional action (championed by the "new teleologists") and a purely reactive or causal behavior, while pragmatism was said to add the notion of a "rule-governed" conduct or "practice"—a notion broadly akin to Weber's "habitual" or "traditional" mode of social life.[2]

In the present chapter I would like to take some cautious and very tentative steps beyond the confines of Weberian categories. For this purpose, I want to correlate praxis with another—admittedly quite complex and multifaceted—notion: that of "experience." In my usage here, the term is not a synonym for "sense experience" or "sensation" (that is, the reception of sensory stimuli) as these concepts have been employed in the empiricist tradition; nor is it equivalent to an "inner sense" as espoused by a skeptical idealism or mentalism. Rather, my use is indebted (albeit loosely) to the Hegelian legacy—where the term signifies a human learning process or a process of seasoning and maturation. Generally speaking, what I find defective or limiting in Weber's categories of both "action" and "behavior" is their treatment of the human agent as "given": given either as a self-propelled source of intentional designs or else as a psychic mechanism reacting to external influences—that is, as either a "subject" (an underlying substrate) or a predictable "object." Against this background, "experience" accentuates the molding and transformation of the agent—a transformation not simply endured in the mode of passive reaction, but undergone as a catalyst and threshold opening up new horizons. My presentation here will proceed in stages, moving from more general philosophical considerations to more concrete political-theoretical arguments. An initial section will focus not on Hegel directly, but rather on two preeminent philosophers of "experience" in our century: namely, Heidegger and Gadamer. In both instances, I shall draw attention to Hegelian affinities—while also indicating important differences (especially the lack of absolute-idealist inclinations). Shifting from philosophy to recent political theory, the second section will examine the notions of political "action" and "praxis," chiefly as they are delineated in the writings of Michael Oakeshott and Hannah Arendt. In the concluding section I shall attempt to trace the implications of these discussions for the theory of political action, with particular attention to Weber's categories and typologies and recent reassessments of the Weberian legacy.

I

In contrast with competing intellectual frameworks like logical empiricism or linguistic analysis, the category of "experience" is central to existential ontology and hermeneutics—mainly because of their opposition to epistemological closure or the conception of a closed universe. Before turning to Heidegger, I want to review briefly some of Gadamer's arguments in this domain, the sequence being motivated primarily by the greater accessibility of his views and also by his deliberate proximity to the Hegelian tradition. A member of the phenomenological movement and a student of Heidegger, Gadamer is known particularly for his formulation of a "philosophical hermeneutics"—a hermeneutics which, moving beyond the narrow confines of textual exegesis, views human existence itself as an ongoing process of interpretation and self-interpretation. A key term in this perspective is the notion of an "effective-historical consciousness" (*wirkungsgeschichtliches Bewusstsein*), that is, a consciousness which discovers itself through confrontation with the past, especially with historically sedimented actions and beliefs. It is chiefly in discussing this concept that Gadamer pays tribute to Hegel. "It is of central importance for the hermeneutical approach," his *Truth and Method* states, "that it should come to grips with Hegel; for Hegel's philosophy of mind claims to achieve a complete mediation of history with the present." Thus, "we shall have to define the structure of effective-historical consciousness both with an eye on Hegel and in differentiation from his thought." *Truth and Method* also distances itself sharply from facile attempts to dismiss or "transcend" Hegel's legacy, including his category of "absolute spirit": "The varied and sundry attacks on this philosophy of absolute reason by his critics cannot withstand the stringency of that total dialectical self-mediation which Hegel has delineated particularly in his *Phenomenology*, the science of phenomenal knowledge. The notion that the Other must be experienced not as the other side of myself encompassed by pure self-consciousness but as different or as a 'Thou'—this prototype of all objections to the infinity of Hegel's dialectic—does not really hit home; for, nothing perhaps determines the dialectical movement in the *Phenomenology* as much as the issue of interpersonal recognition."[3]

In *Truth and Method* these comments on recognition and the *Phenomenology* serve as introduction to a broader discussion of "experience" and its relevance for hermeneutics. Before developing his views, Gadamer critiques some of the main defects or limitations of the empiricist conception of sense experience. Largely because of its enlistment in empiricist epistemology, he notes, the category of experience belongs "among the most opaque concepts we have. Since it plays a leading role in the logic of induction of the natural sciences, the category has undergone an epistemological schematization which, in my view, truncates its original meaning." The chief drawback of the traditional (and still prevailing) conception is that it has been tailored exclusively to the demands of scientific inquiry—whose aim it is "so to objectify experience that it no longer contains any historical ingredient." The modern procedure of induction—as inaugurated primarily by Francis Bacon—accentuates the accumulation of sense data and repetition of processes in such a way as to permit generalization or the articulation of general propositions; in Baconian terminology, the "*interpretatio naturae*" is designed to advance "step by step, through methodically conducted experiments, towards the true and tenable universals, the simple forms of nature." The restrictiveness of this outlook, evident in the reduction of experience to repetition, is not particularly a discovery of hermeneutics, but an insight guiding phenomenology since its inception. According to Gadamer, Husserl in several of his works tried to uncover the experiential matrix underlying modern science—although, in the end, he remained himself hostage to cognitive-epistemological categories. "In constantly renewed investigations," we read, Husserl "attempted to elucidate the one-sidedness of the scientific idealization of experience; to this end he traced a genealogy of experience which, as experience of the life-world, precedes its idealization through science."[4]

In presenting his own thoughts on experience, Gadamer does not so much reject induction as incorporate it into a broader and more complex conception—a conception comprising chiefly three ingredients or "moments," which can be labeled "inductive," "dialectical," and "existential." Regarding the first ingredient, Gadamer takes his bearings in part from Bacon, but mainly from Aristotle. The inductive stress on accumulation and repetition, he observes, captures a "true element in the structure of experience"; for, assumptions or beliefs are commonly considered well-founded unless or until they are disconfirmed by contrary evidence: "The fact that experience is valid so long as it is not contradicted by new experience (*ubi non reperitur instantia contradictoria*) is clearly characteristic of the general nature of experience, no matter whether we are dealing with scientific procedure in the modern sense or with the experience of daily life which men have always had." In his *Posterior Analytics* Aristotle utilized this insight in laying the groundwork for the acquisition of knowledge or "*episteme*"; his guiding concern was to show how repeated individual perceptions, through the retention of common features, yield the unity of experience and ultimately the unity of knowledge. In this portrayal, the "persistence of important perceptions" was basically the "linking motif" through which knowledge of universals could emerge from particular impressions. To be sure, for Aristotle experience and its unity was not simply synonymous with universal knowledge or science; for, experience is "actually present only in the particular observation" and cannot be grasped in a "prior universality." Yet, singular impressions were the "necessary precondition" or stepping-stone for science; once individual observations begin to reveal "the same regular pattern," it becomes possible "to inquire into the reason and hence move forward into science." To illustrate this procedure, Aristotle used the comparison with a fleeing army: if in the general flight an observation is confirmed through repeated experience it begins to stand still, and if other observations are equally supported, the entire army of impressions comes to a halt. The image, Gadamer comments, captures the disarray "in which experience is acquired, suddenly, through this or that feature, unpredictably, and yet not without preparation, and valid from then on until there is a new experience"; it highlights the "universality of experience through which, according to Aristotle, true conceptual universality and the possibility of science comes about."[5]

While appreciating the point of Aristotle's argument, however, Gadamer finds it flawed by its purely epistemological thrust: in stressing the aspect of data gathering and repetition, induction shortchanges and simplifies the relation between knowledge and experience by treating the former as a cumulative result of the latter. Actually, to maintain this view — Gadamer argues — Aristotle already "presupposes that cognitive unity which is said to persist in the flight of observations and to emerge as general proposition; thus, conceptual universality for him is ontologically prior. What really concerns him about experience is merely its contribution to concept formation." What the emphasis on repetition neglects is the element of surprise and puzzlement: the fact that regular expectations can be disappointed by experience — with repercussions on the observer's cognitive framework. According to *Truth and Method*, this element is preserved in linguistic usage which differentiates between at least two main senses of "experience": by referring, on the one hand, to experiences which "accord with and confirm our expectation," and on the other, to an experience which "one encounters or 'undergoes'." The latter sense — the sense of "genuine experience" — always has negative connotations since regular expectations are shattered and corrected; but it also has a "productive" result: by inducing a general reconsideration of the observer's premises and assumptions. Thus, genuine experience involves not only an initial "deception which is seen through and corrected, but the acquisition of a more comprehensive knowledge." In traditional vocabulary, *Truth and Method* states, a negation yielding such productive consequences is termed a "determinate negation"; with reference to the observer, "we call this kind of experience dialectical."[6]

To elucidate this second, innovative feature, Gadamer departs from the inductive paradigm: "It is no longer Aristotle but Hegel who serves as important witness for the dialectical element of experience." In his *Phenomenology of Mind* Hegel outlined how consciousness, in encountering and learning about phenomena and events in the world, at the same time learns about and experiences itself. In his language, experience could be termed the "completion of skepticism"—in the sense that consciousness, in returning from unexpected or unfamiliar phenomena to its own cognitive premises, finds itself in the throes of a transformation induced by this encounter. Differently phrased, experiences which one "undergoes" are liable to induce a dual change: a change both in our cognitive framework and in the sense of encountered objects or events. Innovative experience from this vantage point thus implies a profound reversal: confronting the unfamiliar and finding its expectations disappointed, "the experiencing consciousness has reversed itself, namely, turned back on itself. The experiencer has become aware of his experience—he is 'experienced', which means: he has acquired a new horizon within which something can become an experience for him." In Hegel's portrayal, the reversal of consciousness is a "dialectical" movement, since it involves an encounter of mind and world and a simultaneous change of both partners in this relationship. The same reversal can also be comprehended as a struggle for recognition in which an initial disparity or disunity is eventually overcome on the level of new insight and self-recognition. As Gadamer paraphrases Hegel's thought: "The concept of experience means precisely this: that such a unity with oneself is only gradually accomplished. This is the reversal which consciousness undergoes when it recognizes itself in what is alien or different."[7]

Gadamer's appeal to Hegel, however, is itself (in a sense) dialectical. As in the case of induction, he sees dialectics marred or overshadowed by epistemological prejudgments: by the postulate of a knowledge immune from experience. "For Hegel," he notes, "the path of conscious experience necessarily leads to a self-knowledge that no longer has anything different or alien outside itself. The perfection of experience resides in 'science', the self-certainty attained in knowledge" or self-knowledge. Consequently, "the dialectic of experience must end in the transcendence of all experience, accomplished in absolute knowledge, that is, in the complete identity of consciousness and object." What Gadamer finds dubious in this postulate is that consciousness is shielded from surprises and guarded against unexpected turns of events—in other words, that it ceases to learn further about the world and itself. On Hegelian premises, we read, "the nature of experience is conceived in terms of that which transcends it"; but "experience itself can never be science." Rather, the true mark of experience is its unqualified "orientation towards new experience; this is why a person who is called 'experienced' has not only become such *through* experiences, but also remains open *for* new experiences." According to *Truth and Method*, in fact, the central characteristic of experience resides not in its cognitive contributions, but in its open-endedness and its opposition to every form of dogmatic closure. Seen in this light, the experienced person "proves to be someone who is radically undogmatic—who, because he has undergone so many experiences and learned from them, is particularly well equipped to have new experiences and learn from them in turn. Thus, the dialectic of experience finds its completion not in a definitive knowledge, but in that openness to experience which is fostered by experience itself."[8]

The new aspect or feature which comes into view at this point transgresses epistemological bounds: it relates not so much to cognitive growth as to a process of existential learning and seasoning. What this "qualitatively new element" accentuates is that kind of experience "from which no one can be exempt" and which "inheres in the historical character of the human condition." In Gadamer's presentation, such experience is bound to be painful—because it challenges and breaks open not only cherished views but existential dispositions and an accustomed way of life: "That experience is preponderantly painful and disagreeable is not a particularly pessimistic tenet, but derives directly from its intrinsic nature." Testimony for this "third ingredient" comes chiefly from Aeschylus and early Greek tragedy. Aeschylus, we read, "found the formula—or rather grasped its metaphysical significance—which expresses the inner historicity of experience: 'learning through suffering' (*pathei mathos*)." In Gadamer's view, this formula signifies not only "that we learn through mistakes and acquire a better knowledge of things only through deception and disappointment." Properly interpreted, Aeschylus' formula "means more: he refers to the reason underlying this process. What man has to learn through suffering is not this or that particular information but rather insight into the limits of human existence, insight into the irremovable boundary between man and the divine." In this sense experience means awareness of "human finitude": "The truly experienced person is one who realizes this finitude, who knows that he is master neither of time nor the future; for he recognizes the limit of all prediction and the uncertainty of all plans." Complete experience from this angle signifies not its transcendence in the direction of pure knowledge, but the unfolding of all its intrinsic dimensions—the stage where "experience is fully and genuinely present." Ultimately the lesson garnered through experience is "a religious insight—the kind of insight which gave birth to Greek tragedy."[9]

Having explored the various dimensions of experience, *Truth and Method* proceeds to transfer these findings to the domain of exegesis, in an effort to pinpoint similar dimensions on the level of "hermeneutical experience" and "effective-historical consciousness." Instead of pursuing these explorations further, I want to shift attention to Gadamer's chief mentor and teacher—a shift involving a move into philosophically more uncharted terrain. In several of his writings, both in his early and his later periods, Heidegger elaborated on the notion of "experience," frequently in a manner reminiscent (at a first glance) of Gadamer's third or existential ingredient. Thus, his lectures on "The Nature of Language" specified as chief aim of the inquiry not the gathering of various types of linguistic information but the endeavor to "experience" language itself. The lectures, Heidegger observed, are "intended to guide us toward a possibility of undergoing an experience with language. To undergo an experience with something—be it a thing, a person, or a god—means that this something happens to us, befalls us, comes over us, overwhelms and transforms us." From this perspective, experience is not, properly speaking, the result of a willful or intentional initiative, but rather a process of seasoning which one endures (although not in a purely passive-mechanical manner): "When we talk of 'undergoing' an experience we mean specifically that the experience is not of our own making: to undergo here means to endure, to suffer, to accept what is intended for us by submitting to it." Thus, "to undergo an experience with language signifies that we let ourselves be touched or reached by the claim of language, by responding and yielding to it." Later in the same lectures, "experience" is paraphrased as a process of "attaining something through journeying or being underway. To undergo an experience with something means that this something, which we try to reach by journeying, itself reaches us, touches and claims us, by transforming us in its mold."[10]

Similar passages could be culled without difficulty from several other lectures and essays; most directly pertinent for present purposes, however, is Heidegger's commentary on the introduction to *Phenomenology of Mind*, published under the title *Hegel's Concept of Experience*. The commentary is striking for its subtlety and close attention to detail — of which I can only convey here a few glimpses. Coming from Gadamer the reader is liable to experience a kind of "sea change"; less metaphorically: a change from an existential-hermeneutical to a more ontological level of analysis. In Heidegger's presentation, the maturation process characterizing experience involves a learning not simply about contingent-historical circumstances, but about the dimension of "Being" permeating mundane phenomena; accordingly, the suffering undergone in experience derives less from human finitude than from the claim of Being and its tranformative effects. The difference is particularly evident with regard to Hegel's notion of the "reversal" of consciousness — which Heidegger interprets in a radical-ontological (and less cognitive) sense. "In ordinary experience (*experiri*)," he writes, "we perceive the object to be examined in light of its conditioning by other objects — which situate and determine the status of the object. Thus, when we have to change our earlier views about the examined object, the change derives basically from the other conditioning objects." The situation is entirely different in the case of non-mundane or ontological experience: "If we concentrate on the 'objectivity' of an object, or the 'truth' of something held true, our experience is still with the first object, but in such a manner that the old object gives rise to the new one, its objectivity." While ordinary or natural consciousness "takes its object and its own thinking directly as a given (ontic) entity, paying no heed to Being which is implicitly represented," attentiveness to the "Being of beings" requires a turn from phenomena to the ground of their disclosure or appearance; in Hegel's terms, this turn is a "reversal of consciousness itself." Through this reversal or inversion, Heidegger notes, we open ourselves to "what no natural consciousness

ever discovers—what 'occurs behind its back'," that is, to the "presentation of the appearance of phenomena."[11]

The preceding observations provide clues for Hegel's concept of
experience, as seen in the commentary. Instead of denoting an inductive
process, the term is basically a synonym for phenomena *qua* phenomena
or "the essence of appearance"—which is Hegel's way of construing
the "Being of beings" or the realm of (ontic) beings conceived in their
"beingness." The concept in any case exceeds purely epistemological
confines: it is "no longer the name for a particular mode of cognition;
rather, experience is now the word or claim of Being, insofar as this
claim is heeded or accepted by beings *qua* beings." Concentrating on
reflective awareness, Hegel's *Phenomenology of Mind* delineates the progressive disclosure of the ground or truth of appearance, that is, the
gradual ascent from natural to ontological or "real" consciousness:
"The being of consciousness consists in being in motion or underway.
Thus, the being which Hegel construes as experience has the character
of movement: his sentence pinpointing the nature of experience starts
with the phrase 'the *dialectical* movement'." As Heidegger elaborates,
"dialectics" at this point is not simply a label for familiar formulas
(like "thesis-antithesis-synthesis" or "negation of negation"), but the
outgrowth of an ontological difference. Consciousness, he writes, "is
its own movement, since it is the comparison between ontic pre-
ontological knowledge and ontological knowledge." Consequently,
"dialectics can neither be explained logically in terms of positing and
negating thought, nor ontically as a special activity and movement in
real consciousness; rather, dialectics inheres in Being as the mode of
appearance (of phenomena)." Understood in this fashion, dialectical
experience is a movement in the sense of "undergoing" or "being
underway"—underway toward the truth of appearance and the objectivity of objects: "Experience is the manner in which consciousness
in its being journeys toward its concept, that is, its truth; this journeying
outreach reaches in appearances the apparition of truth." Thus, "experience is a mode of the presence of Being."[12]

While supporting (in its broad outlines) the view of experience
sketched, Heidegger does not equally endorse Hegel's conception of
"ontology"—which is basically a "metaphysical" conception rooted
in the primacy of consciousness and subjectivity. "It is, to be sure, an
altogether different question," we read, "whether and to which extent
subjectivity constitutes a particular phase or destiny in the unfolding

of Being in which the unconcealment of Being (not the truth of particular beings) *withdraws*, thus determining an epoch of its own. For, under the sway of subjectivity, every being as such turns into an object, and all beings are beings only in virtue of this stabilization." In Hegelian philosophy, the unfolding of Being occurs essentially as a maturation of subjectivity and the appearance of truth as an appearance in and for consciousness. In some measure, this outlook also has repercussions on his concept of experience—to the extent that the latter coincides with the essence or "beingness of beings which as '*subjectum*' derives its sense from subjectivity." According to Heidegger, Hegel's concept actually deepens and expands the Cartesian legacy of the *cogito*: "What Hegel has in mind with the term 'experience' first makes clear the meaning of the *res cogitans* seen as the *subjectum co-agitans*. Experience is the presentation of the absolute subject which finds its being in representational thought and thus gains absoluteness. Experience is the subjectivity of the absolute subject; as presentation of an absolute representation it is the apparition (or *parousia*) of the absolute." As he adds, "Everything depends on our conceiving the mentioned 'experience' in terms of the being of consciousness. But being means being present, and the latter manifests itself as appearance; thus appearance now means appearance of knowledge."[13]

II

The foregoing discussions of experience have implications for numerous philosophical and social-theoretical domains; in the present context I want to concentrate on their relevance for "praxis" and the theory of (political) action. In stressing the aspect of "undergoing," the reviewed philosophers seem to undercut or disavow such a relevance; this impression, however, is misleading. Actually, both thinkers provide helpful observations on the topic. In his commentary, Heidegger describes the "reversal" of consciousness explicitly, with Hegel, as "our contribution (*Zutat*)." Although not synonymous with willful-intentional projects, experience in his view does not simply coincide with passivity or the passive endurance of an external fate. In moving from natural to ontological consciousness, it is true, experience has to leave aside personal predilections in order to let the truth of phenomena appear; but—as Heidegger states—this leaving or letting "does not happen by itself. If ever a letting is a doing, it is this letting and leaving aside;

and this doing or acting necessarily has the character of a contribution (on our part)." The reason this doing is not a private whim is that it inserts itself from the beginning into a transpersonal (though not extrinsic) pattern or design: "The contribution of the reversal of consciousness consists in letting phenomena appear as such. This contribution does not impose on experience an alien design; it merely elicits from it specifically what inheres in it as the being of consciousness." In Hegelian philosophy, the truth of phenomena was construed as the purpose or "will of the absolute." Consequently, our contribution can be said to "will in accordance with the will of the absolute." Thus, "the reversal of consciousness does not add to the absolute any self-seeking increment on our part; rather, it restores us to our nature which consists in our standing in the *parousia* of the absolute."[14]

More elaborate comments on praxis have been formulated by Gadamer, especially in his later writings; his *Reason in the Age of Science* is in large portion specifically devoted to the issue. Focusing on the "original notion of praxis," Gadamer criticizes the customary juxtaposition of theory and praxis according to which the latter is simply an implementation of the former. In order to grasp this notion once again and thus "to understand the meaning of the tradition of practical philosophy," he writes, "one has to remove it completely from the context of an opposition to 'science'. Not even the contrast to *theoria*—which, of course, is contained in the Aristotelian classification of sciences—is really crucial or determining here," mainly because Aristotle viewed *theoria* itself as "a mode of praxis." According to Gadamer, the meaning context in which "praxis" is properly located is "not primarily marked by an antithesis to theory or an application of theory. Rather—as especially Joachim Ritter has shown in his writings—'praxis' denotes the behavioral mode of living beings in the broadest sense"; it refers to "the activation of life (*energeia*) of living beings, manifest in a 'life', that is, a way of life which is conducted in a certain manner (*bios*)." Seen in this light, praxis "stands between (individual) activity and sheer (biological) existence"—in Weberian terms, between subjective-intentional action and purely reactive behavior. To be sure, in differentiation from animal life, human praxis exhibits an element of deliberation and choice (*prohairesis*); yet, especially on the social-political level, this element is not identical with private preference or whim. Above all, political action is not oriented toward an extrinsic goal or product; rather, as distinct from technical "making" (or *poiesis*), political "doing" carries its purpose in itself by being inserted into a broader matrix or pattern. In Gadamer's presentation, this matrix is the context of human solidarity: "Praxis is conduct and action in the mode of solidarity. The latter in turn is the decisive condition and basis of social reason."[15]

Considerations of this kind are not the exclusive province of professional philosophers. Among contemporary political thinkers and theorists, no one has contributed more to the clarification of praxis and action than Michael Oakeshott and Hannah Arendt; to some extent, both have also been sensitive to the linkage of praxis and experience. This is particularly obvious in the case of Oakeshott, whose first major publication was entitled *Experience and Its Modes*. The study from the beginning advanced a view of philosophizing at variance with epistemological formulas: namely, a notion of philosophy tied to experience or rather seen itself "as experience without reservation or arrest, experience which is critical throughout, unhindered and undistracted by what is subsidiary, partial or abstract." Regarding intellectual mentors, Oakeshott acknowledged his debt to the Hegelian legacy, especially as filtered through British idealism. "I ought perhaps to say," he wrote, that the view proposed in the study "derives all that is valuable in it from its affinity to what is known by the somewhat ambiguous name of idealism, and that the works from which I am conscious of having learnt most are Hegel's *Phänomenologie des Geistes* and Bradley's *Appearance and Reality*." The actual connection with Hegelian teachings may occasionally be in doubt or hard to gauge, particularly in a book not given to direct citations; but some affinities are unmistakable. Thus, the reader can hardly miss the Hegelian overtones of the following statements, referring to the correction of an erroneous or fallacious conception: "Its refutation is not to be accomplished merely by ignoring or dismissing it. To refute is to exhibit the principle of the fallacy or error in virtue of which a form of experience falls short of complete coherence; it is to discover both the half-truth in the error, and the error in the half-truth."[16]

Concerning the meaning of "experience," the study's perspective was in many ways akin to existential hermeneutics. Together with Gadamer, Oakeshott viewed experience "of all the words in the philosophic vocabulary" as "the most difficult to manage," so that "it must be the ambition of every writer reckless enough to use the word to escape the ambiguities it contains." According to the study, the term basically denoted—in Hegelian fashion—a synthesis or correlation of sensation and judgment as well as subject and object in such a manner that changes in the status of objects reflected changes or a learning process in the experiencer or observer: " 'Experience' stands for the concrete whole which analysis divides into 'experiencing' and 'what is experienced' "—aspects which "taken separately" are "meaningless abstractions." The main position challenged by this view was the empiricist notion of induction, a notion equating experience with sense-experience or a "sensation" uncontaminated by thought or judgment. Radically construed, Oakeshott stated, the empiricist approach implies "that the given in sensation must be isolated, simple, exclusive, and wholly unrelated; transient, inexpressible, unsharable and impossible of repetition"; simultaneously, the observer or experiencer becomes "a mere abstraction, now to be identified with sight, now with hearing, and always devoid of continuity and individuality"—in short, an entity reduced to "the momentary state of an isolated sense." Marshaling the resources of reflective and dialectical philosophy, the study vigorously rejected the pretense of an experience "which presents itself in utter isolation, alone, without a world, generation or relevance. Experience is always and everywhere significant," whereas "experience less than thought is a contradiction and nowhere to be found." This challenge to induction, however, did not mean endorsement of a purely intellectualist conception treating thought as self-contained and immune from experience—in other words, a conception implying that there is "an absolute distinction between what is called 'knowledge of' and 'knowledge about'," that "the object in thought is never reality but a mere being-for-thought," and that "the so-called categories of thought stand between the subject and reality," tenets which Oakeshott denounced as "false and misleading." What the twofold demarcation yielded was a vindication of philosophy as experience: "In its full character thought is not the explicit qualification of existence by an idea, but the self-revelation of existence."[17]

While stressing the wholeness or unity of experience, the study acknowledged a number of different "modes" or accents within this unity—among them the mode of practice or "practical experience." Although not devoid of interest, I shall bypass here discussion of this mode, mainly because Oakeshott has expressed himself more fully (and more perceptively) on this topic on later occasions.[18] His inaugural lecture of 1951 on "Political Education"—reprinted in *Rationalism in*

Politics—offered a detailed account of practice or action, and especially of political action. "Politics," the lecture stated, "I take to be the activity of attending to the general arrangements of a set of people whom chance or choice have brought together." In portraying political action as the practice of "attending to general arrangements," Oakeshott profiled his outlook against competing approaches: especially against empiricist and rationalist or intellectualist construals—in Weber's vocabulary, against the alternatives of reactive behavior and subjective intentional initiative. In line with the earlier study, the accent sought to preserve the wholeness of practical experience: the synthesis of thought and reality, of agency and world; for, "to understand an activity is to know it as a concrete whole" and to recognize it "as having the source of its movement within itself." As presented in the lecture, empiricism treats action basically as stimulus-response behavior governed by induced desires or spontaneous impulses; by stressing the "pursuit of merely what recommends itself from moment to moment," it implies a notion of "politics without a policy" (at least without a deliberate policy)—clearly a truncated and shortsighted view. "To understand politics as a purely empirical activity," Oakeshott countered, "is to misunderstand it, because empiricism by itself is not a concrete manner of activity at all, and can become a partner in a concrete manner of activity only when it is joined with something else." Polemically stated, the empiricist construal could be termed "an approach to lunacy"—more dispassionately, "the product of a misunderstanding."[19]

As commonly perceived, the chief alternative to induction was intellectualism, according to which concrete conduct is predicated on a prior idea or intentional blueprint—more broadly phrased, a preexisting political "ideology." According to the lecture, a political ideology could be defined as "an abstract principle, or set of related abstract principles, which has been independently premeditated" and which supplies "in advance of the activity" a "formulated end to be pursued" (together with a specification of means for reaching the end). Reviewing historical examples of ideological formulas, Oakeshott found the intellectualist position no less defective than behaviorism. "So far from a political ideology being the quasi-divine parent of political activity," he affirmed, "it turns out to be its earthly stepchild"; for, "the pedigree of every political ideology shows it to be the creature, not of premeditation in advance of political activity, but of meditation upon a manner of politics. In short, political activity comes first and a political ideology follows after." As a summary of political goals and recommended policies, an ideology had to be seen "not as an independently premeditated beginning for political activity, but as knowledge (abstract and generalized) of a concrete manner of attending to the arrangements of a society"—as a "catechism" which, in spelling out purposes to be pursued, "merely abridges a concrete manner of behavior in which those purposes are already hidden." Against this background, the accent on "attending to general arrangements" had the advantage of integrating both empirical desires and premeditated ideas into a broader purposive pattern or fabric. Political activity, the lecture concluded, "springs neither from instant desires, nor from general principles, but from the existing traditions of behavior themselves. And the form it takes, because it can take no other, is the amendment of existing arrangements by exploring and pursuing what is intimated in them." Succinctly stated: "In politics, then, every enterprise is a consequential enterprise, the pursuit, not of a dream, or of a general principle, but of an intimation."[20]

The difference between Oakeshott's notion of political practice and the intellectualist position (especially if construed as synonym for a means-ends rationality) was further sharpened in the lead essay in *Rationalism in Politics*. Within the broader confines of experience and also in its various modes, the essay asserted, two types of thought or knowledge could be differentiated (though not neatly segregated): "The first sort of knowledge I will call technical knowledge or knowledge of technique." In many domains or pursuits, "this technical knowledge is formulated into rules which are, or may be, deliberately learned, remembered, and, as we say, put into practice"; generally speaking, its chief trait is to be "susceptible of precise formulation." Standing over against this type was a "second sort of knowledge I will call practical, because it exists only in use, is not reflective and (unlike technique) cannot be formulated in rules." Although not devoid of general features, the means by which the latter kind may "be shared and becomes common knowledge is not the method of formulated doctrine"—an aspect rendering it feasible "to speak of it as traditional knowledge." According to Oakeshott, the chief distinction between the two types resided in the degree of precision: the one aiming at cognitive certainty, the other at commonsense judgment. Technical knowledge, we read, "is susceptible of formulation in rules, principles, directions, maxims—comprehensively, in propositions. It is possible to write down technical knowledge in a book." On the other hand, "it is characteristic of practical knowledge that it is not susceptible of formulation of this kind. Its normal expression is in a customary or traditional way of doing things, or, simply, in practice." As a corollary of their diverse cognitive statuses, the learning process differed in the two instances; for, while the first type "can be both taught and learned in the simplest meanings of these words," the second type "can neither be taught nor learned, but only imparted and acquired. It exists only in practice, and the only way to acquire it is by apprenticeship to a master—not because the master can teach it (he cannot), but because it can be acquired only by continuous contact with one who is perpetually practicing it."[21]

As a collection of essays, *Rationalism in Politics* only offered scattered hints or clues for a "theory" of political action; in the meantime, Oakeshott has provided a more integrated presentation in his book *On Human Conduct* (1975). In good measure, the book fleshed out and correlated (in part also corrected) previously sketched notions regarding political action—now subsumed under the broader category of "conduct." As on previous occasions, action or conduct was sharply distinguished from purely reactive behavior (termed "process") devoid of judgment or thought. An agent's actions and utterances, Oakeshott stipulated, "cannot be 'reduced' to a component of a genetic, a biochemical, a psychological or any other process, or to a consequence of any causal condition." Yet, although implying a "reflective consciousness" and even a mode of "self-disclosure," action was not simply identical with the implementation of a preconceived idea or plan. "Conduct," we read, "is not to be understood (as it is often understood) as performing actions designed to achieve imagined and wished-for ideal satisfactions. The wished-for satisfaction is what the agent 'intends', in the proper sense of 'means', not before he decides what he shall do, but in deciding it." Above all, the goal pursued in an action was never a purely private or "merely subjective" preference; in fact, the phrase "merely subjective" had to be seen as an "empty expression," and the "myth of the necessarily egocentric agent" as a "denial of agency." According to Oakeshott, action occurred typically in an intersubjective setting, and "conduct *inter homines*" was embedded in a larger purposive web made up of distinct "practices"—where "practice" stands for "a set of considerations, manners, uses, observances, customs, standards, canons, maxims, principles, rules, and offices specifying useful procedures or denoting obligations or duties which relate to human actions and utterances." A practice, in turn, might be directed toward the achievement of a common purpose—in which case it could be labeled an "instrumental practice" or a joint "enterprise." However, the most significant mode of practice—manifest in political or "civil" relations and in morality in general—was not preoccupied with ulterior aims, but only with the quality of conduct itself. Such a practice, the study observed, "is not a prudential art concerned with the success of the enterprises of agents; it is not instrumental to the achievement of any substantive purpose or to the satisfaction of any substantive want"; in short, it is "a practice without any extrinsic purpose," having to do "with good and bad conduct, and not with performances in respect of their outcomes."[22]

Like Oakeshott, Arendt has made important contributions to the clarification of political action or praxis; among her many accomplishments, none has been as widely acclaimed as her endeavor—especially in *The Human Condition*—to revive the "*vita activa*," that is, a properly political way of life. Despite several differences of accent (and also differences in philosophical presuppositions), the outlooks of the two thinkers show marked affinities. Together with Oakeshott, Arendt sharply differentiated action from reactive behavior and a purely biological life process. Under the influence of modern science and the rise of mass society, *The Human Condition* stated, "behavior has replaced action as the foremost mode of human relationship," a change fostering "the all-comprehensive pretension of the social sciences which, as 'behavioral sciences', aim to reduce man as a whole, in all his activities, to the level of a conditioned and behaving animal." Closely linked with the stress on reactive behavior was the submergence of human conduct in the biological life process—in what Arendt called "labor" or "laboring." In her definition, labor is "the activity which corresponds to the biological process of the human body, whose spontaneous growth, metabolism, and eventual decay are bound to the vital necessities produced and fed into the life process by labor." In classical thought, to labor "meant to be enslaved by necessity," a view justified by the fact that in laboring the human body is "thrown back upon itself, concentrates upon nothing but its own being alive, and remains imprisoned in its metabolism with nature without ever transcending or freeing itself from the recurring cycle of its own functioning." In

Arendt's portrayal, the restrictive character of labor did not change when, in modern times, it was linked with productivity and increasingly streamlined through "division of labor," automation, and similar devices. "The rather uncomfortable truth of the matter is," she wrote, "that the triumph the modern world has achieved over necessity is due" primarily to the fact "that the *animal laborans* was permitted to occupy the public realm; and yet, as long as the *animal laborans* remains in possession of it, there can be no true public realm, but only private activities displayed in the open."[23]

While clearly distinct from natural-biological processes, action was not synonymous with the making of artifacts, that is, with the instrumental-intentional fashioning of products—in Arendt's vocabulary: with "work." Work, we read, "provides an 'artificial' world of things, distinctly different from all natural surroundings"; it "fabricates the sheer unending variety of things whose sum total constitutes the human artifice." In contrast with both laboring and fabrication, "action"—particularly political action—was neither merely reactive nor technical-productive, but rather "revelatory" of the "human condition" or in an existential sense; in Oakeshott's terms: it was centered neither on processes nor on ulterior aims but on the quality of conduct itself, specifically "conduct *inter homines.*" As Arendt observed, action was "the only activity that goes on directly between men without the intermediary of things or matter," testifying explicitly to "the human condition of plurality"—where "plurality" refers both to the similarity and the difference of human beings, to the circumstance that "we are all the same, that is, human, in such a way that nobody is ever the same as anyone else who ever lived, lives, or will live." From the perspective of the "human condition" seen as plurality, action was an intrinsic requisite, not a contingent accessory: "Men can very well live without laboring, they can force others to labor for them, and they can very well decide merely to use and enjoy the world of things without themselves adding a single useful object to it"; in contrast, a "life without speech and without action" is "literally dead to the world; it has ceased to be a human life because it is no longer lived among men." What renders action (and speech) so crucial for human life is that "with word and deed we insert ourselves into the human world," an insertion which is "like a second birth" and in any case signifies a creative "new beginning" manifesting the "principle of freedom." Beyond the initiation of new events, however, the significance of action resides in the aspect of self-disclosure or self-revelation. "In acting and speaking," *The Human Condition* noted, "men show who they are, reveal actively their unique personal identities and thus make their appearance in the human world, while their physical identities appear without any activity of their own in the unique shape of the body and sound of the voice"; in particular, "this revelatory quality of speech and action comes to the fore where people are *with* others and neither for nor against them—that is, in sheer human togetherness."[24]

Given the stress on human freedom and the relative silence on the issue of "experience," *The Human Condition* might seem to endorse unlimited intentional or subjective initiative; but this is not (or only to a very limited extent) the case. Due to the constitutive role of plurality, action in Arendt's presentation is always embedded in "the 'web' of human relationships," a web "no less bound to the objective world of things than speech is to the existence of a living body." As a result of this embeddedness, the path of individual initiatives tends to be deflected, preventing action from being a straightforward reflection of intentionality or the implementation of premeditated goals. "The disclosure of the 'who' through speech, and the setting of a new beginning through action," we read, "always fall into an already existing web where their immediate consequences can be felt." It is "because of this already existing web of human relationships, with its innumerable, conflicting wills and intentions, that action almost never achieves its purpose." More important, the same insertion in a larger matrix jeopardizes or renders dubious the agent's status as sovereign author or cause of his projects—thus transforming action into a learning process in which "doing" and "undergoing" are closely intertwined. In Arendt's formulation: "Although everybody started his life by inserting himself into the human world through action and speech, nobody is the author or producer of his own life story. In other words, the stories, the results of action and speech, reveal an agent, but this agent is not an author or producer. Somebody began it and is its subject in the twofold sense of the word, namely its actor and sufferer, but nobody is its author." Challenging the juxtaposition—customary in social and political theory—of sovereign initiative and reactive adaptation or implementation, she added, "Because the actor always moves among and in relation to other acting beings, he is never merely a 'doer' but always and at the same time a sufferer. To do and to suffer are like opposite sides of the same coin, and the story that an act starts is composed of its consequent deeds and sufferings."[25]

As *The Human Condition* observed, the noted ambivalence conjures up long-standing philosophical quandaries, especially quandaries surrounding the relation of freedom and necessity or non-sovereignty. The opposed terms—one should realize—are not simply antithetical; for, it is precisely the "human capacity for freedom" which, "by producing the web of human relationships, seems to entangle its producer to such an extent that he appears much more the victim and the sufferer than the author and doer of what he has done." More provocatively put: nowhere else—"neither in labor, subject to the necessity of life, nor in fabrication, dependent upon given material"—does man "appear to be less free than in those capacities whose very essence is freedom." To overcome the antinomy, the study suggested, it was necessary to probe "whether our notion that freedom and non-sovereignty are mutually exclusive is not defeated by reality"; in other words: "whether the capacity for action does not harbor within itself certain potentialities which enable it to survive the disabilities of non-sovereignty." Another, related issue was whether, given the ambivalence of public or political engagement, human agents are "able to bear its burden of irreversibility and unpredictability, from which the action process draws its very strength." It is at this point that two of Arendt's most distinctive and noteworthy contributions come into play: namely, her accent on the "power to forgive" and the "power of promise"—the former seen as a remedy for irreversibility, the second as an antidote to unpredictability. As she pointed out, the function of the "faculty of promising" was to relieve the "darkness of human affairs" and to provide an alternative to "a mastery which relies on domination of one's self and rule over others; it corresponds exactly to the existence of a freedom which was given under the condition of non-sovereignty." On the other hand, forgiveness alleviates the weight of responsibility without succumbing to a merely vengeful reaction; in fact, it is "the only reaction that acts in an unexpected way and thus retains, though being a reaction, something of the original character of action. Forgiving, in other words, is the only reaction which does not merely re-act but acts anew and unexpectedly, unconditioned by the act which provoked it and therefore freeing from its consequences both the one who forgives and the one who is forgiven."[26]

III

Having reviewed the arguments advanced by some contemporary philosophers and political thinkers, the point has now come to pull the various strands together in an attempt to arrive at some theoretical conclusions. My attempt here will be guided by a query mentioned at the beginning: the question whether Weber's basic categories are sufficient and exhaustive. As one may recall, Weber's framework relies centrally on the dualism between subjective-intentional "action" and reactive "behavior" or between activity and passivity. Within the category of social action, Weber further differentiated between four major modes or types: namely, "instrumental-rational action" governed by a means-ends rationality; "value-rational action" guided by belief in ultimate ends or purposes; "affectual action" revealing the agent's emotions or feeling states; and "traditional action" determined by "ingrained habituation." As I have indicated—appealing to Bernstein's *Praxis and Action*—contemporary philosophizing and theorizing are still in large measure indebted to Weber's distinctions and definitions; even the one notable innovation (initiated by pragmatism and continued by analytical philosophy)—the concept of "practice" seen as a conventional or "rule-governed" action—can without great difficulty be reconciled or coalesced with Weber's notion of traditional conduct. My own intent, I should emphasize, is not to dismiss the Weberian categories in their respective domains, but only to see whether room should be made for alternative formulations, especially for a distinct category of political "praxis." Before exploring this question, however, I would like to turn briefly to a recent reassessment of the Weberian framework, and of action theory in general, undertaken by Jürgen Habermas—mainly because his comments (to some extent) yield a refinement and amplification of the pertinent conceptual arsenal.

The reassessment occurs in Habermas's *Theory of Communicative Action*, a broad-gauged study ranging over such themes as secularization and modernization in the West, in addition to or in conjunction with the topic of action theory; Weber's legacy is relevant in this context because of his contributions to all these themes—particularly to the issue of the rationalization of life-forms and of social action or conduct. According to Habermas, Weber's action framework was basically predicated on subjective intentionality, with the four action types representing different modes of subjective orientation. In his words, the framework relied on an "intentionalist theory of consciousness," a theory deriving the "meaning" of action not from "the linguistic medium of possible communicative understanding" but from "the opinions and intentions of an individual agent viewed initially in isolation." In this perspective, the agent's goals or motives coincided either with consciously chosen ends or else with sentiments or conventional habits; whether "utilitarian, value-rational or affectual," the goals were always "manifestations of the subjective meaning which agents can attach to their purposive activities." Regarding the rationalization of social conduct, Habermas argues, Weber actually gave priority among the types mentioned to "instrumental-rational" action, embodying a clear-cut means-ends rationality. At least in the "official" or most widespread construal of Weber's framework, the instrumental-rational type is perceived as the yardstick of social conduct in general, with other types said to exhibit decreasing levels of rationality. As the study acknowledges, some interpreters place relatively more emphasis on the "interactive" or consensual strand in Weber's outlook evident in his notion of "reciprocal" orientation—a strand, however, which was never "clearly developed" and certainly not coherently applied to the "issue of social rationalization."[27]

In an effort to correct the limitations of Weber's outlook, *Theory of Communicative Action* outlines a new or revised classification of action types (although one still broadly compatible, in my view, with Weber's categories). The classification comprises four basic modes—labeled, respectively, "teleological," "norm-regulated," "dramaturgical," and "communicative" action—of which the first three are profiled in existing literature, while the fourth represents Habermas's chief contribution. The "teleological" mode places the accent on the deliberate-intentional pursuit of goals, that is, on the purposive selection of aims by individual agents, where "aims" include both means and ends; the "central criterion" is the "rationally guided decision between practical alternatives directed toward the realization of an aim." Where the purposive decision of one agent is influenced by, or a response to, decisions of other agents, the teleological type—in Habermas's vocabulary—turns into a "strategic action model," exemplified in decision- and game-theoretical approaches. As can readily be seen, the type corresponds roughly to Weber's "instrumental-rational" and "value-rational" options (especially if the element of reciprocity in his framework is stressed). In "norm-regulated" action, the focus is not

on individual choice but on social interaction in conformity with established cultural values and social role patterns; provided "norms"
are interpreted broadly to include not only deliberately chosen standards but conventional rules and habitual ways of life, the type matches
Weber's category of "traditional" behavior as well as the more recent
notion of rule-governed "practices." The "dramaturgical" mode concentrates on the active self-disclosure or "self-representation" of an
agent in front of other agents or a public audience, that is, on the
"more or less deliberate revelation of his subjectivity"; to the extent
that desires and emotions enjoy—as Habermas says—an "exemplary
status" in such self-disclosure, the mode can be linked with the "affectual" type in Weber's scheme. The concept of "communicative
action," finally, involves interaction among social agents oriented toward a deliberate, communicatively achieved and rationally justified
consensus or agreement. In Habermas's portrayal, the category brings
into play the "further presupposition of a linguistic medium in which
the world-relations of agents are directly mirrored"; against the horizon
of "a pre-interpreted life-world, speakers and hearers in this mode
can refer simultaneously to aspects of the physical, social, and subjective
worlds in order to reach a joint definition of their situation."[28]

With this revised or amplified classification in mind, I would like
now to reconsider the correlation of action and "experience," with
particular attention to the discussed philosophical and political-theoretical arguments. Is it possible to discern a distinct mode of political
praxis, or do the reviewed arguments readily blend into Weber's and
Habermas's typologies? In some respects, an answer to these questions
seems simple or straightforward, while in other respects the situation
is more complicated. Throughout my presentation, I have stressed the
differentiation of experiential praxis both from reactive behavior or
biological life processes and from subjective-intentional—especially
instrumental-rational—endeavors, that is, from "teleological" activity
in Habermas's sense. In particular, the distinction from teleology—
the pursuit of aims lying beyond action itself—was an Ariadne thread
linking the various authors and their perspectives. Thus, Gadamer's
Reason in the Age of Science clearly juxtaposes praxis or political "doing"
to both individual activity and technical "making" (or *poiesis*). The same
kind of distinction pervades Oakeshott's *Rationalism in Politics*, where
teleology appears in such guises as "technical knowledge" and "ideological" blueprints, and also his *On Human Conduct*, where political

and moral action is set apart from "instrumental practice" conceived as a joint "enterprise." Regarding the meaning of teleology, Arendt's vocabulary in *The Human Condition* appears relatively restricted—given the equation of "work" with the fabrication of tangible goods or products. Yet, her existential definition of "action" (as conduct not serving ulterior aims) seems to make room for instrumental-teleological activity unrelated to artifacts. This alternative is in fact recognized by Arendt in another context, where she associates Aristotle's "*nous praktikos*" (in one of its senses) with a "calculating reason," a reason prompted "to step in and calculate the best ways and means to obtain" a desired end. "It is this future imagined object of desire," she writes, "that stimulates practical reason; as far as the resulting motion, the act itself, is concerned, the desired object is the beginning, while for the calculating process the same object is the end of the movement."[29]

While the foregoing points are relatively unproblematic, complications arise on other levels—due mainly to hazy terminology employed by the writers reviewed. Gadamer's *Truth and Method* speaks of the need to recognize and restore the "element of tradition" in hermeneutical understanding and experience. More pointedly and explicitly, Oakeshott's *Rationalism in Politics* portrays politics as predicated on "a traditional manner of behavior" and political action as springing "from the existing traditions of behavior themselves"; in line with these notions, practical thought or reasoning is described as "traditional knowledge," as knowledge anchored in "a customary or traditional way of doing things." Using philosophically more nuanced and elaborate language, *On Human Conduct* presents political life as a "practice," and practice in turn as a set of "customs, standards, canons, maxims, principles, rules, and offices" relating to actions and utterances. Although ambiguous in their import, expressions of this kind should not lead us (I believe) to mistake praxis for Weber's "traditional" behavior or else for "norm-regulated" or rule-governed activity. Implicit as well as explicit reasons militate against this construal. In Gadamer's case, attentiveness to tradition cannot be equated with preservation of the past—without jeopardizing the transformative quality of experience, its unqualified openness to new horizons. Regarding Oakeshott, phrases like "traditions of behavior" and "traditional knowledge" must be assessed in light of his broader argument—especially his definition of politics as a manner of "attending to general arrangements" and of probing their "intimations." Clearly, pursuit of intimations implies not only repetition of past patterns of conduct, but also exploration of possibilities opened up by the past—a point Oakeshott himself under-scores by linking intimations with the "amendment of existing ar-rangements." Concerning "practice," its affinity with conventional, rule-governed behavior is attenuated in several passages. The insertion of action in a general practice, *On Human Conduct* states, "does not reduce conduct to a process or impose upon it the character of a *mere* habit. Customs, principles, rules, etc. have no meaning except in relation to the choices and performances of agents; they are *used* in conduct and they can be used only in virtue of having been learned." To this may be added the (stronger) comment in *Rationalism in Politics* that, in contrast to technical knowledge, practical thought "exists only in use" and "cannot be formulated in rules."[30]

Similar complications beset the accent on self-disclosure. Highlighting the contrast with instrumental pursuits, Oakeshott depicts moral-political practice as a mode of human self-disclosure and self-enact-ment—thus approximating it to the "affectual" or "dramaturgical" type of action. The language of moral-political life, *On Human Conduct* asserts, "is an instrument of self-disclosure used by agents in diagnosing their situations and in choosing their responses; and it is a language of self-enactment which permits those who can use it to understand themselves and one another" and "to disclose to one another their complex individualities." The theme of self-disclosure is even more pronounced in *The Human Condition*. "Action and speech are so closely related," Arendt observes, "because the primordial and specifically human act must at the same time contain the answer to the question asked of every newcomer: 'Who are you?' This disclosure of who somebody is, is implicit in both his words and his deeds." Despite terminological similarities, there are again reasons (in my view) pre-venting assimilation of these statements to the action types discussed. In Oakeshott's parlance, self-disclosure coincides by no means with a simple revelation of "subjectivity" or the enactment of subjective pref-erences—mainly because of the ambivalence surrounding "selfhood": the fact that, in Hegelian fashion, the self only discovers himself through self-transcendence or in the course of experiences. A similar point is made by Arendt, who—apart from questioning the notion of "au-thorship"—observes that self-disclosure "can almost never be achieved as a wilful purpose, as though one possessed and could dispose of this 'who' in the same manner he has and can dispose of his (contingent) qualities. On the contrary, it is more likely that the 'who', which appears so clearly and unmistakably to others, remains hidden from the person himself, like the *daimon* in Greek religion."[31]

Among the action types mentioned, political praxis exhibits probably closest kinship to "communicative action," as delineated by Habermas. Focusing on "conduct *inter homines*," Oakeshott portrays it as involving "encounters of reciprocity in which agents converse with one another," adding that "the two most important practices in terms of which agents are durably related to one another in conduct are a common tongue and a language of moral converse." In *The Human Condition*, the linkage of language and action is a central and recurrent theme—reflected, for example, in this comment on Greek thought: "Of all the activities necessary and present in human communities, only two were deemed to be political and to constitute what Aristotle called the *bios politikos*, namely action (*praxis*) and speech (*lexis*), out of which rises the realm of human affairs." Notwithstanding this kinship, however, there are at least two aspects separating political praxis from Haberman's conception: first, the latter's somewhat one-sided rationalism, manifest in the stress on "ideal speech" and the rational validation of actions; and second, the relative neglect of experiential encounter seen as exposure to "otherness." Regarding the first aspect, Oakeshott tends to mitigate the idealized transparency of discourse through attention to "vernacular language" and its mixture of opacity and lucidity—a point echoed in Arendt's concern with the existential moorings of speech. The second (and more important) issue revolves around divergent views of human "plurality." In Habermas's presentation, communicative interaction appears basically as convergence of plural or multiple intentionalities, oriented toward a consensus on common ideas; what is bypassed or downplayed in this focus is the transformative side of experience—the Hegelian "reversal of consciousness" induced by the difference of fellowmen, social institutions, or natural conditions. At this point the character of experience as a learning process gains prominence—together with its corollary: the fusion of doing and undergoing or acting and suffering, crucial to Arendt's notion of plurality. To repeat a previously cited statement, "To do and to suffer are like opposite sides of the same coin, and the story that an act starts is composed of its consequent deeds and sufferings."[32]

By way of conclusion, I would like to return briefly to philosophy—the province from which I took my initial bearings. Arendt's construal of plurality is by no means a whimsical invention; actually, the linkage of doing and suffering, of activity and passivity, is nourished by a long-standing philosophical tradition—as especially Michael Theunissen has reminded us in his writings. Drawing inspiration from Spinoza, Schelling, and dialectical idealism (to mention only some prominent sources), the legacy has been cultivated in our century primarily by dialogical existentialism or the "philosophy of dialogue," a perspective articulated by Martin Buber and a host of other writers. In Buber's thought, interpersonal encounter involves an act of engagement and self-transcendence—but an "act" which, by virtue of its radical openness to fellowmen and the world, turns into a mode of "undergoing" or rather into a mixture of action and suffering or passivity. In his words, human interaction denotes "choosing and being chosen, action and passion at the same time; as a transcendence of all partial activities, an engagement of our entire being must, in fact, be akin to suffering." The mixture mentioned, one should note, does not simply involve a juxtaposition of opposites, nor the submergence of initiative in pure passivity; rather, action through encounter is itself permeated by passion or non-action: "This is the activity of the fully developed human being which has also been called non-action." The blending is particularly evident in dialogue, where every act of speech already anticipates a response—not as an external supplement, but as a condition of speech, manifest in an initial responsiveness or receptivity. Pursued beyond the range of contingent encounters, the same anticipation acquires ontological import. What emerges then, Theunissen comments, is "that the origin of my being or selfhood is a doing which not only simultaneously but primordially is a suffering—a doing which can be my action only because it is initially enacted and constantly renewed by others."[33]

In Heidegger's philosophy, the action-passion theme can be detected in the correlation of "project" and "thrownness" (or situatedness) delineated in *Being and Time*; but the theme is also evident in his commentary on Hegel's *Phenomenology of Mind*. Pondering Hegel's description of his *Phenomenology* as the "golgotha of the absolute spirit," Heidegger observes that, as the completion of skepticism, the experience of consciousness is "the path of despair, the path by which consciousness at each stage loses what in it is not yet true, sacrificing it to the epiphany of truth." Thus, "the science of the phenomenology of mind is the theology of the absolute, the latter seen in its *parousia* on the dialectical-speculative Good Friday." The reference to the "path of despair," to be sure, should not be read as an expression of defeatism or fatalistic surrender—as is clear from Heidegger's stress on "our contribution (*Zutat*)" in the appearance of Being. This kind of misreading is unfortunately quite common. As Arendt has noted, "It is in accordance with the great tradition of Western thought to think along these lines: to accuse freedom of luring man into necessity, to condemn action, the spontaneous beginning of something new, because its results fall into a predetermined net of relationships"; the "only salvation from this kind of freedom seems to lie in non-action, in abstention from the whole realm of human affairs." In her notion of forgiveness, however, she indicated another alternative: the alternative of a passion or reaction which transcends fatalism for the sake of genuine renewal. In *Reason in the Age of Science* Gadamer cites a saying by the "weeping philosopher," Heraclitus, to the effect that "the *logos* is common to all, but people behave as if each had a private reason." And he asks, "Does this have to remain this way?"[34]

3

Pluralism Old and New:
Foucault on Power

Politics and power seem to be naturally paired; according to long-standing beliefs shading over into commonplaces, the two terms are intimately connected, if not actually synonyms. In our own century, proponents of an "empirical" or "scientific" study of politics have frequently emphasized this linkage to the point of making power the central, if not the sole, topic of their inquiries.[1] Commonly, this emphatic focus on power has a polemical edge or purpose: the aim of differentiating politics from such competing conceptions as concern for the "good life," maintenance of public institutions or "regimes," or cultivation of shared beliefs and ideals. In their polemical thrust, recent power theorists thus corroborate or reiterate—albeit less elegantly—such well-known Hobbesian adages as *"auctoritas non veritas facit legem"* and "covenants without the sword are but words." Although united on a polemical level, power arguments differ with regard to the precise locus and scope of power. In the modern age—from the time of Machiavelli to our own—power has predominantly been construed as rooted in human will, and as the attribute or property of distinctive political agents ranging from "princes" or governmental leaders over social groups and classes to semi-private actors and even to the nation at large seen as a collective unit. To the extent that a distinction was made between more derivative and more basic or "foundational" layers of power, modern theorizing (and Western thought in general) has tended to thematize the latter under such rubrics as *"suprema potestas"* and "sovereignty," concepts denoting an ultimate decision-making capacity.

In twentieth-century social science, the sketched view (or a main strand in it) has been articulated most prominently by Max Weber, for whom power denoted basically the ability or probability of social actors, specifically individual actors, to implement their wills against the resistance of others—a formulation which, with varying accents, permeates contemporary literature on the topic. In his study entitled *Power*, Steven Lukes has provided a succinct synopsis of scholarly debates in this area—including the debates between "pluralist" and anti-pluralist factions—in addition to offering his own amendments to the dominant conception. In Lukes's presentation, contemporary thinking can be divided roughly into three major camps, labeled "one-dimensional," "two-dimensional," and "three-dimensional," respectively, and differentiated by the degree to which the exercise of power extends from overt "decision-making" over covert compulsion or manipulation ("nondecision-making") to the broader "mobilization of bias" through institutional and social constraints. While favoring a complex, multidimensional approach, the study stresses the common Weberian core of the three perspectives, portraying them as different "interpretations and applications of one and the same underlying concept of power, according to which A exercises power over B when A affects B in a manner contrary to B's interests." Lukes's account, it is true, is not entirely restricted to Weber's legacy in its various manifestations, but concedes the possibility of "alternative (no less contestable) ways of conceptualizing power, involving alternative criteria of significance." A chief example of this possibility is functional systems theory as championed by Talcott Parsons, where power operates as a general medium of social cohesion rather than an instrument of control. "Parsons's conceptualization of power," he writes, "ties it to authority, consensus and the pursuit of collective goals, and dissociates it from conflicts of interest and, in particular, from coercion and force."[2]

At the time of its appearance, Lukes's study provided (and was meant to provide) a handy summary of the prevailing "state of the art," a state whose parameters were clearly staked out and were unlikely to be unsettled by new theoretical impulses—or so it seemed until the publication of Foucault's writings in the field. The iconoclastic character of Michel Foucault's opus is evident and acknowledged in many areas, ranging from epistemology to historiography; but his attention to political questions is of relatively recent origin—and so is his recognition by students of politics and political thought.[3] Among his numerous contributions in the area of social and political analysis none appears more crucial and fertile than his arguments relating to power—although their precise contours emerge only against the backdrop of traditional political theory. Pointing to the "novelty" of his "reflection on power," Colin Gordon finds this reflection located "outside the fields of force of two antithetical conceptions of power whose conjunction and disjunction determine the ground rules of most modern political thought: on the one hand, the benign sociological model of power as the agency of social cohesion and normality, serving to assure the conditions of existence and survival of the community, and on the other the more polemical representation of power as an instance of repression, violence and coercion, eminently represented in the State with its 'bodies of armed men'." Marking a break with the traditional tendency of tying power to "some substantive instance or agency of sovereignty"—Gordon adds—Foucault's initiative seeks to uncover "the *positive, productive* characteristics" of power undergirding "the installation of what he calls a politics or a regime of truth."[4] In the following I intend to trace the path of Foucault's venture into political analysis by concentrating, first of all, on his initial conception of power, as formulated roughly at the time of *Discipline and Punish* and *The History of Sexuality*; next, I shall review more recent modifications and refinements of this conception, including his differentiation between power and violence. By way of conclusion, I intend to place Foucault's venture into the context of twentieth-century thought, by juxtaposing it both to Hannah Arendt's views on politics and power and to Heidegger's broader philosophical comments on power and domination.

I

In delineating Foucault's conception of power, commentators regularly focus on a host of novel and startling terms like "bio-power," "micropower," and the "capillary" character of power. Thus, Alan Sheridan—author of *Michel Foucault: The Will to Truth*—asserts that "by 'power', Foucault does not mean 'Power', in the sense of a unified state apparatus whose task it is to ensure the subjection of the citizens of a particular society. Nor does it mean a general system of domination exerted by one group over another, the effect of which spreads to the whole of society. Power should be understood as 'the multiplicity of power relations' at work in a particular area"; what exists at this level is "an infinitely complex network of 'micro-powers', of power relations that permeate every aspect of social life." Similarly, in their study *Michel Foucault: Beyond Structuralism and Hermeneutics*, Dreyfus and Rabinow note that "to understand power in its materiality, its day-to-day operation, we must go to the level of the micropractices, the political technologies in which our practices are formed." Foucault's "originality," in their view, consists chiefly in having "isolated the mechanism by which power operates: meticulous rituals of power. He claims to have found the manner in which power is localized: the political technology of the body. He also claims to have revealed the dynamics of how power works: the microphysics of power." Similarly, in an essay concentrating entirely on questions of power, another commentator states, "Foucault's account demonstrates that modern power is 'capillary', that it operates at the lowest extremities of the social body in everyday social practices"; in this manner he "enables us to understand power very broadly, and yet very finely, as anchored in the multiplicity of what he calls 'micropractices', the social practices which comprise everyday life in modern society. This positive conception of power has the general but unmistakable implication of a call for a 'politics of everyday life'."[5]

Although clearly capturing important facets of Foucault's argument, an exclusive reliance on the terms mentioned appears misleading in several respects. First of all, one may query why a "call for a politics of everyday life" should necessarily be tied to a "microphysics of power," that is, to a "bio-politics" concerned with the production and reproduction of human and social life or to what Foucault elsewhere terms the methods of "disciplinary power." Other recent authors, among them Maurice Merleau-Ponty, have championed a concrete "everyday" politics without endorsement of disciplinary techniques.[6] More important, one may wonder why the notion of microphysics should encapsulate a "positive conception of power"—in Gordon's words "the positive, productive characteristics" of power—and thus be less repressive, less bent on the "subjection of citizens," than earlier conceptions of a "unified state apparatus" or of class domination. As it seems to me, treating the notion as plainly "positive" renders unintelligible Foucault's critical comments on the emergence of bio-power—to the effect that "a kind of animalization of man through the most sophisticated political techniques results. Both the development of the possibilities of the human and social sciences, and the simultaneous possibility of protecting life and of the holocaust make their historical appearance."[7] On a more general level, the identification of Foucault's perspective with bio-power militates against the demands of historical concreteness, that is, the need to differentiate between historical modes of power—a neglect particularly disturbing in the case of an author so persistently concerned with history. Although "repressive" and "positive" dimensions of power may plausibly be distinguished for many purposes, it seems odd to associate the former entirely with the past and the latter with modern disciplinary regimes; precisely in seeking to transcend purely repressive construals, Foucault might be expected to explore both the constructive and negative features in varying constellations of power and thus to uncover different historical modes of "a politics or regime of truth."

In my view, Foucault's perspective cannot be detached from historical nuances; moreover, apart from the difference between historical periods, attention must also be given to the evolving, non-static character of his own argument. Foucault himself has been the first to recognize the slow and sometimes tortuous path of his theorizing. As he stated in an interview in 1977, with specific reference to the issue or "question of power," "I am struck by the difficulty I had in formulating it. When I think back now, I ask myself what else it was that I was talking about, in *Madness and Civilization* or *The Birth of the Clinic*, but power? Yet, I am perfectly aware that I scarcely ever used the word and never had such a field of analyses at my disposal." According to Foucault's account, his turn to power was obstructed or complicated primarily by the prevailing clamor of ideological polemics, especially by the denunciation of "socialist power" in terms of "totalitarianism" and of Western capitalist power under the rubric of "class domination." In contrast with the profusion of polemical rhetoric, he continued, "the mechanics of power in themselves were never analyzed. This task could only begin after 1968, that is to say on the basis of daily struggles at the grass roots level, among those whose fight was located in the fine meshes of the web of power. This was where the concrete nature of power became visible, along with the prospect that these analyses of power would prove fruitful in accounting for all that had hitherto remained outside the field of political analysis."[8]

To be sure, while animated chiefly by epistemological concerns, Foucault's early writings were not entirely unaware of politics; yet, awareness was limited to what he later called the "repressive," coercive, or purely negative aspect of power. Comparing this aspect with broader ideological slogans, the same interview termed the "notion of repression" a "more insidious one," in the sense that "I myself at all events have had much more trouble in freeing myself of it, insofar as it does indeed appear to correspond so well with a whole range of phenomena which belong among the effects of power. When I wrote *Madness and Civilization*, I made at least an implicit use of this notion of repression." A similar admission occurs in another interview of the same year which differentiates clearly between an early epistemological and a later, more politically astute phase of thinking. Commenting on his inaugural address of 1970, translated as "The Discourse on Language," Foucault remarked, "Till then, it seems to me, I accepted the traditional conception of power as an essentially judicial mechanism, as that which lays down the law, which prohibits, which refuses, and which has a whole range of negative effects: exclusion, rejection, denial, obstruction, obfuscation, etc. Now I believe that conception to be inadequate. It had, however, been adequate to my purpose in *Madness and Civilization*." As in the previously mentioned context, the shift of attention or change of awareness was again attributed to the aftermath of 1968, and especially to some direct social-political experiences in France. "There came a time," we are told, "when this (negative conception) struck me as inadequate: it was during the course of a concrete experience that I had with prisons, starting in 1971–72. The case of the penal system convinced me that the question of power needed to be formulated not so much in terms of justice as in those of technology, of tactics and strategy, and it was this substitution for a judicial and negative grid of a technical and strategic one that I tried to effect in *Discipline and Punish* and then to exploit in *The History of Sexuality*."[9]

In line with earlier considerations, one might ask again at this point why a "judicial" approach should necessarily yield a repressive version, and a "technical and strategic" approach a positive or constructive model of power: surely, "judicial mechanisms" entail not only legal prohibitions but also legal rights, not only rules of exclusion, but also modes of entitlement—while techniques and strategies carry distinct overtones of manipulation and coercion. Leaving aside this quandary for the moment, it is clear that Foucault's studies on punishment and sexuality marked a break with a narrow or restrictive view of power and a tentative move toward a more complex or multidimensional type of analysis. Both the break and initial steps toward reorientation are highlighted in two lectures delivered at the Collège de France in January of 1976. The lectures spelled out in some detail the historical ramifications of the restrictive-legalistic model by tracing it from the liberal-capitalist era back to its roots in royal absolutism and medieval kingship; in doing so, however, they also revealed a basic ambivalence in Foucault's argument: namely, his vacillation regarding the basic flaw of the criticized model. Regarding the origins of the model, the lectures placed the accent chiefly on medieval and absolutist royal power. "It seems to me," Foucault noted, "that in Western societies since medieval times it has been royal power that has provided the essential focus around which legal thought has been elaborated. It is in response to the demands of royal power, for its profit and to serve as its instrument or justification, that the judicial edifice of our own society has been developed." The crucial nexus between royal power and legality, in this analysis, resided in the notion of "sovereignty," defined originally (though later extended to non-monarchical regimes) as the supreme authority of the king: "I believe that the king remains the central personage in the whole legal edifice of the West."[10]

As portrayed in the lectures, the kingship model was continued and refashioned subsequently by both liberal and Marxist construals, the first characterized by the treatment of power as a kind of legal property, the second by the association of power with class domination. In Foucault's words, "I consider there to be a certain point in common between the juridical, and let us call it 'liberal' conception of political power (found in the *philosophes* of the eighteenth century) and the Marxist conception, or at any rate a certain conception currently held to be Marxist: I would call this common point an economism in the theory of power. By this I mean that in the case of liberal-juridical theory, power is taken to be a right, which one is able to possess like a commodity, and which one can in consequence transfer or alienate, either wholly or partially." As exemplified chiefly in the "social contract" tradition, the perspective concentrates on "that concrete power which every individual holds, and whose partial or total cessation enables political power or sovereignty to be established." Regarding the Marxist conception, on the other hand, Foucault speaks of an "economic functionality of power," in the sense that power is functionally dependent on a given mode of production and its attendant class structure: "The economic functionality is present to the extent that power is conceived primarily in terms of the role it plays in the maintenance simultaneously of the relations of production and of a class domination which the development and specific forms of the forces of production have rendered possible." Thus, in the liberal-juridical version political power "obeys the model of a legal transaction involving a contractual type of exchange," whereas in the Marxist interpretation "the historical *raison d'être* of political power and the principle of its concrete forms and actual functioning, is located in the economy" and the prevailing mode of class domination.[11]

As is apparent from this portrayal, the central flaw or restrictiveness of traditional accounts resides not so much or not primarily in their emphasis on repression (as opposed to positive or constructive aspects); rather, what vitiates them is a certain "patrimonial" or "proprietary" outlook—the assumption that power is the attribute of kings, entrepreneurs, or classes—and their neglect of the broader, "capillary" network of power relations. The deemphasis of repression is evident in the discussion of kingship, where, in addition to absolutist tendencies, Foucault mentions also the long-standing practice "of imposing limits upon this sovereign power, of submitting it to certain rules of right, within whose confines it had to be exercised," adding, "The essential role of the theory of right, from medieval times onwards was to fix the legitimacy of power." With reference to liberal and Marxist construals the lectures question not principally their repressiveness but the "subordinate position" assigned to power relative to the economy, and especially the thesis according to which power is "modelled upon the commodity." Is power, Foucault asks, "something that one possesses, acquires, cedes through force or contract, that one alienates or recovers, that circulates, that voids this or that region"—or do we not, on the contrary, "need to employ varying tools in its analysis?"[12]

The contrast between "patrimonial" and "capillary" views, it is true, is by no means the only or even the predominant theme of Foucault's presentation: persistently the issue of repression infiltrates, and sometimes overshadows, the contrast mentioned. In commenting on the limitations imposed on kingship since medieval times, Foucault claims that "the essential function of the discourse and techniques of right has been to efface the domination intrinsic to (royal) power" and thus to conceal the repressiveness of sovereignty. In a more elaborate (and somewhat convoluted) fashion, the discussion of liberal and Marxist interpretations is linked with the thesis or theorem—articulated among others by Freud and Reich—which defines power as "a relation of force" or "an organ of repression" in the sense that "power represses nature, the instincts, a class, individuals." When this theorem is joined or fused with the liberal-juridical account, one obtains a peculiar model—termed "contract-oppression schema"—in which power "risks becoming oppression whenever it over-extends itself," that is, where power has "oppression as its limit, or rather as the transgression of this limit." To complicate matters further, Foucault introduces a second, more radical version of the "relation of force" theorem, a version associated in the lectures with Nietzsche and which analyzes politics "primarily in terms of struggle, conflict and war" and in effect treats power as "war, a war continued by other means." According to this Nietzschean alternative, the role of power is "perpetually to re-inscribe this relation (of force) through a form of unspoken warfare; to re-inscribe it in social institutions, in economic inequalities, in language, in the bodies themselves of each and every one of us." In this manner, the moderate "contract-oppression schema" is augmented by a "war-repression schema for which the pertinent opposition is not between the legitimate and illegitimate, as in the first schema, but between struggle and submission."[13]

The topic of repression, one should add, is not abandoned in subsequent, more "constructive" segments of the lectures: just as traditional accounts were not unequivocally marked by repressiveness, Foucault's counter-model—the model of modern "micro-power" or "disciplinary power"—is not distinguished by its absence. "My general project over the past few years," Foucault observes, has been "to give due weight to the fact of domination, to expose both its latent nature and its brutality." Yet, the term "domination" at this point refers no longer to the royal-juridical model but rather to new forms of social control emerging in bourgeois society in the wake of the industrial revolution: "In speaking of domination I do not have in mind that solid and global kind of domination that one person exercises over others, or one group over another, but the manifold forms of domination that can be exercised within society. Not the domination of the king in his central position, therefore, but that of his subjects in their mutual relations:

not the uniform edifice of sovereignty, but the multiple forms of subjugation that have a place and function within the social organism." In contrast with older, more compact and stationary types of constraints, the new power mechanisms, according to Foucault, are "more dependent upon bodies and what they do than upon the earth and its products"; they allow "time and labor, rather than wealth and commodities, to be extracted from bodies" by means of "continuous and permanent systems of surveillance." As he adds, "This new type of power which can no longer be formulated in terms of sovereignty is, I believe, one of the great inventions of bourgeois society; it has been a fundamental instrument in the constitution of industrial capitalism and of the type of society that is its accompaniment. This non-sovereign power, which lies outside the form of sovereignty, is disciplinary power."[14]

Actually, in Foucault's analysis, disciplinary power has not entirely supplanted the royal-juridical tradition but rather has tended to coalesce with it—with the result that politics today exhibits a mixture of sovereign and disciplinary controls. "The powers of modern society," we are told, "are exercised through, on the basis of, and by virtue of, this very heterogeneity between a public right of sovereignty and a polymorphous disciplinary mechanism." Despite its innovative and richly textured features, Foucault's disciplinary power is readily compatible (I believe) with the functionalist theory of power, and especially with Parsons's view of systemic integration and cohesiveness. The convergence is evident in the description of modern power as "a closely linked grid of disciplinary coercions whose purpose is in fact to assure the cohesion" of the social organism. The affinity is equally obvious in Foucault's stress on the "normalizing" effects of disciplines and his distinction between "natural" or quasi-mechanical rules, on the one hand, and juridical or properly "normative" rules, on the other. "The disciplines may well be the carriers of a discourse that speaks of a rule," he notes, "but this is not the juridical rule deriving from sovereignty, but a natural rule or norm. The code they come to define is not that of law but of normalization; their reference is to a theoretical horizon which of necessity has nothing in common with the edifice of right. It is human science which constitutes their (statutory) domain, and clinical knowledge their jurisprudence." Under the impact of disciplines, what modern industrial (and post-industrial) developments usher in is a "society of normalization," a society deriving its rules not from sovereign commands but from a more muted "microphysics" of subliminal constraints.[15]

From the juxtaposition of traditional-juridical and disciplinary modes of control Foucault's lectures derived a number of theoretical and methodological lessons—lessons which potentially exceeded the bounds of functional cohesion. In contrast with the older patrimonial and proprietary model, these lessons shifted the accent to the fragmented, "capillary" (and if you will: ontologically dispersed) character of power; in lieu of the customary "pluralist" doctrine—tied to willful designs of individuals and groups—the shift adumbrated the notion of a non-proprietary and non-voluntaristic pluralism. The basic lesson spelled out in the lectures was the need to depart from sovereignty and the Hobbesian vision of "Leviathan." The analysis of power, Foucault observed, "should be concerned with power at its extremities, in its ultimate destinations, with those points where it becomes capillary, that is, in its more regional and local forms and institutions. Its paramount concern, in fact, should be with the point where power surmounts the rules of right which organize and delimit it and extends itself beyond them, invests itself in institutions, (and) becomes embodied in techniques." As he realized, this outlook was strongly non- or anti-traditional in orientation, especially to the extent that traditional political thought subscribed to a uniform structure of rules and sanctions: "I would say that we should direct our researches on the nature of power not towards the juridical edifice of sovereignty, the State apparatuses and ideologies which accompany them, but towards domination and the material operators of power, towards forms of subjection and the inflections and utilizations of their localized systems, and towards strategic apparatuses. We must eschew the model of Leviathan in the study of power."[16]

Other lessons mentioned in the lectures were closely associated with this aspect of fragmentation and dispersal. A corollary of the deemphasis of sovereign commands was the general advice that analysis in this area "should not concern itself with power at the level of conscious intention or decision" and thus should avoid the "labyrinthine" question, "Who then has power and what has he in mind? What is the aim of someone who possesses power?" Without entirely neglecting conscious designs, the study of power in Foucault's view should concentrate on "the point where its intention, if it has one, is completely invested in its real and effective practices" or where it is manifest "in its external visage." In fact, rather than tracing power to deliberate or purposive aims, subjective intentions and human "subjects" themselves should be seen as produced by, or at least enmeshed in, prevailing constellations of power: "We should try to grasp subjection in its material instance as a constitution of subjects. This would be the exact opposite of Hobbes' project in *Leviathan*, and of that, I believe, of all jurists for whom the problem is the distillation of a single will— or rather, the constitution of a unitary, singular body animated by the spirit of sovereignty—from the particular wills of a multiplicity of individuals." Instead of being preoccupied with will formation and the establishment of a central will or "spirit," Foucault's lectures argued in favor of attempting "to study the myriad of bodies which are constituted as peripheral subjects as a result of the effects of power." In line with the departure from voluntarism the lectures counseled against construing power relations in terms of a deliberate antithesis between rulers and ruled, between the powerful and powerless. Power, we are told, "is not to be taken to be a phenomenon of one individual's consolidated and homogeneous domination over others, or that of one group or class over others." What, in contrast, should "always be kept in mind" is that power is "not that which makes the difference between those who exclusively possess and retain it, and those who do not have it and submit to it," but that it is "something which circulates" or "which only functions in the form of a chain."[17]

The notion of a "chain" or capillary network, one should add, was not meant to suggest a complete equality or equal distribution of power—which in the end would coincide with non-power or an absence of power. In Foucault's analysis, the critique of patrimonial sovereignty was not intended to vindicate the functionalist treatment of power as a neutral currency or the liberal utopia of an "end of power" as the external limit of power politics. While opposed to traditional hierarchies, his perspective did not rule out the assumption of a power differential— although this differential needed to be studied from the bottom up, rather than from the top down. "I do not believe," Foucault stated, that "power is the best distributed thing in the world, although in some sense that is indeed so. We are not dealing with a sort of democratic or anarchic distribution of power through bodies." What the notion of a capillary network rejected was not power itself, but only the endeavor "to attempt some kind of deduction of power starting from its center and aimed at the discovery of the extent to which it permeates into the base." Instead of this deductive endeavor, what was required was "an *ascending* analysis of power, starting, that is, from its infinitesimal mechanisms which each have their own history, their own trajectory, their own techniques and tactics," in order to determine "how these mechanisms of power have been—and continue to be—invested, colonized, utilized, transformed, displaced, extended, etc., by even more general mechanisms and by forms of global domination." Thus, in lieu of causal derivations from a presumed source (or sources) of power, the lectures urged a concrete historical inquiry, beginning at the "lowest level," into the operation of power mechanisms in given situations. In the modern age, for example, one needed to see how disciplinary controls, "at a given moment, in a precise conjuncture and by means of a certain number of transformations, have begun to become economically advantageous and politically useful"— that is, how "apparatuses of surveillance, the medicalization of sexuality, of madness, of delinquency, all the micro-mechanisms of power" came "from a certain moment of time, to represent the interests of the bourgeoisie."[18]

Summarizing the preceding account, one might say that Foucault's thoughts on power—at the time in question—were marked by a number of distinctive accents or orientations. First, there was his break with tradition: more specifically, his break with sovereignty and with the patrimonial-juridical conception according to which power is the property of individuals, groups, or collectivities. Next, and closely linked with this break, we find his effort to offer a concrete analysis of non-patrimonial or systemic constraints operative in modern industrial society—an analysis highlighted by such labels as "bio-power" and "disciplinary power" and compatible in large measure with the functionalist treatment of society as an integrated organism governed by standards of normalcy. Finally, meandering through these arguments, we discover his critique of simple repressiveness and his search for a "positive, constructive" approach to power—where repressiveness (as I have tried to show) functions as an ingredient in the patrimonial and the disciplinary model alike. Both the critique and the mentioned search surface again at the end of the discussed 1976 lectures. "If one wants to look for a non-disciplinary form of power, or rather, to struggle against disciplines and disciplinary power," Foucault remarks, "it is not towards the ancient right of sovereignty that one should turn, but towards the possibility of a new form of right, one which must indeed be anti-disciplinarian, but at the same time liberated from the principle of sovereignty." In moving in this constructive direction, one needs to differentiate power from repression, since, he adds, "the critical application of the notion of repression is found to be vitiated and nullified from the outset by the two-fold juridical and disciplinary reference it contains to sovereignty on the one hand and to normalization on the other."[19]

II

Foucault's analysis cannot be laid to rest at this point. Despite a powerful display of critical verve—evident in his critiques of sovereignty, disciplinary constraints, and repressiveness—his arguments so far still leave too many issues unresolved: above all, the issue of a notion of power not synonymous with repression. As previously indicated, reviewers of his work often collapse his thought into the micro-mechanisms outlined in *Discipline and Punish* and *The History of Sexuality*—a treatment I consider lopsided and misleading. Apart from paradoxes and oddities mentioned before, the portrayal tends to land Foucault squarely in the positivist camp, including the positivist fact-value dilemma or the bifurcation between empirical description and normative aspirations. Actually, if seriously pressed, the portrayal conjures up the danger of fatalism or determinism—by intimating the futility of resistance to a network of inescapable disciplines.[20] For these and other reasons, Foucault's "positive" alternative in my view cannot simply be "positivist" in the sense of coinciding with micro-mechanisms factually operating in modern "societies of normalization." Instead of merely capturing factual-empirical constraints, the conception of capillary networks must point toward underlying (or ontological) premises of political life. Seen in this light, Foucault's approach necessarily transcends the antithesis of power and non-power, repression and liberation—thus bringing into view a notion of human "freedom" which is no longer the opposite, but rather simply the other side and, in fact, the condition of possibility of power.

In the meantime, these comments are no longer merely personal opinions but are buttressed by Foucault's more recent writings—especially an essay of 1982 to which I now turn, entitled "The Subject and Power." The essay differentiates between three main modes or dimensions of human experience: namely, language and signification;

labor and technical production; and political power. While linguistics and semiotics are said to provide good instruments for studying the first dimension, and while economic history and theory offer keys to the second, power relations are claimed to be a less clearly demarcated domain, lacking so far adequate "tools of study." Somewhat later in the essay, the differentiation is rephrased in terms of the distinction between three kinds of relationships: relations of communication; relations to external objects or things; and power relations. It is necessary, Foucault insists, "to distinguish power relations from relationships of communication which transmit information by means of a language, a system of signs, or any other symbolic medium. No doubt communicating is always a certain way of acting upon another person or persons; but the production and circulation of elements of meaning can have as their objective or as their consequence certain results in the realm of power: the latter are not simply an aspect of the former." Similarly, it is important not to confuse power with objective or instrumental modes of endeavors. There is a kind of control, we read, "which is exerted over things and gives the ability to modify, use, consume, or destroy them—a power which stems from aptitudes directly inherent in the body or relayed by external instruments. Let us say that here it is a question of 'capacity'. On the other hand, what characterizes the 'power' we are analyzing is that it brings into play relations between individuals (or between groups)"—relations which do not take the form of "a zero-sum game."[21]

Although emphasizing their analytical differentiation, Foucault does not endorse a rigid segregation of the mentioned dimensions. "Whether or not they pass through systems of communication," he notes, "power relations have a specific nature"—which also demarcates them from technical capacities; but "this is not to say that there is a question of three separate domains." Instead of mutual isolation, what one encounters rather are "three types of relationships which in fact always overlap one another, support one another reciprocally, and use each other mutually as means to an end." Relying on concrete historical examples, the essay suggests that the correlation of dimensions yields a distinctive blend of communication, power, and technical control— whose respective weights shift with changing circumstances. "In a given society," we are told, "there is no general type of equilibrium between instrumental activities, systems of communication, and power relations; rather, there are diverse forms, diverse places, diverse circumstances or occasions in which these interrelationships establish themselves according to a specific model." In addition, it is possible to discern various "blocks" in which "the adjustment of capacities, the resources of communication, and power relations constitute regulated and concerted systems." As Foucault indicates, particularly compact or stable "blocks" of correlations might be called "disciplines" (in a slight reformulation of previous usage of the term). Such disciplines, he notes, reveal "according to artificially clear and decanted systems, the manner in which modes of productive capacity, communication, and power can be welded together. They also display different models of articulation, sometimes giving preeminence to power relations and obedience (as in those disciplines of a monastic or penitential type), sometimes to instrumental activities (as in the disciplines of the workshops or hospitals), sometimes to relations of communication (as in the disciplines of apprenticeship), sometimes also to a saturation of the three types of relationship (as perhaps in military discipline)."[22]

Turning to the "specific nature of power" or power relations, Foucault advances a number of important stipulations which together give a captivating, new profile to this theme. The first stipulation concerns the operation of power and places power squarely in the context of action theory or a theory of political "praxis." "The exercise of power," the essay states, "is not simply a relationship between partners, individual or collective; it is a way in which certain actions modify others." Instead of denoting an abstract cognitive category or an invariant structure, power is said to exist "only when it is put into action, even if, of course, it is integrated into a disparate field of possibilities brought to bear upon permanent structures." Viewed in the light of action theory, power signifies a relation between actors or agents, and not simply between human beings seen as physiological organisms or as reactive-behavioral mechanisms. "In effect," Foucault asserts, "what defines a relationship of power is that it is a mode of action which does not act directly and immediately on others. Instead it acts upon their actions: an action upon an action, on existing actions or on those which may arise in the present or the future." As an action or set of actions bearing on other actions, power yields effects in a manner which exceeds the bounds of causality and of subjective-intentional designs: in contrast to the former, its operation is less pre-determined or predictable; in comparison with the latter, it is less pre-meditated or planned. Although extremely manifold or diversified in its manifestations, power never strays too far from the confines of action and agency: "It incites, it induces, it makes easier or more difficult; in the extreme case it constrains or forbids absolutely; it is nevertheless always a way of acting upon an acting subject or acting subjects by virtue of their acting or being capable of action."[23]

Being demarcated from causality and intentional designs, power-action or action-power also deviates from external-physical and ideal-mental occurrences—which means: it coincides neither with external compulsion or violence nor with consensus. At this point, the two dimensions adjacent to power relations—objective capacities and communication—emerge in Foucault's analysis as limits or boundaries of power properly speaking. Unwilling to reduce actors or agents either to pure "mind" (that is, subjectivity) or "matter," his presentation equates power relations neither with rational "meetings of minds" nor with empirical-objective modes of constraint. Power, he argues, is "not a function of consent; in itself it is not a renunciation of freedom, a transference of rights." Although sometimes obliquely related to "a prior or permanent consent," power-action is "not by nature the manifestation of a consensus." Equally important is the demarcation of power relations from thing-relations or external compulsion. Putting aside an earlier fascination with "force" or the "war-repression" model, the essay refuses to collapse power into a "violence" alleged to be "its primitive form, its permanent secret and its last resource." Contrary to the demands of action theory, we read, "a relationship of violence acts upon a body or upon things; it forces, bends, breaks on the wheel, or closes the door on all possibilities." What distinguishes power-action from such violence is that it "can only be articulated on the basis of two elements which are each indispensable for a genuine power relationship: that 'the other' (the one over whom power is exercised) be thoroughly recognized and maintained to the very end as a person who acts; and that, faced with a power relationship, a whole field of responses, reactions, results, and possible inventions may open up." Again, as in the case of the three dimensions of experience, the point here is not a simple isolation of power from its limits or boundaries: "Obviously the bringing into play of power relations does not exclude the use of violence any more than it does the obtaining of consent; no doubt the exercise of power can never do without one or the other, often both at the same time. But even though consensus and violence are the instruments or the results, they do not constitute the principle or the basic nature of power."[24]

Given this delimitation of its boundaries, Foucault is led to associate power-action with the notions of "government" or "regime"—in Gordon's words, with a "politics or a regime of truth"—notions which, in his portrayal, transgress both pure enmity and pure consensus. "Basically," he states, "power is less a confrontation between two adversaries, or a linking of one to the other, than a question of government"—provided the word is "allowed the very broad meaning which it had in the sixteenth century," when government "did not refer only to political structures or to the management of states," but "designated the way in which the conduct of individuals or of groups might be directed: the government of children, of souls, of communities, of families, of the sick." In the older and broader sense, to govern means to create an "open field of possibilities" in the sense of inaugurating and maintaining a public or political space for possible action—differently put: it means "to structure the possible field of action of others" (and of those involved in governing). The emphasis on government as a public space of possibilities clarifies further the concept of political action or agency by underscoring its difference both from mechanical reaction and from subjective-consensual (or intersubjective) interaction. "The relationship proper to power," we read, "would not therefore be sought on the side of violence or of struggle, nor on that of voluntary convergence (all of which can, at best, only be instruments of power), but rather in the area of that singular mode of action, neither warlike nor juridical, which is government."[25]

Together with the valorization of terms like government and regime, Foucault's essay places in the foreground another category (previously not very prominent in his writings): that of human "freedom" seen as a basic requisite of action and thus of power. "When one defines the exercise of power as a mode of action upon the actions of others," he observes, "when one characterizes these actions as government of men by other men in the broadest sense, one includes an important element: freedom. Power is exercised only over free subjects and only insofar as they are free"—by which "we mean individual or collective subjects who are faced with a field of possibilities in which several ways of behaving, several reactions and diverse comportments may be realized." Against this background, power-action necessarily conflicts with doctrines of strict determinism or (cosmological) fatalism—doctrines which, in more subdued form, reverberate in physicalism and social-scientific behaviorism: "Where the determining factors saturate the whole, there is no relationship of power; slavery is not a power relationship when man is in chains (in this case there exists only a physical relationship of constraint)." Given the linkage between power and freedom, resistance or challenges to power are not simply side effects or avoidable hazards; in fact, Foucault's essay portrays "forms of resistance" as a particularly promising and fruitful focus in the study of power relations, outlining a set of criteria characterizing such antagonisms in contemporary society. More important still, the same linkage militates against the time-honored assumption—cherished by Enlightenment thinkers and liberals of every persuasion—according to which power necessarily negates freedom, whose ascendancy, in turn, heralds the "end of power." In Foucault's words, "There is no direct clash of power and freedom which would render them mutually exclusive (such that freedom disappears wherever power is exercised), but rather a much more complicated interplay. In this interplay, freedom may well appear as the condition for the exercise of power (both its precondition, since freedom must exist for power to be exerted, and also its permanent support, since without the possibility of resistance, power would be equivalent to a physical determination)."[26]

Returning to the liaison between dimensions of experience, the concluding portion of the essay focuses on the intersection between power relations and objective "capacities" or between power and external coercion. Terming the persistent pursuit of coercion "strategy" and more specifically "strategy of confrontation," Foucault finds the central trademark of this endeavor in the attempt to incapacitate an opponent, that is, "to act upon an adversary in such a manner as to render the struggle impossible for him." In this usage, the term "strategy" is defined "by the choice of winning solutions," while "confrontation" has the character of a "zero-sum" game. Employed as a backdrop, confrontation strategies serve to throw power still more clearly into relief. In Foucault's presentation, "every power relationship implies, at least *in potentia*, a mode of struggle in which the two forces are not superimposed, do not lose their specific nature, or do not finally become confused"—a mode where "each constitutes for the other a kind of permanent limit, a point of possible reversal." In contrast, a confrontation strategy "reaches its term, its final moment (and the victory of one of the two adversaries) when stable mechanisms replace the free play of antagonistic reactions" and when the winning party "can direct, in a fairly constant manner and with reasonable certainty, the conduct of others." While power relations require tension or "points of insubordination which, by definition, are means of escape," and while every intensification or extension of power to the point of making "the insubordinate submit" necessarily reveals the "limits of power," strategies find their fulfillment "either in a type of action which reduces the other to total impotence (in which case victory over the adversary replaces the exercise of power) or at least in a confrontation with those one governs and their transformation into enemies."[27]

Although profiled against each other in their intrinsic features, power relations and strategies are not immune to each other in actual political life. In Foucault's account, every confrontation strategy "dreams of becoming a relationship of power," while every power relation toys with, or leans toward, the notion of becoming "the winning strategy"— a notion implemented only at the price of the erosion of power. Thus, the two types of relations are simultaneously joined and separated; they are, he says, connected through "a reciprocal appeal, a perpetual linking and a perpetual reversal." At any moment, a power relation may turn into enmity or a "confrontation between two adversaries," just as enmity may, at a given moment, make room for the "operation of mechanisms of power." In concrete practice, the two modes of relationships tend to shade over into each other, with the result that the same phenomena or events can sometimes be interpreted either from the perspective of strategy or the vantage point of power. To designate the interpenetration of the two modes Foucault uses the term "domination," giving to the term a more distinctive connotation than it commonly carries: "Domination is in fact a general structure of power whose ramifications and consequences can sometimes be found descending to the most incalcitrant fibers of society; but at the same time it is a strategic situation more or less taken for granted and consolidated by means of a long-term confrontation between adversaries."[28]

III

Foucault's views on power are innovative, perhaps provocative, but not erratic; although marked by uncommon features and a sometimes unusual vocabulary, his arguments are not simply the outgrowth of personal idiosyncracies. In order to situate these arguments more clearly in the parameters of twentieth-century thought, I would like at this point to compare the notion of power sketched with, first, the political theory of Hannah Arendt and, next, the philosophical opus of Martin Heidegger. Affinities between Foucault's and Arendt's writings can be detected on numerous levels. Echoing the former's critique of patrimonial or proprietary conceptions of power, Arendt's *The Human Condition* contains a spirited attack on sovereignty and the entire Western metaphysical legacy which construes politics as the implementation of causal-intentional designs originating in the human will. Similarly, comparable with Foucault's analysis of "bio-power" and the modern micro-mechanisms of power, *The Human Condition* offers a far-flung historical account portraying the progressive submergence of public-political life in the imperatives of the "social domain" and of the "life-process" sustaining the *"animal laborans."*[29] Important and well-known is also Arendt's elaboration of "action" or the *"vita activa"* and its differentiation from both instrumental fabrication ("work") and reactive behavior ("labor")—a differentiation loosely akin to Foucault's distinction between power relations and objective "capacities." For present purposes I want to concentrate chiefly on this last distinction and its affinity with Arendt's juxtaposition of power and violence.

Arendt's thoughts on power have been repeatedly reviewed and assessed—but not always with sufficient attention to its intrinsic character or her broader theoretical framework. In his study *Power*, Steven Lukes associates Arendt's views on the topic closely with Parsons's functionalist perspective, arguing that both approaches ultimately submerge power in consensual interaction or harmonious cooperation. Just as, in the functionalist treatment, power is simply a medium of social-systemic cohesiveness, Arendt's conception is said to be tied "to a tradition and a vocabulary which she traces back to Athens and Rome"—a tradition according to which "the republic is based on the rule of law," which, in turn, is founded on popular endorsement and consensus. In Lukes's judgment, the aim of "these rather similar definitions of power" is to "lend persuasive support" to broader theoretical preferences. While, in Parsons's case, "the linking of power to authoritative decisions and collective goals serves to reinforce his theory of social integration as based on value consensus," Arendt's portrayal likewise plays a "persuasive role": namely, the role of buttressing "her conception of 'the *res publica*, the public thing' to which people consent" and in which they "behave nonviolently and argue rationally," in contradistinction to "the reduction of 'public affairs to the business of domination' and to the conceptual linkage of power with force and violence." According to the study, both theorists offer "revisionary persuasive redefinitions of power" which, though interesting and "rationally defensible," are "out of line with the central meanings of 'power' as traditionally understood and with the concerns that have always centrally preoccupied students of power"—chiefly concerns with "the conflictual aspect of power, the fact that it is exercised *over* people."[30]

Lukes's assessment is not exceptional or unique; to some extent its general thrust is seconded by Jürgen Habermas—although with greater sensitivity to the difference between systemic mechanisms and interpersonal or intersubjective consensus. In his memorial essay on Arendt (published shortly after her death in 1975), Habermas demarcates her outlook both from Weber's instrumental-teleological account and from Parsons's notion of systemic capacity, locating the demarcation precisely in what he calls "Hannah Arendt's communications concept of power." In contrast with Weber's equation of power with "control over means to influence the will of another"—an equation still reverberating in functionalist theory—Arendt is said to start "from a different, namely, a communicative model of action": one which sees the basic character of power "not in the self-seeking instrumentalization of another's will, but rather in the formation of a common or joint will through a communication directed toward consensual agreement." The emergence of agreement, in this approach, is seen not as the result of manipulation or inculcation, but rather as synonym for the generation of "power" to the extent and insofar as the latter is "founded on conviction and thus on that peculiarly forceless force with which insights assert themselves." Through her consensual orientation, Arendt is claimed to disengage "the concept of power from the teleological model: power is produced in communicative interaction; it is a collective effect of discourse in which all participants regard agreement as an end-in-itself." In Habermas's presentation, this outlook ultimately reflects Arendt's endeavor to salvage or recover "structures of an unimpaired intersubjectivity" in the midst of contemporary social-economic constraints. "Communicative action," he writes, "is the medium in which the intersubjectively shared life-world is formed"; by relying on "the formal properties of communicative action or praxis," Arendt seeks to "read off the general structures of an unimpaired intersubjectivity—structures which establish the criteria of normalcy for human existence, indeed for an existence worthy of human beings." Given this ambition, her "central hypothesis" can be stated as follows: "No political leadership can with impunity replace power through violence or coercion; and it can gain power only from a nondeformed public realm."[31]

Evaluating Arendt's conception, Habermas finds it simultaneously attractive and restrictive. As he notes, "We are faced here with a dilemma: on the one hand, the communications concept of power discloses important boundary phenomena to which political science has become largely insensitive; on the other hand, it is linked with a notion of politics which, when applied to modern societies, leads to absurdities." Through her focus on "praxis," that is, the "mutual discourse and interaction among individuals," Arendt is said to capture a significant political dimension—specifically the communicative "generation" of power—but at the price of disregarding the harsher features of political life. What the focus chiefly neglects, in Habermas's view, is the broad domain of political strategies or the "strategic competition" for power, as well as the field of political domination or control: "The (strategic) acquisition and maintenance of political power must be distinguished both from domination or the employment of power and from the original generation or constitution of power; in the latter case, but only there, does the concept of praxis prove useful." While the employment of power, in Habermas's presentation, carries functional-systemic connotations, strategic competition basically denotes a collective-manipulative endeavor or pursuit, an endeavor patterned on the model of warfare and guided by the criterion of a "winning solution." Despite the merits of Arendt's consensualism, he argues, neither strategies nor their successful implementation in modes of domination can sensibly be banished from politics. "The concept of the political," he concludes, "must extend to the strategic competition for political power and to the employment of power within the political system; politics cannot, as with Arendt, be identified with the praxis of those who talk together for the purpose of joint action. Conversely, the prevailing theory narrows this concept to phenomena of strategic competition and power allocation, thereby slighting the distinctive phenomenon of the generation of power." At this last juncture, Arendt's "segregation of power from violence becomes salient."[32]

My concern here is not so much with the range and adequacy of Arendt's view of politics, but only with the meaning and status of power. As it seems to me, both preceding accounts tend to truncate or unduly simplify this status; Habermas's portrayal in particular leaves room only for strategic coercion and communicative agreement—in Foucault's vocabulary: the alternatives of "confrontation strategies" and consensus—while collapsing power into the second option. Despite the undeniable ambivalence of some of Arendt's formulations,[33] this equation of power and agreement appears to me implausible for a number of reasons. The main reason is Arendt's distinction between praxis and cognition, between the *vita activa* and the *vita contemplativa*, and her emphatic insertion of power in the context of practical life— an insertion approximating Foucault's notion of action-power or power- action. Since politics in her view is not a theoretical-cognitive but a practical enterprise, political interaction and the generation of power cannot simply coincide with a "meeting of minds" or, as Habermas claims, with a "communication directed toward consensual agreement." In the concluding portion of his essay, Habermas himself acknowledges Arendt's differentiation of politics from knowledge and cognitive con- sensus—but attributes this difference simply to an inconsistency, if not timidity, in her thinking. Referring to the distinction between political "opinions" and cognitive truth claims—elaborated in her essay "Truth and Politics"—he comments, "An antiquated concept of theo- retical knowledge based on ultimate evidential certainty prevents Ar- endt from construing the process of reaching agreement on practical issues as rational discourse." Once knowledge is properly defined, however, "then a cognitive foundation can also be assigned to the power of common convictions—a power anchored in the factual rec- ognition of validity claims amenable to criticism and discursive re- demption. Yet, Arendt sees a yawning abyss between knowledge and opinion that cannot be closed with arguments."[34]

In my opinion, Arendt's outlook cannot fairly be ascribed to in- consistency or to an unawareness of present-day theories of knowledge; nor does her notion of power conform to Habermas's reduction of politics to cognition (and ultimately of power to non-power). Apart from the distinction between theory and practice, this non-conformity is also evident in her portrayal of human "plurality" seen as the

backbone of public-political life. In Habermas's rendition, politics denotes an intersubjective praxis devoted to the "formation of a common
or joint will" or the pursuit of "joint action"—a rendition which lands
Arendt squarely in a Rousseauan model of popular "sovereignty"
which she has taken great pains to criticize. Instead of coinciding with
a merger of ideas and wills, "plurality" in *The Human Condition* signifies
primarily an "agonal," though not hostile, mode of interaction, a
competitive striving for excellence and public virtue (manifest in great
"deeds") which does not degenerate into enmity or "confrontation."
As she writes, "Human plurality, the basic condition of both action
and speech, has the twofold character of equality and distinction."
Without equality, no political or public space would be available; but
without distinction or distinctiveness, human beings "would need neither speech nor action to make themselves understood; signs and
sounds to communicate immediate, identical needs and wants would
be enough." Thus, human plurality is a "paradoxical plurality of unique
beings"; speech or communicative interaction in particular reveals "the
fact of distinctness and is the actualization of the human condition of
plurality, that is, of living as a distinct and unique being among equals."
Similar views also emerge in her comments on political "friendship"
based on mutual respect: "Respect, not unlike the Aristotelian *philia
politike*, is a kind of 'friendship' without intimacy and without closeness"
(that is, without merger or identity); "it is a regard for the person from
the distance which the space of the world puts between us."[35]

The aspect of distinctness or non-identity also provides a warrant
for Arendt's linkage of political power and freedom—a linkage which
otherwise would be spurious. Countering the modern reliance on private
autonomy seen as a counterpoint to governmental restraints, *The Human
Condition*—in line with classical teachings—connects freedom with
public or political life, viewing it as internal mainspring rather than
as the "end" of power. "What all Greek philosophers, no matter how
opposed to *polis* life, took for granted," we read, "is that freedom is
exclusively located in the political realm, that necessity is primarily a
prepolitical phenomenon characteristic of the private household organization, and that force and violence are justified in this (latter)
sphere because they are the only means to master necessity." Thus,
while freedom was basically a political category, violence was assumed
to function both as antidote and accomplice to "prepolitical" necessity
or external compulsion. In Arendt's account, public-political freedom

obviously clashes with external-manipulative control or violence; but neither does it coincide with the unfettered designs of individuals or groups, designs ultimately coalescing in structures of "sovereignty." "If it were true that sovereignty and freedom are the same," she insists, "then indeed no man could be free, because sovereignty, the ideal of uncompromising self-sufficiency and mastership, is contradictory to the very condition of plurality. No man can be sovereign because not one man, but men, inhabit the earth." Like freedom, power is essentially a political category, characterized by human plurality or an "agonal" pluralism; as condition of possibility of political life, it cannot be reduced to a stable attribute or patrimonial possession of rulers. "Power is what keeps the public realm, the potential space of appearance between acting and speaking men, in existence," Arendt notes. If it were more than this "potentiality" of interaction, power "could be possessed like strength or applied like force instead of being dependent upon the unreliable and only temporary agreement of many wills and intentions." While manifold in its shapes, power's basic limitation resides in "the existence of other people"—a limitation which is "not accidental, because human power corresponds to the condition of plurality to begin with. For the same reason, power can be divided without decreasing it, and the interplay of powers with their checks and balances is even liable to generate more power, so long, at least, as the interplay is alive and has not resulted in a stalemate."[36]

The conception of freedom and power sketched finds a broader philosophical corroboration (I believe) in Heidegger's writings. Together with Arendt, Heidegger presents human existence as governed by neither external constraints nor individual (or collective) whims or impulses; overarching the antimony of fatalism and subjective designs, freedom is found to mark man's "essence"—which consists in care for, or attentiveness to, "Being." Likewise, power in Heidegger's thought does not primarily signify strategic manipulation or coercion; nor is it a proprietary adjunct of human will. As presented in his works, power signifies first of all an ontological potency or "empowerment," that is, a condition of possibility of human and public life—a view which does not rule out, but rather supports, the "agonal" operation of power in concrete political settings.[37] Only when it is appropriated or wantonly usurped by particular rulers or ontic structures does power progressively shade over into oppressive political

domination and violence. By stressing the primacy of ontological empowerment, Heidegger makes room for the critique of mundane strategies and modes of domination—but without relinquishing the role
of power as a requisite of public life. While not endorsing the utopia
of powerlessness or an end of politics, his work basically pays tribute
or homage to a "peculiarly forceless force"—which is not so much
the force of human reason (with its strictures against unreason) as the
generative potency and generous largesse of Being.[38]

4
Ontology of Freedom:
Heidegger and Political
Philosophy

The theme announced in the title of this chapter contains a paradox, or rather a number of paradoxes. As is well known, Heidegger has never developed or elaborated a "political philosophy" properly speaking; on the contrary, he has explicitly denied any such intent. On the other hand, it is precisely politics—more specifically: Heidegger's presumed political outlook—which for many complicates or obstructs access to his work. Thus, an opus largely devoid of overt political ambitions is curiously encumbered by a heavy political mortgage. At the same time, the term "freedom" as used in modern philosophical discussions tends to denote a human property and capacity for spontaneous initiative divorced or severed from "ontological" moorings, just as "ontology" is widely assumed to imply a denial of free human choice.

The mortgage encumbering Heidegger's work dates back to the years 1933–1934, that is, to the time of his service as rector of the University of Freiburg. The episode has been frequently recounted in the literature—not always with a sober attention to factual details.[1] Heidegger's endorsement of the Nazi regime at the time is undeniable; but the precise character of his motives and expectations is hard to pinpoint. Probably an array of factors influenced his attitude during

A modified version of this chapter appeared under the same title in *Political Theory*, vol. 12 (May 1984), pp. 204–234, published by Sage Publications Inc.

that period: among them a distaste for the chaotic condition of the late Weimar Republic; the desire for a political reorientation or rebirth beyond the spectrum of traditional ideologies; perhaps also—as Otto Pöggeler suggests—the hope for a strengthening of central Europe and a "great (European) politics," as a counterpoint to the emerging technological superpowers in the East and the West.[2] That such expectations were egregious misjudgments or else the outgrowth of gross political naiveté is beyond question. Still, in view of the relative brevity of his official role as rector (altogether ten months) and his vast productivity both before and afterward, an exclusive focus on the episode seems to me both lopsided and unfair.

The chorus of accusations and condemnations has almost but not entirely been able to drown out more balanced and conciliatory voices. Already in 1953 the philosopher Max Müller remarked about Heidegger's political venture, "We encounter here the limits of his concrete political judgment—limits which, in the end, do not jeopardize his philosophical stature and the integrity of his endeavors." Almost two decades later, at the time of his eightieth birthday, Hannah Arendt placed the episode into the gentle light of personal catharsis and absolution. "Now we all know," she wrote at the time, "that Heidegger, too, once succumbed to the temptation to change his 'residence' and to get involved in the world of human affairs. As to the world, he was served somewhat worse than Plato, because the tyrant and his victims were not located beyond the sea, but in his own country. As to Heidegger himself, I believe that the matter stands differently. He was still young enough to learn from the shock of the collision, which after ten short hectic months thirty-seven years ago drove him back to his residence, and to settle in his thinking what he had experienced. What emerged from this was the discovery of the will as 'the will to will' and hence as the 'will to power'."[3]

Arendt's phrase of the native "residence" (angestammter Wohnsitz) is, of course, a reference to philosophical reflection or the philosophia perennis. What renders the exclusive emphasis on 1933 frequently annoying is its complicity with a strategy of avoidance: the tendency to ignore or bypass Heidegger's philosophy in favor of a time-bound set of political speeches. This tendency was noted by Bernard Willms in 1977, shortly after Heidegger's death, when he portrayed the fascination with 1933 as an attempt "to circumvent the confrontation with the thought and philosophy of Martin Heidegger." As he added,

"The superficial dispute about the topic 'Heidegger and the Nazis' or—seemingly more penetrating—'Heidegger and fascism' only solidifies ideological preoccupations; it does not unlock a single political problem, including the problem of politics or 'the political' in Heidegger's philosophy. To probe the latter, however, is far from unimportant."[4] A decade earlier, François Fédier had formulated a similar opinion perhaps even more poignantly. Following a critical review of some polemical books on Heidegger's politics, Fédier reached this conclusion: "The first step which no one can skip," he wrote, "is the serious study of Heidegger's opus. However, one realizes immediately that there is also a means to prevent *ab limine* the possibility of objective appraisal; namely, by moralistically sealing off access to his work. This can be and is done by surrounding the author with a dense fog of rumors and innuendos." Fédier also pointed to Heidegger's increasingly non- or anti-fascist attitude after 1934—an aspect I consider particularly important and which Beda Alleman (in his commentary on Fédier) seconded with these words: "Only an analysis of the lectures given between 1934 and 1944—of which several are assembled in the Nietzsche-volumes (of 1961)—would enable us to grasp the precise sense of Heidegger's opposition to the Nazi regime, and conversely to clarify the reasons underlying Heidegger's belief in 1933 to contribute to the rise of something *other* than what national socialism turned out to be."[5]

Together with Willms, Fédier, and Alleman, I am convinced that the episode of 1933 holds the key neither to Heidegger's philosophical opus nor to the "problem of the political" in his thought—differently put: the latter problem really can be decoded only via a close interpretation of the general philosophical work. I am aware that this view conflicts with another major thesis or verdict in this area: the verdict—probably first pronounced by Leo Strauss—that Heidegger's thought signals the "end" of political theory or its terminal stage of decay. According to Strauss, Heidegger represents the zenith of modern "historicism," a perspective which, in his judgment, undermines the condition of possibility of political reflection. As he wrote in 1971, "There is no room for political philosophy in Heidegger's work. . . . One is inclined to say that Heidegger has learned the lesson of 1933 more thoroughly than any other man. Surely he leaves no place whatever for political philosophy."[6] Strauss's verdict implies a series of premises which I consider highly questionable, primarily these: that a viable political philosophy did exist sometime in the past; that this philosophy could or might have been readily preserved or restored; but that this opportunity has been spoiled by Heidegger and historicism. Clearly, Strauss himself harbored doubts regarding the viability or robustness of "modern" political thought prior to the rise of historicism. More important, the verdict militates, I think, against the notion of political "philosophy" itself—to the extent that "philosophy" designates not so much a fixed doctrine as rather a mode of radical inquiry and perpetual questioning (a view endorsed by Strauss on several occasions).[7] Seen in this light, Strauss's verdict can readily be reversed: instead of signaling a stage of terminal decay, Heidegger's work emerges as an attempt at a radical philosophical reorientation—a reorientation, it is true, complicated by the prevailing congealment of philosophical reflection either into logical technique or into ideological doctrines or *Weltanschauungen*.

My own approach to Heidegger, and to the linkage between Heidegger and politics, takes its point of departure from this latter assumption; in contrast with both a narrow polemical treatment (focused on 1933) and a restorative conception of political theory, I prefer to stress the inquiring, innovative or *"en route"* character of his thought. In the present chapter I intend to profile him chiefly as a non-traditional or post-metaphysical philosopher of "freedom," including political freedom. In the course of my presentation, it should also become evident why, in addition to the stress on freedom, I consider him likewise a philosopher of human "solidarity"—and thus as the oblique heir of at least two Enlightenment maxims: "liberty" and "fraternity." As we all know, we find ourselves today, once again, in an increasingly threatening confrontation between East and West, a confrontation in which the latter is commonly designated as the "free world" or as the bastion of human "freedom." Little inquiry, however, is required to show the deep opacity shrouding the concept of freedom in contemporary Western thought and its deterioration into an ideological slogan (akin to the status of "socialism" or fraternity in the East). Mankind, one has the impression, is steadily drifting toward a political cataclysm, on both sides propelled by watchwords or doctrines whose significance is only barely intelligible. In this situation, I believe, Heidegger's work offers some aid, by encouraging a rethinking of key phrases of traditional philosophy. As I propose to show, his thought, from the earliest to the latest writings, is permeated by the endeavor to grapple with the category of "freedom"—in a manner which decisively moves beyond the confines of traditional liberalism and libertarianism. In the following I shall first of all highlight the relevance of the issue of freedom in the context of prevailing Heidegger interpretations; next I shall review some of his major texts dealing with the category (with some emphasis on his "middle" period). By way of conclusion I intend to indicate parallels between Heidegger's initiative and some arguments in contemporary social and political thought.

I

My focus on freedom is prompted not only by the unquestionable centrality of the category in Western political philosophy, and in philosophy *per se*; an additional and more immediate motivation derives from its role in the literature surrounding Heidegger's opus: no theoretical aspect of his work has occasioned more controversy and heated debate than his attitude toward freedom. On the one hand, he is reproached for having carried the modern concept of freedom to an absurd extreme and thus for having promoted a blind and arbitrary "decisionism." On the other hand, his writings are sometimes claimed to endorse a complete dismantling or eradication of human freedom and willing and thus to sanction a deterministic "fatalism." Leo Strauss has the distinction of having raised both accusations simultaneously and more or less indiscriminately. Reminiscing about his own student years and "giving an account" of his background, Strauss concedes the fascination which Heidegger's teaching exerted on him at the time, but adds, "What I could not stomach was his moral teaching, for despite his disclaimer, he had such a teaching. The key term is 'resoluteness' (*Entschlossenheit*) without any indication as to what are the proper objects of resoluteness. There is a straight line which leads from Heidegger's resoluteness to his siding with the so-called Nazis in 1933." The term "resoluteness" in this portrayal clearly stands for a kind of arbitrary willfulness or spontaneity. At the same time, Strauss's essay "What Is Political Philosophy?" links Heidegger's outlook with what he calls "a mysterious dispensation of fate," that is, with a somewhat occult fatalism. "It was the contempt for these permanencies [that is, the realm of eternal values]," we read, "which permitted the most radical historicist in 1933 to submit to, or rather to welcome, as a dispensation of fate, the verdict of the least wise and least moderate part of his nation while it was in its least wise and least moderate mood."[8]

In a more nuanced and temporally more differentiated manner, the same two-pronged indictment has been formulated by Jürgen Habermas (hardly suspect as a Straussian). In his *Philosophical-Political Profiles* Habermas refers first of all to Heidegger's early work, that is, to *Being and Time*, where he detects a "Lutheran radicalism manifest in the projection or 'project' of one's 'authentic' *Dasein*, a *Dasein* gaining wholeness through the anticipation of death." According to the *Profiles*, this secularized Protestantism shades over quickly and readily into a simple "decisionism purged of Kierkegaardian and all theological remnants," although one "parading in antique costumes." On the other hand, Heidegger's thought after the so-called *"Kehre"* (or "turning") is claimed to leave no more room at all for human will or freedom of choice, granting "complete primacy" instead to Being and its various disclosures. "Out of this hand (of Being)," Habermas writes, "human existence emerges as a fated or fateful event. Man now is called the shepherd and guardian of Being."[9]

At this point, particularly in light of Habermas's periodization, it may be appropriate to cast a quick glance at the overall development of Heidegger's opus. In this context, the notion of the so-called *"Kehre"* has played, and continues to play, a prominent and largely disorienting role. In the view of many commentators, the *"Kehre"* represents a sharp dividing line neatly segregating the early from the later writings— an opinion which Heidegger himself has repeatedly disavowed. In lieu of this neat bifurcation I consider more plausible another scheme which arranges the opus into three successive and only partially discontinuous phases: an early period extending roughly until 1930; a middle period until the end of World War II; and a late period up to the time of Heidegger's death in 1976. This arrangement finds a good deal of support from Heidegger himself. Thus, in his seminar held at Thor in 1969 he portrayed his own development as a path marked by the three successive concerns with the "meaning," the "truth," and the "topology" of Being. Referring to the early phrase "meaning of Being," Heidegger observed at the time, "This formulation was replaced somewhat later by the 'question concerning the truth of Being,' and still later by the 'question of the place or locality of Being' (hence the expression 'topology of Being'). Thus, we have here three interlocking terms which simultaneously mark stages along the route of thought: *meaning, truth, place* (topos). If one seeks to clarify the question of Being, it becomes necessary to grasp both what links and what differentiates these three successive formulations." In his *Philosophie und Politik bei Heidegger* (1972), Pöggeler embraces the same arrangement, stating, "If one wishes to avoid the misleading partition into a phase prior to and after the '*Kehre*', one can readily divide the path of Heidegger's thought in accordance with his respective orientation toward the meaning of Being, the truth of Being, and the clearing or locality."[10]

This is not the place to discuss in detail the characteristic features of the successive phases and their interconnections; a few cursory comments must suffice. The early phase was dominated by the question of the "meaning of Being" and thus by a first, tentative revival of an ontological problematic. As presented in *Being and Time*, human existence or *Dasein* was a distinctive and particularly important mode of being because it provides a forum for the mentioned question, thus rendering possible an "understanding" of Being. Despite its ontological thrust, however, the early phase was still permeated by remnants of modern subjectivity and intentionality—an aspect giving rise in due course to a more radical revision. In Pöggeler's words, the question of the meaning of Being "was apparently replaced by the phrase 'truth of Being' because the former was still impregnated by tenets of modern historicism and neo-Kantianism" (one might add: of transcendental phenomenology as well).[11] The middle phase is the period of Heidegger's intensive preoccupation with the entire tradition of Western metaphysics—in ontological terms: with the "history of Being." This is the time of his protracted confrontation with Nietzsche, of his renewed and probing study of German idealist philosophy (especially Hegel and Schelling), and of his growing fascination with Hölderlin. This is also the time of those lecture courses and seminars mentioned by Fédier which testify to a growing critical distantiation from the Nazi regime. Particularly instructive for Heidegger's outlook during this period is the lecture series "The Origin of the Work of Art" (of 1935–1936), which—in lieu of the previous juxtaposition of things "at-hand," things "to-hand," and human *Dasein*—differentiates between "thing," "equipment," and "art-work," with a decisive shift of accent from *Dasein* to the creation of works. The last period is inaugurated by the *Letter on Humanism* and includes such publications as *Wegmarken*, *On the Way to Language*, and *On Time and Being*. Heidegger's reflections during this phase culminate in a radical, ontological critique of modern technology under the label "*das Ge-stell*" (the "framing"), and also in a reformulation of the history and disclosure of Being by means of such categories as "*Ereignis*" (appropriating event) and "*das Geviert*" (the four-fold); particularly the comments on "*das Geviert*" reveal a modification of the earlier hierarchy of thing-equipment-work in favor of a more attentive appreciation of "thinghood" as a central manifestation of Being.

Attempts to derive political or political-theoretical lessons from Heidegger's work can be correlated, without great difficulty, with the three stages mentioned; again I limit myself to a few hints. Thus, the focus in the early period on *Dasein* and authentic human self-enactment has given rise to an existentialist type of political theorizing which places the accent squarely on individual choice, decision, and activity. In a broad review essay of 1970, Beat Sitter compiled the relevant secondary literature which used *Being and Time* as a warrant for individual-political activism and decisionism; foremost among the authors reviewed is Count Christian von Krockow, whose book *The Decision* (*Die Entscheidung*) placed Heidegger in tandem with the early perspectives of Carl Schmitt and Ernst Jünger. On the other hand, in the reading of the early Marcuse, *Being and Time* furnished impulses for a philosophical rejuvenation of Marxism in which "project" and "decision" resurfaced in the guise of "revolutionary praxis."[12] The writings of the middle period likewise have inspired or influenced a number of political-theoretical interpretations and arguments. As it seems to me, Hannah Arendt's *The Human Condition* displays many affinities with this Heideggerian phase; thus, the hierarchical tripartition of thing–equipment–art-work, elaborated in the lectures of 1935–1936, finds a loose parallel in Arendt's differentiation between "labor," "work" (or instrumental fabrication) and political "action." The "Art-Work" lectures also stand at the center of the most comprehensive critical analysis of Heidegger's political perspective available so far: Alexander Schwan's *Politische Philosophie im Denken Heideggers* (1965). Relying on the correlation between art-work and *polis* (or "*Staatswerk*"), Schwan applauds Heidegger's quasi-classical conception of politics as "work" or "praxis" or as the practical enactment of "truth"—but finds fault with his post-classical leanings, especially his alleged tendency to ascribe Promethean, if not outright demonic qualities, to artistic creation and the production of works.[13] Writings of the late period provide the chief inspiration for Pöggeler's study, already mentioned, of 1972 which states, among other things, that our "world civilization" is decisively shaped by "the preeminence of technology" and that the proper "starting point for a political philosophy in Heidegger's opus resides consequently in his thinking on '*Technik*' (as it is elaborated in his discussion of the *Gestell* and the *Geviert*)." A similar outlook animates Hans Köchler's study on *Skepsis und Gesellschaftskritik im Denken Martin Heideggers* (1978), where "skepsis" designates Heidegger's critical distantiation from objectifying analysis, while "social criticism" revolves around the predominance of technology or the "*Gestell*."[14]

A common theme running through much of the secondary literature mentioned is the meaning and status of human "freedom" (which brings me back to my own topic). The thesis of an arbitrary "decisionism" is perhaps nowhere more baldly asserted than in Count Krockow's study *The Decision*. According to Krockow a key category in *Being and Time* is the notion of decision, styled as "resoluteness" (*Entschlossenheit*)—a notion allegedly severed from rational motivations or intelligible purposes. "This peculiar formalism and absolutism of human decision," he writes, "characterizes that mode of thought which, following Carl Schmitt, we shall call decisionism." In formalizing and absolutizing human choice, Heidegger is said to have joined ranks with Schmitt, Jünger, and similar intellectuals of the Weimar Republic radically opposed to the established order. By emptying resoluteness of "all substantive content," he adds, "Heidegger moves in the same direction as did Jünger with his notion of 'struggle' (*Kampf*) and Schmitt with the concept of 'decision' (*Entscheidung*). . . . And while, in the domain of politics, Schmitt portrays parliamentary government as the systematic avoidance of all real decisions, Heidegger affirms that 'the They' (*das Man*) in the ambiguity of their everyday 'public chatter'— as contrasted with the 'silence' of authentic, resolute *Dasein*—abscond from any substantive choice or commitment." In contrast with this radical voluntarism, Krockow detects in a later phase a sharp reversal or "*Kehre*": namely, in the direction of an "essential reflection" (*wesentliches Denken*) in the case of Heidegger and Jünger, and of a "concrete thought of order" (*konkretes Ordnungsdenken*) in the case of Schmitt. In Heidegger's writings this reversal is claimed to manifest itself in the blind submission to an ontological destiny (*Seins-Geschick*), a destiny completely at odds with human freedom. From this vantage point, he notes, authentic decision "must now appear as a mere 'errance', as an embroilment in subjectivity."[15]

Similar arguments, though with greater attention to the middle period, are advanced also in Schwan's book. In his view, *Being and Time* and the "Art-Work" lectures are subterraneously linked by the common emphasis on a blind activism. Artistic creativity as displayed in the production of "works" is shown to be rooted ultimately in the "resoluteness of the spontaneous and violent deed of the creator (artist)"; in the case of the *polis*, where creativity is monopolized by political leaders, the lectures allegedly support the fascist model of a correlation of "leaders" and "followers" (*Führer-Gefolgschaft-Staat*). As Schwan concedes, experiences of the time as well as his study of Nietzsche prompted Heidegger increasingly to muffle his voluntaristic stance—but at the price of an ultimate lapse into quietism; by turning to the history or "destiny" of Being, Heidegger, in this view, cut himself adrift from political practice *per se* and from the possibility to develop "guiding frameworks for a politics of the future."[16] Comments or passages to this effect could readily be multiplied from the available literature. To round out my survey let me mention a last example: Ernst Tugendhat's *Der Wahrheitsbegriff bei Husserl und Heidegger* (1967). Tugendhat accuses Heidegger of vacillating precariously between arbitrariness and fatalism. While, as presented in the early work, freedom was completely devoid of binding yardsticks or guideposts, the same freedom is sacrificed after the *"Kehre"* to the mandates of Being. In the later works, he writes, submission to Being tends to "take the place of choice" and thus to function "as an alibi" in practical-political matters.[17]

II

After this rapid overview it is time to turn to Heidegger himself. As I have indicated, and as the commentaries readily attest, Heidegger's opus revolves to a significant extent around the problematic of freedom. What I wish to show, however, is the unconventional character of his conception of freedom: the fact that this conception can be reduced to neither arbitrary choice nor fatalism. In a sense his entire work can be read, I believe, as an intense and persistent endeavor to find a way pointing beyond this traditional-metaphysical antinomy beleaguering practical thought. For the sake of brevity I shall concentrate here chiefly on writings of the middle period—although I shall also cast a quick glance at the early and late phases of Heidegger's work.

As even its proponents recognize, the charge of a blind "decisionism" is relevant—if at all—mainly to the early stage of Heidegger's thought, especially to *Being and Time*. In effect, *Being and Time* does place human *Dasein* in the center of its analyses and thus, in a sense, carries "anthropological" (or anthropocentric) overtones. Yet, even in this limited context, the charge is in my view untenable, for the simple reason that the transition from "inauthentic" to "authentic" *Dasein* is not simply an act of free will or choice, and that the unfolding of human "freedom" accordingly is not synonymous with a blind or arbitrary decision. In *Being and Time*, the portrayal of "authentic" *Dasein*—which coincides with human freedom or, in Heidegger's terms, with the mode of "being free" (*Freisein*)—occurs on the level of an existential analytics or descriptive ontology, not that of ethics or practical imperatives. The turn toward authenticity signifies not properly a choice between ontic goals or objectives, but rather *Dasein*'s move toward its own intrinsic "essence" or ontological ground—a ground which is always already implicit in everyday existence. The assumption of a free choice of human authenticity seen as *Dasein*'s essence is predicated on a conception of "free will" which presupposes already what needs to be shown: namely, the possibility of freedom. Differently put: freedom of will is based on human *Dasein* construed as freedom or a mode of "being free," and not vice versa. Viewed as *Dasein*'s ontological core, "being free" is neither imposed on *Dasein* as an external fate or destiny, nor can it be arbitrarily chosen or discarded.

It would lead me too far afield here to review Heidegger's existential analytics in its breadth and complexity—to show, for example, how *Dasein* is centrally marked by "care" for its own "being" and how this "care" in turn permeates the category of "resoluteness" (*Entschlossenheit*). In Heidegger's concise formulation, "Resoluteness is nothing but the carefully nurtured and only through this cultivation conceivable authenticity of care." In *Being and Time*, incidentally, resoluteness is intimately linked with the notion of "openness" (*Er-schlossenheit*), that is, with *Dasein*'s availability for its own essence or ontological ground. This openness is manifest primarily in the call of "conscience" which as the "call of care" summons *Dasein* into the realm of its innermost potential. To cite Heidegger again, "This unique and distinctive openness witnessed in the call of conscience—this silent and anxious self-projection toward proper accountability and guilt—this is what we call resoluteness." In light of the linkage between resoluteness, conscience, and innermost potential, *Being and Time* finds it legitimate to describe resoluteness as "the most original because authentic truth of *Dasein*."[18]

Still with reference to the early work, one might mention the untenability of the view which regards resoluteness simply as a private preference or as a solipsistic decision severed from contextual or environmental constraints. According to Heidegger, resoluteness places *Dasein* into the concrete "existence of its situation," just as "the call of conscience, in summoning to an ontological potential, does not merely hold up an empty ideal, but rather calls (*Dasein*) into a situation." Similarly, resoluteness or existential authenticity does not simply remove *Dasein* from all intersubjective bonds. In Heidegger's words, "Seen as authentic mode of self-being, resoluteness does not cut *Dasein* loose from its world, nor reduce it to a free-floating ego. How could this happen—given the fact that, as authentic openness, resoluteness is nothing but the authentic mode of being-in-the-world? Actually, resoluteness prompts *Dasein* to deal in a concerned manner with things-at-hand and to nurture with solicitude the co-being (*Mitsein*) with others." Perhaps a last citation from *Being and Time* highlights the theme of these pages. In authenticity, Heidegger writes, "the resolute *Dasein* sets itself free for its world. It is resoluteness to itself which enables *Dasein* to let fellow-beings 'be' in their own innermost potential and to help open up this potential in the mode of anticipative-liberating solicitude (*vorspringend-befreiende Fürsorge*). . . . Thus, it is the authentic selfhood of resoluteness which gives rise to authentic co-being."[19]

On the threshold to the middle period—in 1930—we encounter one of Heidegger's most famous essays (which, as we know, he chose to deliver repeatedly during subsequent years): the essay "On the Essence of Truth." In the essay truth is no longer, or not primarily, presented as the openness or disclosedness (*Erschlossenheit*) of *Dasein*, but rather as the "unconcealment" (*Unverborgenheit*) of Being. Despite this slight shift of accent, the essay maintains a close linkage between truth and freedom—the latter defined as mode of "being free" for the disclosure of Being. With reference to the traditional theory of truth as "correspondence" or "correctness," Heidegger points to an underlying "openness of comportment" (*Offenständigkeit des Verhaltens*) as the "condition of possibility" of such correspondence or correctness.

"How can something like a correctness or an insertion into a correspondence happen or be engendered?" he asks, and responds, "Only
if this engendering (or enabling) act has already freed itself for an
open region and for a disclosure occurring in this region which binds
every cognition or representation. To free oneself for a binding direction
is possible only by *being free* for the disclosure in the open region. . . .
The openness of comportment as the inner condition of possibility of
correctness is grounded in freedom. *The essence of truth is freedom.*"
Heidegger is well aware of the doubts and objections conjured up by
this formulation—especially the charges of relativism and subjectivism.
"To place the essence of truth in freedom," he continues, "doesn't
this mean to submit truth to human caprice? Can truth be any more
radically undermined than by being surrendered to the arbitrariness
of this 'wavering reed'?" From the standpoint of common sense it
must appear as if truth "is here reduced to, or levelled into, the
subjectivity of the human subject," while the "essence of truth 'in
itself,'" that is, its "imperishable and eternal" quality, is ignored.[20]

As is clear from its general tenor, the argument of the essay proceeds
again on an ontological rather than a practical-ethical level. From this
perspective, freedom signifies not so much an exercise of free will or
the willful enactment (or omission) of particular deeds, but rather a
mode of "being free" for the disclosure or unconcealment of Being,
differently put: a mode which "lets" all beings "be" what they are
without constraint or manipulation. "Freedom for disclosure in an
open region," Heidegger writes, "lets beings be what they are; freedom
now reveals itself as letting beings be." As one should note, freedom
in the sense of letting-be is by no means synonymous with indifference,
but rather an expression of liberating (or emancipatory) "care": "The
phrase required in this context—to let beings be—does not refer to
neglect and indifference, but rather the opposite: to let be is to engage
oneself (*Sicheinlassen*) with beings"—an engagement, it is true, which
is not akin to willful management, planning, or manipulation: "To let
be—that is, to let beings be what they are—means to engage oneself
with the open region and its openness into which every being comes
to stand and which it carries along like an aura. This open region was
conceived by Western thought in its origins as *ta alethea*, the uncon-
cealed." According to Heidegger, freedom for the disclosure of Being
also carries with it the possibility of concealment and distortion, that
is, the possibility of "untruth" or of the "non-being of truth" (*Unwesen*

der Wahrheit). "Because truth is in its essence freedom, however," the essay states, "historical man—in letting beings be—can also *not* let beings be what they are and as they are; in this case, beings are concealed and distorted. Thus, semblance becomes dominant; with it the non-being of truth comes to the fore." Yet, Heidegger adds, since freedom designates not simply a willful human decision but rather the essential mode of human being, therefore "the non-being of truth cannot arise subsequently from mere human incapacity or negligence; rather untruth must derive from the essence (or being) of truth."[21]

As the essay repeatedly stresses, freedom for truth and untruth is not simply equivalent to the traditional notion of free will or choice; in fact, freedom as "being free" coincides with neither arbitrary choice nor an external constraint or destiny. "Freedom," Heidegger observes, "is not merely what common sense is content to let pass under this name: the caprice, occasionally present in our choosing, of moving in this or that direction. Freedom is not mere arbitrariness in what we can and cannot do; nor, on the other hand, is it the mere submission to a requirement or necessity (and thus to an ontic standard or object). Rather, prior to all such 'negative' or 'positive' construals, freedom is engagement in the disclosure of beings as such." Viewed as an ontological engagement (or as an engagement with Being and beings), freedom cannot simply be regarded as a human trait, quality, or property. In Heidegger's words, "Human caprice does not have freedom at its disposal. Man does not 'possess' freedom as a property; at best, the converse holds: freedom—synonymous with ek-static, disclosive *Dasein*—possesses man, and this so fully and originally that only *it* (freedom) secures for humanity that distinctive relatedness to Being as a whole which first founds all history." As the essay adds, anticipating later formulations regarding the "history of Being," "That man ek-sists now means that for historical humanity the history of its essential possibilities is conserved in the disclosure of beings as a whole. The rare and simple decisions of history arise from the way the original being of truth unfolds."[22]

Roughly contemporaneously with the first version of the "Truth" essay—in the summer of 1930—Heidegger presented in Freiburg a lecture course "On the Essence of Human Freedom" ("*Vom Wesen der menschlichen Freiheit*"), subtitled "Introduction to Philosophy." The lecture course—only recently published—is important here mainly for two reasons: first, its clear ontological treatment of freedom; and second, its detailed and sustained critique of the most prominent modern counter-conception: Kant's construal of freedom as a kind of transcendental "cause" or "causality." In its opening pages, the lecture text raises the query how and to what extent a discussion of freedom can serve as an "introduction to philosophy" as such; Heidegger's reply consists basically in the argument that freedom involves always in some manner the notion of "Being" or of "beings as a whole" and thus touches at the central or guiding question of philosophy. In his view, this is true even in the case of a mere "negative" freedom conceived as "man's independence from world and God"; even here freedom carries ontological implications: "In the negative concept of freedom, world and God are not merely accidentally co-represented, but rather belong to the essence of the concept itself." However, "in their unity world and God comprise the universe of beings. Thus, in thematizing freedom initially only from a negative angle, we already inquire necessarily into the whole or totality of beings." The situation is still more evident in the case of "positive" freedom defined as radical human "self-determination" and "spontaneity" (a conception chiefly inaugurated by Kant). In this case freedom functions as a type of initial cause or starting point. As Heidegger notes, however, "To be a cause means among other things: to begin, to let follow or make happen"; it belongs in the context of "what is happening" or of "movement in the broader sense." Yet, movement is nothing else but a "basic category attaching to everything to which we ascribe Being, that is, to beings in general." Thus, the problem of movement leads back to the question of the "Being" of everything, or of beings as such. With the latter query, however—Heidegger adds—we find ourselves face to face with "that question which from earliest times has been the first, last, and decisive question of genuine philosophy—that is, the guiding question (*Leitfrage*) of philosophy: *ti to on*, what is being" or what is "being as such?" Consequently, from whatever angle the issue of freedom is approached, we always "stand in the midst of the question regarding being as such."[23]

The first part of the lecture course offers a wide-ranging overview of the treatment of the so-called "guiding question" in Western philosophy from antiquity to Hegel—an overview which I bypass at this point. I want to turn directly to the second major theme of the lectures: Kant's conception of freedom. According to Heidegger, Kant construed freedom basically in a "positive" sense as human self-determination and self-enactment; his construal, moreover, proceeded on two levels: a "cosmological" or transcendental level and a practical-moral level. In the cosmological dimension freedom signified for Kant "absolute spontaneity" or the possibility of an absolutely new beginning, while its practical meaning coincided with "autonomy of willing" in the sense of an independence of will from external constraints. Cosmological and practical conceptions were correlated in Kant's scheme via the subordination of the latter to the former; in other words: autonomy of will denoted a type or subcategory of absolute spontaneity, a type operative in the special domain of practical-moral action (but grounded in the transcendental-cosmological domain). As Heidegger tries to show, full spontaneity in Kant's presentation meant the free capacity for a new beginning—where freedom served as ground or cause of subsequent events, thus shading itself over into a mode of causality. Within the range of empirical phenomena, it is true, cognition was tied by Kant to the strict category of natural "causality" which was counterposed to (noumenal) freedom. Since nature made no room for a radical new beginning, absolute spontaneity in his view pointed beyond nature in a transcendental (noumenal) direction. As Heidegger comments, "The new beginning of a condition or series of events, and more specifically the absolutely new beginning is (for Kant) a grounding or causing radically different from the causality of nature or a completely distinctive mode of causality. Kant designates the latter—that is, absolute spontaneity—as 'causality of freedom'. Thereby one point becomes evident: the really problematic aspect of absolute spontaneity is the issue of causality or causation. Kant basically views freedom as the capacity for a unique and distinctive causation."[24]

According to Heidegger, however, the Kantian linkage of freedom with causation is profoundly suspect; more sharply put: the linkage is ontologically untenable—provided the "guiding question" of philosophy regarding the Being of beings is taken seriously. Kant's conception, he concedes, is historically important because freedom was here "for the first time explicitly and directly connected with the basic problems of metaphysics," albeit in a "one-sided" manner. "If we force a confrontation with Kant," he states, "our motivation is precisely to focus on the correlation between freedom and causation or causality. The necessity of such a confrontation is all the more urgent since we ourselves construe freedom as condition or grounding of the possibility of *Dasein*—which conjures up the issue of the relationship between causation and such a grounding." The central theme dominating the remainder of the lectures is the question whether freedom is somehow reducible to, or derivable from, causation or whether causality is ultimately reducible to, or grounded in, freedom. "In the latter case where freedom provides the grounding," the lectures ask, "how must freedom itself be conceived?" Moreover, and more important, is the essence of freedom "exhaustively defined by seeing it as a grounding for causality"—or is it not rather imperative both to reconceptualize causality and to construe freedom itself "more radically and not simply as a mode or type of causation"?[25]

In investigating this theme and its alternative resolutions, Heidegger analyzes in detail the Kantian opus, focusing first on the cosmological or transcendental formulation and next on the practical-moral conception of freedom; the briefest synopsis of this analysis must suffice here. Especially on the cosmological level, the lectures highlight the close interplay of natural causality and "causality of freedom." In Kant's presentation of the latter notion, we read, we witness "the intrusion of the general concept of causality into the definition of freedom. Thus, we grasp still more clearly the general ontological horizon in which Kant viewed freedom to the extent that freedom signified a mode of causation." According to Heidegger, despite the concern with clear metaphysical delimitations Kant ultimately remained vague or hazy regarding his own "ontological horizon" in which causality functioned as a basic category: in its linkage with causation his transcendental notion of freedom continued to be indebted to traditional "cosmology" or the philosophy of nature. "If freedom is placed in the context of the world or universe and if 'world' designates the totality of phenomena and their concatenations," Heidegger observes, then freedom as a cosmological theme "moves into the closest proximity to the causality of nature—even if freedom is differentiated from natural causality as a special type of causation. . . . Briefly put: freedom emerges as a unique mode of natural causality." As presented in the lecture course, the "limits" or limitations of the Kantian doctrine result basically from this contamination of freedom and causation. The "questionable character" of both Kantian approaches or formulations, we read, arises from "the fact that in both instances freedom is placed under the auspices of the category of causality, while causality itself is never thematized as a problem on the level of a radical ontological inquiry." To thematize causality in this manner would require a reinterpretation of cosmology, that is, of empirical reality and natural phenomena—namely as manifestations of Being and its disclosure in an open region; such a reinterpretation, however, is predicated on the notion of "truth" as freedom.[26]

From this perspective the Kantian scheme of priorities is reversed, with the result that causality emerges at best as a subsidiary or derivative category. "*One* ontological category among others," Heidegger asserts, "is that of causality. Causality, however, is grounded in freedom; thus the issue of causality belongs to the problematic of freedom and not the reverse." Actually, the lecture course assigns to freedom an ontological status which even antedates the correlation of "being" and "time." "The essence of freedom," we read, "comes properly into view only once we perceive it as the condition or ground of possibility of *Dasein*, as something which precedes the nexus of being and time." As Heidegger emphasizes, reiterating a point of the "Truth" lecture, to treat freedom as the grounding of philosophy does not denote a simple subjectivism or a relativization of metaphysics, but rather a "*reductio hominis*," that is, an attempt to return *Dasein* to its ontological essence or condition. "Freedom," he writes, "is not a particular notion among others, not part of a series of concepts, but rather underlies and permeates the totality of beings as a whole. In furnishing the ground of possibility of *Dasein*, freedom itself is in its essence still more primordial than man; thus man is only a guardian of freedom." More sharply phrased: "Human freedom signifies now no longer: freedom as a property of man; but the reverse: man as a possibility of freedom. Human freedom is a freedom which invades and sustains man, thereby rendering man possible."[27]

Heidegger's subsequent works modified or reformulated his conception of freedom in some details—without, however, jeopardizing its central philosophical status. A crucial question arising from his ontological approach can be pinpointed by the label "fatalism." Is ontology, one may ask (as many commentators have persistently done), really compatible with freedom? Can a category enmeshed in Being or the "history of Being" properly claim to capture the essence of human liberty? In the summer of 1936 Heidegger offered in Freiburg a lecture course entitled "Schelling's Treatise 'On the Essence of Human Freedom' (1809)." The lectures deserve attention here for a number of reasons. Perhaps even more than Nietzsche, Schelling emerged during this (middle) period as a key figure in Heidegger's thought—

a fact attested by his repeated return to Schelling in courses and seminars during subsequent years. Broadly speaking, Schelling represented for him one of the few great philosophers after Kant, perhaps the only one, who managed to push the problematic of freedom beyond the bounds of causality in the direction of ontology (or at least a quasi-ontological metaphysics). A central point addresssed in Schelling's treatise is precisely the issue of "fatalism," that is, the issue of the relationship between ontology and freedom. Together with this issue, the treatise also investigates the problem of "evil"—in religious terms: the compatibility of evil and divine providence. At this point, some of the political or political-theoretical overtones come into view to which Fédier and Alleman alluded. 1936, one may recall, was the year following the enactment of the Nuremberg laws and thus the beginning of concentrated racial-ethnic persecution—a policy which coincided with a progressive intensification of militarism and chauvinism. Was it simply an accident, one may query, that Heidegger in 1936 and subsequent years turned his attention to Schelling and the philosophical problematic of evil?

The political relevance of the lecture course is hardly only a matter of conjecture. As it seems to me, several passages are unmistakably political in character or clear manifestations of political dissent; a few examples must suffice. In pointing to the historical context of Schelling's treatise—Napoleonic expansionism and growing German resistance to Napoleon—Heidegger comments on the political aspirations of the Prussian leadership (von Humboldt, vom Stein, and others) at the time. "All these new figures," he writes, "were united in their goals. What they aimed at was expressed in a motto which circulated among them; among themselves they called the emerging Prussian State the 'state of intelligence,' that is, of spirit. Ahead of all others the soldier Scharnhorst demanded with increasing insistence for wartime bravery, but for peacetime knowledge and more knowledge and genuine education (*Bildung*). Genuine education meant: an essential insight penetrating all basic dimensions of historical experience, an insight which is the precondition of great acts of will. And soon the deep untruth of that phrase became evident which Napoleon had uttered to Goethe in Erfurt: 'Politics is destiny.' No," Heidegger adds, "the spirit is destiny and the destiny is spirit; but the essence of spirit is freedom. In 1809 Schelling published his treatise on freedom; it is Schelling's greatest achievement and simultaneously one of the profoundest works of

German and Western philosophy." Here is another passage directed against chauvinism which occurs in the middle of the lectures; it is a citation from Schelling's late manuscripts (but in 1936 unequivocally addressed to the Germans): "A truly general philosophy can impossibly be the property of a single nation; and so long as a philosophy does not transgress the limits of a single people (*Volk*), one can confidently assume that it is not yet a true philosophy (although it may be heading in that direction)."[28]

Considering its overall thrust or tenor, Heidegger's lecture course is anything but an academic or antiquarian exercise; basically it constitutes an exhortation to a radical philosophical (and perhaps political) reorientation. "We are only going to enter and truly penetrate the sphere of Schelling's treatise," the opening pages state, "if we grasp what pushes it beyond itself. Whether or not we fulfill this condition is equivalent to whether we philosophize or only talk 'about' philosophy; but we philosophize only if the condition of our *Dasein* engenders the genuine need of the question regarding Being as a whole." Schelling's significance is highlighted still more urgently and pointedly in a later passage—whose pathos contrasts sharply with the prevailing racial biologism of the time: "Being deserves preeminence of dignity because it occupies the highest rank before, in, and for all beings. Being is the pure air which man breathes and without which he degenerates into a mere animal and all his activity into animal husbandry. Because Schelling's treatise on human freedom is basically a metaphysics of evil; because it carries an essential new impulse into the basic philosophical question of Being; and because this impulse has so far been deprived of any effect—although such effectiveness could only happen in a still further transformation—this is why we attempt here an interpretation of the treatise. This is the real philosophical motivation for our choice."[29]

In the present context I can only offer a few glimpses of Heidegger's richly detailed commentary on Schelling. For brevity's sake I shall focus here on three aspects: the distinction between ontological freedom and the traditional conception of "free will"; the issue of fatalism in its connection with an ontological "pantheism"; and last the metaphysics of evil (seen as a non-voluntaristic or ontological ethics). The critique of the doctrine of "free will" stands at the threshold of the entire lecture course and thus can serve as starting point. Regarding the question of the essence and proper definition of freedom, Heidegger observes, "One knows this question under the familiar label of the 'problem of free will'; what is debated under this rubric is whether human will is free or unfree and how the one or the other can be convincingly demonstrated. Freedom is viewed here as a trait or property of man; but what and who man is, one presupposes to know." Against this assumption or presupposition the course articulates a radical ontological counterposition: "With this question of free will—which in the end is wrongly put and thus not even a proper question—Schelling's treatise has nothing whatever in common. For in this treatise freedom is not a property of man, but rather the reverse: man is at best a property of freedom. Freedom is the comprehensive and pervasive dimension of being in whose ambience man becomes man in the first place. This means: the essence of man is grounded in freedom; freedom itself, however, is a category transcending human *Dasein*, that is, a category of authentic Being as such." In portraying his (and Schelling's) ontological perspective, Heidegger is emphatic about the trans-human (and also trans-existentialist) character of the problematic discussed. "In asking about the essence of man," he writes, "we ask a question pointing beyond man—in the direction of a more basic and potent dimension, namely, that of freedom, construed not as an attribute or quality of human will, but as the essence of Being seen as the ground of beings as a whole. Our investigations thus carry us necessarily and *ab limine* beyond the pale of man into the question regarding the essence of Being as such."[30]

The issue of fatalism arises in Schelling's treatise primarily because of his attempt to formulate a comprehensive ontological "system" of thought—an objective which may be claimed to conflict with human freedom seen as spontaneous (and anti-systemic) self-determination. The more immediate source of the issue is the "pantheistic" character of Schelling's system, his assumption that all beings are somehow "immanent" in God or that "God is everything"; in its traditional construal, however, pantheism has typically been equivalent to fatalism—as especially F. H. Jacobi tried to demonstrate in his polemic against Spinoza (in 1785). As Schelling concedes, pantheism in most of its traditional formulations has indeed tended to coincide with fatalism and thus a denial of freedom. What his treatise tries to show, however, is that the pantheistic notion of immanence renders "a fatalistic construal merely possible, not necessary." More sharply put: pantheism according to the treatise is not only compatible with human freedom, but actually requires such freedom as its complement, since "the original experience of freedom embraces simultaneously the experience of the unity of all beings in their common ground." In the formula "everything is (in) God" or "God is everything," the crucial issue for Schelling is the meaning of the copula or of the asserted identity. In his view, the basic defect of traditional conceptions lies in the misunderstanding of the "is," that is, the "misconstrual of the law of identity and of the meaning of the copula in judgments." The treatise categorically rejects the construal of the copula in the sense of an "empty sameness" or "uniformity," opting instead for a notion of identity as the "harmony of difference within unity" or as the "unity of sameness and its opposite." With reference to the issue of pantheism (and fatalism), this means that God coincides with all beings not "in the sense of an indistinct stew" but in that of a harmonious and creative difference. Turning to the particular question of human freedom, Heidegger comments, "God *is* man—where 'is' does not signify uniformity. Identity is the unity of differences; thus man is from the first differentiated from and against God. Identity here denotes . . . the relation between ground and what is grounded as a consequence." This relation, however, is not synonymous with causation or a causal determinism (or fatalism). Rather, "The phrase 'God *is* man' says: God, as ground, lets man 'be' as a consequence—which means: to the extent he is a genuine consequence, man must somehow 'be' or have autonomous being." In his capacity as a free creator, God can properly manifest himself only in a being endowed with free creativity. Thus, "the grounded must itself be a freely active being, precisely because it is grounded in God." To sum up: "God *is* man, that is, man is in God as a free agent, and only free beings can properly be in God."[31]

Schelling's treatise does not limit itself to the stipulation of a mere theoretical compatibility, but presses on to consider the concrete "reality" of human freedom. It is at this point that his argument unfolds into a "metaphysics of evil," for the simple reason that, concretely viewed, freedom is not merely a capacity for good but "the capacity for *good and evil*"—which conjures up the issue of the relation between evil and God (or a comprehensive conception of Being).[32] Again, I cannot enter into the details of Schelling's presentation—except to say that it revolves centrally around a new or reformulated version of ontological difference: the difference between "ground" and "existence," where "ground" signifies the dark embryonic latency of Being or God, while "existence" denotes God's fully revealed manifestation in his creation. Schelling designates the distinction by the term "*Unterscheidung*" (difference), while Heidegger uses the expression "*Seynsfuge*" (ontological juncture or fugue) with the explanation that its components "taken together comprise the determination of the Being of beings." The two terms "ground" and "existence" are related not in the sense of causality but in that of a co-being or mutual "letting-be" which renders possible both their differentiation and their reconciliation and harmony. According to Schelling man is a being rooted as a creature in the "ground" or womb of nature but also one in which God's "existence" can become most fully manifest. More important, man is the creature in which the correlation between ground and existence reveals itself most acutely as tension and possible conflict. As Heidegger writes, paraphrasing Schelling, "Implanted in man are 'the deepest abyss and also the highest heaven'." What is unique about man is that, in his case, the two terms are not only autonomous and co-equal, but peculiarly "variable" against each other in the direction of a rigid self-assertion and enmity—which is the source of evil. In Schelling's words, "If in man the identity of the two principles were just as indissoluble as it is in God, no distinction could emerge, which means: God as spirit could not become manifest. Thus, that same unity which in God is indivisible must in man be divisible—and this division is the possibility of good and evil."[33]

In the treatise, it is thus the special variability of ground and existence against each other which furnishes the ontological foundation for human freedom and also for a metaphysics of evil. The possibility of evil arises here from the dissolution or reversal of divine unity, that is, from the rebellion of ground against existence and vice versa, and thus from the revolt of a stubborn particularity against universality. "Since human will is lodged in inner selfhood," the course states that "this will can attempt in human endeavor to put itself in the place of the universal will; thus, self-will can . . . as separate selfishness pretend to be the ground of the whole. . . . This ability is the capacity for evil." Seen in this light, evil is not simply immoral conduct but the synonym for a profound ontological perversion of divine unity and harmony—a perversion giving rise, as Heidegger says, to "a reverse God or anti-spirit" and to the "reversal of the ontological juncture (*Seynsfuge*) into disjuncture (*Ungefüge*)." As an ontological perversion of the ground-existence correlation, evil is not merely a human quality or the result of individual arbitrariness. In Heidegger's words, "Man alone is capable of evil; but this capability is not a property of man. Rather, to be capable in this sense is a constitutive (ontological) feature of the essence of man." From a purely moral-ethical perspective, the good is what "ought" and evil what "ought not" to be; what this perspective neglects is that good and evil "could not oppose each other if they were not already constituted as opposites, and that they could not *be* opposites, if they did not reciprocally condition each other and thus were not ultimately correlated in their being." For Schelling (and with slight modification for Heidegger), good and evil signify first and primarily distinct modes or variations of ontological difference. Evil in that view denotes "that unity of ground and existence in which a selfish ground or selfishness usurps the place of universality." Goodness, in contrast, signifies that unity in which ground and existence are differentiated and placed in tension, but where they recognize and thus "let" each other "be" as ground and existence. To designate this concordance or mutual letting-be, Schelling employs the term "love" (*Liebe*). "Love must condone the (independent) will of the ground," we read, "because otherwise love would annihilate itself. Only by letting this independence operate, love has that foil or counterpoint in or against which it can manifest its supremacy. . . . Thus, love is the original union of elements of which each might exist separately and yet does not so exist and cannot really be without the other."[34]

To complete this review of Heidegger's conception of freedom I shall glance briefly at a few passages taken from his later writings— which frequently are claimed to surrender human freedom to a blind destiny. The essay "The Question Concerning Technology" (of 1953) portrays the disclosure or unconcealment of Being as "mission" or "destiny of Being" (*Seinsgeschick*). "We shall call that gathering commission which first starts man upon a path of disclosure, the mission or destiny (*Geschick*)," Heidegger writes. "The essence of all history is determined by this mission." Although primarily a mode of concealment, even technology—styled as a general cast or "framing" (*Gestell*)— in his view is such a mission. No matter how concealment or unconcealment occur, he observes, "the destiny of disclosure always holds sway over man. But that destiny or mission is never a fate that compels; for man becomes truly *free* precisely insofar as he belongs to the realm of mission and thus is one who listens, though not one who simply obeys. The essence of freedom," the essay adds, "is *originally* not connected with the will and even less with the causality of human willing. Rather, freedom governs the free or open space in the sense of a clearing, that is, of disclosure. It is the happening of disclosure, that is, of truth, to which freedom stands in the closest and most intimate kinship." According to the essay, "all disclosure arises in, points to, and conducts into freedom (as a free or open space). But the freedom of the free consists neither in unfettered arbitrariness nor in the constraint of mere (external) laws." The freeing or liberating quality of disclosure prevails even in modern technology to the extent that the latter harbors an ontological "mission" or reveals the "destiny of disclosure." As Heidegger emphasizes, however, these phrases "express something different from the talk one hears quite frequently, to the effect that technology is the fate of our age, where 'fate' means the inevitability of an unalterable course." Rather, by treating technology as a "mission of disclosure," "we already find ourselves in the free space of a mission which by no means confines us to a mute compulsion to push on blindly with technology or, what comes to the same, to revolt helplessly against it and curse it as work of the devil. Quite the contrary: by opening ourselves properly to the essence of technology, we find ourselves unexpectedly addressed by a liberating claim."[35]

Liberty or freedom also figure prominently in Heidegger's essay "Building Dwelling Thinking" (1951). In a manner reminiscent of the Schelling lectures, the essay elaborates on the linkage between freedom and reconciliation or harmony—a linkage not fully disrupted by the danger and constant possibility of enmity and discord. In discussing the notion of "dwelling" from the perspective of the ontological "fourfold" (*Geviert*), Heidegger comments: "The Old Saxon *wuon*, the Gothic *wunian*, like the old word *bauen*, mean to remain, to stay in a place; but the Gothic term says more distinctly how this remaining is experienced. *Wunian* means: to be contented, to be stilled, to be and remain in peace. The word for peace, *Friede*, means the free(d) or what is set free, in Gothic: the '*Frye*'; and *fry* means preserved from harm and danger, preserved and thus spared or saved. To free actually means to spare; but sparing itself consists not only in not inflicting harm on what is spared. Real sparing is something *positive* and occurs whenever, from the beginning, we let something 'be' in its essence; when we return it properly into its own essence; when we 'free' it in the genuine sense of the word by preserving it in peace. To dwell, to be stilled, thus means to remain at peace within that free space which safeguards everything in its essential being."[36]

III

The implications of Heidegger's conception of freedom for contemporary political and social theory are numerous and, I believe, far-reaching. Clearly the most important feature is the dislodging of freedom from human willfulness and subjectivity—a decentering deviating radically from the modern tendency to treat freedom as individual (or collective) property and thus as a particular quality of individual (or collective) decisions. From his earliest to his latest writings, Heidegger has tried to explore the pre-subjective or ontological grounding of freedom—an exploration, however, which did not sacrifice free initiative or action to a blind fate or to the mechanical operation of environmental or structural constraints. In addition to challenging the traditional doctrine of "free will," his conception also implies a departure from the conventional framework of causality and especially from the view that willing, as the core of freedom, signifies the causation or causal production of effects. In light of the frequent charge of amoralism (if not immoralism), it is important to note the "ethical" connotations of Heidegger's perspective—although this perspective is patently incompatible with both naturalistic and voluntaristic versions of ethics. As it seems to me, instead of simply perpetuating (or abolishing) traditional value theories, Heidegger's work seeks to uncover the ontological conditions of possibility of "valuing" or—more appropriately phrased—of "goodness" and "evil."[37] Particularly his lectures on Schelling adumbrate the intimate connection between freedom and the "capacity for good and evil." From this vantage point, the genuine or unperverted exercise of freedom is shown to be a persistent tendency or inclination toward the "good life," that is, toward human reconciliation and peace—an aspect which casts a stark new light on such customary ideological antitheses as liberalism and socialism. Instead of vouchsafing individual isolation and selfishness, freedom in this view is not merely an accidental ingredient, but the essential grounding of human solidarity (or socialism)—just as solidarity properly construed denotes a reciprocal effort of liberation or a mutual "letting-be."

Rather than elaborating further on such implications, I want to draw attention briefly to some social and political thinkers who, in my view, have made tentative steps in the direction sketched by Heidegger. In her remarkable essay "What Is Freedom?" (contained in *Between Past and Future*), Hannah Arendt notes that, in raising this question, one becomes entangled in "age-old contradictions and antinomies" which are "lying in wait to force the mind into dilemmas of logical impossibility so that, depending which horn of the dilemma you are holding on to, it becomes as impossible to conceive of freedom or its opposite as it is to realize the notion of a square circle." Turning to Kant's resolution of the dilemma—his distinction between "inner" freedom and "outer" unfreedom, or between natural causality and "causality of freedom"— Arendt comments, "This solution, pitting the dictate of the will against the understanding of reason, is ingenious enough and may even suffice to establish a moral law whose logical consistency is in no way inferior to natural laws. But it does little to eliminate the greatest and most dangerous difficulty, namely, that thought itself, in its theoretical as well as its pre-theoretical form, makes freedom disappear—quite apart from the fact that it must appear strange indeed that the faculty of the will whose essential activity consists in dictate and command should be the harborer of freedom." What renders the focus on "inner" freedom or freedom of will so obnoxious, in her view, is that it involves ultimately a denial of politics and political praxis. Together with Heidegger, Arendt regards freedom as coterminous with an open space or a space of "disclosure"—in political terms, with a "polis" making room for human action and interaction. Freedom, she writes, "is not only one among the many problems and phenomena of the political realm properly speaking, such as justice, or power, or equality"; rather, it is "actually the reason that men live together in political organization at all." Thus, "the *raison d'être* of politics is freedom, and its field of experience is action." This freedom, however, she adds, "which we take for granted in all political theory and which even those who praise tyranny must still take into account is the very oppposite of 'inner freedom,' the inward space into which men may escape from external coercion and *feel* free."[38]

Again in concordance with Heidegger, Arendt perceives a close proximity between genuine freedom and human solidarity. "We first become aware of freedom or its opposite," she observes, "in our intercourse with others, not in the intercourse with ourselves. Before it became an attribute of thought or a quality of the will, freedom was understood to be the free man's status, which enabled him to move, to get away from home, to go out into the world and meet other people in deed and word." Basically, "without a politically guaranteed public realm, freedom lacks the worldly space to make its appearance." Given its connection with human solidarity or "plurality," freedom cannot coincide with voluntarism or the mere exercise of "free will"; even less can it coincide with an "absolute" free will or an absolute will power as it has traditionally been formulated in the doctrine of "sovereignty." "Politically," Arendt asserts, "the identification of freedom with sovereignty is perhaps the most pernicious and dangerous consequence of the philosophical equation of freedom and free will. For it leads either to a denial of human freedom—namely, if it is realized that whatever men may be, they are never sovereign—or to the insight that the freedom of one man, or a group, or a body politic can be purchased only at the price of the freedom, i.e., sovereignty, of all others. Within the conceptual framework of traditional philosophy, it is indeed very difficult to understand how freedom and non-sovereignty can exist together or, to put it in another way, how freedom could have been given to men under the condition of non-sovereignty." As she adds, "Under human conditions, which are determined by the fact that not man but men live on earth, freedom and sovereignty are so little identical that they cannot even exist simultaneously. Where men wish to be sovereign, as individuals or as organized groups, they must submit to the oppression of the will, be this the individual will with which I force myself, or the 'general will' of an organized group. If men wish to be free, it is precisely sovereignty they must renounce."[39]

The Heideggerian linkage between freedom and both an ontological and inter-human space is also affirmed by Maurice Merleau-Ponty in the concluding chapter of his *Phenomenology of Perception*. "The idea of an initial choice," he writes, "involves a contradiction. If freedom is to have *room* in which to move, if it is to be describable as freedom, there must be something to hold it away from its objectives; it must have a *field*, which means that there must be for it special possibilities or realities which tend to cling to being. . . . Our freedom is not to be sought in a spurious discussion on the conflict between a style of life which we have no wish to reappraise and circumstances suggestive of another: the real choice is that between our whole character and our manner of being in the world." Freedom's insertion in "being" and the "world" also entails for Merleau-Ponty its correlation with human solidarity. "The other-person-as-object," he observes (criticizing an extreme version of existentialism), "is nothing but an insincere modality of others, just as absolute subjectivity is nothing but an abstract notion of myself. I must therefore, in the most radical reflection, apprehend around my absolute individuality a kind of halo of generality or a kind of atmosphere of 'sociality'. . . . I must apprehend myself immediately as centered in a way outside myself, and my individual existence must diffuse round itself, so to speak, an existence of (general) quality." Thus, "my life must have a significance which I do not constitute; there must strictly speaking be an intersubjectivity." Or as he phrased the same thought, perhaps more radically, at a later point: There is "reversibility"; we are "each the other side of each other."[40]

Is Critical Theory a Humanism?

"Humanism" today is an embattled notion; while some philosophers treat the term as the capstone of past illusions, others vindicate it as an emblem of imperishable values.[1] Over three decades ago, Jean-Paul Sartre in a famous lecture probed the question whether existentialism could be viewed as a form of humanism, answering that query in the end affirmatively. In the following pages I would like to raise a similar question with regard to "critical theory," especially (though not exclusively) that version of critical theory articulated by Jürgen Habermas. In trying to disentangle this issue, I shall adhere loosely to the meaning of "humanism" outlined by Sartre—though without his peculiarly existentialist pathos. In his lecture, Sartre did not present humanism as an ideological creed and certainly not as synonym for a cult; rather, the core of the term was simply that man had to be seen as center or source of all his actions, beliefs, and propositions (where "source" does not designate an empirical fact or solid plank but a condition of possibility). To regard "man" as central, he noted, means that "it is in projecting and losing himself beyond himself that he makes man to exist" and that "there is no other universe except the human universe, the universe of human subjectivity. . . . This is humanism because we remind man that there is no legislator but himself." Sartre's conception of the term, one should add, was not narrowly individualistic, but sought to embrace mankind as a whole: "The subjectivity which we thus postulate as the standard of truth is no narrowly individual subjectivism, for as we have demonstrated, it is not only one's own self that one discovers in the *cogito*, but those of others as well."[2]

The proposed inquiry, I believe, is not an idle or unmotivated intellectual exercise. Both traditional and contemporary theoretical perspectives are currently under scrutiny, by philosophers as well as social scientists, with respect to their ties with the legacies of humanism, Cartesianism, and speculative "metaphysics." Recently, in a study entitled *Sociology and the Twilight of Man*, Charles Lemert has associated all the prevalent sociological frameworks or approaches—including Habermasian critical theory—with a particularly pronounced and restrictive type of humanism which he calls "homocentrism" and which, in his presentation, is the outgrowth of Kantian philosophy and subsequent trends in the nineteenth century. What his study tries to show is "that all of the major alternatives within recent sociological theory are, in fact, centered; and furthermore, that they are centered in a particular and common fashion. There is evidence to demonstrate that even the most recent of presumed sociological 'inventions' are *homocentric*: One way or another, they all return to the peculiarly nineteenth-century idea which holds that *man* is the measure of all things." Regarding the specific meaning of "homocentrism," Lemert finds its distinguishing traits mainly in the focus on human finitude in opposition to the constancy of the physical world, and on subjectivity and historical creativity in contrast with nature. "Strictly defined," he writes, "homocentrism is that discursive formation which centers itself upon man as a finite subject who dominates his own history. Finitude, subjectivity, and historicism—these nineteenth-century inventions are the marks of man as center." Shorthand formulas for the conception are that "man-expelled-from-nature was given history as the place of which he became the central principle," or simply: *"Man, the finite subject of history."*[3]

In this chapter I intend to pursue, expand, and evaluate Lemert's assessment. In view of his stress on the nineteenth century, it seems desirable first of all to glance at the parentage of critical theory and examine possible homocentric leanings in the writings of Marx (and Engels). As a link between this parentage and Habermas's outlook, the beginnings of the Frankfurt School—especially Horkheimer's programmatic statement of 1937—also deserve brief attention. Following this historical recapitulation, I shall turn to a review of Habermas's opus, without limiting myself strictly to his sociological contributions. The accent here will be placed on three main topics or problem areas: epistemology, theory of social evolution, and language theory. Taking Lemert's arguments as road markers or direction signals, I shall sift pertinent publications for their manifest or latent homocentric premises. By way of conclusion I intend to comment more generally on the issue of humanism and homocentrism, its relevance to critical theory, and its broader philosophical implications.

I

The correlation of "classical" Marxism with humanism is relatively uncontroversial, except among its doctrinaire opponents. Scholarly experts and nonacademic readers generally concur regarding the strong humanist streak evident in many of the classical texts; widespread agreement also prevails to the effect that this streak is particularly pronounced in Marx's early works, that is, those written prior to his move to London. Dispute surrounds mainly the overall significance of the humanist strand within the larger corpus. While some students are inclined to locate the core of Marx's teachings in his early, more philosophical writings and virtually to bypass *Capital*, others consider his humanist leanings as a youthful aberration remedied by his "mature" economic analysis. This is not the place for me to settle this dispute—although I confess a slightly greater sympathy for the first than for the second interpretation. On the whole I tend to agree on this point with Robert Tucker, the renowned Marx scholar, when he states that "there is an underlying basic continuity of thought not only between the 1844 manuscripts and *The German Ideology*, but more broadly between the early Marx and the Marx of the later writings culminating in *Capital*."[4]

In trying to pinpoint the brand of humanism embedded in classical Marxism, initial consideration needs to be given to Ludwig Feuerbach. It seems safe to say that it was mainly Feuerbach's influence that drove a wedge between Marx and orthodox as well as left-wing Hegelianism and prompted him to develop his new perspective of "historical materialism." In his *Essence of Christianity* (published in 1841), Feuerbach had attacked Hegelian philosophy as an abstract metaphysical speculation, or rather as a doctrine containing a valid kernel of truth—mainly the notion of "self-alienation"—but a kernel which was cloaked in mystification and could be rescued only through rigorous "transformative criticism." While, for Hegel, the essence of reality resided in a transcendent (or divine) "spirit" whose self-alienation and self-recovery constituted the path of history, Feuerbach's study insisted on the need to invert the idealist scheme by giving center stage to man or the human species. Once this was done, idealism itself emerged as a form of human self-alienation, in the sense that "spirit" (a philosophical equivalent for God) appeared as a mystified image of man projected onto heaven; above all, the changed focus cast a new light on historical evolution: instead of denoting the progressive self-formation of spirit, history was revealed as the story of man's progressive self-realization through various detours or stages of alienation. There is evidence that Marx was strongly impressed by Feuerbach's study — although he did not entirely embrace the latter's "humanism." Marx's main complaint was that Feuerbach stopped short of pursuing the implications of "transformative criticism" and remained satisfied with an abstract conception of individual man or human "essence," without probing the concrete tensions and conflicts besetting the human condition in different social contexts.[5]

Notwithstanding his reservations, several of Marx's early writings followed the general strategy of Feuerbach's critique, extending its thrust mainly into the domain of politics and economics. Thus, in an essay entitled "For a Ruthless Criticism of Everything Existing" (written in 1843), Marx depicted the modern "state" and its array of political institutions as rationalist-idealist structures deriving ultimately from human self-alienation. Although conceding that, in comparison with the feudal past, the "political state in all its modern forms" reflects somehow "the demands of reason," Marx noted that the same state "everywhere presupposes that reason has been realized," thereby concealing its actual functions behind a cloak of mystification. "Out of this conflict of the political state with itself, therefore, one can develop social truth," the essay stated. "Just as religion is the catalogue of the theoretical struggles of mankind, so the political state is the catalogue of its practical struggles." In the political domain what the inversion of idealism required was mainly an effort to raise the conflict mentioned to the level of consciousness and thereby to wake society "from its dream about itself": "Our whole task can consist only in putting religious and political questions into self-conscious human form — as is also the case in Feuerbach's criticism of religion. Our motto must therefore be: reform of consciousness not through dogmas, but through analysing the mystical consciousness, the consciousness which is unclear to itself, whether it appears in religious or political form."[6]

The scrutiny of modern political institutions was continued in greater detail in Marx's justly famous "Contribution to the Critique of Hegel's *Philosophy of Right*" (written in the same year as the preceding essay). The opening pages of that manuscript clearly spelled out the linkage between political and social criticism and Feuerbach's transformative approach; they also provide evidence of Marx's attachment to a radical humanism or, if one prefers, "homocentrism." In the wake of Feuerbach's study, the first sentence argued, "the criticism of religion has been largely completed, and the criticism of religion is the premise of all criticism." The basic tenet of Feuerbach's strategy according to Marx was this: "Man makes religion; religion does not make man." The strategy revealed that "religion is indeed man's self-consciousness and self-awareness so long as he has not found himself or has lost himself again. But man is not an abstract being, squatting outside the world; man is the human world, the state, society. This state, this society, produce religion which is an inverted world consciousness, because they are an inverted world." As Marx added, the attack on religion was not designed to rob man of consolation or hope, but rather to give him grounds for hope by laying the foundation for human self-realization and fulfillment. "Criticism has plucked the imaginary flower from the chain," we read, "not in order that man shall bear the chain without caprice or consolation but so that he shall cast off the chain and pluck the living flower. The criticism of religion disillusions man so that he will think, act and fashion his reality as a man who has lost his illusions and regained his reason; so that he will revolve about himself as his own true sun. Religion is only the illusory sun about which man revolves so long as he does not revolve about himself." Seen in this light, Feuerbach's work opened up vast arenas for philosophical and social-political inquiry: "The immediate task of philosophy, which is in the service of history, is to unmask human self-alienation in its secular form now that it has been unmasked in its sacred form. Thus the criticism of heaven is transformed into the criticism of earth, the criticism of religion into the criticism of law, and the criticism of theology into the criticism of politics."[7]

Turning to Hegel's political theory, Marx found the mainstay of the *Philosophy of Right* in the identification of the modern "state" with the rule of reason—an identification which correctly captured the advance in enlightenment manifest in modern politics, but at the same time obscured this advance by camouflaging the state's shortcomings and concrete underpinnings. Just as, in Hegel's *Logic*, the absolute spirit was an idealized image of human thought, so his notion of the state could be grasped as an idealist projection and self-alienation of concrete human practice and power. Applying transformative criticism to the *Philosophy of Right*, Marx pleaded for an inversion or at least complete reformulation of the Hegelian dichotomy of "state" and "civil society": instead of viewing society simply as content molded by the state as ideal "form," the latter had to be seen as outgrowth of the real tensions and contradictions of social and economic life. In terms of Marx's analysis, the inversion and ultimate abolition or supersession of the dichotomy could be achieved only through a radical endeavor of human emancipation and self-realization, an endeavor which in turn could be successfully pursued only by the concrete agents or producers of the social world, that is, the working class—a class shunned by the modern political system. To overturn political mystification and oppression, the manuscript observed, it was necessary to discover a social layer or component "which cannot emancipate itself without emancipating itself from all the other spheres of society, without, therefore, emancipating all these other spheres—which is, in short, a *total loss* of humanity and can only redeem itself by a *total redemption* of humanity. This dissolution of society, as a particular class, is the proletariat."[8]

Regarding emancipation and its relation to modern political institutions, the essay "On the Jewish Question" (dating from the same year) gives additional indications of Marx's humanism. Differentiating between "political emancipation" under the auspices of the modern state and genuine human emancipation, the essay argued that the former liberated from feudal bonds merely isolated individuals with their empirically given (including religious) preferences, without tapping the richer potential of man seen as a genuine social agent or "species-being."[9] According to Marx, the creation of the modern (bourgeois) state produced a rigid bifurcation "between individual life and species life, between the life of civil society and political life." From the vantage point of the state, man was indeed "considered a sovereign being, a supreme being"; but it was "uneducated, unsocial man, man just as he is in his fortuitous existence, man as he has been corrupted, lost to himself, alienated, subjected to the rule of inhuman conditions and elements, by the whole organization of our society—in short, man who is not yet a real species-being." In the wake of political liberation, Marx noted, "feudal society was dissolved into its basic element, *man*, but into egoistic man who was its real foundation." Treated as an isolated entity, this egoistic man was "the passive, given result of the dissolution of society, an object of direct apprehension and consequently a *natural* object. The political revolution dissolves civil society into its elements without revolutionizing these elements themselves or subjecting them to criticism." Concrete human agency could only be uncovered by moving beyond the schism between "state of nature" and abstract-rational politics: "Political emancipation is a reduction of man, on the one hand, to a member of civil society, an independent and egoistic individual, and on the other hand, to a citizen, to a moral person. Human emancipation will only be complete when the real individual man has absorbed into himself the abstract citizen; when as an individual man, in his everyday life, in his work, and in his relationships, he has become a species-being; and when he has recognized and organized his own powers as *social* powers so that he no longer separates this social power from himself as *political* power."[10]

Having criticized modern politics from a transformed or inverted Hegelian perspective, Marx turned his attention progressively to the domain in which "social" and "political power" intersect: that of political economy. His *Economic and Philosophic Manuscripts* (of 1844) were the first main step along this road, a step which revealed the continuing relevance of both Hegel and transformative criticism. Commenting on the *Phenomenology of Mind*, Marx acknowledged that "the outstanding thing in Hegel's *Phenomenology* and its final result—that is, the dialectic of negativity as the moving and generating principle—is primarily that Hegel conceives the self-development of man as a process, objectification as loss of the object, as alienation and transcendence of this alienation; that he thus grasps the essence of *labor* and comprehends objective man, authentic because actual, as the outcome of his *own labor*." In terms of the *Phenomenology*, genuine human nature could be revealed only by man's "bringing out of himself all the *powers* that are his as species-being—which in turn is only possible through the totality of man's actions, as the result of history." Despite this acknowledgment, however, the *Manuscripts* were quick in denouncing Hegel's purely speculative approach. It was only "within the sphere of abstraction," we read, that Hegel viewed "labor as man's act of self-genesis" and thus grasped "man's relation to himself as an alien being and the disclosure of himself as an alien being as the catalyst of species-consciousness and species life." The chief shortcoming of Hegelian philosophy was that human nature was reduced to an "abstract, thinking essence" and history to "the divine process of man, a process traversed by man's abstract, pure, absolute essence that is distinct from him." From the vantage point of "absolute self-consciousness" or the "self-knowing and self-manifesting idea," "real man and real nature become mere predicates—symbols of this esoteric, unreal man and of this unreal nature. Subject and predicate are therefore related to each other in absolute inversion."[11]

Employing the transformative method, the *Manuscripts* insisted on the central role of concrete human "labor" and on the need to view past historical developments as a succession of distinct modes of economic production—modes in which human initiative and self-genesis were invariably thwarted or repressed. Man's intrinsic vocation or his "species-character," according to Marx, resided in his capacity to be a "free conscious producer" or to engage in "free, conscious activity." By working upon and thus imprinting himself on the "objective world," we read, "man first really proves himself to be a species-being. This production is his active species life; through and because of his production, nature appears as his work and his reality." Instead of fostering and enhancing species life, however, traditional modes of production typically subjected human labor to exploitation and external forces or constraints; in the context of the capitalist system, these constraints were embodied in the laws of the market and in the privileged status of the owners of the means of production. Governed by the dictates of commodity production, the worker's life was increasingly regimented, while labor was turned into "estranged" or "alienated labor": "Labor's realization is its objectification. In the conditions established by political economy, this realization of labor appears as loss of reality for the worker; objectification as loss of the object and object-bondage; appropriation as estrangement, as alienation." In terms of the *Manuscripts*, estrangement at this point had multiple connotations: separation of the producer from his products; alienation of man from man in a competitive, atomistic setting; and betrayal of the worker's species-character through his transformation into a commodity. Removal of these combined ills could only be effected through a dismantling of the capitalist system and the abolition of its class structure. In its deeper or essential thrust, communism—in Marx's words—had to be seen "as the positive transcendence of private property or human self-estrangement, and therefore as the real appropriation of the human essence by and for man"; differently phrased: the "annulment of private property" was "the justification of real human life as man's possession and thus the advent of practical humanism"—of a "positively self-deriving humanism, *positive humanism.*"[12]

The themes discussed in the *Manuscripts* were subsequently subjected to more detailed and rigorous analysis, but they were never really abandoned. Regarding self-production viewed as man's species-character, *The Holy Family* (of 1845) applied the notion concretely to the proletariat and its struggle with the "possessing class." "To use Hegel's expression," the treatise stated, "this (proletarian) class is, within depravity, an indignation against this depravity, an indignation necessarily aroused in this class by the contradiction between its human nature and its life-situation, which is a blatant, outright and all-embracing denial of that very nature." The "practical humanism" *motif* was strongly reaffirmed in *The German Ideology* (written by Marx jointly with Engels during the following year). The "premises" of their study, the authors asserted, were "not arbitrary ones, not dogmas, but real premises": "They are the real individuals, their activity and the material conditions under which they live, both those which they find already existing and those produced by their activity." In their species-character men were said "to distinguish themselves from animals as soon as they begin to produce their means of subsistence, a step which is conditioned by their physical organization. By producing their means of subsistence men are indirectly producing their actual material life." Self-production in this sense also embraced mental life, for men had to be perceived as "the producers of their conceptions, ideas, etc.," and consciousness as "directly interwoven with the material activity and the material intercourse of men, the language of real life." According to *The German Ideology*, human activity and productivity always occurred in a concrete setting or a distinct mode of production. In the prevailing capitalist mode of economics, human productivity was transformed into "estranged labor," and labor itself was degraded to the point that it "lost all semblance of self-activity." Only the reappropriation of the productive forces by the proletariat could remedy this spoliation of human self-genesis: "The appropriation of a totality of instruments of production is, for this very reason, the development of a totality of capacities in the individuals themselves. This appropriation is further determined by the persons appropriating: only the proletarians of the present day, who are completely shut off from all self-activity, are in a position to achieve a complete and no longer restricted self-activity, which consists in the appropriation of a totality of productive forces and in the thus postulated development of a totality of capacities."[13]

Owing largely to their more technical subject matter, Marx's later writings exude a less overtly humanist posture; but their animating principle continues to be human emancipation. In *Capital*, the effect of this principle is clearly manifest in the discussion of such categories as "labor value," "surplus value," and "commodity fetishism." In a passage delineating the latter notion as a mode of estranged labor or self-activity, Marx stated that a commodity is "a mysterious thing simply because in it the social character of men's labor appears to them as an objective character stamped upon the product of that labor; because the relation of the producers to the sum total of their own labor is presented to them as a social relation, existing not between themselves, but between the products of their labor." In this manner, a "definite social relation between men" assumes for the producers "the fantastic form of a relation between things." The same animating impulse also pervades the concluding comments on the "realm of freedom" as the goal of emancipation. Genuine freedom, we read, "can only consist in socialized man, the associated producers, rationally regulating their interchange with nature, bringing it under their common control, instead of being ruled by it as by the blind forces of nature; and achieving this with the least expenditure of energy and under conditions most favorable to, and worthy of, their human nature." In light of these and many similar passages, Richard Bernstein seems entirely justified in saying that "the thrust of *Capital* is to reveal that under seemingly abstract, impersonal, economic categories, a great *human* drama is taking place," the drama of human self-realization: "The thrust of *Capital*, and all of Marx's thinking, is *not* to affirm the impotence of man in the face of impersonal forces but rather to affirm the *real* possibility of a critical understanding of the world which allows man's eventual mastery of his own fate."[14]

Mediated by the more empiricist leanings of the later Engels and the entire *fin-de-siècle* period, the humanist thrust of the classical texts was bequeathed as a legacy to the Marxist movement seen as both an intellectual and a practical-political enterprise. This is not the place to review the changing fortunes and misfortunes of this strand among Marx's intellectual heirs. At this point I would like to shift attention to the beginnings of the Frankfurt School—and particularly to Max Horkheimer's programmatic formulation of its posture in his essay "Traditional and Critical Theory" (of 1937). As presented in that essay, the "traditional" mode of theorizing was limited to the registration and explication of phenomena in abstraction from their social contexts and origins, whereas "critical theory" focuses on the concrete genesis of factual-social conditions and especially on the role of human agency and productivity in this process. "As inaugurated by Descartes and now practiced everywhere in the specialized sciences," Horkheimer wrote, theory in the traditional sense "organizes experience in the light of questions concerned with the reproduction of life in the prevailing context of contemporary society." Although clearly endowed with pragmatic utility, this perspective treats "the social genesis of problems, the real situations in which science is applied, and the purposes it is made to serve as extraneous or external to itself." In contrast, "critical theory deals with human beings as the producers of their entire historical way of life. The real situations which are the starting point of science are not regarded here simply as data to be verified and to be predicted according to the laws of probability." For, Horkheimer added, "a given context or situation depends not on nature alone but also on the control man has over it. The objects and modes of perception, the kinds of questions asked and the meaning of the answer given—all bear witness to human activity and the degree of man's power."[15]

According to the essay, the traditional mode of theorizing was part and parcel of concrete trends in modern society, especially the growing division of labor, the fragmentation of society into atomistic components, and the transformation of interaction into commodity relations. "The traditional conception of theory," we read, "is abstracted from the scientific enterprise such as it functions in the context of the division of labor at a given stage of social development; it corresponds to the activity of the scientist such as it is carried on alongside all the other activities in society but in no immediately transparent connection with them." Specialized scientific activity in turn was a reflection of the disjointed economic structure of the market; enjoying an "apparent independence," particular agents in that structure "believe they are acting according to individual decisions, whereas in reality even their most complicated calculations exemplify the working of an incalculable social mechanism." As an antidote to social atomization and reification, the essay outlined a perspective which would overcome "the one-sidedness that necessarily arises when limited intellectual endeavors are detached from their matrix in the total practice of society." Such a perspective had to be critical both of the general structure of prevailing society and of its corollary: the spurious notion of private independence. "The separation between individual and society," the essay stated, "in virtue of which the individual accepts as natural the limits prescribed for his activity is relativized in critical theory. The latter considers the overall framework as it arises from the blind conjunction of isolated activities (that is, the existing division of labor and the class distinctions) to be a situation which, originating in human action, is potentially amenable to planned decision and a rational determination of purpose." A major trait of critical thought, in Horkheimer's presentation, is its rejection of the customary bifurcation between scientific analyst and observed data, in favor of a closer subject-object correlation. The distinction between the two postures, he noted, "springs in general from a difference not so much of objects as of subjects. For proponents of the critical outlook, the 'facts' as they emerge from the operation of society are not in the same degree extrinsic as they are for the specialized scientist and members of other professions modeled after the sciences. The former are concerned with a reorganization of labor; but insofar as the objective conditions given in perception are conceived as products which in principle are subject—or in the future should become subject—to human control, these conditions lose the character of pure factuality."[16]

Paralleling Marx's Hegelian affinities, the essay drew some of its inspiration from the German idealist legacy: "In relating the complex of seemingly irreducible facts (which the scientific specialist must respect) to human production, the critical theory of society accords with German idealism; ever since Kant the latter has pitted this dynamic thrust against blind objectivism and the social conformism connected with it." To be sure, like Marx, the essay insisted on the need to correct this legacy through transformative criticism. As construed by idealism, Horkheimer observed, human production was a purely "mental or spiritual" activity, anchored in a "transempirical consciousness per se, an absolute ego or spirit" removed from mundane predicaments; Hegel's recourse to the "world spirit," in particular, had to be seen as "a private belief, a personal peace treaty between the philosopher and an inhuman world." In contrast, in line with historical materialism, critical theory treats human production and self-production as a mode of "social labor whose stratified (or class-divided) structure puts its stamp on all forms of human behavior, including theorizing." Instead of denoting an unobstructed mental process, production from this perspective necessarily has a conflictual character. "Critical thinking," we read, "is motivated by the effort concretely to transcend the tension (in present-day society) and to overcome the contrast between individual purposefulness, spontaneity and rationality, and the socially regulated conditions of labor. Critical thought harbors a concept of man which is in conflict with itself until this contrast is removed; if rationally guided action is proper to man, then prevailing social arrangements which shape existence in all details are inhuman and this inhumanity affects everything that happens in society." The outcome or goal of social struggle, as envisaged by critical theory, is human emancipation on a large scale in a fully "rational society"; in other words: the "vision of self-determination for the human species, that is, the idea of a state of affairs in which man's actions no longer flow from a mechanism but from his own decisions." Without endorsing an easy optimism or utopianism, Horkheimer's account pointed in the direction of "a condition free from exploitation and oppression in which an all-embracing subject, namely self-aware mankind, actually exists and when it becomes possible to speak of coherent theory construction and of a thinking transcending individuals."[17]

II

As a branch or offshoot of the Frankfurt School, Habermas's perspective can be expected to exhibit some of the central accents of the essay discussed and of the Marxist legacy in general; despite a considerable diversification of arguments and focal concerns, his version of critical theory can plausibly be assumed to share the "vision of self-determination" sketched in Horkheimer's formulation. In his *Sociology and the Twilight of Man*, Lemert portrays Habermas's outlook as a distinct type of sociological homocentrism. Adopting a classificatory scheme concentrating on different aspects of "discursive practice," his study places Habermas under the rubric of a "syntactical" sociology—in contradistinction to the "lexical" (or empirical-analytic) and "semantical" (or interpretive-hermeneutical) brands. As he observes, the notion of a syntactical sociology refers to "approaches that give primary attention to the normative basis of social science and which develop sociological theory with reference to explicitly stated values." Just as syntax is the "normative aspect of language," he adds, "syntacticality" in social-scientific parlance denotes "that type of sociological writing which derives from an interest in the norms governing both science and social life"; intrinsic to this type of inquiry is that it "concerns itself with the grammar of the good life."[18] In trying to vindicate the label of a syntactical homocentrism, Lemert's analysis ranges broadly over Habermas's writings. In the following, I intend to pursue a somewhat similar path, by concentrating in greater detail on a more limited set of problem areas: those of epistemology, individual and social evolution, and language theory.

There can be little doubt that epistemology—seen as philosophically reflective theory of knowledge and justification of knowledge claims—occupies a central place in Habermas's overall conception. His *Knowledge and Human Interests* (first published in 1968) was basically an attempt to rejuvenate epistemological inquiry as an antidote to positivistic "scientism" and as a prelude to a critically reflective theory of society. In large measure, this rejuvenation was effected through recourse to "quasi-transcendental" cognitive orientations and human endowments. In Lemert's view, the study offered in essence a "modified transcendental philosophy"—more specifically: "a general metatheory of knowledge which is able to refer both action and theory back to their constitutive foundations."[19] Recourse to constitutive categories or faculties evoked not only by implication but explicitly the legacy of Kantian philosophy. According to Habermas, the latter represented the last major effort in the modern epoch to provide a full-fledged philosophical grounding for knowledge claims of all kinds. As he noted, it was through Kant's "transcendental-logical perspective" that "epistemology first became conscious of itself and thereby entered its own unique dimension," attributing to rational reflection a "sovereign role in relation to (empirical) science." Ever since Hegel's metacritique of Kant's framework, however, reflective epistemology underwent a process of decline or disintegration—a decline which was accelerated by Marx's writings (who "misunderstood his own premises") and was finally completed by positivism. "I should like to put forth the thesis," the opening section affirmed, "that since Kant science has no longer been seriously comprehended by philosophy. For, epistemologically—that is, as *one* category of possible knowledge—science can only be comprehended as long as cognition is not equated either effusively with the absolute knowledge of a great philosophy or blindly with the scientistic self-understanding of the ongoing research enterprise."[20]

To be sure, *Knowledge and Human Interests* did not simply counsel a refurbished Kantianism. Repeatedly the study acknowledged the limits or shortcomings of Kant's transcendental logic, limits which provided a warrant for the new departures of Hegel and Marx (as well as later thinkers). Yet, despite this acknowledgment, one cannot overlook the extent to which post-Kantian departures were in turn subjected to a renewed Kantian—and sometimes Fichtean—counter-critique. Hegel, Habermas noted, "quite properly" criticized the "hidden premises of epistemology" by showing the involvement of transcendental categories in an intellectual learning process or in the "phenomenological self-reflection of mind." Epistemology, he added, "presumes to take nothing for granted except its pure project of radical doubt. In reality, however, it relies on a critical awareness that is the result of a complex learning process; thus it is the beneficiary of a stage of reflection which it disavows and therefore also cannot legitimate." To the extent that it undermined the pretense of a categorial foundation or "first philosophy," Hegel's argument had to be accepted as "conclusive"; for, "the circle in which epistemology inevitably ensnares itself is a reminder that critical reflection cannot claim the spontaneity of an origin, but remains dependent on a prior process which it contemplates and from which it simultaneously originates." As developed primarily in the *Phenomenology of Mind*, Hegel's approach challenged mainly three presuppositions of Kantian epistemology: its underlying conception of "science" (borrowed from mathematics and eighteenth-century physics); its assumption of a "fixed knowing subject" (or its "normative notion of the ego"); and last, its dichotomy of theoretical and practical reason. With these challenges Hegel destroyed "the secure foundation of transcendental consciousness in which the a priori demarcation between transcendental and empirical categories, between genesis and validity, seemed solidly lodged."[21]

While conceding the cogency of these correctives, however, Habermas chided Hegel's posture for its epistemological evasiveness.

According to *Knowledge and Human Interests*, Hegel's ambition in focusing on the phenomenology of self-reflection was not so much to radicalize as to overcome and abolish epistemology—an ambition curiously linked with his stress on "absolute" philosophical knowledge or insight (which itself required epistemological legitimization). In unmasking "the absolutism of an epistemology based on unreflected premises," we read, Hegel "fancied himself to be transcending the critique of knowledge as such"; this view arose because "from the beginning Hegel presumed access to absolute knowledge—whose very possibility demanded corroboration according to the criteria of a radicalized epistemology." In Habermas's view, Hegel's move beyond epistemology was plausible "only on the assumption that there can be something like knowledge as such or absolute knowledge independent of the subjective conditions of possible cognition." This assumption, however, had already been demolished by Kant's arguments: "For a critical philosophy unafraid of its implications—and mindful of Kant's principle of the synthetic unity of apperception as the highest warrant of cognitive understanding—there can be no concept of knowledge divorced from the subjective conditions of the objectivity of possible cognition." Against this background, Hegel's phenomenological observations—instead of offering an alternative—provided at best a refinement of epistemology: "The experience of reflection records those eminent moments in which the subject looks back (so to speak) over its own shoulder and perceives how the transcendental relation between subject and object changes behind its back; it thus recollects the emancipation thresholds of human history." Yet, this hindsight or double vision could not affect the crucial constitutive role of consciousness or human subjectivity: "Under contingent circumstances, the conditions under which a new transcendental framework for the appearance of possible objects arises may be produced by the knowing subject itself: for example, through a development of the forces of production (as Marx assumes). This would preclude an absolute unity of subject and object—a unity or identity which alone would confer upon critical awareness, at the end of phenomenological recollection, the status of absolute knowledge."[22]

In contrast with Hegel's speculative aberration, Marx—in Habermas's judgment—moved with Hegel beyond the confines of transcendental logic without entirely obfuscating epistemological issues; in the words of the study, he "pursued Hegel's critique of Kant without sharing the basic premise of identity which prevented the former from unambiguously radicalizing the theory of knowledge." Together with Hegel, Marx insisted on embedding transcendental categories in a historical genesis or formative process—although this process was seen not as the maturation of self-reflection but as a concrete human praxis or activity. Commenting on the *Theses on Feuerbach*, Habermas noted that "Marx, on the one hand, construes objective activity as a transcendental constitution or accomplishment" tying reality to conditions of possible experience, while "on the other hand, he views this transcendental accomplishment as rooted in real human labor. The subject of world constitution, from this vantage point, is not transcendental consciousness per se but rather the human species concretely reproducing its life within natural parameters." In lieu of Kant's transcendental-logical matrix, Marx thus placed the emphasis on the active self-formation of the species or a "historical constitutive nexus." At the same time, his approach departed from Hegel's model not only by substituting activity for reflection but also (and more important) by rejecting the subject-object identity. From Marx's perspective, the constitutive role of social labor did not yield an "absolute" synthesis; for, "anything like absolute synthesis can be conceived only on (Hegelian) identity premises." Since Marx did not comprehend nature as an alienated subject "but conversely the subject under the rubric of another nature," he did not envisage their relation as an "absolute unity." This rejection of identity, however, carried potential epistemological significance. Marx's concept of social labor, we read, was "not only a basic anthropological but also an epistemological category: The system of concrete activities creates the factual conditions of the possible reproduction of social life and *simultaneously* the transcendental conditions of the possible objectivity of experience. The conception of man as a tool-making animal implies a schema both of action and cognition."[23]

Despite advances over his predecessors, Marx failed to develop this epistemological potential; in the end he even muffled and curtailed epistemology to the point of giving aid and comfort to scientism. According to *Knowledge and Human Interests*, Marx "did not properly conceptualize" the knowledge-constitutive role of labor but only had "a more or less vague intuition of it." In his attempt to unearth and reconstruct this implicit epistemology, Habermas pointed to important Kantian as well as Fichtean ingredients in Marx's approach. The main linkage with Kant resided in the separation of subject and object and in the stress on the constitutive function of human faculties: "Like Kant's original synthesis of apperception, the materialist concept of synthesis preserves the distinction between form and matter." The materialist concept thus "retains from Kant the fixed framework within which the subject forms a substance that it encounters; this framework is established once and for all by the equipment respectively of transcendental consciousness or of man as *homo faber*." In Habermas's view, the Kantian component of Marx's outlook foreshadowed an "instrumentalist epistemology" or theory of knowledge (as sketched later by pragmatism)—a theory explicating "the transcendental structure of labor processes within which the organization of experience and the objectivity of cognition become possible from the standpoint of the technical manipulation of nature." The Fichtean ingredient was evident mainly in the replacement of purely cognitive faculties by human praxis or activity. Countering Kant's focus on transcendental consciousness and self-reflection, Fichte had postulated a prior act of self-constitution or self-production preceding consciousness (differently phrased: a primal or "absolute ego" generating the conscious distinction between ego and non-ego). In Habermas's reconstruction, Marx translated self-constitution into concrete social labor, while simultaneously reasserting nature's function in human genesis: "Confronted with its environment the social subject at every stage relates to past processes of production and reproduction in the same manner as (in Fichte) the ego confronted with its non-ego relates to the act of self-constitution which as 'absolute ego' produces itself as ego in contraposition to the non-ego. It is in the process of production that the species posits itself as a social subject. Production—that praxis which Marx treats as continuous sensuous labor and creativity—gives rise simultaneously to the specific formations of nature confronting the social subject and to the forces of production enabling the subject to transform nature and thus to shape his own identity."[24]

As indicated, the epistemology sketched was only implicit and not fully developed in Marx's writings; more important, even this reconstructed version offered only a truncated view of human cognition, a view ultimately unable to stem the tide of positivism. In Habermas's presentation, the curtailment was basically the result of Marx's preponderant (if not exclusive) preoccupation with labor or "instrumental action" and his comparative disregard of meaning-formation and cultural interaction: "The philosophical basis of this materialism proves itself insufficient to sustain an unconditional phenomenological self-reflection of cognition and thus to prevent the positivist atrophy of epistemology. Considered immanently, I see the reason for this deficiency in the *reduction of the self-production of the human species* to labor." Habermas's epistemological counterproposal, as articulated in *Knowledge and Human Interests*, involved the juxtaposition of at least two modes or dimensions of human self-production: those of instrumental-technical activity and of symbolic-communicative praxis or interaction. Broadly speaking, the two modes provided the cognitive underpinnings for the natural and human sciences respectively: the former construed as empirical-analytic sciences concerned with the uniformities of nature, the latter as critical-hermeneutical inquiry (or "critique of ideology") devoted to the decoding of meaning. According to Habermas, both orientations served in different ways an emancipatory goal: the first by promoting control over external nature, the second by removing ideological blinders (or the constraints of "internal nature"). In his words, "Society owes emancipation from external nature to labor processes, that is, to the production of technically useful knowledge"; on the other hand, "emancipation from the compulsion of internal nature succeeds to the degree that social institutions based on force are replaced by an organization of social interaction wedded only to non-repressive communication." The process of social genesis, against this background, had to be seen both as the unfolding of the capacities of labor and as a struggle against class domination. In view of their cognitive implications, the two trends buttressed Habermas's claim of a linkage of epistemology and social theory—the notion that "ultimately a radical epistemology can be carried out only through a reconstruction of the history of the species while, conversely, given the self-constitution of the species through social labor and class struggle, social theory is possible only as self-reflection of the knowing subject."[25]

Exceeding the confines of epistemology narrowly construed, the preceding citations pointed to the importance of social evolution and linguistic communication in Habermas's overall project—topics which he explored with growing intensity in subsequent years. The theme of social evolution occupied center stage in two major studies, *Legitimation Crisis* and *Zur Rekonstruktion des Historischen Materialismus* (of 1973 and 1976, respectively); as in the case of epistemology, my comments will be restricted to aspects relevant to the issue of humanism. In *Legitimation Crisis*, social evolution was presented basically as a dual process of human genesis or self-production: as a process involving both the growth of instrumental capacities for environmental control and the maturation of symbolic-communicative understanding. The two dimensions were discussed under the rubrics of "system integration" and "social integration" and, more briefly, under the labels of "system" and "life-world." In line with functionalist systems theory, the term "system" was said to capture "a society's steering mechanisms and the expansion of its scope of operational capacity"; the "life-world" focus, on the other hand, was designed to "thematize the normative structures (values and institutions) of a society." Correspondingly, "system integration" was portrayed as referring to "the specific steering performances of a self-regulated *system*; social formations (or societies) are considered here from the vantage point of their capacity to maintain their boundaries and their continued existence by mastering the complexity of a fluctuating environment." In contrast, "social integration" was essentially a synonym for symbolic meaning formation and communicative interaction: "We speak of social integration in reference to a system of institutions in which speaking and acting subjects are socially interrelated; social systems are seen here as *life-worlds* which are symbolically structured."[26]

Having specified central categories of the adopted framework, *Legitimation Crisis* proceeded to delineate a number of "universal properties" or features characterizing typical patterns of social evolution. One of these features concerned the relationship between man and nature. As in the earlier epistemological study, social genesis or self-production was depicted as a two-fold emancipatory movement, entailing progressive liberation from both external and internal constraints. According to Habermas, evolutionary advances in the two dimensions of systemic and social integration have the effect of promoting society's mastery over external and internal environment or its "appropriation" of "outer" and "inner" nature. As he wrote, "For the specific form in which the reproduction of socio-cultural life takes place, the exchange processes with outer and inner nature are of decisive importance." While the forces of external nature are harnessed through economic "production processes," inner nature becomes tractable through "processes of socialization"; thus, "with expanding steering capacity a social system extends its boundaries into nature both outside and inside." The two modes of development and emancipation were claimed to be linked with not only distinct types of praxis but also different cognitive strategies: the strategies of instrumental-technical knowledge and of normative-cultural inquiry, respectively. "Social systems," we read, "adapt outer nature to society with the help of the forces of production: they organize and train labor power, and develop methods and technologies; for this purpose they require technically usable knowledge." On the other hand, the same systems "adapt inner nature to society with the help of normative structures in which needs are interpreted and actions licensed or made obligatory." Another typical "property" or feature identified in the study was the notion of an evolutionary learning process occurring in both dimensions of integration and leading from spontaneous or pre-reflective behavior to the steady cultivation of reflexivity and discursive rationality. In Habermas's words, "Evolution in both dimensions takes place in the form of directional learning processes which yield discursively redeemable validity claims: the development of productive forces and the transformation of normative structures follow a logic, respectively, of growing theoretical and practical insight." Accordingly, the evolutionary level of a society was said to depend on its "institutionally permitted learning capacity," more particularly on the degree to which a society encouraged, first, "the differentiation between theoretical and practical questions," and second, "the transition from non-reflective (or pre-scientific) to reflective learning."[27]

These and related arguments were subsequently expanded and further refined in *Zur Rekonstruktion des Historischen Materialismus*; at the same time, the later study made a concerted effort to correlate social evolution or "phylogenesis" with patterns of individual-psychological development or "ontogenesis"—with the result that, in both domains, changes were seen as processes of human maturation and self-production. One essay in the volume, focusing on the problem of identity-formation in advanced or "complex" societies, sketched a stage sequence of individual maturation leading from "natural identity" over "role identity" to "ego-identity," a sequence which then was matched with corresponding phases of phylogenetic evolution. While early infancy was said to be characterized by an undifferentiated, "natural" selfhood lodged in the "boundary-maintaining human organism," and pre-adolescence by a "role identity" fashioned through internalization by the child of "symbolic role-properties" of family and peer groups, late adolescence was claimed to witness the emergence of a properly autonomous selfhood anchored in an abstract ego-core "behind the lines of all particular roles and norms." Turning to social evolution, Habermas discovered in the mythical world-views of "archaic societies" an organismic "fabric of cosmic substances and forces"—which encouraged the comparison of "human identity in archaic society with the natural identity of the infant." Corresponding roughly to preadolescence, "early civilizations" gave rise to differentiated but nonuniversal role structures and behavioral norms centered around empire, monarchy, or city-state; the universalistic claims advanced by "developed civilizations" and especially by the "great world religions" finally promoted "the formation of an ego-identity divorced from all concrete roles and norms." Another chapter in the volume, also dealing with identity formation, sought to buttress the ontogenic sequence mentioned through recourse to Piaget's theory of cognitive development and Kohlberg's analysis of the stages of moral consciousness. Among the theses advanced in the chapter were the notions that ego-identity is a "competence formed in social interactions" and thus linked with the evolution of communicative praxis, and that human maturation in general is marked by an emancipatory thrust, that is, by a growth of autonomy deriving from the ego's "increasing problem-solving capabilities" in dealing with external and internal nature. At another point, development—on both the individual and phylogenetic levels—was portrayed as involving an "ever more precise categorical demarcation of the subjectivity of internal nature from the objectivity of external nature, as well as from the normativity of social and the intersubjectivity of linguistic reality."[28]

The lead essay, carrying the same title as the volume itself, tried to adapt the framework of "historical materialism" to contemporary phylogenetic and ontogenetic teachings; the basic aim of the essay was to bring the Marxist legacy more closely in line with the strict requirements of an evolutionary or developmental "logic." Elaborating on the Marxist concept of a "history of the species" revolving around successive "modes of production," Habermas acknowledged its potential utility, especially to the extent that "forces" and "relations" of production were seen, respectively, as manifestations of cognitive-instrumental and moral-practical learning processes; however, he also stressed defects of traditional or orthodox formulations. As he pointed out, traditional Marxism typically portrayed changes in production relations as dependent on the growth of cognitive-instrumental productive forces—a view which neglects that instrumental knowledge "can be applied to develop productive forces only once the evolutionary step to a new institutional framework and a new form of social integration has been accomplished." Reiterating earlier arguments, Habermas insisted on the dual or two-layered character of social development. In his words, "The species learns not only in the dimension of technically useful knowledge decisive for the development of productive forces, but also in the dimension of moral-practical consciousness crucial for structures of interaction. The rules of communicative action, to be sure, evolve in reaction to changes in the domain of instrumental and strategic behavior; but in doing so they follow *their own logic*." Regarding possible ontogenetic underpinnings of historical materialism, the essay relied again on Piaget's and Kohlberg's models and also on a newly devised scheme of linguistic maturation, moving from the level of "symbolically mediated interaction" over that of "propositionally differentiated speech" to the stage of discursive or "argumentative speech." Phylogenetically the scheme was paralleled by the phases of neolithic kinship systems, early and developed civilizations, and modern society.[29]

In the area of language theory, Habermas's main concern has been with the "pragmatics" of speech and with the articulation of a theory of "communicative competence" seen as quasi-transcendental or universal human endowment (although one nurtured in processes of individual and social maturation). Linguistic "pragmatics" focuses on the performance of speaking subjects and their relations to various (natural and social) contexts; its chief sources of inspiration are communications and speech-act theory. As Habermas pointed out, in one of his early essays on the topic (of 1970), "In the case of normal speech, the speakers are aware of the categorical difference between subject and object; they differentiate between outer and inner speech and separate the private from the public world. Moreover, the differentiation between being and appearance depends on the distinction between the language sign, its significative content (*significatum*), and the object which the symbol denotes (referent, *denotatum*)." Paralleling arguments in the fields of epistemology and social evolution, the paper distinguished between two major levels or functions of language: an empirical-referential and a communicative-self-disclosing function. "On the one hand," we read, "the analytic use of language allows for the identification of objects (thus the categorization of particular items, the subordination of elements under classes, and the inclusion of sets). On the other hand, the reflexive use of language assures a relationship between the speaking subject and the language community which cannot be sufficiently presented by the analytic operations mentioned." In the latter case, "an intersubjectivity of mutual understanding, guaranteeing ego-identity, develops and is maintained in the relation between individuals who acknowledge one another." The two levels or functions were said to be closely intermeshed, with the communicative aspect taking precedence: "The analytical use of language is necessarily embedded in the reflexive use, because the intersubjectivity of mutual understanding cannot be maintained without reciprocal self-representation on the part of the speaking subjects."[30]

The referential-communicative distinction was later fleshed out and further profiled through recourse to speech-act theory. In "What Is Universal Pragmatics?" (first published in 1976), Austin's differentiation between "illocutionary" and "locutionary" or propositional components of speech acts was invoked as evidence or telling illustration of the "double structure of speech"—the fact that communication typically occurs on (at least) two levels simultaneously: namely, first, "the *level of intersubjectivity* on which speaker and hearer, through illocutionary acts, establish the relations that permit them to come to an understanding with one another," and second, "the *level of propositional content* which is communicated." In Habermas's view, this double structure pointed to the inherent "reflexivity" or self-referential (and self-clarifying) character of ordinary language: "The peculiar reflexivity of natural language rests in the first instance on the combination of a communication of content—effected in an objectifying attitude—with a communication concerning the relational aspect in which the content is to be understood—effected in a performative attitude." As he added, the double structure could be harnessed for a general classification of speech acts, and especially for the distinction between two major types, labeled "constative" and "regulative" speech acts and characterizing, respectively, the "cognitive" and the "interactive" use of language: "In the cognitive use of language, with the help of constative speech acts, we thematize the propositional content of an utterance; in the interactive use of language, with the help of regulative speech acts, we thematize the kind of interpersonal relation established." The intersubjective-communicative dimension was amplified or supplemented in the essay by a third mode or function, called "expressive use of language" and manifest in "expressive speech acts" or "avowals" articulating the intentionality and sincerity (or truthfulness) of the speaker: "Truthfulness guarantees the transparency of a subjectivity representing itself in language; it is especially emphasized in the expressive use of language." As a fourth dimension, the essay mentioned the syntactical-grammatical "comprehensibility" of speech—a function presupposed in communication without being thematized in specific speech acts.[31]

Habermas's ambition in "What Is Universal Pragmatics?" was not simply to give a descriptive account of contingent-empirical speech patterns, but rather to uncover the rational-universal structure of speech—in his words, to offer a "rational reconstruction of the double structure of speech" by identifying the "universal conditions of possible reciprocal understanding." In contrast with a purely empirical approach, universal pragmatics pursued the goal of explicating "the rules that a competent speaker must master in order to form grammatical sentences and to utter them in an acceptable way." In focusing on universal categories, this perspective resembled Chomskyan linguistics, but went beyond the latter by encompassing communicative performance. Whereas linguistics, we read, "starts from the assumption that every adult speaker possesses an implicit, reconstructible knowledge embodying his linguistic rule competence," universal pragmatics "postulates a corresponding communicative rule competence, namely, the competence to employ sentences in speech acts," while stipulating at the same time that "communicative competence has just as universal a core as linguistic competence." In Habermas's presentation, the rational-universal structure of speech was evident in the "universal validity claims" implicitly or explicitly raised in any communicative exchange. Insofar as a speaker "wishes to engage in a process of reaching reciprocal understanding," he wrote, "he cannot avoid raising the following—and indeed precisely the following—validity claims": he must "choose a comprehensible expression," must have the aim of "communicating a true proposition," must want "to express his intentions truthfully," and finally must "choose an utterance that is right" in the context of "a recognized normative background." The four claims of "comprehensibility, truth, truthfulness, and rightness" were intimately correlated with the previously mentioned dimensions or functions of speech—in the sense that cognitive use involves an "obligation to provide grounds," interactive use an "obligation to provide justification," and expressive use an "obligation to prove trustworthy" (with comprehensibility being presupposed in any exchange). These and related arguments finally led Habermas to sketch a "model of linguistic communication" conceived as a system of boundaries drawn around the speaker: "Language is the medium through which speakers and hearers realize certain fundamental demarcations. The subject demarcates himself: first, from an environment that he objectifies in the third-person attitude of an observer; second, from an environment that he conforms to or deviates from in the ego-alter attitude of a participant; third, from his own subjectivity that he expresses or conceals in a first-person attitude; and finally, from the medium of language itself. For these domains of reality I have chosen somewhat arbitrarily the terms: *external nature, society, internal nature, and language.*"[32]

III

Despite divergences of accent and formulation, the topical areas discussed are not devoid of common themes and linkages. As it seems to me, Habermas's outlook in all three areas can with some legitimacy be described as a "humanism"—where this term stands for a more or less man- or subject-focused orientation. The distinctions between empiricism and hermeneutics, system and life-world, and propositional and reflective speech can, without undue violence, be reconciled with the Cartesian and Kantian subject-object bifurcation (and thus with the basic framework of modern metaphysics). To be sure, critical theory does not simply coincide with this legacy. Epistemologically, Habermas finds it important to correct Kant's subjectivity through recourse to Hegel's notion of a cultural learning process, a notion further stripped of idealist premises by Marx's concrete-materialist approach; but, as has been shown, Marx's arguments are in turn refracted through Kantian and Fichtean categories. As a result, "cognitive interests" are presented as a set of species-specific, quasi-transcendental and quasi-contingent endowments crucial both for the generation of knowledge and human self-constitution. In the domain of evolution, Habermas emphatically rejects the concept of a universal agent or "species-subject" as carrier of historical change; but this rejection does not affect the role of concrete social groupings and human actors in the process of human self-production through labor and symbolic meaning-formation—a process entailing the progressive appropriation of external and internal nature.[33] The concern with "cognitive interests" and ontogenetic structures operative in evolution is paralleled, in the field of language theory, by the stress on a "communicative rule competence" through which speakers can demarcate themselves from different environmental settings. These and related arguments lend plausibility even to Lemert's label of "homocentrism" which, as previously mentioned, is defined as "that discursive formation which centers itself upon man as a finite subject who dominates his own history."

While acknowledging departures from the Cartesian and Kantian tradition, Lemert views Habermas's approach as an attempt to "resurrect" man or subjectivity "beyond the tomb of language." Pointing especially to the "linguistic turn" in critical theory, he notes that "syntactical sociology has moved in the direction of inserting language into the center of sociology's discursive space, thereby displacing man"— or at least displacing the "critical philosophy of the subject" inherited from the past. By virtue of his concern with language and social-cultural learning processes, Habermas is said to occupy "an eccentric place relative to subjectivism" and traditional humanism: "On the one hand, he is quite intentionally at odds with the pure subjectivity of critical philosophy; on the other hand, it is clear that self-reflection is central to his theoretical program. Thus, while pure phenomenological subjectivity is rejected, subjectivity remains central in the form of intersubjectivity." More sharply formulated: "Against the transcendental subject, Habermas poses a quasi-transcendental *inter*subjectivity." In line with his Hegelian and (unorthodox) Marxist sympathies, Habermas's writings are claimed to disclose "a subjectivity interdependent with intersubjectivity, that is, a subjectivity analyzed from the point of view of social context" and "bound up in an intersubjective nexus encompassing the totality of social and anthropological organization." In Lemert's opinion, however, attention to social context does not eliminate the underlying homocentric thrust. In his words, "to embed subjectivity in intersubjectivity is not to destroy it but to bring it to life," since subjects are assumed to discover themselves through interaction: "The original experience of the subject is constituted in communication with others. Therefore, to explain subjectivity by means of intersubjectivity is not at all the same as expelling the subject from thought."[34]

According to *Sociology and the Twilight of Man*, the homocentric outlook is evident in Habermas's entire opus, including the three topical areas highlighted before. In the field of language theory, manifestations of the outlook can be found in the accent on speech-act theory and communicative competence. Although competence is by no means synonymous with a transcendental category or mental faculty, "there is consciousness nonetheless: Syntactical man emerges as the creature able to speak by virtue of an innate consciousness of the ideal rules of speech, which consciousness is gained intersubjectively and which reacts back to secure the validity of speech itself." Epistemologically, cognitive interests play a role akin to competence. The term "quasi-transcendental," as an epithet for such interests, signifies simultaneously that cognition is anchored in the natural genesis of the species and that knowledge can only be fully secured through man's "transcendence" of nature. Knowledge, Lemert writes, "appears only with the birth of man." Although man through labor is "tied to nature," the latter is "not sufficient to emancipated knowledge." Thus, "while nature is not pictured as death to knowledge, it is that which must be overcome in order for knowledge to exist." The same ambivalence regarding nature surfaces also in Habermas's ontogenetic and phylogenetic arguments which depict human genesis as a self-production effected through mastery of external and internal nature: "Man becomes man only when he is technically able to control outer nature (resources) and practically able to shape inner nature (biological needs) to social purposes." Since neither accomplishment, Lemert comments, is "a given in human nature," both must be "gained by cultural, historical man"—a theme which leads him back to the crucial motif of homocentrism: "Man, the finite subject of history." From Habermas's historical perspective, we read, human life "depends upon an unattainable ideal of communicative freedom"; this goal or *telos* of freedom, however, "is simply another name for man."[35]

Critiques of homocentrism, as articulated in *Sociology and the Twilight of Man*, are not entirely a homegrown product of American sociological thought. Since Lemert repeatedly stresses his indebtedness to Michel Foucault, a brief glance at his mentor may be in order. In *The Order of Things* (1966), Foucault had examined the development of the "human sciences" or humanities (broadly construed) since the dawn of the modern age, recording in detail their initial ascent and then their progressive decay and eventual dissipation. The notion of a dissipation or reversal of the humanities, seen as disciplines dealing with the nature and "meaning" of man, was developed more systematically and with attention to epistemological implications in *The Archaeology of Knowledge* (of 1969). The opening section of the study placed the main focus on the status of "history" as linchpin of the human sciences—a theme which had only been adumbrated in the earlier work;[36] in its basic thrust, the argument of the section was a full-fledged assault on traditional historiography and its guiding motto: "Man, the finite subject of history." In Foucault's presentation, the traditional aim of historiography was to grasp history as a collection of "documents" disclosing human purposes and meanings; recent historical research, however, points in a different direction. In the past, he noted, "the document was always treated as the language of a voice since reduced to silence, its fragile, but possibly decipherable trace. Now, through a mutation that is not of very recent origin, but which has still not come to an end, history has altered its position in relation to the document." In lieu of a concern with exegesis and a primary reliance on "memory," history tends to be viewed more like an archaeological site. "To be brief, then," we read, "let us say that history, in its traditional form, undertook to 'memorize' the *monuments* of the past, transform them into *documents*, and lend speech to those traces which, in themselves, are often not verbal, or which say in silence something other than what they actually say; in our time, history is that which transforms *documents* into *monuments*." Differently phrased, contemporary history "aspires to the condition of archaeology, to the intrinsic description of the monument."[37]

The change in outlook, according to Foucault, had a number of significant methodological and general-philosophical consequences. Methodologically, one important result was the stress on "discontinuity" in place of the previous preoccupation with continuity and the progressive unfolding of purpose. "For history in its classical form," the study argued, "the discontinuous was both the given and the unthinkable"; it was "the stigma of temporal dislocation that it was the historian's task to remove from history." Recent research, in contrast, witnesses the transfer of discontinuity "from an obstacle to the work itself; its integration into the discourse of the historian, where it no longer plays the role of an external condition that must be reduced, but that of a working concept." On a broader philosophical plane, the changed perspective affected a cherished premise of modern thought: the central function of man or human subjectivity. Viewed as a continuous unfolding of reason or meaning, Foucault asserted, history could "provide a privileged shelter for the sovereignty of consciousness," a shelter guarding this sovereignty against the constant threat of erosion. Historical continuity, in other words, was "the indispensable correlative of the founding function of the subject: the guarantee that everything that has eluded him may be restored to him; the certainty that time will disperse nothing without restoring it in a reconstituted unity; the promise that one day the subject—in the form of historical consciousness—will once again be able to appropriate, to bring back under his sway, all those things that are kept at a distance by difference, and find in them what might be called his abode." The dream of such a shelter or abode was shattered by a discontinuous, archaeological approach. In fact, this approach has produced a profound "crisis" in contemporary (Western) thought—a crisis which, in terms of a later passage, "concerns that transcendental reflexion with which philosophy since Kant has identified itself; which concerns that theme of the origin, that promise of the return, by which we avoid the difference of our present; which concerns an anthropological thought that orders all these questions around the question of man's being" and "which, above all, concerns the status of the subject."[38]

In large measure, the crisis mentioned operates in a covert or subterranean fashion because of repression. Despite the tremors touched off by Marx, Nietzsche, and later thinkers, contemporary thought tends to cling desperately to the traditional legacy, in an effort "to preserve, against all decenterings, the sovereignty of the subject, and the twin figures of anthropology and humanism." Despite the challenges issuing from economic-materialist analyses and from "Nietzschean genealogy," our century on the whole has remained wedded to "the search for an original foundation that would make rationality the *telos* of mankind, and link the whole history of thought to the preservation of this rationality, to the maintenance of this teleology, and to the ever necessary return to this foundation." As Foucault noted, opponents of this legacy tend to be quickly branded as destructive or villainous and as enemies of man's finer aspirations: "One will be denounced for attacking the inalienable rights of history and the very foundations of any possible historicity. But," he added, "one must not be deceived: what is being bewailed with such vehemence is not the disappearance of history, but the eclipse of that form of history that was secretly, but entirely related to the synthetic activity of the subject; what is being bewailed is the 'development' that was to provide the sovereignty of consciousness with a safer, less exposed shelter than myths, kinship systems, languages, sexuality, or desire," and finally, "what is being bewailed is that ideological use of history by which one tries to restore to man everything that has increasingly eluded him for over a hundred years."[39]

To the extent that Lemert relies on Foucault's writings, his review of Habermasian humanism can enlist a battery of powerful arguments. On the whole, I find persuasive the critique of homocentrism or anthropocentrism—the notion that the Cartesian-Kantian legacy of subjectivity has been eclipsed and is unable to play a foundational role. Nevertheless, despite my sympathies for this notion, I want to conclude by alerting the reader to some drawbacks or hazards involved in a single-minded pursuit of "archaeology." First of all, I wish to point to a certain bluntness or sweeping quality in Foucault's (and Lemert's) approach: the broad-scale attack on modern subjectivity cannot possibly make room for the nuances and differentiations among types of humanism. Clearly, there are important differences of accent between the conceptions of consciousness and human nature as expounded by Descartes, Kant, Hegel, and even (at some points) Marx. In the case of Habermas, a categorical anti-humanism is bound to shortchange or contract the peculiar "quasi-transcendental" character of his perspective: in particular, the subtle and ingenious blending of Kantian, Fichtean, Hegelian, and Marxist ingredients (not to speak of more recent accretions). The same bluntness also affects the distinction between the modes of humanism found in Habermasian critical theory and classical Marxism (as seen by Habermas): the distinction between a human self-production through labor and a self-production effected simultaneously by means of instrumental activity and cultural-symbolic praxis. As an aside, one may wonder in this context whether Foucault's own portrayal of Marx as a precursor of anti-humanism can be reconciled with Marx's writings (especially those cited earlier in this chapter).[40]

More important are other hazards associated with anti-humanism. Irrespective of its eventual shortcomings, the modern legacy of subjectivity has from the beginning served to buttress human self-reflection and moral autonomy—in other words, the perennial quest for "truth" and the "good life." Foucault occasionally writes as if the notion of "an ideal truth as a law of discourse" were a completely optional bias or preference and might as well be replaced by an opposite commitment, or at least by a decision to suspend "our will to truth." But, in this case, how would his own works be deserving of attention (as containing possibly "true" arguments)? Lemert makes light of Habermas's concern with reflection and normative "goodness," commenting that the call to reflexivity is set forth "as the ideal calling of man" and that "with Habermas the primacy of language always points beyond itself to the good life"; as a result, syntactical discourse "becomes a normative theory of man in spite of the presumably fatal blow delivered to consciousness by language." However, does indifference to normative standards not precisely presuppose the kind of spectatorial neutrality or transcendental stance which is claimed to be overcome by the turn to language? Lemert's observations on autonomy strike me as equally precipitous. Formulated by an anti-humanist, the statement that "the telos of freedom is simply another name for man" can hardly be read without uneasiness—especially in a time when freedom seems everywhere in short supply.[41] On these and related topics I find it advisable to get my bearings from Martin Heidegger's writings—whose teachings are sometimes invoked as primary warrants for contemporary anti-humanism. As it seems to me, Heidegger's critique of traditional philosophy or "metaphysics" at no point was designed to invalidate philosophical reflection construed as a meditative mode of thinking. Similarly, his strictures against the traditional infatuation with (deductive or inductive) "truth" were never the expression of a simple indifference or unconcern—as is evident in his turn to the early Greek notion of truth as "unconcealment" (*aletheia*). Regarding freedom, his *Being and Time*—although sharply opposed to traditional subjectivity—made room for an "emancipatory" type of "care," that is, for a free and unregimented mode of being-in-the-world and being-with-others.

These observations lead me to a final comment on humanism or homocentrism. Perhaps humanism cannot be radically denied or disavowed—at least not by a human voice. In recoiling from consciousness and intentionality, Foucault sometimes takes refuge in a factual "positivity" (of texts or discourses) and even in a kind of epistemological positivism. However, apart from the circumstance that positive-factual accounts presuppose a predicating consciousness, his positivism is belied by the secret passion or zeal pervading all his writings—the passion to strip man of his self-centeredness and narcissistic pretense (what he at one point calls his "transcendental narcissism"). What sort of positivism would have the slightest use, and even the required intellectual antennae, for Foucault's notion of an "incorporeal materialism," as a characteristic of "discursive events"? And which positivist would empathize with the arduous, quasi-metaphysical "transgression" delineated in some of his works? As it seems to me, the attempt to move beyond or "transgress" traditional subjectivity cannot take the form of a straightforward negation—without succumbing to an unacknowledged and purely schematic Hegelian dialectic. Possibly, what this move requires is a renewed, post-Hegelian type of double vision: a willingness of the subject to glance back over his own shoulder—but without the (Hegelian) hope to capture his own image. Instead of indifference, such a double vision may well hold the key to a rethinking of epistemology and ethics, as well as language theory and social evolution. Although written several decades ago and in response to somewhat different issues, Heidegger's *Letter on Humanism* may still provide some guideposts for this endeavor. "If we decide to keep the label," the *Letter* stated, "the term 'humanism' signifies that human nature is crucial for the truth of Being—but crucial precisely in a way where everything does not depend on man as such."[42]

6

Public Policy and Critical Discourse

For a long time now, the study of politics has been in search of itself—in search of its characteristic premises, its proper procedures, and its distinctive focus of inquiry. During the modern era, this search has had all the earmarks of a far-flung journey, if not an aberrant odyssey. Machiavelli's writings, appearing at the threshold of that era, were still steeped in the older legacy of practical political wisdom, a wisdom nurtured by historical erudition and the "topical" common sense of the rhetoricians; but his recommendations to the "Prince" were leaning more in the direction of expert counsel or of carefully calculated "policy" advice. With the rise of modern science, both common sense and applied expertise tended to be subordinated to the formulation of relatively abstract, explanatory frameworks constructed *more geometrico*—an approach evident, to some extent, in Hobbes's *Leviathan*. The preference for theoretical constructs persisted even after the geometrical model was replaced by, or coupled with, empirical investigations of sensory experience and after the concepts of "State" and "sovereignty" were reduced to marginal constraints on market exchanges and economic interests. Yet, explanatory frameworks remained elusive in the face of haphazard social and political customs; the full sway of rationality required the "rationalization" of actual life patterns.

A shorter version of this chapter appeared under the title "Critical Theory and Public Policy" in *Policy Studies Journal*, vol. 9, Special Number 2 (1980–1981), pp. 522–534, published by the Policy Studies Organization, University of Illinois at Urbana.

It was chiefly concern with the gap between theory and practice or between theoretical models and social conditions which, in the nineteenth century, triggered a broad-scale "turn" toward applied knowledge and "social engineering," a turn entirely faithful to scientific imperatives and exemplified mainly by utilitarianism, Saint-Simonism, and, at the beginning of the next century, (strands in) American pragmatism.[1]

The motive of recalling historical precedents is not simply antiquarian curiosity. As it seems to me, such recollection can provide helpful background for present dilemmas in at least two respects. First, one can (and I shall) argue that, in its recent shift to a "policy" orientation, the study of politics has undergone a similar turn as had been experienced by the study of "society" and political economy over a century ago, in the transition from Enlightenment rationalism to utilitarianism. Second, and perhaps more important, historical recollection brings back into view the notions of common sense and practical wisdom, notions which became almost apocryphal after Machiavelli. Meandering through the collective memory of the discipline of "politics" (or "political science") there is still the legacy of a tripartite division between types of inquiry inaugurated by Aristotle: the division between "theoretical," "technical," and "practical" knowledge. While the first type was meant to provide knowledge for its own sake (and thus is distantly but awkwardly related to modern "pure" science), and while the second supplied knowledge needed for the "making" of artifacts (thus paving the way for modern applied science and technology), the category of "practical" thought was reserved for insights garnered through life experience and through practical conduct, preferably in public affairs.[2] I intend to invoke these memories and precedents in the following discussion of the present state of the study of politics construed as the study of "policy." I propose to approach this topic successively from three angles. After initially delineating the recent rise of policy studies and the meaning commonly attached to "policy analysis," I shall, in a second section, sketch diverse reactions provoked by these developments among prominent students of politics or the theory of politics. In the last section, turning to the issue of "policy evaluation" and legitimation, I intend to discuss arguments advanced in this domain both by some American commentators and (especially) Jürgen Habermas, the leading contemporary champion of a critical public "discourse"—adding, by way of conclusion, some of the reasons which lead me to believe that policy evaluation needs to be expanded into a critical evaluation of the very meaning and status of "policy."

I

Within the larger context of the study of politics, the contemporary preoccupation with policy issues constitutes a departure from an earlier consensus which, during preceding decades, had unified professional practitioners (particularly in America) and which had insisted on the primacy of theoretical frameworks capable of explaining and predicting political conduct seen as empirical "behavior." As a broad professional reorientation, the departure obviously resists rigid periodization. Nevertheless, despite the diffuseness of the change, there is an event in recent memory which, I believe, handily pinpoints something like the "birth date" of the policy movement (and simultaneously the birth date of what has come to be known as the period of "post-behavioralism"): this was the presidential address delivered by David Easton in 1969 at the annual meeting of the American Political Science Association, under the title "The New Revolution in Political Science." The address, one may recall, came at the height of intense intellectual ferment in the social sciences and also in the midst of widespread social and political unrest in the nation. Noting these troubled conditions, Easton found unsatisfactory the focus on abstract explanatory schemes, characteristic of the prevailing consensus, or the simple cultivation of science for science's sake. As he observed, the wellspring of the "new" or "post-behavioral revolution" was not hard to discern: "It consists of a deep dissatisfaction with political research and teaching, especially of the kind that is striving to convert the study of politics into a more rigorously scientific discipline modelled on the methodology of the natural sciences." In light of the noted dissatisfaction and of the steadily "increasing social and political crises of our time," Easton's address urged a radical or "revolutionary" realignment of the discipline, namely, a shift of attention which would channel professional energies toward the solution or amelioration of the major social and political problems of the time—although problem solving in his view was bound to honor "the findings of contemporary behavioral science."[3]

Easton's counsel to the profession, offered in his presidential role, was not without delicacy or irony, given the fact that he had been one of the main spokesmen of the erstwhile consensus and one of the chief advocates of the conversion of the study of politics into a "more rigorously scientific discipline" modeled on natural science canons. As is well known, his earlier writings had been influential in promoting a macro-framework for political analysis termed "systems theory," a framework translating the behavioristic "stimulus-response" model into the more holistic terminology of systemic "inputs" and "outputs." Despite the stress placed in this scheme on the "authoritative allocation of values" and despite a complex differentiation between types of "outputs" and between outputs and "outcomes," Easton's perspective at this point had paid only scant attention to the formulation and implementation of "policies" and to the assessment of policy alternatives. In fact, one of his major studies, *A Framework for Political Analysis* (1965), had disclaimed any direct concern with policy questions. "My approach to the analysis of political systems," he wrote at the time, "will not help us to understand why any specific policies are adopted by the politically relevant members in a system. Furthermore, the capacity to adapt (to system needs) does not thereby dictate that any specific, successful way of doing so is morally better or worse than any other if, under the circumstances, someone might prove that it was a necessary and, therefore, inescapable condition of persistence." The same study also had put forth a list of basic assumptions and priorities characteristic of "behavioralism" or the behavioral consensus (a list which subsequently became known as something like a "behavioral creed"). As one central assumption the list stressed the priority of "pure science" over applied research, predicated on the fact that "the understanding and explanation of political behavior logically precede and provide the basis for efforts to utilize political knowledge in the solution of urgent practical problems of society."[4] Viewed against this background, Easton's presidential address signaled in essence a reallocation of priorities: a move from pure to applied science.

Easton's call for a "new revolution" or a realignment of priorities, one can say in retrospect, was heeded by the profession more eagerly than he could possibly have anticipated—and heeded not because it was issued in a presidential address. Clearly, despite the author's prominence, the address would have been entirely ineffectual if it had not somehow meshed with powerful intellectual and social-political trends operative during the past decade. By themselves, the notion of applied research and the need for political "relevance" were not completely absent or overlooked even during the ascendancy and predominance of "pure" behavioralism; in fact, the first steps toward the conversion of the study of politics to scientific methodology were accompanied by efforts to maintain or salvage the applicability of professional expertise. Thus, in 1927, at the time when Charles E. Merriam and other members of the so-called Chicago School spearheaded endeavors to create a new, empirical "science of politics," the American Political Science Association officially established a national Committee on Policy charged with the tasks of both clarifying the organization's role in the public domain and fostering professional involvement in the resolution of urgent "policy" problems. However, apart from issuing a number of hortative reports and assuaging the lingering "progressive" conscience of many practitioners, the committee failed to exert a significant impact on the discipline and ceased functioning within less than a decade. During World War II, many social and political scientists served governmental agencies in an advisory capacity; but for most the experience was a short-lived interlude and only intensified concern with the refinement of scientific methodology. The postwar years saw the emergence of a professional Committee on Citizenship Participation in Politics and of a national Citizenship Clearing House designed to acquaint political scientists with the needs and dilemmas of "practical politics"; yet, initiatives of this kind were hardly more than marginal glosses on the consolidation of the behavioral consensus during that period.[5]

Thus, irrespective of Easton's persuasiveness, the recent change in the direction of policy issues must be traced to a set of conditions congenial to this move; in my view, both "endogenous" or internal-professional factors and environmental or social-political motives must be taken into account. Among the latter, primary emphasis should probably be placed on the manifest or immediate predicaments of the past decade, that is, on the "increasing social and political crises" mentioned by Easton. At the time of his address, these predicaments derived mainly from the experiences of the Vietnam War, racial tensions, and urban riots; subsequent years brought to the fore a host of additional problems and crisis conditions: problems revolving around economic stagnation, energy shortages, and unemployment—not to mention the Watergate episode and the disclosure of corruption in high governmental circles. On the whole, the turbulence and agitation of the Vietnam era has given way to a time of scarcity and austerity, a situation which tends to place a heavy premium on pragmatic "problem solving" and on the efficient handling of urgent public needs. The dilemmas mentioned, I believe, can and should be seen in conjunction with more pervasive or long-range trends of our age. As was suggested before, contemporary developments in the study of politics find a distant parallel in the earlier transition from Enlightenment rationalism to utilitarianism and also from classical economics to post-classical and Keynesian economic analysis. In large measure, the delay or retardation in political inquiry can be ascribed to the marginal or subsidiary status of politics during the era of laissez-faire liberalism. In our own time, the progressive amalgamation of the "polity" and the economy has as one of its consequences the absorption of the former by the distinctive rationality and concrete "rationalization" processes characteristic of modern social-economic evolution; epistemologically and methodologically, this absorption entails the alternating (and sometimes combined) predominance of pure and applied science or, in Aristotelian language, of "theoretical" and "technical" knowledge.

In terms of endogenous or internal-professional factors, some attention should be given to theoretical antecedents or precursors. There is ample evidence to indicate that the present policy focus is not a sudden innovation but was prepared and nurtured by analytical and methodological initiatives, on the levels of both macro- and micro-analysis, stretching back over the last several decades. On the level of macro-frameworks, one may point to the progressive replacement of static equilibrium models by models stressing effective systemic "steering" and crisis management, a change evident, for example, in Gabriel Almond's shifting emphasis from the description of systemic "functions" to the stipulation of basic "capabilities" seen as required "output" criteria for handling domestic crises and environmental challenges; the same trend was also manifest in the emergence of political "cybernetics," a perspective which, according to one of its leading spokesmen, was meant to capture "a shift in the center of interest from drives to steering, and from instincts to systems of decisions, regulation, and control."[6] On the level of micro-approaches or models, one must mention especially the so-called "decision-making" framework which, in past decades, was developed both along the lines of an empirical scrutiny of decision-making processes and in the direction of a more formalized "rational choice" or decision theory. As it seems to me, the approaches cited bequeathed to policy analysis not only their respective strengths or merits, but also all their quandaries and ambiguities. One such quandary concerns the status of "politics" or political practice—notions which tend to be submerged, on the one hand, in general management categories and, on the other, in the dimension of individual or social psychology. More directly apparent is the ambivalent character of "steering," "control," and "decision"— labels which, in professional usage, hover precariously between causal "behavioral" processes and voluntary-purposive activities; the "decision-making" model, in particular, leaves hazy the import of "intentionality" and the role and range of human "rationality." All the frameworks listed are beset by the positivist "fact-value" dichotomy and its implications, especially the unresolved query whether choices and decisions are amenable to not only empirical testing and prediction but also normative evaluation and judgment.

Given its inherited quandaries and dilemmas, contemporary policy analysis is not an entirely homogeneous enterprise, but makes room for different accents and formulations; like the earlier behavioral consensus, the post-behavioral realignment signals not so much a rigid doctrine as a broad intellectual tendency or outlook. Yet, despite internal flexibility and variations, it is not impossible to pinpoint a common denominator or shared thrust linking adepts of this outlook: in my view, this thrust consists in a primary concern with "outputs," with pragmatic problem solving, and with applied knowledge. Without venturing too far afield, this affinity is readily evident from a quick glance at some of the literature which inaugurated the policy focus, writings which appeared roughly at the time of Easton's address. Thus, in a book entitled *The Study of Policy Formation*, Raymond Bauer (in 1968) defined "policy" as a "course-setting involving decisions of the widest ramifications and longest time perspective in the life of an organization," decisions designed to cope with internal or environmental problems of any kind. Similarly, Charles Lindblom's *The Policy-Making Process* treated "policy" as the outcome of decision-making processes set in motion in response to existing stimuli or challenges. What is immediately obvious in these examples is that a distinction is lacking between politics and non-politics or between political and general managerial policies; equally manifest is the non-differentiation (or obscure relation) between empirical behavior and purposive action, as both Bauer and Lindblom relied chiefly on social-psychological categories. Even where the first issue is partially attended to, incidentally, the second dilemma may still persist. Thus, in his *Public Policymaking Reexamined*, Yehezkel

Dror concentrated more strongly on political aspects, defining policy as the "direct output of public policy making"; but as in the other examples the subject matter "reexamined" were essentially behavioral processes. All three studies demonstrated the effects of the positivist legacy: the focus on empirical behavior for all practical purposes barred normative inquiry.[7]

Perhaps, to gain a stronger sense of the policy focus and its quandaries, it may be advisable to take a somewhat closer look at one of the most widely used texts in the field: Thomas R. Dye's *Understanding Public Policy* (first published in 1972). From its opening pages, the text illustrated the concern with "outputs" and the treatment of prevailing social-political ills. In Dye's definition, "public policy is whatever governments choose to do or not to do"; additionally it involves "why they do it, and what difference it makes." As he acknowledged, the preoccupation with policy issues was prompted by mushrooming domestic and international problems; however, in contrast with "many of the currently popular approaches to policy questions," like "rhetoric, rap sessions, dialogue, confrontation, or direct action," policy analysis was identified (in the subtitle of the first chapter) as "the thinking man's response to demands for relevance." According to the text, such analysis was not an entirely "new concern of political science"; however, in the past the main stress of the discipline had "never really been on policies themselves, but rather on the institutions and structures of government and on the polical behaviors and processes associated with policy making." Actually, regarding the historical development of the discipline, the study delineated two prior phases, labeled, respectively, "traditional" and "behavioral" periods. Traditional political science was said to have concentrated "primarily on the institutional structure and philosophical justification of government" and, in terms of governmental performance, on "the *institutions* in which public policy was formulated." Modern behavioral political science, on the other hand, was described as concerned chiefly with "the processes and behaviors associated with government"; although intent on analyzing "the *processes* by which public policy was determined, it did not deal directly with the linkages between various processes and behaviors and the content of public policy." Deviating from preceding approaches, the text noted, "today the focus of political science is shiftig to *public policy* — to the *description and explanation of the causes and consequences of government activity.*"[8]

Despite the suggestiveness of this periodization, its plausibility was offset by the sentence last cited. Given the stress placed on causal explanation of decisions, the text shared the ambivalence of earlier volumes regarding the relation between empirical behavior and intentional action; the recommended policy focus thus amounted not so much to an abandonment as an application of the behavioral model (or to an "applied behavioralism"). Dye's study also—and in a deliberate fashion—shared the dilemmas and constraints deriving from the positivist heritage. As he indicated, policy analysis could be undertaken by students of politics for a limited number of reasons: first, for "purely *scientific reasons*" with the aim to "improve our understanding of the linkages between environmental forces, political processes, and public policy"; second, for *"professional reasons"* or reasons of professional expertise, since "an understanding of the causes and consequences of public policy permits us to apply social science knowledge to the solution of practical problems"; and third, for practical or *"political reasons"* in order "to insure that the nation adopts the 'right' policies to achieve the 'right' goals." Among these motives, Dye's own sympathies were clearly with the first two (and particularly with the second). Elaborating on the fact-value dichotomy, he insisted that, whatever the causes for studying public policy may be, "it is important to distinguish *policy analysis* from *policy advocacy. Explaining* the causes and consequences of various policies is not equivalent to prescribing what policies governments ought to pursue." According to the text, policy analysis was marked by three main tenets or traits: "*a primary concern with explanation rather than prescription*"; next, "*a rigorous search for the causes and consequences of public policy*"; and last, "*an effort to develop and test general propositions about the causes and consequences of public policy and to accumulate reliable research findings of general relevance.*" Given these tenets, practical (including normative) considerations were bound to be marginal. In lieu of "the skills of rhetoric, persuasion, organization, and activism" needed for policy advocacy, Dye concluded, "policy analysis encourages scholars and students to attack critical policy issues with the tools of systematic inquiry"; in short, it "might be labeled the 'thinking man's response' to demands that social science become more 'relevant' to the problems of our society."[9]

The abstinence from practical-normative issues which characterized the literature cited soon proved to be a straitjacket. Given the fact that policy "choices" or "decisions" (if these terms are to have meaning) involve options among alternative courses of action, some attention had to be given to the criteria for such options. Yet, at least during the early phase of the policy movement, such attention did not necessarily imply a departure from positivist premises. A brief illustration is the symposium on "Current Problems of Policy Theory," published three years after Dye's study in the *Policy Studies Journal* (the official organ of the Policy Studies Organization). In his contribution to the symposium Dror sketched "Some Features of a Meta-Model for Policy Studies," features which included a combination of "descriptive-explanatory" and "prescriptive" categories and a stress on "preferization" as the major standard of policy studies and their acceptability. "The first yardstick to be applied to any improvement-directed policy study," he noted, "is the quality of the relevant policies as they are or would be without that study. If the study can improve policy-results" (in some discernible way) "so they will be 'preferable' to those otherwise achieved, then the 'preferization' test is met and the policy study should be judged acceptable." While thus seemingly venturing in a prescriptive direction, however, the author strongly insisted on the "instrumental" and "relativistic" character of the proposed "preferization" test. Basically, what relativism meant here was the reendorsement of the fact-value distinction, this time in the form of the dichotomy between politics and policy science or between subjectively chosen political goals and objective means-ends research: " 'Preferization' is to be considered in terms of the values and goals of 'legitimate value judges' who may range from democratically elected leaders to a general assembly of a Kibbutz or, not acceptable in my personal ideology, various kinds of totalitarian leaders." Although policy scientists could clarify politicians' values, they were not to trespass into the latter's domain; for "the values and goals of the 'legitimate value judges' serve as preferization yardsticks—not those of the policy researcher. Here lies a primary distinction between policy studies as a scientific, academic and/or professional activity and other orientations or roles such as advocacy-researcher, social critic, change agent, and social prophet of radical scientists." The same symposium volume contained an essay by Robert Bish, who argued that "most policy proposals are supposed to enhance the well-being of identifiable citizens, and policy analysis is used to determine which of several policies may do the better job." However, the paper failed to shed light on "the assignment of 'values' citizens place on the policy outputs."[10]

II

Instead of pursuing the rise of the policy movement further, I would like to interrupt the historical account at this point in order to glance briefly at repercussions of the nascent focus among students of politics (and especially of the theory of politics). As it seems to me, a major and perhaps central issue raised by the professional realignment sketched is its compatibility with older and broader conceptions of "politics" or its effects—benign or detrimental—on such conceptions. Needless to say, in view of the multifaceted character of the discipline, I shall have to limit myself to a condensed synopsis. On the whole, among political scientists attentive to the movement, the realignment was greeted with mixed emotions. For some, the dawn of policy research signaled an advance to professional maturity, that is, a break-through from inept speculation to applied expertise; in the eyes of others, in contrast, the innovation heralded trouble for the discipline and even the potential corruption of the genuine study of politics.

To exemplify the first approach one need not look far: no one has been a more fervent spokesman of the new focus than Eugene Meehan, a political theorist drawing his inspiration mainly from modern empiricism, pragmatism, and utilitarianism. His attitude toward policy research—seen as springboard for large-scale "social engineering"—is clear from an essay entitled "What Should Political Scientists Be Doing?" published in 1972 in a book entitled *The Post-Behavioral Era*. As the author emphasized right away, the answer to his question could not be derived from any presumed "essence" of politics or from the administrative structure of contemporary academic disciplines, said to be based on "guild membership"; rather, the yardstick had to be found in social utility, just as the standard of medicine was effectiveness of remedies: "The physician learns to justify his interests by referring to impact on the patient; the social scientist must learn to do likewise." For Meehan, cognitive investigations in all fields were ultimately prompted by man's precarious condition in a complex and frequently threatening world and by his effort and need to master enviromental challenges. "The point of departure for my own approach to inquiry," he wrote, "is the human need to cope with the external environment (which includes other humans, of course) using human capacities to create instruments for achieving human needs and purposes. For survival is predicated on man's capacity to anticipate events in the environment, to control events in the environment, and to make choices (i.e., adopt policies) from among the alternative situation states that can be achieved in the environment through human intervention."[11]

Several aspects, I think, should be noted in the preceding formulation: first of all, the reliance on "human needs and purposes" and the connection of both with imperatives of "survival"; second, the stress on the human capacity to "create instruments" and tools or on man's quality as *homo faber*; and third, the focus on man's ability to "control" the environment by means of his instruments and through the adoption of effective choices or strategies. Regarding the first aspect, the essay pointed (validly enough) to the importance of linking empirical and evaluative or "explanatory and normative dimensions" of political inquiry; however, the manner proposed for effecting the linkage implicitly reduced the latter to the former. On the whole, in referring to "needs and purposes" the author's assumption seemed to be either that both are pre-given and self-explanatory or else that "purposes" are derivable from factual "needs" and equally governed by survival standards. As he pointed out, concern with survival "requires man to make and justify propositions asserting what is the case, what can be expected under given circumstances, and what should be preferred in particular situations"; thus, "man must organize what he perceives and use it to forecast changes in the environment, to explain changes in ways that allow intervention to inhibit or further them, and to express preferences or make value judgments." Some additional light on the proposed linkage can be gleaned from the second aspect relating to *homo faber*. According to Meehan, pursuit of survival needs and their cognitive elucidation presupposed a combination or convergence of instrumentalism and pragmatism. "Two assumptions," we read, "are needed to bridge the gap between observation and choice or expectation: instrumentalism—the doctrine that concepts, explanations, value judgments, and so on are tools created by man for dealing with the environment; and pragmatism—the belief that the quality of the instrument is measured by its use in the environment to achieve purpose." The two assumptions or yardsticks were said to be equally applicable to empirical and normative questions: "In normative inquiry, human purposes are construed as tools for the betterment of human life, and evaluated by comparison with other purposes that might have been pursued in the same situation with different effect."[12]

The core of the essay, however, was clearly the third aspect: the achievement of human "control" through instrumental implementation of needs and purposes. "Systematic inquiry," Meehan asserted, "springs from, indeed cannot exist without, a desire to modify the environment; it consists in a search for dimensions of the environment that need changing and for the most efficient (least costly in normative terms) means of achieving such changes. The principal tasks of social science are social criticism and social engineering." Past professional performance of these tasks, in the author's view, was dismal and uninspiring; not only had social scientists "thus far failed miserably," they "failed even to try": "For the most part, they have fled from policy making, eyed social criticism with distaste, and studiously refused to accept the principle that inquiry should be directed to the solution of human problems." Only recently was there a noticeable disenchantment and hence movement away from "scholasticism"; Meehan's own contribution was meant to accelerate this change: "We need to identify the conditions in society that can and should be altered (or maintained), determine the available alternatives and find means of assessing their respective costs, develop priority structures for allocating resources to deal with them, and create the tools that can bring them about as efficiently as possible. The goal is simply maximization of reasoned control over the environment, including its human dimension."[13]

A few words should probably be added regarding the notion of "social criticism" which occurs in the preceding passages. As employed by Meehan, the notion stands entirely in the service of policymaking and social engineering: its critical edge is directed against useless or inefficient human pursuits or against conditions obstructing instrumental control. In his essay, the phrase clearly does not serve as a synonym for "critical reflection" or critical moral and political "judgment," as these terms are used in the philosophical tradition. Actually, Meehan's posture toward reflection and philosophy varied from indifference to open contempt. "The questions posed by traditional philosophy," he asserted, "bear little relation to the kinds of questions for which social scientists must have answers—most particularly, what reasons can be given for preferring to live in one situation rather than another, where both are attainable and the choice is real." The trouble with much philosophical literature, however, was not only that it was irrelevant but that it was detrimental and obnoxious: "The fact is that the traditional philosophers have made an awful mess of normative inquiry without being subjected to criticism, despite the amount of destruction that has taken place in the scientific and epistemological areas of traditional philosophy." Among reflective or philosophical orientations Meehan reserved his most cutting and devastating remarks for non-instrumental or non-utilitarian types of speculation, or—in his words—for "those who indulge freely their soaring imaginations": "Prophets and poets, utopians and idealists, ultras of every persuasion, share an utter unwillingness to be bound by the limits of fact and logic. At their worst, the result is mysticism, anti-intellectualism, prophecy, affect manipulation; easily destroyed by argument, though with little observable effect on the speculator."[14]

Meehan's distaste for philosophical reflection was displayed even more forcefully in a subsequent essay entitled "Philosophy and Policy Studies" (published a year later in the *Policy Studies Journal*). The central query raised in the article was what contributions, if any, philosophy in its various branches could make to the nascent field of policy analysis. The reply was blunt and unambiguous. "With some relatively minor exceptions," we are told, "those involved in the study of public policy will find little or nothing in philosophy, either substantive or procedural, that can be used productively in their work and much that is actually misleading and counterproductive." As before, the main defect of philosophical reflection was seen in the lack of a consistently technical-instrumental orientation; for, "when the products of philosophy are measured against human needs, and particularly against the need for a body of cumulable, testable, transferable, and useful knowledge that can tell us when and how to go about changing the world—which is what policy studies *must* have—their irrelevance is unmistakable." In lieu of traditional speculation or " 'philosophic' activities of a scholastic sort," the author advocated concrete problem solving or an approach designed to produce "specific solutions to specific situations." Properly defined and pursued, he affirmed, "knowledge supplies man with the capacity to anticipate events in the environment and in some degree to control them by his own actions. By doing so, it forces man to solve the normative problem of choosing one world from among those worlds he has the capacity to bring about. Policies I take to be the instruments to make such choices." Toward the end of his paper, Meehan's irreverence lost its occasionally humorous quality and began to show its teeth; the yardstick of environmental and social "control" shaded over into a plea for thought control: "There are some few signs that a weary population is demanding to know why society should provide an unending feast for a horde of unproductive locusts."[15]

Although provocatively formulated and hardly typical even of committed policy analysts, Meehan's views have been discussed here at some length—for a reason: I think it is instructive to savor in detail the implications of an unabashed instrumentalism. To be sure, among professional political scientists his posture has not gone unopposed. To the extent that it is identified with "social engineering," policy analysis has been severely denounced by practitioners concerned with the integrity of both "politics" and the academic study of politics. At this point, in order to illustrate this opposing outlook, I want to glance briefly at important counter-arguments articulated by Theodore Lowi, a political scientist known for his contributions both to the elucidation of contemporary politics and to the non-instrumental study of public policy. In a splendid essay, "The Politics of Higher Education" (published also in *The Post-Behavioral Era*), Lowi resumed and reformulated the basic theme of Julien Benda's *Betrayal of the Intellectuals*, by castigating not so much or not only the "politicization" as rather the "technocratization of the intelligentsia," that is, the inroads of technocratic engineering into academia and its progressive sway over theoretical reflection and reflective judgment. "Technocratization," he stated, "takes the organized disciplines and turns them toward a direct problem-solving and policy-oriented *relationship* to the society." This relationship, moreover, was not simply an innocuous liaison, but was prone to lead to subservience: "With technocratization, the university enmeshes itself with regimes. This means purposive social action, master-servant relationships, rather than merely the older functional relationship expressing the needs of a given social class." The detrimental effects of an instrumental relationship were bound to be particularly evident in the case of an "applied" political science; for, "technocratic education focuses on real social problems" and thus produces "a high degree of consonance between the scholar and the policy maker." This consonance, in turn, diminishes the accountability both of politics or politicians and of students of politics: "To help the policy maker solve problems is to make the conduct of his responsibilities a good deal more comfortable. And the problem and the solution are made more legitimate by virtue of the academic help rendered him. But most importantly, *it means that the intellectual agenda of the discipline is set by the needs of the clientele, not by the inner logic of political science.*"[16]

Proceeding from a critique of technocratization, Lowi's essay attacked instrumentalism with all its connotations: including its glorification of *homo faber* and its fusion of knowledge and "control." Taking his cues from Lord Acton's dictum, the author exposed the corrupting effects of academia's flirtation with technocracy: "Technocratization involves a power that also corrupts, but this power corrupts in a culturally more important sense. It involves a corruption of the intellect, of the purpose of academic freedom," because it embroils "the academic with the immediate and the concrete; corruption means a blurring of the difference between theory and rationalization." The main warnings of the essay, however, were sounded against the perils accruing from instrumentalism to the integrity of the study of politics. Lowi's arguments on this count are important and eloquent enough to deserve a longer quotation. "A political science," he wrote,

dedicated to better solutions to society's problems cannot in the long run be radical *or* science, because it will be too closely tied to the very regimes whose roots it must constantly question. There is danger in realism. There is danger in problem solving. There is certainly danger in setting up an entire curriculum that stresses problem solving. There is danger in defining science as nothing more than a collection of rigorously stated individual hypotheses aimed at manipulating the real world. There is danger in these because each one tends to reduce the autonomy of political science as a learned society. We need look no further than public administration to find a mature example. Each of these dangers is a virtue of technocratization that tends to reduce the alienation and the detachment of political science from the society which sustains it.[17]

To ward off the dangers cited, Lowi's essay relied on the force of "radical," that is, non-instrumental, reflection and non-utilitarian judgment; only critical reason or reflection, he asserted, can salvage academia from subservience. Like any other discipline, we read, political science "is radical or conservative by virtue of its conceptual apparatus rather than by virtue of the distribution of individuals and substantive attitudes. It is radical insofar as it is out of mesh with society, rather than insofar as the individual member of the discipline may feel or act in a personally radical way about certain social issues." For Lowi, the remedy to technocratization derived "from theory, not from practice," at least not from instrumental practice. If the theoretical insights or conceptions of the discipline are "energetic and relevant," he added, teachers of political science are bound to create "a generation of students who simply do not think like their older policy makers. This is deeply radical"—provided the latter term is interpreted as having to do with the foundation of the discipline: Such students "will not be necessarily radical in the sense of being dedicated to cutting out the old roots. The important thing is that the capacity to deal critically with the roots of the polity is a capacity without which political science would indeed be nothing but a handmaiden."[18]

III

Lowi's strictures against instrumentalism, in my view, are cogent and salutary in their main thrust—although the remedies are perhaps not very clearly delineated in the essay discussed. Thus, one may wonder how a commitment to professional "detachment" and even "neutrality" can simultaneously yield theories which are "energetic and relevant"; likewise, the wholesale aversion from "practice" seems farfetched and not readily compatible with Lowi's own concern with policy research. However these quandaries may be resolved, the author's arguments clearly point beyond the confines of technical rationality and beyond the reduction of normative issues to problems of environmental adaptation. Along the latter lines, the need for "policy evaluation"—in the sense of a non-instrumental assessment of policy goals or preferences—has been explicitly stressed by Lowi on other occasions. In a wide-ranging review of "policy-making" literature, he noted that an approach focusing exclusively on means-ends questions and policy procedures "becomes essentially technocratic and instrumental in values, in analysis, and in ultimate impact. When one assumes that 'policy making is policy *making* is decision making' and therefore does not enter into *a priori* analysis of the character of the choices being made, one almost inevitably becomes incrementalist and manipulative." The tendency was reinforced by the positivist legacy of fact-value segregation: "When the goals of policies are not questioned because they are the values which must be kept separate from facts, the analyst becomes committed to the value context of those policies even if his political ideology would not support them if he looked more carefully at them."[19]

In the meantime, efforts have been undertaken by numerous scholars to overcome the most glaring defects or limitations of policy analysis noted by Lowi. In the domain of policy evaluation, one of the most significant developments has been resort to the notion of critical or "valuative discourse" as a correlate and possible antidote to a narrowly empiricist or procedural approach. In the following, I intend to illustrate this development by reference to two examples: one taken from the American, the other from the Continental European setting. In the first context, the concept of "valuative discourse" has been articulated primarily by Duncan MacRae in a series of writings, beginning in 1971 and culminating in a study published in 1976 under the title *The Social Function of Social Science*. As it seems to me, the study constitutes an important contribution to social science literature during the past decade and certainly one of the most searching and thoughtful publications in the field of policy analysis. MacRae's point of departure in his study was the "post-behavioral" malaise in the social sciences, especially the widespread dissatisfaction with the conception—characteristic of the behavioral consensus—which viewed the social disciplines as self-contained analytical or "nomothetic" enterprises governed by the motto: "Science for science's sake." In contrast with more ambitious recent ventures trying to banish or exorcise behavioral "scientism" altogether, his proposal was in essence to correlate and reconcile empiricism and "valuation." Bypassing both positivist and radical anti-positivist formulas, the study noted "that there is another path to follow: that reliable scientific knowledge of man and nature is an important resource for policy choice but can coexist with rational ethical discourse; that some of the values of science may be transferred to this ethical discourse; and that scientific propositions and ethical assertions, while clearly distinguishable, may be fruitfully combined in academic disciplines concerned with the study of man and society."[20]

According to MacRae, the combination of scientific knowledge and valuation was particularly desirable and appropriate in the field of policy analysis construed as an "applied" social discipline. To implement its tasks, such a discipline could not limit itself to the investigation of empirical conditions but had to probe normative questions; it had to be guided by the conviction "that science should serve human welfare, not simply scientists' satisfaction or the discovery of truth as an end in itself." While advocating the strengthening of "applied" inquiry, one should note, MacRae's study held no brief for technocracy and was careful to differentiate its proposals from an instrumental model of "social engineering." Positivism and academic specialization, he observed, had produced either an infatuation with "pure science" divorced from values and intentional purposes, or else a narrowly technical or instrumental type of applied analysis. In the latter case—where research was typically the handmaiden of economic or political organizations—ends or values were treated as fixed or given and thus removed from critical scrutiny and discussion. As the author commented (echoing some of Lowi's concerns), the engineering model was damaging both to science or academic inquiry and to politics, especially to democratic politics. Operating instrumentally, science betrayed its own rational ethos by subservience to non-rational dictates: "To separate valuative questions from science is perhaps to strengthen science, but also to weaken applied science by making it totally dependent for its guidance on unreflective standards and modes of valuation. The values that guide the application of science are thus deprived of the rational component that is so essential to science's own internal functioning." At the same time, definition of values by client organizations—or by such organizations in conjunction with experts or applied scientists—encouraged elitist and undemocratic proclivities: in particular, the tendency to bypass the views of "informed citizens" described as "the ultimate decision makers in a democracy."[21]

Despite the concern for democratic participation, MacRae's study did not entrust the formulation of values and policy goals entirely to the "educated public" or to generally informed citizens. In order to overcome the opacity and "sluggishness" of public opinion and to facilitate the rational resolution of policy issues, ethical argument in his view had to partake of some of the qualities of scientific discourse. It was at this point that his conception of the "function of social science" came most clearly into view: social scientists were accorded a special role in the discussion of values because of both their empirical knowledge of social conditions and their attachment to rigorous canons of inquiry and communication. The specific recommendation of the study was "to transfer to valuative discourse some of the norms that a well-organized scientific community imposes on its own communications." With the exception of empirical testing, the norms of ethical argument were said to be "analogous to those that govern the discussion of scientific theories and hypotheses." The central yardstick of valuative discourse, as delineated in the study, was "that before anyone enter into ethical argument he first render his own ethical system clear, consistent, and general—modifying it in detail if necessary." Apart from stipulating standards for each individual participant, MacRae also outlined a set of rules governing normative debate: first, that such debate be conducted between proponents of "ethical systems" or "ethical hypotheses" which are "specified in writing in advance"; second, that "each discussant (shall) have equal opportunity to argue for his own system, and against the opposing one, by pointing out presumed shortcomings in the other system"; and third, that after each exchange "the proponent of the ethical system under criticism (shall) decide whether he wishes to alter his ethical system or make the choice dictated by it."[22]

In my view, MacRae's study was distinguished by numerous impressive qualities, including its interdisciplinary outlook, its sober and careful mode of presentation, and the cogency of many of its proposals; one of its strongest virtues was its appeal to the "common good" as ultimate yardstick of policy choice, in lieu of the separate interests of either (detached) academics or politicians and client groups.[23] Unfortunately, such merits were marred by several drawbacks or limitations besetting the argument—drawbacks affecting both the status of ethical discourse and the range of public deliberation. In stressing the affinity between science and ethics and the role of "ethical hypotheses," the study injected into policy evaluation some of the contingent qualities of empirical research: treated as heuristic frameworks, normative propositions can yield at best hypothetical, not "categorical," obligations. Deference to science, I think, also colored the notion of application. By treating policy analysis as an "applied" discipline implementing the canons of scientific research (canons which themselves are rarely open to debate), MacRae's approach courted the danger of instrumentalism—a peril which was reinforced by his own ethical preference for utilitarianism, a doctrine traditionally associated with instrumentalist premises and convictions. The preference for utilitarianism or efficient utility calculations may also have something to do with the study's deemphasis of citizen participation in favor of social-scientific discourse. As John Ladd has noted at one point, "Like utilitarianism, policy studies often operate with a very limited picture of what morality and politics are all about; namely, they conceive of morality and politics as principally concerned with the production and (just) distribution of *consumer goods* for society." In Ladd's view, such a conception easily encourages moral "paternalism," that is, a "functional division" between moral producers and consumers: "A clear understanding of the relationship of the individual to public policy, not as a receiver (consumer), but as an active moral agent seems to me to present the most important challenge to policy studies from the point of view of morality."[24]

Many or most of the drawbacks mentioned, I believe, are remedied in the second example taken from the Continental setting: the version of "critical theory" articulated by Jürgen Habermas in a series of writings during the past decade. To some extent, the central thrust of critical theory was anticipated or intimated in Lowi's reference to a type of theorizing which is "out of mesh" with society and yet "energetic and relevant." Broadly speaking, Habermas's perspective parallels MacRae's approach with respect to the juxtaposition or combination of empirical science and moral evaluation; the parallel extends to the stress on disciplined normative deliberation, termed by Habermas "practical discourse." In contrast with MacRae's focus on application or applied analysis, however, Habermas intensifies and broadens the significance of practical-moral argument vis-à-vis empirical-scientific inquiry. While empirical science, in his view, is ultimately geared to the goal of human mastery or "control" of the environment and thus guided by a "technical interest," ethical evaluation is rooted in interpersonal contacts and communicative interaction, which, in turn, are governed by a "practical interest" in mutual understanding and in the maintenance of just or justifiable norms of conduct. As used in this context, incidentally, practice and practical interaction are not synonyms for a blind activism opposed to thought, but rather are closely linked with the capacity for radical "reflection" and self-reflection—a capacity described in Habermas's earlier writings as man's interest in "emancipation" and later as the basis and mainspring of rational "discourse."[25] In the present context, instead of surveying Habermas's sprawling opus, I intend to concentrate on two studies particularly relevant to policy issues: *Toward a Rational Society* (first published in 1970) and *Legitimation Crisis* (whose English translation appeared in 1975).

The first volume is a collection of essays not all of which are equally pertinent here. Taking its cues from Lord Snow's "two cultures" theme, an essay entitled "Technical Progress and the Social Life-World" explores the complex relationship between empirical science and cultural understanding and self-understanding fostered by the humanities. In our technological era, Habermas observes, this relationship is "only one segment of a much broader problem: *How is it possible to translate technically exploitable knowledge into the practical consciousness of a social life-world?*" What emerges in this question is a "true life-problem of scientific civilization," which can be couched in these terms: "How can the relation between technical progress and the social life-world, which today is still clothed in a primitive, traditional, and unchosen form, be reflected upon and brought under the control of rational discussion?" Following a review of historical antecedents, the essay applies this problem chiefly to the life-world of politics, particularly democratic politics, where it yields this query: "How can the power of technical control be brought within the range of the consensus of acting and transacting citizens?" In probing this query, Habermas rejects as too facile two customary responses: that science and technology are the automatic harbingers of democracy, or else that technology necessarily destroys democracy. "Today, in the industrially most advanced systems," he writes, "an energetic attempt must be made consciously to take in hand the mediation between technical progress and the practical conduct of life in the major industrial societies, a mediation that has previously taken place without direction, as a mere continuation of natural history." To accomplish this mediation, it suffices, in his view, by no means that society matches "the conditions of technical rationality"; for, "even if the cybernetic dream of a virtually instinctive self-stabilization could be realized, the value system would have contracted in the meantime to a set of rules for the maximization of power and comfort; it would be equivalent to the biological base value of survival at any cost, that is, ultrastability." Thus, the contemporary "challenge of technology cannot be met with technology alone"; rather, it is a question of "setting into motion a politically effective discussion that brings the social potential constituted by technical know-how into a rationally defined and controlled relation to our practical knowledge and will."[26]

Another essay in the same volume probes the relation between the "scientization of politics" (what Lowi called "technocratization") and democratic "public opinion," starting from the premise that if such "scientization" is not yet a reality, it is today "a real tendency for which there is evidence": "It is only recently that bureaucrats, the military, and politicians have been orienting themselves along strictly scientific guidelines in the exercise of their public functions—indeed this practice has only existed on a large scale since World War II."

Three theoretical accounts or construals of the relationship are discussed in the paper: a "decisionistic model" dating back to Hobbes and Max Weber; a "technocratic model" deriving from Bacon and Saint-Simon; and a practical-dialectical (or "pragmatistic") model. Whereas in the first account the politician is the ultimate authority, making arbitrary political choices while employing technical expertise only in the selection of means, in the second construal "the dependence of the professional on the politician appears to have reversed itself," with the result that the latter "becomes the mere agent of a scientific intelligentsia which, in concrete circumstances, elaborates the objective requirements of available techniques and resources as well as of optimal strategies and steering regulations." Habermas's own preference is clearly for the third model, in which "the strict separation between the function of the expert and the politician is replaced by a critical interaction," and where the transposition of technical recommendations into practice is "increasingly dependent on mediation by the public as a political institution." As he recognizes, the feasibility of this model today is hampered by numerous obstacles, including the erosion of the "public sphere" and the pervasive collusion of bureaucracy and expertise. The integration of technology into social self-understanding and thus the interpenetration of "political will" and scientific rationality, he argues, could be effectively pursued only "under the ideal conditions of general communication extending to the entire public and free from domi- nation." The emphasis on unconstrained communication recurs also in a third essay, which distinguishes "two concepts of rationalization," a symbolic-communicative type and a truncated technocratic type. "At the level of subsystems of instrumental action," we read, "scientific- technical progress has already compelled the reorganization of social institutions and sectors, and necessitates it on an increasingly larger scale." On the other hand, *"rationalization at the level of the institutional framework* can occur only in the medium of symbolic interaction itself, that is, through *removing restrictions on communication."* In the latter context, "public, unrestricted and unconstrained discussion of the suit- ability and desirability of action-orienting principles and norms in the light of the socio-cultural repercussions of developing subsystems of instrumental behavior—such discussion at all levels of political and repoliticized decision-making processes is the only medium in which anything like (genuine) 'rationalization' is possible."[27]

Public discussion of alternative courses of social action, one should add, is meant here to entail not only the stipulation and confrontation of hypothetical maxims, but the articulation and clarification of valid or categorical yardsticks—whose binding character, to be sure, derives not from dogmatic acceptance but from the cogency of a "practical discourse" yielding a rational consensus among all participants. Elaboration of the character and implications of such discourse is one of the central themes of Habermas's *Legitimation Crisis*. As he points out, norms have obligatory effects and thus raise validity claims, claims which cannot be redeemed on a strictly empirical or voluntaristic basis. For, "if only empirical motives (such as inclinations, interests, or fear of sanctions) sustain an agreement, it is impossible to see why a party to the contract should continue to feel bound to norms once his original motives change"; the same situation obtains if reliance is placed on arbitrary will. In general terms, he notes, "we cannot explain the validity claim of norms without taking recourse to a rationally motivated agreement or at least to the conviction that consensus on a recommended norm could be brought about *with reasons*." Consequently, the "model of contracting parties" merely enacting preferences or heuristic maxims is inadequate: "The appropriate model is rather the communicative community of those affected, who as participants in a practical discourse test the validity claims of norms and, to the extent that they accept them with reasons, arrive at the conviction that in the given circumstances the proposed norms are 'right'." The "rightness" or validity of norms, from this perspective, is predicated on the rational structure of the validating discourse—its openness to all affected parties and the absence of extrinsic constraints: "Discourse can be understood as that form of communication that is removed from direct contexts of experience and action and whose structure assures us that possible validity claims of assertions, recommendations or warnings are the exclusive object of discussion; that participants, topics and contributions are not restricted except with reference to the goal of testing validity claims; and that no force is exercised except that of the better argument."[28]

Critical theory as formulated by Habermas—and especially his notion of "practical discourse"—undoubtedly goes a long way toward overcoming the pitfalls of technocracy and giving policy evaluation its proper due. Yet, I cannot conclude these comments without adding a further consideration or proviso. There are reasons for holding that critical evaluation should extend not only to the assessment of substantive policies, but to the status and role of "policy" itself. Despite the stress on interaction, Habermas's arguments at various junctures still carry overtones of instrumentalism. The connotation is evident in his commitment to broad-scale "rationalization" and a "rational society"—notwithstanding the distinction between symbolization and technological progress. The aspect is also manifest in the frequent emphasis on human (though not purely technical) "control"—an emphasis illustrated by the references cited for the need to "bring under control" the traditional relation between technology and the social life-world. As it seems to me, primary preoccupation with rational action and goal-oriented human designs cannot entirely avoid instrumentalist effects; even when endorsed by a consensus of participants, such designs are liable to reduce the environment—and potentially other human beings—to the level of means. Against this background, political scientists should be reluctant to submerge their discipline in policy analysis or to identify "politics" with policy making. In a radical sense, non-instrumental action must be construed as action unconcerned with outcomes or goal attainment and even receptive to (what one may call) the inroads of "non-action" into purposive designs.

Some guidance along these lines may be obtained from Michael Oakeshott's study *On Human Conduct*, a book which has been poorly received by students of politics but probably deserves another look.[29] In his study, Oakeshott differentiates between two main manners or aspects of human conduct: namely, substantive conduct or performance concerned with the pursuit of substantive goals or satisfactions; and rule-governed practices in terms of which particular goals are pursued and among which the most important are non-instrumental or "moral" practices. Building on this distinction, the volume further opposes two modes of interpersonal relationships, termed, respectively, "enterprise association" and "civil association" or *civitas*. While in the first case agents are "related in the joint pursuit of some imagined and wished-for common satisfaction," that is, in the pursuit of "some common purpose, some substantive condition of things to be jointly procured, or some common interest to be continuously satisfied," members of the second type (termed *cives*) are "not partners or colleagues in an enterprise," nor are they "individual enterprises related to one another as bargainers for the satisfaction of their individual wants"; rather, they are related in terms of a non-instrumental practice "which has no extrinsic purpose and is not related to procuring any substantive satisfaction." Correlated with these modes of association is the difference between "policy" and "politics." In a joint enterprise, Oakeshott observes, "the associates are related in terms of their choice to pursue a common purpose and of their continuous agreement upon a 'policy'; that is, upon 'managerial' decisions concerned with the actions and utterances in which, from time to time, this purpose shall be pursued." Politics, in contrast, has to do with the maintenance or modification of the "practice of civility"; it is "concerned with determining the desirable norms of civil conduct and with the approval or disapproval of civil rules which, because they qualify the pursuit of purposes, cannot be inferred from the purposes pursued."[30] Whether or not one agrees with Oakeshott's separation of the two associational types (or with his dichotomy of matter and form), the distinction between substantive pursuits and a non-purposive matrix permitting such pursuits seems worth pondering. What the distinction suggests is that the "good life" or "good society" is not simply a goal to be implemented, but depends on, or is intimated by, an ongoing cultivation of civility.

7

Conversation, Discourse, and Politics

Language has emerged as a prominent, perhaps the predominant, philosophical and intellectual concern in our century. Although first noticeable in the context of the positivist and analytical movement, the so-called "linguistic turn" is an unmistakable feature of all brands of contemporary philosophy, and also of many versions of social and political thought. Apart from Anglo-American investigations of "ordinary language" patterns and their relation to artificially constructed idioms, one only needs to point to efforts—pursued especially on the Continent—to articulate a phenomenology of language, a hermeneutics of understanding and interpretation, a "grammar" of culture, as well as the social-theoretical ramifications of speech and linguistic interaction. On the whole, the overall effect of the turn to language has been an increased attentiveness to communication and the intersubjective matrix of thought and action, in contradistinction to the focus— prevalent in much of modern philosophy—on individual consciousness and solitary reflection. Yet, the noted effect is not free of ambivalence. In the case of some philosophical perspectives, the changed outlook serves mainly as an amplification or expanded corroboration of traditional premises regarding the structure of cognition (in the sense that a plurality of subjects is substituted for the *cogito*); in the case of other thinkers, in contrast, preoccupation with language signals a break with the same premises and with the entire thrust of traditional epistemology (and metaphysics). In his recent book entitled *Philosophy and the Mirror of Nature*, Richard Rorty has formulated this break in a radical manner: by opposing hermeneutics to epistemology, and philosophy seen as "conversation" to the inveterate urge for "commensuration." As Rorty points out in his study, the traditional urge for a "theory of knowledge" is basically "a desire for constraint—a desire to find 'foundations' to which one might cling, frameworks beyond which one must not stray, objects which impose themselves, representations which cannot be gainsaid"; differently phrased, the urge proceeds "on the assumption that all contributions to a given discourse are commensurable"—where commensurable signifies the proclivity "to be brought under a set of rules which will tell us how rational agreement can be reached or what would settle the issue on every point where statements seem to conflict." Thus, a philosophy wedded to epistemology and commensuration "sees the hope of agreement as a token of the existence of common ground which, perhaps unbeknown to the speakers, unites them in a common rationality." On the other hand, a philosophical hermeneutics views "the relations between various discourses as those of strands in a possible conversation, a conversation which presupposes no disciplinary matrix which unites the speakers, but where the hope of agreement is never lost so long as the conversation lasts." Accentuating the contrast between the two perspectives, Rorty asserts that "for hermeneutics, to be rational is to be willing to refrain from epistemology" and "to pick up the jargon of the interlocutor rather than translating it into one's own," whereas "for epistemology, to be rational is to find the proper set of terms into which all the contributions should be translated if agreement is to become possible." Succinctly put: "For epistemology, conversation is implicit inquiry. For hermeneutics, inquiry is routine conversation."[1]

By and large, I consider Rorty's book an insightful and (especially in the Anglo-American context) a pathbreaking study; his vindication of "conversation," in particular, strikes me as captivating and potentially very fruitful. The proposed move beyond traditional epistemology, one may note, is by no means a whimsical or purely idiosyncratic preference; repeatedly, in advancing this proposal, the study acknowledges a debt to such mentors as Wittgenstein, Dewey, Gadamer, and Heidegger. Nevertheless, despite my sympathy with his aims, I cannot refrain from detecting some quandaries besetting Rorty's argument. Above all, the notion of "conversation"—used as a designation for non-epistemological philosophy—is not fully elaborated in the study and gives rise to various doubts. Supposing the term to stand as a synonym for the kind of verbal exchanges probed by ordinary language analysts, one might wonder whether philosophy is meant to be leveled into everyday, conventional "chitchat" (if not into the stylized rhetoric of daytime television). Rorty strongly resists this conclusion by associating conversation with "abnormal discourse," and the entire distinction between epistemology and hermeneutics with the dichotomy between "normal" and "revolutionary" inquiry. "Normal discourse," he writes, "is that which is conducted within an agreed-upon set of conventions about what counts as a relevant contribution, what counts as answering a question, what counts as having a good argument for that answer or a good criticism of it. Abnormal discourse is what happens when someone joins in the discourse who is ignorant of these conventions or who sets them aside."[2] Taking one's cues from these comments, however, one might legitimately ask, Is conversation here seen as the conjunction of mutually unintelligible (or barely intelligible) soliloquies, and how can this view be reconciled with the prevalent conception of hermeneutics?

Partially in an effort to buttress his approach, Rorty appeals to the teachings of Michael Oakeshott, especially his arguments regarding "civility" and the "conversation of mankind." In a justly celebrated essay on the latter topic, Oakeshott observed that "in a conversation the participants are not engaged in an inquiry or a debate; there is no 'truth' to be discovered, no proposition to be proved, no conclusion sought. They are not concerned to inform, or to refute one another, and therefore the cogency of their utterance does not depend upon their all speaking in the same idiom; they may differ without disagreeing."[3] Yet, notwithstanding a similarity of tenor, Oakeshott's testimony does not entirely remove the quandaries mentioned—mainly because the two authors do not completely concur. Conversation, in Oakeshott's presentation, is not (or not unequivocally) an "abnormal" enterprise; also, epistemological inquiry or "science" constitutes not so much the antithesis as rather an integral partner of ongoing conversational exchanges (alongside other equally respectable partners). The present chapter seeks to disentangle some of the issues encountered in this domain. Following the lead of Rorty and Oakeshott, I intend to probe the meaning and implications of human "conversation," and of related notions, such as "dialogue" and "discourse." In order to gain my bearings in the complex arena demarcated by these terms

I shall, in a first section, turn to some prominent contemporary philosophers and social theorists whose writings have focused in detail on questions of language and communication. By assimilating the diverse perspectives and formulations offered by these thinkers, a second section will try to delineate a typological panorama comprising major modes of communicative interaction. By way of conclusion I intend to explore the significance of these various modes for different dimensions of political life.

I

Under philosophical auspices a discussion of "conversation" may feasibly take its point of departure from the work of Hans-Georg Gadamer, the chief spokesman of "philosophical hermeneutics": no one in our century, it seems to me, deserves more properly to be labeled as philosopher of conversation and dialogue. Rorty in his study pays special tribute to this mentor, noting that the rise of hermeneutics as an antidote to epistemological inquiry is "largely due to one book — Gadamer's *Truth and Method.*" The latter's cultivation of *Geisteswissenschaften*, he adds, can be seen largely as an endeavor "to prevent education from being reduced to instruction in the results of normal inquiry. More broadly, it is the attempt to prevent abnormal inquiry from being viewed as suspicious solely because of its abnormality." While Rorty's indebtedness is explicit, the affinities between Oakeshott and Gadamer are latent or implicit — but no less evident. Something like Gadamer's stress on the role of "prejudgments" in understanding and interpretation is intimated in Oakeshott's observation that "long before we are of an age to take interest in a book about politics we are acquiring that complex and intricate knowledge of our political tradition without which we could not make sense of a book when we come to open it." Similarly, echoes of *wirkungsgeschichtliches Bewusstsein* (the reverberations of the past in the present) and of the intimate connection between understanding and concrete "application" seem manifest in Oakeshott's comments that "the past, in whatever manner it appears, is a certain sort of reading of the present" and that "every society, by the underlinings it makes in the book of its history, constructs a legend of its own fortunes which it keeps up to date and in which is hidden its own understanding of its politics."[4]

For present purposes Gadamer's linkage of hermeneutics and conversation is most directly relevant. According to *Truth and Method*, hermeneutical understanding can and should be seen against the backdrop of interpersonal "experience": more particularly, of a communicative "I-Thou" relationship. "Tradition," we read, "is not simply a process that inductively we learn to know and to master; rather it is *language*, that is, it speaks to us like a 'Thou'." Thus, tradition is, or can be, "a genuine partner in communication to which we are tied like the 'I' is to a 'Thou'." In Gadamer's presentation, interpersonal contact can take several forms, some of which are relatively defective or non-communicative: from a scientific perspective, fellow humans may be viewed simply as specimens of a general species, a treatment yielding an expertise ("knowledge of human nature") permitting prediction and control of behavior; in a less abstract vein, others may be regarded as unique individuals living in concrete settings—but on a par with ethnological museum exhibits (analyzed by means of "historical consciousness"); finally, others may be accepted as partners in a personal relationship which exerts reciprocal claims and is predicated on mutual recognition. In genuine human relations, Gadamer notes, the important point is "to experience the 'Thou' truly as a 'Thou,' that means, not to ignore his claim and to listen to what he has to say"—an attitude which requires complete existential "openness" and availability. Since openness implies readiness to interrogate and listen to one another, genuine encounter can be said to have the character of a conversation (*Gespräch*)—a conversation which, far from being a series of monologues, is governed by the "dialectic of question and answer" and whose distant ancestor is the Platonic dialogue. The same openness also is crucial for historical understanding and interpretation; in this case, "I must permit tradition to exert its claim on me—not by simply acknowledging the past in its otherness or remoteness, but by accepting it in a way which allows it to speak to me." Such acceptance is the hallmark of the experience of effective historical continuity (*wirkungsgeschichtliches Bewusstsein*).[5]

To be sure, Gadamer does not ignore the difference between historical or textual exegesis, on the one hand, and personal encounter, on the other: in the former case, one partner has to be awakened and rendered "vocal" (so to speak) for communication to take place. Texts, he notes, "are 'permanently fixed expressions of life' that have to be understood—which means that one partner of the hermeneutical conversation, the text, is given voice only through the other partner, the interpreter." Yet, to the extent that this revival is accomplished (which is possible only through interrogation), hermeneutical understanding partakes of the central traits of conversation, expecially of the "structure of question and answer." "Precisely this is what characterizes conversation," we read, "that, in the process of questioning and answering, giving and taking, talking at cross purposes and concurring, language performs that communication of meaning which, with regard to the written tradition, is the task of hermeneutics. Hence it is more than a metaphor: it is a recollection of original experience if the purpose of hermeneutics is construed as a conversation with the text." Through the work of hermeneutical exegesis, "literary or textual tradition is brought back from the estrangement in which it finds itself into the living presence of conversation whose fundamental procedure is always question and answer." Properly pursued or conducted under proper auspices, the dialectic of mutual interrogation ultimately yields a "fusion of horizons" between the partners of conversation—in the case of literary exegesis between text and intepreter; instead of being distanced like a mute object or embraced as an authoritative doctrine, the text is found to disclose meaning only as a result of questioning which, in turn, is open to the text's claims. This merger or fusion is another emblem or manifestation of effective historical continuity and its operation in human experience.[6]

Actually, despite the phrasing of some previous citations, conversation and hermeneutical understanding in Gadamer's treatment are not strictly equivalent to an "I-Thou" relationship—if such a relationship signifies a contact between individual subjectivities. First of all, conversation partners are not simply Cartesian egos but rather "beings-in-the-world" enmeshed in concrete historical horizons. More important, conversation denotes not so much a confrontation of subjective views as rather the endeavor to grasp a topic or subject matter common to all participants. The reference to an "I-Thou" relationship, Gadamer states, "should not be misconstrued in the sense that what is experienced in tradition is grasped as the opinion of another person or a 'Thou.' Rather, we want to emphasize that hermeneutical exegesis treats the text not as the life expression of a 'Thou' but as a meaning content detached from all ties to individual intentions, of an 'I' or a 'Thou'." According to *Truth and Method*, what counts in a conversation is not so much individual viewpoints as rather the attachment to a common subject matter—that is, to "a logos which is neither mine nor yours and which so far transcends the subjective opinions of the interlocutors that even the person leading the conversation remains (in a sense) ignorant." What basically permits the comparison between exegesis and conversation is the central role of the topic: "The chief element linking these apparently so disparate situations—textual understanding and conversational understanding—is that both are concerned with a subject matter placed before them; just as one person seeks to agree with his interlocutor on a given topic, so the interpreter comes to understand the substance stated in the text." From this perspective, the customary notion of "leading" or "conducting" a conversation appears dubious: "We say that we 'conduct' a conversation, but the more genuine a conversation is, the less its conduct lies within the discretion of either partner. Thus, a genuine conversation is never one that we wanted to conduct; rather, it is generally more correct to say that we stumble into a conversation or become embroiled in it."[7]

Another crucial feature characterizing conversation and overarching individual aims is language or the "linguisticality" (*Sprachlichkeit*) of understanding. Akin to the role of subject matter, language in Gadamer's presentation is not reducible to subjective intentions; instead of functioning as a mere tool or instrument, it constitutes a basic presupposition and the joint product of communication. As he insists, "the fusion of horizons that occurs in understanding is the proper achievement of language." This means that "the language in which something is uttered is not a possession at the disposal of one or the other of the interlocutors. Rather, every conversation presupposes— or better: generates—a common language." In this sense, language provides the medium or "the middle ground, as the Greeks said, in which the speakers participate and regarding which they converse with each other." These considerations also apply to the domain of hermeneutical understanding and textual exegesis. As in the case of actual, interpersonal conversation, Gadamer notes, "hermeneutical conversation" also "has to generate a common language"—a task which, just as in real-life situations, "does not involve the fashioning of a tool for purposes of communication, but rather coincides with the very act of understanding and the attempt to reach agreement." Thus, "as between two interlocutors, a communication takes place between the partners of this 'conversation' that is more than mere adaptation." In the field of historical and literary hermeneutics, the importance of language is evident primarily in the prominence of texts; for, "it is the nature of tradition to exist in the medium of language, so that the preferred target of interpretation has a linguistic character." In more general terms, language provides the fabric for the fusion of historical horizons; from this angle, the linguisticality of understanding is the concrete implementation of *wirkungsgeschichtliches Bewusstsein*.[8]

The preceding brief synopsis of Gadamer's approach yields a number of inferences or conclusions relevant to the discussion at hand. First of all, the notion of "conversation" obviously constitutes a basic and pervasive category in Gadamer's thought—a category applicable both to everyday, real-life interaction and to historical-hermeneutical exegesis. To the extent that the central goal is mutual understanding and agreement, conversation cannot plausibly be described as an abnormal enterprise (if abnormality is seen as counterpoint to intelligibility). As is manifest both from the title of the book reviewed and from the appeal to the Platonic model of dialogue, communicative understanding always is oriented toward some kind of truth—although "truth" here denotes not so much a propositional doctrine as rather an experienced quality constantly renewed through interrogation. Together with the deemphasis of propositional content, *Truth and Method* also deemphasizes the argumentative insistence on individual assertions and validity claims; in a sense, argumentation is subordinated to existential encounter and understanding. Despite its broad sway and relevance, it is possible to indicate some limits or boundaries of conversational understanding in Gadamer's treatment. As it seems to me, conversation is hedged in by two main boundary cases: the one where the effort at understanding is lacking or insufficiently developed, the other where understanding is hampered by the complexity of subject matter or language. Examples of the first type can readily be supplied. Thus, where communication partners, out of indifference or haste, lack concern for promoting an "I-Thou" relationship, conversation may degenerate into routine exchanges or "chitchat" (if not into soliloquies), exchanges characterized by the predominance of clichés and linguistic stereotypes. To some degree, interpersonal indifference is also evident in the case of scientific inquiry, where (as mentioned before) fellow humans are objectified into specimens; a corollary of this inquiry is frequently the replacement of ordinary language by an artificial idiom. From Gadamer's vantage point, both examples are only partially outside the pale of conversation: both can be reintegrated through a reminder of the purpose of communication and the underlying premises of inquiry.[9]

The second boundary case is harder to pinpoint and to assess: the issue here is not the lack of a desire for understanding but the difficulty of reaching it. The difficulty may stem from the intricacy of an explored topic or from unfamiliarity with a given language. Gadamer offers as an example the case of a foreign-language text whose exegesis requires the intervention of a specially trained translator. In this instance, the conversation between text and interpreter is only mediated and indirect; in other words, there exists "a gap between the spirit of the original text and its interpretation" which "can never be completely closed." Yet, as he adds, translation presents no absolute bar to understanding and only highlights general hermeneutical dilemmas: "The encounter with a foreign, unfamiliar language only involves an intensified version of hermeneutical labor, that is, of initial strangeness and its conquest. Actually, all topics dealt with in traditional hermeneutics are alien in the same sense." A more extreme type of unfamiliarity arises in the case of poetry or poetic language. Gadamer at this point refers to Hölderlin's claim that "finding the language of a poem involves the total dissolution of all customary terms and phrases." Elaborating on this notion, he defines poetry not as a mode of representation or description but as a mode of disclosure "opening up a world of the divine and the human" or "a new vision of a new world." Despite the innovative and radically unfamiliar character of poetry, however, *Truth and Method* seeks to depict the "poetic word" simply as "an intensification of everyday speech," by alluding to the intangible or "speculative" quality of language and (genuine) conversation. "The words," we read, "which are put into the mouth of a poetic figure are speculative in the same manner as is the speech of daily life: the speaker always articulates in his speech a relationship to being. Moreover, in talking of a poetic statement we do not really mean the utterance of a literary figure but rather the statement of the poem itself as poetic word. This poetic statement is as such speculative, in that the linguistic event of the poetic word discloses a unique relationship to being."[10]

The boundary cases mentioned, it seems to me, can be profiled more sharply through reference to Gadamer's own philosophical mentor: Martin Heidegger. In his *Being and Time* (1927), Heidegger had delineated a conventional and inauthentic mode of communication which he labeled "idle talk" or "chatter" (*Gerede*) and which consisted chiefly in the reiteration of clichés or of the way everybody else (*das Man*) talks. "Things are such and such," he wrote, "because everybody says so. This kind of mimicking or parroting talk—in which an initial inauthenticity may lapse into complete superficiality—forms the essence of chatter." Even more emphatically than in Gadamer's treatment, chatter in Heidegger's sense derived less from deficient individual intentions than from a general obtuseness to subject matter and language itself; instead of yielding genuine insight, public clichés reflect the spurious view that everything is already well understood: "Chatter means the possibility to understand everything without a prior probing of the subject matter. Since anybody can engage in it at any time, chatter not only absolves from the labor of genuine comprehension but cultivates an indifference which presumably grasps everything."[11] Regarding the second main boundary case—difficulties arising from unfamiliarity—Heidegger's later writings provide important and helpful clues. With respect to poetry in particular, his essays on language stressed the undomesticated and unconventional character of the poetic idiom and its special openness or vulnerability; the poet's central vocation was seen in the task "to guard the word as the disclosure or font of being," while ordinary, everyday language was described as "a forgotten and therefore used-up poem." In another context, Heidegger outlined the contours of a kind of conversation or dialogue whose central traits were akin to the qualities of poetry. His well-known "Dialogue on Language" (with a Japanese) depicted as the core of a genuine conversation its respect for the indefinite and unregimented character of the discussed subject matter and the linguistic medium. Instead of denoting "every form of communicative interaction," dialogue properly speaking was said to designate a "joint attentiveness to the nature of language."[12]

Contemporary philosophical reflection on communication is not restricted to the writings of Gadamer and Heidegger; for purposes of comparison, a few other perspectives may be briefly highlighted. In the context of French existentialism and existential phenomenology, Georges Gusdorf has provided a dramatic account of different communicative modes. His *Speaking (La Parole)* contained arguments which in some respects were similar to, and in others were radically different from, the hermeneutical approach; his comments on communicative interaction, in particular, evoked echoes of Gadamer's boundary situations—but recast in terms of an existentialist (and emphatically egological) "I-Thou" relationship. The study took its point of departure from what it called a "fundamental antimony of human speech," namely, the contrast between "the self-affirmation of the subject" and "the search for others" or between self-expression and communication. "On the one hand," Gusdorf stated, "we have the expressive function of language: I speak in order to make myself understood, in order to emerge into reality, in order to add myself to nature. On the other hand, we have the communicative function: I speak in order to reach out to others, and I can join myself to them all the more insofar as I set aside what is mine alone. This polarity of expression and communication," he added, "corresponds to the opposition between the first person and the third, between individual subjectivity and the objectivity of meaning held in common." Under the auspices of the communicative function, speaking was liable to be reduced to "a falling into step, a forced alignment with others, in other words, a definitive alienation." As a result, from the expressive vantage point, a common tongue was equivalent to bondage: "To say that language is other people is tantamount to saying that we are from childhood on reduced to captivity by our forced submission to the ready-made formulas of the established language."[13]

Confronted with these polar opposites, Gusdorf himself opted in favor of a compromise—but without abandoning the study's existentialist premises. The conflicting extremes of expression and communication, in his view, were in danger of jeopardizing not only the coherence of language but also "the entire destiny of man," by rigidly bifurcating human existence. Actually, what had to be realized was that "human unity and identity is given initially: man is at once the collective consciousness, reason, and the pure self who refuses society and reason." Every "concrete person achieves a balance for himself between these various aspects."[14] Consequently, the two main modes or "intentions" of speech had to be seen as "complementary" rather than standing in an inverse relation. In elaborating on the meaning of complementarity, *Speaking* replaced the initial bipolarity essentially with a tripartition or a three-layered hierarchy leading from conventional usage, as lowest common denominator, over self-expression to the apex of "authentic communication." In this scheme, an "impersonal 'basic' language" or common tongue was said to represent merely "the lowest degree of intention and expression." In fact, however, a tongue "only exists as a necessary condition for the act of speaking"; this means that "it has to be recovered and realized by that effort of expression thanks to which the person establishes himself as a function of verbal reality." Self-expression, in turn, served chiefly as a gateway to genuine dialogue and linguistic communion: "Just as the established tongue is only the terrain for speech, so too speech appears as the necessary means of communication that fixes the moment in which speaking establishes a new language, the moment in which the *we* is realized in the union of *I* and *you*."[15]

From the existentialist milieu I want to shift attention to the Frankfurt School, and particularly to the "critical theory of society" formulated by Jürgen Habermas. While Gusdorf deviated from Gadamer's hermeneutics through his stress on speakers' intentions, Habermas accentuates this departure through his additional elaboration of the notion of "discourse." The latter notion did not feature explicitly in Gusdorf's arguments—but it was not unknown to French existential phenomenology. Thus, at one point, Paul Ricoeur employed the term to designate human speech seen as communicative utterance or as "expression" with a communicative intent—in contradistinction to the objectified systems of signs studied by linguistic science.[16] In Habermas's usage, "discourse" retains some of the qualities of Gusdorf's (and Ricoeur's) "authentic communication"; but the authenticity or genuine character of communication is further protected through the stipulation of formal-rational criteria. Basically, his focus on the notion is prompted by epistemological motivations: the desire to disentangle the pursuit of knowledge from underlying cognitive "interests" or commitments and thus to reduce the impact of "prejudgments" on rational understanding—an impact still left somewhat undefined in *Knowledge and Human Interests* (1968). The aim is implemented chiefly through the sharp differentiation between everyday experience and interaction, on the one hand, and the domain of "discursive" validation, on the other.

In contrast with the opacity prevailing in everyday experience and communicative interaction, "discourses" in Habermas's presentation pursue the goal of a rationally grounded knowledge or insight; while reciprocal understanding in ordinary life is normally taken for granted, discursive validation seeks to scrutinize factual beliefs and practical objectives. As he wrote in one of his early formulations of the concept,

"Discourses are enterprises in which we seek to validate cognitive utterances. Whereas, in actions, the factually raised claims implicit in the underlying consensus are naively accepted, discourses serve to provide grounds for problematic validity claims involving opinions and norms." The distinction between the two levels or domains involves not so much a difference between experiential topics, or even between the claims or propositions advanced in each case; rather, what is at issue is the radical disengagement of discourses from ordinary experience and the replacement of everyday talk by argumentation. "The system of action and experience," we read, "yields compellingly to a form of communication in which the participants are not concerned to exchange information, to direct or perform actions, or to have or communicate experiences, but where they search for arguments and offer reasons. Thus, discourses require a virtualization or bracketing of action constraints, a virtualization which is designed to render inoperative all motives except solely that of a cooperative readiness for communicative understanding and to segregate questions of validity from questions of genesis." Under the auspices of such bracketing, factual beliefs are "transformed into states of affairs which may or may not be the case," just as moral standards and action goals are transmuted into "recommendations and warnings which may be right or appropriate, but also incorrect or inappropriate." In Habermas's view, discourses constitute the warrant of human rationality and the gateway to "truth" in the strong or categorical sense of the term: "Only the structure of this peculiarly unreal form of communication guarantees the possibility of a discursively attained consensus which deserves to be called rational. Since truth (in the comprehensive traditional sense of rationality) differs from mere certainty by its claim to be absolute, discourse is the condition of the unconditional."[17]

Habermas's notion of discourse was further fleshed out in his subsequent writings on epistemology, legitimation problems, and language philosophy. His "Epilogue" (1973) to *Knowledge and Human Interests* sharpened the distinction between ordinary talk and validation into the dichotomy between "discourse and life praxis" or between the "a priori of experience" and the "a priori of argumentation," while simultaneously differentiating, on the level of life praxis, between "sensory experience" (guided by observation) and "communicative experience" (oriented toward mutual understanding). "In life praxis," he observed, "we acquire and exchange action-related *experiences*"; in contrast, "discursive procedures generate nothing but arguments." *Legitimation Crisis* (first published in the same year) contained a long section on normative or "practical discourses" devoted to the validation or justification of norms and action standards. Concurring with Stephen Toulmin's concept of "nondeductive" argumentation, the study insisted that, in the normative field, "the appropriate model is that of a communicative community of individuals who, as partners in a practical discourse, examine the validity claims of norms and, to the extent that they accept them with reasons, arrive at the conviction that the proposed norms are 'right' in the given circumstances."[18] In the area of language philosophy, Habermas's writings articulated not only the perspective of a "universal pragmatics" integrating elements of speech-act theory with deep-seated linguistic endowments, but also as benchmark an authentic type of communication called "ideal speech situation" (derived through "rational reconstruction" of the premises of communicative interaction). Somewhat reminiscent of Gusdorf's views, authentic communication was linked with an authentic and emancipated mode of human existence—in the sense that genuine interaction presupposes a fully developed "communicative competence" enabling all participants to raise and test validity claims, if necessary and feasible, through the medium of discourses.[19]

To round out this survey of philosophical literature, I want to cast a glance on Michel Foucault's work, specifically on his inaugural address entitled "Discourse on Language" (more literally "Discourse on Discourse"). The basic thesis or hypothesis advanced in this address concerns the invariably circumscribed and socially regulated character of discourse. "I am supposing," Foucault states, "that in every society the production of discourse is at once controlled, selected, organized and redistributed according to a certain number of procedures, whose role is to avert its powers and its dangers, to cope with chance events, to evade its ponderous, awesome materiality." Several "rules of exclusion" or forms of control are mentioned in the address—some establishing external boundaries around topics and substance of discourses, others providing internal guidelines, and still others regulating practical implementation. In the first category, Foucault lists the attempt to neutralize "politics and sexuality," the segregation of "reason and folly," and finally—as most radical principle of delimitation—the "opposition between true and false." As he notes, it was in Greek antiquity that "a division emerged between Hesiod and Plato, separating true discourse from false; it was a new division for, henceforth, true discourse was no longer considered precious and desirable, since it had ceased to be discourse linked to the exercise of power." Regarding internal control, the main types of delimitation have to do with the standard-ization of the cultural tradition, with the reliance on author or speaker "as the unifying principle in a particular group of writings or state-ments" and "as the seat of their coherence," and last with the rise of scientific or professional disciplines prescribing "a certain type of theoretical field" as matrix of legitimate propositions. In the area of practical implementation, regulation is evident mainly in specified qualifications required of speakers and writers, the cultivation of "fel-lowships of discourse" controlling access and membership, and the operation of educational systems seen as "political means of maintaining or modifying the appropriation of discourse."[10]

Probably the strongest claim advanced in the address refers to phi-losophy's long-standing complicity in the limitations mentioned. Ac-cording to Foucault, traditional philosophy has manifested this complicity "first of all, by proposing an ideal truth as a law of discourses, and an immanent rationality as the principle of their operation." As a result of these guideposts, Western thought has tended to ensure "that *to discourse* should appear merely as a certain conduit between thinking and speaking; that it should constitute thought, clad in its signs and rendered visible by words." The same collusion is shown in the stress on intentional subjectivity—on the "theme of the founding subject" whose task it is "to animate the empty forms of language with his objectives" and who, "through the thickness and inertia of empty things, grasps intuitively the meanings lying within them." In modern times, the philosophical yardsticks cited have been institu-tionalized in formal disciplines and thus have come to vindicate the predominance of scientific reason. "I believe," Foucault writes, "that this will to knowledge, reliant upon institutional support and distri-bution, tends to exercise a sort of pressure, a power of constraint upon other forms of discourse—I am speaking of our own society. I am thinking of the way Western literature has, for centuries, sought to base itself in nature, in the probable, upon sincerity and science—in short, upon true discourse. I am also thinking of the way economic practices, erected into precepts and recipes and even into a moral code, have tried since the eighteenth century to ground themselves, to rationalize and justify their sway in a theory of wealth and production." As he adds, "True discourse, liberated by the nature of its form from desire and power, is incapable of recognizing the will to truth which pervades it; and the will to truth, having imposed itself upon us for so long, is such that the truth it seeks cannot fail to mask it."[21]

II

The preceding review offers a complex and perhaps bewildering panorama of arguments and perspectives. Is it possible to find a path in this terrain without being overwhelmed by conflicting road signals or markers? Is it feasible to sort out modes of communication in a manner which renders them at least broadly compatible, without truncating their intrinsic diversity? There are a number of available strategies or approaches which, while plausible in some contexts, I do not find particularly helpful for present purposes. One such strategy involves an arrangement according to number of speakers. Gusdorf at one point employs this approach — which he calls "the simplest method" — in an attempt "to enumerate the various kinds of language" or linguistic settings. "In every case," he observes, "the number of participants changes the laws and the very nature of language, according to whether it is a monologue, a dialogue, a conversation with a greater or fewer number of participants, or finally a mass phenomenon." Despite the significance of the distinction between monologues and other kinds of linguistic behavior, the obvious drawback of this "quantitative point of view" is that it shortchanges the qualitative differences of texture and temper between forms of communicative interaction. Another strategy concentrates on subject matter and speakers' intentions. Thus, in elaborating on patterns of communicative interaction, Ricoeur speaks of the "pluralism of forms and levels of discourse," mentioning as prominent examples "poetic discourse, scientific discourse, religious discourse, speculative discourse, and so on." To explain this pluralism, he refers to "the semantic intentions of each type of discourse that are capable of being taken up in reflection," invoking explicitly the notion of "intention or semantic aim, borrowed from Husserlian phenomenology." Yet, given the linkage between this notion and subjectivity, the approach seems to prejudge communication too readily in terms of speakers' objectives.[22]

To make some modest headway in this field, I would like to return to my starting point: Rorty's and Oakeshott's comments on conversation. As previously mentioned, Rorty's study establishes an antithesis between epistemology and hermeneutics or between "normal" (or commensurable) and "abnormal" discourse—a contrast which, on one occasion, is described as "the distinction between inquiry and something which is *not* inquiry, but is rather the inchoate questioning out of which inquiries—new normal discourses—may (or may not) emerge." In other passages, the same contrast is depicted as the difference between "systematic" and "edifying" (or broadly educational) philosophies. "The mainstream philosophers," Rorty states, "are the philosophers I shall call 'systematic,' and the peripheral ones are those I shall call 'edifying.' These peripheral, pragmatic philosophers are skeptical primarily *about systematic philosophy*, about the whole project of universal commensuration." From the angle of communicative interaction, the chief import of the distinction lies in the linkage of edification and conversation—in the fact that "edifying philosophy aims at continuing a conversation" rather than setting up principles of inquiry or argumentation. "One way to see edifying philosophy *as* the love of wisdom," we read, "is to see it as the attempt to prevent conversation from degenerating into inquiry, into an exchange of views. Edifying philosophers can never end philosophy, but they can help prevent it from attaining the secure path of a science."[23]

Earlier I expressed some reservations regarding the cogency of this antinomy. Actually, on a closer reading of the study, the entire dichotomy seems less solid than it appears at first sight and tends to give way to subtle nuances and differentiations. As the terms "commensuration" and "abnormality" indicate, the dichotomy turns to a large extent on the criterion of familiarity. In Rorty's poignant formulation, "hermeneutics is, roughly, a description of our study of the unfamiliar and epistemology is, roughly, a description of our study of the familiar." Still more forcefully expressed: "Edifying discourse is *supposed* to be abnormal, to take us out of our old selves by the power of strangeness, to aid us in becoming new beings." As he recognizes, however, our approach to strangeness may take different forms: we may seek to integrate the unfamiliar by connecting it with our pre-understandings, or we may venture into entirely new directions. "The attempt to edify (ourselves or others)," he writes, "may consist in the hermeneutic activity of making connections between our own culture and some exotic culture or historical period, or between our own discipline and another discipline which seems to pursue incommensurable aims in an incommensurable vocabulary. But it may instead consist in the 'poetic' activity of thinking up such new aims, new words, or new disciplines, followed by, so to speak, the inverse of hermeneutics: the attempt to reinterpret our familiar surroundings in the unfamiliar terms of our new inventions." These observations clearly introduce a tension into the notion of "edification," unsettling the previously cited antinomies. What emerges is the distinction between an ordinary and an extraordinary hermeneutics or, more simply, between hermeneutics (in the narrow sense) and poetry. The tension is reinforced by the later comment that the fear of science or "scientism" is "the fear that all discourse will become normal discourse"—a prospect which is "frightening because it cuts off the possibility of something new under the sun, of human life as poetic rather than merely contemplative."[24]

While hermeneutics thus appears internally diffracted, another tension and differentiation—though one less openly recognized—surfaces on the level of normal discourse. Despite his manifest sympathies for hermeneutics and edification, Rorty at one point emphasizes the importance of normal discourse as an antidote to whimsical extravagance and pathological disorders. Countering the claim, advanced by extreme "existentialist" thinkers, that "normal participation in normal discourse" is purely optional, he insists "that abnormal and 'existential' discourse is always parasitic upon normal discourse, that the possibility of hermeneutics is always parasitic upon the possibility (and perhaps upon the actuality) of epistemology, and that edification always employs materials provided by the culture of the day." To sever this dependence, that is, "to attempt abnormal discourse de novo, without being able to recognize our own abnormality, is madness in the most literal and terrible sense." In its broad intent, one may readily agree, this caveat is surely commendable—and would no doubt be applauded by spokesmen of hermeneutics; in fact, Gadamer's concepts of *Wirkungsgeschichte* and of a "fusion of horizons" are intelligible only in reference to an ongoing cultural tradition and the "culture of the day." What is not immediately obvious is the identification of this culture with epistemology seen as disciplined scientific inquiry. Equally unobvious is the equation of "acculturation" with "the search for objectivity and the self-conscious awareness of the social practices in which objectivity consists."[25] Is popular culture really synonymous with science; and does "normal" everyday interaction necessarily coincide with the exchange of "objective" information—rather than being a mélange of beliefs, sentiments, and aspirations, most of which are simply taken for granted and unquestioned? If the latter alternative is granted, does normal talk not acquire some of the overtones of Gusdorf's "pragmatic language," if not of Gadamer's and Heidegger's notion of "chatter"? Conversely, could epistemology not plausibly be viewed as a comparatively stylized and "abnormal" mode of communication?

As one may note, the differentiations mentioned approximate Rorty's approach more closely at the boundary situations discussed in *Truth and Method*. The rapprochement is equally manifest in Oakeshott's case. In his previously cited essay, Oakeshott not only opposes in general terms the conversational to the argumentative stance, but also distinguishes a number of "idioms" or "voices" in the comprehensive "conversation of mankind." The chief or "most familiar" voices listed are those of "practical activity," "science," and "poetry"—with "history" occasionally being added as a fourth companion (although its idiom seems to permeate the other partners). Despite their distinctness, the various voices are presented as in principle "conversable" or compatible—except for the intolerance of some of their proponents. "The defect to which some of the voices are liable," we read, "is a loosening (even a detachment) of what is said from the manner of its utterance, and when this takes place the voice appears as a body of conclusions reached (dogmata), and thus, becoming eristic, loses its conversability." Moreover, conversational interaction "may not only be destroyed by the intrusion of the eristic tendencies of the voices; it may suffer damage, or even for a time come to be suspended, by the bad manners of one or more of the participants." In Oakeshott's view, conversation in recent centuries has become "boring" because it has been dominated by practice (narrowly understood) and science: "To know and to contrive are our pre-eminent occupations." Scientific inquiry, in particular, has tended to reduce human utterance effectively to "one mode": under the auspices of modern scientific rationality, a virtual monopoly has been accorded to "the voice of argumentative discourse, the voice of 'science,' and all others are acknowledged merely in respect of their aptitude to imitate this voice."[26]

In an effort to counteract intolerance and one-sided predominance, the essay delineates the peculiar features and linguistic characteristics of each idiom. Basically, every voice is portrayed as a kind of practice or activity, namely, the activity of an "imagining self"—where the "self" does not emerge except through or in the course of the activity.[27] In Oakeshott's presentation, everyday "practical activity"—the "commonest manner of imagining"—is a complex mixture of desire, will, and moral aspiration. "The aspect of practical imagining which calls first for our attention," he observes, "is its character as desire and aversion: the world of practice is the world *sub specie voluntatis*, and its constituents are images of pleasure and pain." Viewed from this angle, practical activity reveals "a desiring self engaged in constructing its world and in continuing to reconstruct it in such a manner as to afford it pleasure." Fellow humans on this level are not entirely disregarded, but are treated simply as instruments of personal satisfaction: "Another self is known as the consumer of what I produce, the producer of what I consume, one way or another the assistant in my projects, the servant of my pleasure." Yet, everyday life is not restricted to this self-serving and manipulative mode; apart from manifesting desire, practical activity is also "the world *sub specie moris*: it is composed not merely of images of desire and aversion but also of images of approval and disapproval." With regard to fellow humans, the "I-It" contact of desire gives way to an incipient "I-Thou" relationship: "The merely desiring self can go no further than a disingenuous recognition of other selves; in the world *sub specie moris*, on the other hand, there is a genuine and unqualified recognition of other selves. All other selves are acknowledged to be ends and not merely means to our own ends." According to Oakeshott, the rule of will and desire inaugurates a kind of proto-science, involving the ordering of external "facts" for purposes of control: "In short, there is *scientia* in practical activity, but it is *scientia propter potentiam*." Similarly, the rule of approval yields a proto-ethics, revolving around the skill of "knowing how to behave in relation to selves ingenuously recognized as such."[28]

Although everyday practice reveals itself mainly in concrete action or conduct, it also exhibits a peculiar linguistic or communicative idiom. By and large, this idiom coincides with the speech patterns studied by "ordinary language" analysts: it is chiefly a means allowing us "to identify and describe images of desire and approval, to explain, argue, instruct and negotiate; to advise, exhort, threaten and command; to purify, encourage, comfort and console." Despite the rich profusion of performative utterances, "practical language" in Oakeshott's view is not a completely open-ended arsenal, but tends to be governed by routines and conventions; its words and expressions have a "symbolic" quality—in the sense that they are "so many agreed signs which, because they have relatively fixed and precise usages, and because they are non-resonant, serve as a medium for confident communication." In some contexts and for some purposes, the practical idiom is entirely stereotyped and akin to "a coinage": "the more fixed and invariable the value of its components, the more useful it is as a medium of exchange." Since it is adapted to everyday needs, the routinized character of the idiom is not so much a defect to be deplored as a benefit. "The *clichés* of the business-man's letter are unobjectionable," we read, "indeed they are to be preferred to elegance because they are familiar and more genuinely symbolic. So far as this sort of language is concerned there would be an unquestionable advantage if a single set of symbols were current throughout the world: a 'basic' language of this sort, understood by all, is both possible and desirable."[29]

In contrast with the dictates of desire and moral approval, science or scientific "imagining," according to Oakeshott, is a purely rational pursuit, governed by the yardstick of inductive or deductive validity. "Scientific investigation, the activity of being a scientist," he states, "is mankind in search of the intellectual satisfaction which comes from constructing and exploring a rational world of related concepts in which every image recognized to be relevant 'fact' in the idiom of this inquiry is given a place and an interpretation." Instead of catering to everyday needs or concerns, the goal of science is simply to design "a system of conceptual images related to one another consequentially and claiming universal acceptance as a rational account of the world we live in." Accentuating the mutual independence of idioms, the essay insits (perhaps slighting unduly the modern linkage of science and technology) that "properly speaking, *scientia* is what happens when we surrender ourselves to this impulse for rational understanding: it exists only where this impulse is cultivated for its own sake unhindered by the intrusion of desire for power and prosperity." Congruent with its rational bent, the linguistic or communicative mode of science stresses logical and conceptual accuracy, a goal epitomized in mathematical equations. In response to the "requirement of exactness," statements "become measurements according to agreed scales, relationships are mathematical ratios, and positions are indicated by numerical co-ordinates: the world of science is recognized as the world *sub specie quantitatis*." Actually, in Oakeshott's account, the scientific idiom is more routinized and "more severely symbolic" than practical language and "the range of its utterance is both narrower and more precise." Although the voice of science is invariably "argumentative," its argumentation is peculiarly non-eristic—shading over into monologue—due to conceptual agreement: "All who participate in the construction of this rational world of conceptual images invoking universal acceptance are as if they were one man, and exactness of communication between them is a necessity."[30]

The constraints of everyday practice and scientific rationality are set aside in poetry or "poetic imagining." Like every idiom, poetry in the essay is seen as a practice or activity—but as the activity of "contemplating" and "delighting": contemplating images for their own sake and delighting in their appearance. In calling poetry "contemplative," Oakeshott writes, "I do not mean that poetic imagining is one species among others of contemplative imagining; I mean that the voice of contemplation is the voice of poetry and that it has no other utterance. And just as activity in practice is desiring and obtaining, and activity in science is inquiring and understanding, so poetry is contemplating and delighting."[31] What distinguishes poetic imagining from other types of imagining is that images here are "not recognized either as 'fact' or as 'non-fact' "; nor do they "provoke either moral approval or disapproval"; rather, they are simply "made, remade, observed, turned about, played with, meditated upon, and delighted in." Due to its disengagement from practical and empirical concerns, poetry constitutes a unique or peculiar enterprise and might be more appropriately called (in Aristotle's terms) "a non-laborious activity— activity which, because it is playful and not businesslike, because it is free from care and released from both logical necessity and pragmatic requirement, seems to participate in the character of inactivity." Paralleling this disengagement or release, poetic language exhibits an open-ended texture and resonance not found in other idioms. In poetry, the essay notes, "words, shapes, sounds, movements are not signs with preordained significances; they are not like chessmen behaving according to known rules or like coins having an agreed current value." In contrast with the fixed "symbols" of everyday talk and scientific inquiry, we encounter here "a language without a vocabulary, and consequently one that cannot be learned by imitation." Against this background, poetry signals a journey into unfamiliar terrain: "As in science there is no room for ambiguity, so in poetry there is no room for stereotypical images. What, therefore, has to be 'dissolved' before poetry can appear is not the images of a 'primary,' non-modal manner of imagining but the authority of the symbolic language of practical activity and of the even more precisely symbolic language of science."[32]

By integrating Rorty's and Oakeshott's comments with the previously reviewed philosophical literature a path may be cleared in the thicket of communicative modes. As it seems to me, the broadest or most ample type of communication—a general background category—can be found in the notion of "conversation" as discussed by Gadamer. Conversational interaction is conducted in a dynamic kind of ordinary language, a language relatively free from clichés and formalized jargon. The basic purpose of this interaction is to achieve mutual understanding between the participants relative to respective horizons of experience and subject matters of joint concern. To this extent, conversation overarches the distinction between "sensory" and "communicative" experience introduced by Habermas, as well as Oakeshott's differentiation between desire and moral purpose. The conversational mode is indifferent also with regard to another dichotomy: that between subject and object or between a "subject-language" and an "object-language." In this respect my sympathies are with Gadamer's stress on the relative "I-lessness" of communication—and with Oakeshott's view of the emergence of "self" in the course of practice—rather than with Gusdorf's (and partially Habermas's) focus on "I-Thou" relations and the constitutive role of intentional speech. The rise of subjectivity and of ego-*alter ego* relations, it appears to me, already carries with it a degree of rigidity and formalization; "authentic" communication, in any event, may depend more on reciprocal attentiveness than on an existentially construed selfhood. Conversation in Gadamer's sense is akin to Oakeshott's usage of the same term—and also to the latter's "practical language," at least where it functions *sub specie moris*. The notion also seems synonymous with Rorty's treatment of "ordinary" hermeneutics—a hermeneutics bent on appropriating and rendering familiar what is alien. Yet, despite the role of appropriation and understanding, an element of strangeness always is endemic to conversation. In Gadamer's words, attentiveness or "openness toward the other implies the recognition that I have to let some things count against myself, even if there were no one else pressing the claim."[33]

Against the foil of conversation, several other communicative modes can readily be profiled. In comparison with the former's relatively open texture, some linguistic patterns are more restricted or routinized; two such patterns seem particularly significant: one operating on the commonsense level, which may be termed "everyday talk" or "chatter"; the other guided by rational standards, which, following Habermas, I shall call "discourse." Everyday talk proceeds in an ordinary-language idiom which is strongly molded by linguistic conventions; its favorite utterances are commonplaces and clichés. In Gadamer's presentation, this type of interaction appears as a boundary situation arising mainly from negligence or indifference; Heidegger portrayed it more vividly as a "parroting talk" or the endeavor to speak like everybody else (*das Man*). In large measure, chatter coincides with Gusdorf's "pragmatic language" or "established tongue"—which at one point he derides as a "devalued" and "pruned" idiom or as a "centrifugal language because its center is everywhere and its circumference nowhere."[34] Against a purely pejorative treatment, however, it is probably well to heed Oakeshott's reminder of the practical usefulness of chatter (in some contexts). A main reason for the prevalence of clichés is that, in large measure, pragmatic language is speech governed by immediate desire or the dictates of pleasure and pain—dictates which are either universally shared or else socially preformed and transmitted. Together with the imprint of desire, practical life *sub specie voluntatis* also bears the marks of social-political power—since desire basically seeks to control the environment and to subjugate or manipulate fellow humans. In Habermas's vocabulary, ordinary "life praxis" is strongly under the sway of "instrumental" interests and ambitions, connected with "sensory" experience. Even where life praxis assumes a "communicative" orientation and thus places itself *sub specie moris*, one should add, pragmatic language only makes room for conventional norms and ritualized codes.

A different kind of limitation prevails on the level of rational inquiry. While everyday talk obeys the dictates of custom and habit (and also of social-political pressure), "discourse" operates under the auspices of rational argumentation and precisely stipulated procedures for obtaining results.[35] The language of discursive inquiry favors precision and a univocal terminology: hence the tendency among its proponents to replace ordinary language by an "ideal" (or artificially constructed) idiom. Rorty's comments on epistemology and "normal discourse" are pertinent in this area—provided these comments are not read as a simple dismissal of argumentation. Perhaps, his observations on the relation between hermeneutics and epistemology should be construed not in terms of a one-sided dependence, but in those of an inevitable tension—the tension between inquiry and common sense (or, if one prefers, between reason and folly). Oakeshott's essay seems to point in this direction—given his simultaneous emphasis on the intrinsic rationality of "science" and its limited scope. The range of discursive language, however, is not restricted only to natural or empirical science, but extends to methodologically disciplined versions of the human and social sciences, and even to ethical and meta-ethical inquiry. In this respect, Habermas's analysis of the discursive validity basis of communicative interaction, and especially his distinction between "theoretical" (scientific) and "practical" (normative) discourses, is an important contribution to a proper grasp of this domain. In regard to practical-purposive questions, his endeavors are seconded by proponents of a rational, but non-scientific, mode of argumentation, such as Toulmin, Kurt Baier, and others. Notwithstanding their importance for the advancement of knowledge, discourses seen as disciplined group enterprises tend to be circumscribed by exclusionary rules and prohibitions—constraints which Foucault has cogently enumerated and described. Especially in institutionalized settings, it seems to me, Foucault's criteria have invariably circumscribed inquiry—except perhaps the so-called "will to truth" (if "truth" is viewed not as a doctrine but as an open horizon and as a standing invitation to return to the *docta ignorantia* extolled by Gadamer).[36]

The restrictions operative in everyday talk and discourses are revoked and transcended in poetry and poetic modes of colloquy or dialogue. With regard to pragmatic language, the possibility of such transcendence is recognized by Gusdorf when he cautions against treating it as a completely "closed system": "A living tongue appears to be animated by a mysterious movement, as if the collective agreement that sustains it were in a state of constant renewal." In a sense, the potential for renewal is endemic in hermeneutical conversation properly understood; however, poetry represents (as it were) a distilled challenge or antidote to linguistic sclerosis—an antidote particularly significant in an age governed by science and practical needs. Contrary to Gusdorf's portrayal, the poetic idiom, in my view (and in Oakeshott's), signals not so much a heightened mode of self-expression as rather a heightened openness to strangeness and unfamiliarity. To this extent, Rorty's observations on "poetic activity" strike me as plausible and persuasive when he describes it as an extraordinary hermeneutics and even as "the inverse of hermeneutics": that is, as "the attempt to reinterpret our familiar surroundings in the unfamiliar terms of our new inventions." In an effort to discover "intimations of contemplative imagining" in other voices and thus to bridge the gulf between poetry and ordinary understanding, Oakeshott at one point appeals to the mediating role of friendship and "moral goodness" (he might also have mentioned the search for truth); but he particularly singles out the "recollections of childhood"—of an age depicted as "a delightful insanity, a miraculous confusion of poetry and practical activity in which nothing has a fixed shape and nothing has a fixed price." However "immersed we may become in practical or scientific enterprise," he adds, the confusion of childhood preserves our linkage with poetry seen as "a sort of truancy" or "a wild flower planted among our wheat."[37]

III

A discussion of communication or communicative modes, no matter from which vantage point it is undertaken, inevitably carries implications for politics and its theoretical study. Most of the protagonists presented in these pages have been explicit about this aspect. In a well-known passage, Oakeshott has claimed that politics is "the pursuit of intimations; a conversation, not an argument" and that consequently political education involves "learning how to participate in a conversation." Similarly, in reviewing the respective merits of linguistic idioms, his cited essay notes that "the proper context in which to consider poetic utterance, and indeed every other mode of utterance, is not a society engaged in practical enterprise, nor one devoted to scientific inquiry," but rather a "society of conversationists." Invoking a later work of the British theorist, Rorty observes that "epistemology views the participants as united in what Oakeshott calls an *universitas*—a group united by mutual interests in achieving a common end. Hermeneutics views them as united in what he calls a *societas*—persons whose paths through life have fallen together, united by civility rather than by a common goal, much less by a common ground." Disclosing his own preferences or inclinations, he portrays hermeneutics as "an expression of hope that the cultural space left by the demise of epistemology will not be filled—that our culture should become one in which the demand for constraint and confrontation is no longer felt."

On the other hand, Habermas has been eloquent in stressing the "institutionalization" of discourses and its political importance. In Western history, he writes, "discourses have lost their sporadic character only at a relatively late stage. Only when in certain domains discourses are *institutionalized* to such an extent that, under specifiable conditions, discursive exchanges can be expected to take place as a matter of course, are they able to function as relevant learning mechanisms for a given society."[38]

Comments of this kind, of course, provide only broad orientation signals and need to be fleshed out to gain concrete significance. Efforts in this direction have not been lacking among students of politics. Recently, in a paper addressed to fellow practitioners, a competent observer examined the role of communicative interaction in the "policy process as a whole," that is, in politics comprehensively construed. Referring explicitly to Oakeshott's teachings, the paper presented political life as a large-scale conversation in which "different universes of discourse meet" and which is conducted on different levels or in various stages of the policy process. For purposes of discussion, four main stages were outlined: the domain of public opinion and relevant public clienteles; the field of "pregovernmental institutions" including interest groups and political parties; the level of policy deliberation and "promulgation" in the legislative and executive branches; and finally, the phase of policy implementation through administrative agencies and the judicial system.[39] Although valuable in terms of approach or general framework, the paper did not fully explore its ramifications: while attentive to questions of communication, it refrained from probing the characteristics of the various "universes of discourse" and their role in different dimensions of political experience. In the following, I want to undertake a few tentative steps along this road. Adopting a somewhat similar framework regarding political levels or policy phases, I would like to scrutinize distinct communicative patterns and their contributions to diverse junctures of the political fabric. Needless to say, only a rough outline can be offered in this context.

The most comprehensive, and perhaps the ultimately decisive, level of politics is the "public" or the citizenry at large. In modern times, endeavors to establish a democratic form of government have almost invariably been accompanied by educational efforts designed to foster a politically informed citizenry and thus the operation of an enlightened or reasonable "general will." The communicative mode most suitable to this conception, it seems to me, is the hermeneutical conversation outlined by Gadamer—an interchange neither governed rigidly by formal rationality nor swayed by arbitrary whims, but permeated by practical wisdom and prudence; this is also the type of interaction where, in Oakeshott's terms, diverse idioms or "universes of discourse" are able to "meet, acknowledge each other and enjoy an oblique relationship." In recent times, it is true, this conversational mode has fallen on bad days in the political arena. Under the impact of various political and intellectual trends, the traditional public or "public sphere" has largely given way to the notion of "public opinion" viewed as the aggregation or conglomeration of factual preferences and wishes. To this extent, public interaction has increasingly come under the sway of Gusdorf's pragmatic language and the more restrictive portion of Oakeshott's practical voice—an idiom in which vivid communication is replaced by linguistic conventions or stereotypes, and the goal of mutual understanding by the pursuit of immediate desire. Construed narrowly *sub specie voluntatis*, the "general will" shades over into the sum of private wills, or at least into the will of the most vocal and preponderant segment of society. Since, unrelieved by practical judgment, desire is not so much a spontaneous personal as a socially generated and fashioned impulse, pragmatic language easily succumbs to political control and manipulation. Even in the absence of direct political constraints, mass media effectively channel public opinion, adapting it to the *idola fori* or fashions of the day.[40]

The prevalence of pragmatic language spills over into the field of "pregovernmental institutions," especially into the operation of private organizations and interest groups. The basic purpose of such groups is to bring pressure to bear on public authorities and the "public sphere," for the sake of advancing the preferences or inclinations of group members. As in the case of the public or the citizenry at large, the pursuit of interest or desire is not necessarily or as such objectionable. Clearly, individuals and groups have a primary stake in assessing their own needs and in deciding "where the shoe pinches"; pleasure-pain estimates provide a useful, *prima facie* yardstick—although they cannot settle the merits between competing claims. Where preferences clash solely *sub specie voluntatis*, the outcome can only be a compromise of interests—or else the imposition of the strongest will. The situation is bound to be more complex in the case of political parties. The central ambition of parties is not only to éxert pressure on public authorities but, if possible, to assume the mantle of government or public authority and thus to guide the fortunes not only of party members but of the political community as a whole. In pursuing their aims, parties therefore have to be attuned not only to private preferences but to the "general will"; differently put: they have to blend the dictates of desire with interaction *sub specie moris*—an interaction directed ultimately toward mutual understanding and recognition. Reflecting their precarious position between private and public realms, parties in a sense have to be at least bilingual: by combining the pragmatic language of desire with the more open-ended idiom of genuine conversation (and sometimes with the voice of argumentation). To be sure, even in dealing with their own members or constituencies, parties (and other organized groups) cling to pragmatic routines only at the risk of becoming dogmatic; thus, intra-group relations cannot entirely neglect a conversational element—provided group members are meant to function as part of an enlightened public.[41]

Openness to diverse wills and judgments has traditionally been the hallmark of such policy-deliberating and -promulgating institutions as legislative assemblies and similar representative bodies. Since delegates in such assemblies represent not only the public but constituencies with distinct aims—and also due to the operation of tight parliamentary procedures—legislative interaction frequently has the character of discursive or quasi-discursive argumentation rather than a flowing conversation (although assemblies can be differentiated in terms of communicative style). In Habermas's view, modern parliaments and representative bodies are chief examples of the progressive institutionalization of discourses, an institutionalization going hand in hand with the rise of an enlightened public sphere. "With precursors in the Italian cities of the Renaissance," he notes, "a political public sphere emerged first in England during the seventeenth century and later on the Continent and in America; and in conjunction with this development, we witness the growth of representative forms of government, that is, of constitutional (bourgeois) democracy." In our own century, legislative communication has been simultaneously refined and blunted. The refinement has occurred through a strengthening of the role of committees, and especially through an increasing reliance on formal "hearings" and expert testimony; in this manner, science or scientific language has come to exert a growing impact on policy formulation.

Yet, this trend has exacted a price by truncating debate "on the floor"; the ascent of scientific discourse thus has been accompanied by a decline of practical-political deliberation, making room frequently for prepared soliloquies. This decline, one should add, has been accelerated or reinforced by the advent of political mass movements and the corrosive effect of class divisions in society.[42]

Discussion and deliberation are traditionally less strongly anchored in executive and administrative branches involved in promulgating and implementing policies. In critical situations, it is true, chief executives have often found it useful to blend pragmatic decision-making with a recourse to conversational language aimed at the public at large; however, apart from being one-sided exercises (as in the case of "fireside chats"), conversational attempts of this kind have more recently tended to be streamlined by mass media and professional "image" makers. Owing to the doctrine of a "neutral" civil service, public administration in the past was widely assumed to be entirely removed from practical-political questions—or else to be governed only by narrow pragmatic rules. Subsequently, concurrent with the upsurge of positivism, administrative behavior was claimed to be amenable to strictly scientific analysis and prediction, through formal means-ends calculations. Of late, these claims have come under attack by observers stressing the broader, practical-political ramifications of policy implementation. Thus, at a time when deliberation on other levels is receding, students of public administration and "policy analysis" have begun to vindicate the importance of argumentation and of practical-normative considerations—although there is no full consensus on appropriate methods and procedures (beyond a common plea for effective rational yardsticks). According to one leading practitioner, Duncan MacRae, the most urgent need in policy studies is an effort to supplement empirical research and analysis by what he terms "valuative" or "rational ethical discourse," a mode of inquiry closely patterned on the canons of scientific methodology. In the view of other writers, the desirable road to follow is indicated by Toulmin's notions of "substantive" arguments and a "logic-in-use," by Habermas's model of "practical discourse," by the "good reasons" approach in ethics, or by a combination of these perspectives.[43] Most practitioners would concur, however, concerning the distance separating academic recommendations from administrative performance in contemporary post-industrial society.

While pragmatic language and discursive argumentation occupy an acknowledged place in public proceedings, the poetic idiom seems to be a stranger to political life. Yet, its strangeness does not render this idiom negligible or marginal—as long as politics is not reduced to the simple reenactment of established routines. Periods of crisis or profound reorientation are liable to have an ear for the voice of unfamiliarity and innovation; this may also be true of our own century—a time marked by the dislocation of time-honored premises and the intrusion, in many fields, of abnormal into normal discourse.[44] Oakeshott at one point refers to the non-pragmatic qualities of the Greek polis, noting that "in ancient Greece (particularly in Athens) 'politics' was understood as a 'poetic' activity in which speaking (not merely to persuade but to compose memorable verbal images) was pre-eminent and in which action was for the achievement of 'glory' and 'greatness'." In the modern era, poetic activity of this kind has increasingly been submerged in everyday practice (and science)—though not exclusively so. As it seems to me, founders of new regimes both on the Continent and in America have frequently displayed a practical wisdom and imaginative foresight exceeding daily routines and formal rationality; moving beyond pragmatic language (and beyond purely rational discourses), members of constitutional conventions were compelled to weigh their own experiences against those of alien cultures in charting their course into an unknown future. Even after the inauguration and institutionalization of a regime, the voice of unfamiliarity cannot entirely be silenced or ignored. Apart from formal amendment procedures, the highest courts of the land are sometimes charged with the task—or are constrained to assume the function—of adapting and reinterpreting the established framework in the light of broader considerations of practical and poetic wisdom.[45]

Indicating the role or significance of individual idioms does not yet amount to showing their compatibility. As previously mentioned, Oakeshott's essay contains suggestive passages regarding a possible linkage or "channel of common understanding" between the different voices; in the political domain, his comments on friendship seem most directly pertinent. As he points out, human interaction takes many forms, and it is possible to move from limited, pragmatic contacts to a deepened relationship and thus to find in everyday practice "intimations of contemplative imagining." In ordinary interactions governed by dictates of profit and pleasure, such as "those of producer and consumer, master and servant, principal and assistant," he writes, "each participant seeks some service or recompense for service, and if it is not forthcoming the relationship lapses or is terminated." The interaction remains partially utilitarian even in cases where partners seek a common end or where they value each other for reasons other than the partnership itself: "In the world *sub specie voluntatis* we normally reject what is not to our liking; and in the world *sub specie moris* we normally reject what proves itself to be irrational or imperfect." But, Oakeshott adds, "there are relationships, still unmistakably practical, where this is not so. It is not so, for example, in love and in friendship. Friends and lovers are not concerned with what can be made of each other, but only with enjoyment of one another." Thus, what remains constant between levels is human interaction—although it is capable of radical transformation: "In short, the world *sub specie amoris* is unmistakably the world of practical activity; there is desire and frustration, there is moral achievement and failure, there is pleasure and pain"; nevertheless, love and friendship generate a peculiar contemplative engagement, an acceptance of "whatever it turns out to be." There are echoes in these lines, I think, of Aristotle's distinction between hedonistic, utilitarian, and "perfect" friendship—where the last is said to "include" the other two—and also of his statement that "wishing to be friends is quick work, but (real) friendship is a slow-ripening fruit."[46]

Appendix: Life-World and Communicative Action

As in the case of literature and philosophy, "classical" texts in social theory are usually a matter of the past; only rarely does one witness the emergence of such a text as a contemporary. Habermas's *Theorie des kommunikativen Handelns* is one of the few exceptions to this rule: in terms of both its range of coverage and its trenchant mode of analysis the sprawling, two-volume study carries all the earmarks of a sociological "classic."[1] Apart from its intrinsic merits, the classical quality attaches to the work also through a kind of osmosis; over long stretches the study offers a detailed discussion of the classical founders of modern sociology, notably Weber, Durkheim, Mead, and Parsons — a discussion which, in my view, has no equal in recent literature. To be sure, *Theorie des kommunikativen Handelns* differs from its classical forebears by a number of innovative features: both by the incorporation of recent, sophisticated methods of inquiry (like "reconstruction") and, more important, by its attunement to pervasive intellectual changes characterizing our age. On the latter plane, the most significant innovation is Habermas's departure from the traditional "philosophy of consciousness" (or subjectivity) dating back to Descartes and Kant, and his resolute turn toward language and intersubjective communication. Moving beyond initial steps made in this direction by Mead and Durkheim, the study elevates speech and communication to primary categories of sociological theory. Given its central status, a chief question raised by the study is whether, as formulated in its pages, the "linguistic turn" constitutes an adequate response or remedy to the dilemmas bequeathed by the philosophy of consciousness.

The wealth and complexity of issues covered in *Theory of Communicative Action* (to use the English title) militates against a comprehensive review in the confines of a short essay. For present purposes I intend to focus on two major topics or conceptual themes, those of "communicative action" and the so-called "life-world"—although I shall also attempt to indicate the significance of these themes in Habermas's broader theoretical frame of reference. The choice of the two topics, I believe, is not the result of idiosyncratic preference. The importance of "communicative action" is already amply attested by the overall title of the work. In addition, Habermas underscores the weight of the themes by devoting to them two "theoretical interludes" ("*Zwischenbetrachtungen*") which punctuate the argument of the two volumes: the first deals with social action and "communication," and the second with the relation between "system and life-world."[2] In the following I shall, first of all, recapitulate in some detail Habermas's own presentation of the two concepts in his study. Next, I shall point to some quandaries or unresolved issues besetting these concepts both singly and in their mutual relation. Finally, by way of conclusion, I endeavor to project these quandaries against the larger tapestry of the work—using them as a sort of fulcrum to detect more deep-seated fissures or antinomies—while simultaneously suggesting alternative pathways of thought conducive to a lessening of such tensions.

I

Communicative action, as any attentive reader will recognize, is not a novel feature in the Habermasian opus. One of his earliest publications, entitled *Strukturwandel der Öffentlichkeit*, deplored the progressive dismantling of public debate and communication in favor of technical-functional imperatives. His main epistemological work, *Knowledge and Human Interests* (1968), focused more directly on the notion, attributing to it a quasi-transcendental cognitive status. In discussing Peirce's theory of science the study observed, "The community of investigators, however, requires a use of language not confined to the limits of technical control over objectified natural processes—a use which arises from symbolically mediated interactions between social subjects who know and recognize each other as unique individuals. Such *communicative action* forms a system of reference that cannot be reduced to the framework of *instrumental action*."³ The "Postscript" to the same study (written some five years later) differentiated more carefully between experiential "interests" and knowledge claims or between the domains of "life-praxis" and "praxis of inquiry"—but without abandoning the distinction between empirical-instrumental and communicative endeavors. Communicative action or interaction was now assumed to occur both on the level of everyday experience and on that of reflectively refined, "discursive" inquiries. As Habermas elaborated, the "linkage between knowledge and interests had been developed in the study without sufficient attention to the critical threshold separating communications embedded in experiential and action contexts from 'discourses' permitting rationally grounded and thus properly cognitive knowledge."⁴

Following *Knowledge and Human Interests*, the theme of communicative action surfaced repeatedly in Habermas's publications, including his writings on linguistic competence, universal pragmatics, and cognitive and moral development; for the sake of brevity, however, I shall omit citation of relevant passages.⁵ In *Theory of Communicative Action* the theme is first introduced in an epistemological context, namely, during a discussion of modes of rationality and rationalization. Critiquing the Baconian focus on science as technical control—a focus strongly reverberating in Max Weber's perspective—the study comments, "By concentrating on the non-communicative use of propositional knowledge in purposive action we make a prior choice in favor of *cognitive-instrumental rationality*, a concept which, via empiricism, has strongly shaped the outlook of modernity and which carries with it connotations of successful self-preservation, rendered possible through informed control over, and intelligent adaptation to, the conditions of a contingent environment." In contrast, "when starting from the communicative use of propositional knowledge in speech acts, we opt in favor of a broader meaning of rationality linked with older notions of 'logos'. This latter concept of *communicative rationality* carries with it connotations which ultimately derive from the central experience of the quietly unifying, consensus-producing function of argumentative speech where participants overcome their initial subjective views and, through the bond of rationally grounded convictions, assure themselves both of the unity of the objective world and the intersubjectivity of their life context." The differential use of knowledge, according to the study, determines in the end the basic direction or objective of reason: "In the one case the intrinsic telos of rationality is *instrumental control*, in the other *communicative consensus* or agreement."[6]

Communication and communicative rationality, in the new work, are by no means limited to "propositional" knowledge or propositions about empirical phenomena (in the external or "objective world"). In line with arguments familiar from his "universal pragmatics," Habermas extends the range of rational speech from factual assertions to intersubjective norms and modes of self-reflection and self-expression (in his terms, the dimensions of the "social" and the "subjective world"). "Norm-regulated actions, expressive self-presentations and evaluative utterances," he writes, "complement and round out constative-factual speech acts to form a broad communicative praxis. Against the backdrop of a 'life-world' this praxis aims at the attainment, preservation and renewal of consensus—more specifically of a consensus resting on the intersubjective recognition of arguable validity claims. The rationality inherent in this praxis manifests itself in the fact that a communicatively reached consensus must *ultimately* be grounded on reasons." Regarding the rational validation of cognitive claims, some types of communication are said to be amenable to "discursive" scrutiny (especially the domains of factual propositions and intersubjective norms), while other types permit only more limited versions of "critique" (such as the critical analyses operative in individual therapy and aesthetics). "We can summarize our views by saying," Habermas affirms, "that rationality is a disposition of speaking and acting subjects that manifests itself in forms of behavior backed up by good reasons." Accordingly, "any explicit examination of controversial validity claims requires an exacting mode of communication satisfying the conditions of argumentation."[7]

So far, the presentation has concentrated chiefly on the rational-discursive aspect of communication, while, in comparison, neglecting its "active" or practical connotations. The latter topic is broached in a subsequent section of the study dealing with "sociological concepts of action" and their linkage with modes of rationality. Habermas at this point differentiates communicative action from three competing action types prominent (in his view) in recent sociological literature: namely, "teleological (or purposive-rational) action," "norm-regulated action," and "dramaturgical action." As the study emphasizes, the first type has at least since Aristotle been the focus of theoretical attention. Acting teleologically, an actor seeks to implement his objective or "telos" by choosing the means appropriate to his aims, that is, by selecting a given course of action among available alternatives. Individual teleological choice is transformed and amplified into "strategic action" whenever the decision of one actor is influenced by, or a response to, decisions by another agent (or agents). In its strategic guise, the teleological model forms the bedrock of the theory of "economic choice," as developed by the founders of classical economics, and also of more recent formulations of "games of strategy." In terms of its linkage with rationality, the model, according to Habermas, is basically guided by the standard of rational "efficiency"—although this standard cannot be entirely divorced from valid propositional knowledge. As he points out, teleological action necessarily involves a relation between an actor and the external or "objective world," where "objective world" means the "totality of states of affairs which either exist or can be made to exist through purposive intervention." While, in principle, such a relation can support a purely cognitive or contemplative stance, action becomes teleological (or strategic) through the accent on intervention and efficiency.[8]

As portrayed in the study, other action types or models can be understood in terms of the progressive differentiation of actor-world relations. In contrast with the individualistic and "one-world" mentality operative in teleological endeavors, "norm-regulated action" refers to consensual activity among members of a social group, that is, to activity in accordance with accepted cultural norms and values, where the latter express "a prevailing consensus among group members." In Habermas's account, this action type was first introduced by Durkheim and subsequently fleshed out by Parsons and other spokesmen of sociological "role theory"; action from this vantage point always means compliance with socially prescribed behavior expectations. Regarding its rationality potential, the type is said to involve basically a "two-world" orientation, namely, orientation to both the objective and the "social world"—where "social world" means a given "normative context" specifying the "totality of legitimate interpersonal interactions" and where legitimacy is judged by the standard of (normative) "rightness." While role theory points to the normative-social dimensions of behavior, "dramaturgical action" uncovers the domain of subjectivity by concentrating on the self-disclosure of agents in front of each other or in front of an audience. In this case, Habermas writes, the actor "evokes in his audience a particular image or impression by means of a more or less deliberate revelation of his subjectivity." With this action type, he adds, a new "world" or dimension of behavior comes into view: namely, the agent's "subjective world," defined as the "totality of subjective experiences to which the actor has privileged access" and governed by such (potentially rational) standards of truthfulness and authenticity. Despite its discovery of this new terrain, Habermas finds dramaturgical action still restricted to a "two-world" outlook: the correlation of inner and outer, subjective and objective worlds.[9]

In Habermas's presentation, communicative action is distinguished from the action types mentioned by both its range of coverage and its uniquely reflective-rational capacity: that is, by both its ability to encompass the "three worlds" simultaneously and its rootedness in language seen as a reflective "medium" of interaction. In his words, the concept refers to the interactive "negotiation of definitions of situations amenable to consensus"; with this action type "the further premise of a *linguistic medium* comes to the fore in which the world-relations of actors are mirrored as such." First initiated by Mead, the category was subsequently developed—though insufficiently and sketchily—by interactionism, speech-act theory, and sociological hermeneutics. According to the study, the chief advantage of communicative action resides in its ability to correct the one-sidedness of alternative approaches, mainly through its reliance on language. While, in the teleological type, language serves merely as a subordinate means for utilitarian calculations, and while normative and dramaturgical actions thematize language only as a reservoir of cultural values or an instrument of self-display, the communicative model alone "presupposes language as a medium of unrestricted consensual interaction in which speakers and hearers make simultaneous reference to aspects of the objective, social, and subjective worlds, against the backdrop of their pre-interpreted life-world." As Habermas adds, this multidimensional use of language can be explicated more fully in a theory of "formal" or "universal pragmatics"—a theory which transcends narrow linguistic concerns with syntax. While conducive to mutual comprehensibility, adherence to syntactical rules alone does not yield access to the "pragmatic" dimensions of speech, that is, its embeddedness in world-contexts or "world-relations," which, in turn, can be reflectively scrutinized: "In the communicative model of action, language is relevant only from the pragmatic angle that speakers, by uttering statements in a communicative fashion, enter into distinct world-relations" and that they do so "in a reflexive manner." Against this background, communication functions "as a mechanism of coordination" in the sense that participants "reach agreement on the claimed *validity* of their utterances, and thus grant intersubjective recognition to reciprocally raised *validity claims*."[10]

In *Theory of Communicative Action*, the formal or "universal-pragmatic" underpinnings of communicative exchanges are elaborated in greater detail in the first "theoretical interlude" dealing with action theory and communication. Following a critical review of Weber's typology of actions, Habermas at this point introduces a broad distinction between "success-oriented" and "consensus-oriented" actions, where "success-orientation" is basically a new description of the teleological model (comprising both instrumental and strategic behavior), while "consensus-orientation" serves as a trademark of communicative action or interaction: "I call *communicative* those actions in which the behavioral goals or plans of actors are coordinated not via egocentric calculations of success but through consensual exchanges." In Habermas's portrayal, consensus or consensual interaction (*Verständigung*) does not merely denote a psychological convergence of feelings or dispositions or a purely factual-prudential accord, but rather points to a rationally achieved and grounded agreement. Communicative processes, he writes, "aim at a consensus that satisfies the conditions of a rationally motivated assent to the content of an utterance"; thus, consensus rests on "common *convictions*" supported by "potential reasons." To buttress the dichotomy mentioned, the interlude takes recourse to contemporary linguistic analysis and speech-act theory, and especially to Austin's differentiation between "locutionary," "illocutionary," and "perlocutionary" speech acts (or rather components of speech acts). While locutionary utterances report on given states of affairs, and while illocutionary acts signal the "pragmatic" sense of speech, perlocution in essence has to do with the impact of speech on listeners. Transplanting Austin's differentiation to the plane of action theory, the study associates communicative action chiefly with locutionary and illocutionary utterances, while finding the central trait of success-orientation in its emphasis on perlocution. "The self-sufficiency of an illocutionary act," we read, "is to be understood in the sense that both the communicative intent of the speaker and his pursued illocutionary goal result from the manifest meaning of the utterance." In contrast, teleological behavior is guided by extrinsic and instrumental objectives: "Just as for illocutionary acts the *meaning of the utterance* is constitutive, so for teleological behavior it is the *intention* of the actor" — an intention directed at exerting influence or at the "performance of a *perlocutionary* act." As Habermas adds, "I thus label 'communicative' those linguistically mediated interactions in which all participants pursue with their utterances *exclusively* illocutionary aims; on the other hand, interactions in which at least one participant seeks to produce perlocutionary effects I regard as linguistically mediated strategic action."[11]

Having stressed the illocutionary character of communication, the study proceeds to delineate the pragmatic ingredients of consensus, that is, the conditions required for the consensual coordination of behavior. In a nutshell these conditions include, first of all, comprehension of the semantic meaning of an utterance; second, understanding and acceptance of the pragmatic motivations and implications of the utterance ("acceptability conditions"); and last, implementation of the obligations deriving from the utterance. Differently phrased: a hearer must be able to grasp the meaning of a statement as well as to take a stand toward it (by responding with "yes" or "no") and orient his actions accordingly. In Habermas's view, semantic meaning cannot be rigidly divorced from pragmatic connotations, since (to use an example) understanding a command implies knowing how and why to comply with the command. In the case of communicative interaction, understanding a statement typically implies knowing the conditions which would validate, justify, or argumentatively corroborate it. Habermas at this point returns to the theme of validation and validity claims familiar from his earlier writings. Narrowly construed, communicative interaction is said to include "only such speech acts in which the speaker advances validity claims amenable to critical scrutiny." As in previous publications, these claims assume mainly three forms, and include claims regarding the "truth" of propositions, the "rightness" of normative obligations, and the "truthfulness" of self-disclosure — a tripartition which again is linked with the actor's (or speaker's) "world-relations": his relation to the "objective," "social," and "subjective" worlds. "A communicatively achieved consensus," we read, "depends on precisely three reviewable validity claims because — in deliberating about something and articulating their views — actors cannot help but embed their speech acts in exactly three world-relations and claim validity for them in each of these dimensions."

Habermas proceeds to define three types of speech acts ("constative," "regulative," and "expressive") corresponding to the three validity claims and all sharply distinguished from perlocutionary or strategic behavior.[12]

In its concluding paragraphs the interlude draws attention to the second major topic I wish to explore in this context: the concept of the "life-world." As Habermas notes, the focus on rationality or rational validation shortchanges the domain of everyday experience against which processes of rationalization are silhouetted. The concept of the "life-world"—defined as the arena of "implicit knowledge"—serves at this point as supplement or corrective designed to remedy this defect and to provide rationality with concrete social or sociological moorings. In Habermas's words, the concept refers to the "background or implicit knowledge which enters into cooperative efforts of interpretation *a tergo*; communicative action always occurs within a life-world that remains in the back of communicative participants." In the same context the concept is also circumscribed as an "implicit knowledge not representable in a finite number of propositions"; as a "holistically structured knowledge"; and as a kind of knowledge "which is not at our disposal insofar as we are unable to render it conscious or subject it to doubt at our discretion."[13] Although elaborated at length for the first time in *Theory of Communicative Action*, the topic is not an entirely new ingredient in Habermas's vocabulary. As previously indicated, his earlier works on cognitive interests already made reference to a diffuse "life-praxis" seen as a foil or backdrop to the "praxis of inquiry" in which validity claims are scrutinized. In *Legitimation Crisis* the notion of the "life-world" was specifically introduced to counterbalance the category of "systemic" imperatives, that is, imperatives geared to the instrumental-rational efficiency of social systems. We speak of "life-world," the study noted, when focusing on patterns of institutions "in which speaking and acting subjects are socially integrated" or which are "symbolically structured." While, from the systemic angle, "we thematize a society's steering mechanisms and the extension of the scope of contingency," the life-world perspective accentuates "the normative structures (values and institutions) of a society."[14]

Only loosely sketched in such earlier passages, the life-world is a persistent theme running through the two volumes of *Theory of Communicative Action* and culminating finally in the second "theoretical interlude"; here only a few glimpses of this recurrent treatment must suffice. In the opening chapter, the notion surfaces first during a discussion of modes of rationality and particularly of Alfred Schutz's concept of "mundane reasoning." Appealing to the insights of phenomenological sociology, Habermas defines the life-world as an "intersubjectively shared" or "collective life-context" comprising the "totality of interpretations which are presupposed as background knowledge by members of society." The topic reemerges again in a section devoted to the differentiation between primitive-mythical and modern-rational "world-views." In every instance, the life-world is said to be a reservoir of implicit knowledge, that is, a collection of "more or less diffuse, always unproblematical background convictions" providing a "source of situation definitions." The difference between world-views, however, resides in the potential for rationalization. In Habermas's portrayal, primitive-mythical world-views exhibit relatively closed and unquestioned patterns of belief and behavior: "To the extent that the life-world of a social group is governed by a mythical world-view, individual members are relieved of the burden of interpretation and also of the chance to bring about a critically reviewable consensus. As long as it remains 'sociocentric' (in Piaget's sense) the world-view prevents the differentiation between the 'worlds' of existing states of affairs, of valid norms and of subjective experiences amenable to expressive display." Modernization or rationalization from this angle signifies chiefly the progressive differentiation between dimensions of the taken-for-granted life-praxis, and particularly the segregation of reviewable "worlds" from the matrix of the traditional "life-world"— what Habermas describes as the "decentering of world-views." "Only to the extent," he writes, "that the formal reference system of the three worlds is differentiated, is it possible to formulate a reflexive concept of 'world' and to gain access to this world through the medium of common efforts of interpretation understood as cooperative negotiation of situation definitions. . . . In performing their interpretation members of a (modern) communicative group delimit the objective world as well as the intersubjectively shared world against the subjective worlds of individuals and (other) collectives."[15]

The most elaborate treatment of the concept occurs in the second "theoretical interlude" (which forms the centerpiece of the second volume). Drawing on arguments borrowed from Mead and Durkheim, the interlude initially contrasts the concept as a purposive category to purely instrumental or functional criteria. On Mead's interactive premises, we read, "society is construed from the participant perspective of acting subjects as *life-world of a social group.*" On the other hand, "from the observer perspective of an outsider society appears simply as a *system of behavior* where behavior is more or less functionally related to system maintenance." Pursuing the insider's approach, Habermas in the following appeals again to the precedent of phenomenological sociology. Invoking Schutz's distinction between "situation" and "horizon" (or context), he writes, "A *situation* is a thematically focused, action-pertinent segment of patterns of relevance in the life-world which are concentrically ordered and whose anonymity and diffuseness increases with growing social and spatio-temporal distance." Situations, in this terminology, are always embedded in broader "horizons," which, in turn, are grounded in the life-world. For participants, we are told, the concrete situation is "always the center of their life-world; but it has a moving horizon because it points to the complexity of the life-world"—a life-world which is constantly "present" but only as "background of actual events." Noting certain subjectivist limitations of Schutzian phenomenology (deriving from the Cartesian legacy), Habermas seeks to correct this defect through recourse to hermeneutics and ordinary language theory. From a linguistic angle, he observes, "communicative actors always move *within* the horizon of their life-world"—a life-world which now can be defined as "a culturally transmitted and linguistically organized reservoir of meaning patterns." The fabric and structures of the life-world, from this perspective, can be said to "determine the forms of possible intersubjective communication and consensus."[16]

Despite this invocation of phenomenology and hermeneutics, Habermas does not limit his discussion to the level of taken-for-granted convictions and implicit meanings. Reacting against a narrowly "culturalist" construal of the life-world—and also against a pre-cognitive focus inhibiting sociological analysis—the interlude translates background convictions into the concept of "everyday practice" ("*Alltagspraxis*") by means of which distinct life-world spheres and their modes of reproduction can be scrutinized. The reformulation yields three "structural components," labeled, respectively, "culture," "society," and "personality"—where culture denotes a reservoir of shared knowledge and pre-interpretations, society a fabric of normative rules, and personality a set of faculties or "competences" enabling individuals to speak and to act. In terms of generative potential, the three components are said to undergird processes of cultural reproduction, group and solidarity formation, and individual socialization. "Under the functional aspect of consensual agreement," we read, "communicative interaction serves tradition and the renewal of cultural knowledge; under the aspect of action coordination it promotes social integration and the establishment of solidarity; under the aspect of socialization, finally, it supports the achievement of personal identity." In light of previous descriptions of communicative action, the three components can readily be grasped as life-world underpinnings of the "three worlds" characterizing rational argumentation (with culture being related at least in part to "objective" cognition, society to the "social," and personality to the "subjective world"). Underscoring the internal connection, Habermas proceeds to depict modernization as the gradual replacement of implicit by explicit meaning patterns—a change involving the progressive "differentiation" of life-world components and the move away from everyday exchanges to rational communication thematizing reviewable validity claims. In his words, "A directional transformation of life-world structures prevails to the extent that evolutionary changes can be analyzed in terms of a structural differentiation between culture, society, and personality. Distinct learning processes can be postulated for this structural differentiation if it can be shown that such differentiation signifies a growth in rationality."[17]

Modernization (one needs to add) does not entirely coincide, however, with the differentiation of communicative structures or components—an emphasis which would shortchange processes of material reproduction. Habermas at this point returns to the distinction between instrumental (or functional) and communicative rationality and also to the dichotomy between "system" and "life-world" familiar from *Legitimation Crisis*. As he affirms, long-range social development involves not only the internal diversification of life-world components but also the growing segregation of symbolic-communicative patterns from reproductive endeavors governed by standards of technical efficiency—a process which can be described as the "uncoupling" of system and life-world. "If we view the cohesion of society exclusively as 'social integration'," he writes, "we opt for a conceptual approach concentrating on communicative action and construing society as human life-world." If, on the other hand, we grasp the same phenomenon "from the angle of 'system integration', we adopt an approach which conceives society after the model of a self-regulating system." Seen jointly from the two angles, society as a whole emerges as "an entity which in the course of evolution is increasingly differentiated both as system and as life-world. Systemic evolution is measured by the growth of a society's steering capacity, while the segregation of culture, society, and personality indicates the evolutionary stage of a symbolically structured life-world." According to Habermas, the main social domains dedicated to the enhancement of "steering capacity" are the economy and the state; with the disintegration of mythical and traditional world-views, the two domains are said to be steadily transformed into "subsystems" ruled by efficiency criteria and "uncoupled" from symbolic interaction: The "steering mechanisms of money and power" sanction an "instrumental concern with calculable quantities and thus permit a generalized strategic manipulation of the decisions of other agents bypassing modes of linguistic communication." Once instrumental subsystems are no longer merely coordinated with communicative patterns but begin to invade and subdue the latter, the uncoupling of system and life-world is converted into a direct "colonization of the life-world," that is, its subjugation to alien standards of technical control.[18]

II

Before entering into a critical review of Habermas's arguments, I want to stress again some of the obvious merits of *Theory of Communicative Action*. As suggested previously, these merits include the departure from narrowly individualistic premises and the turn to "language" and "intersubjectivity" (although the meaning of these terms is at this point still opaque). Another obvious achievement is the sheer size of the study and the vast range of coverage: a coverage extending from the exegesis of sociological "classics" over discussions of social development to the analysis of modes of rationality and rational argumentation. The very size of the study, however, may also be one source (although not the only source) of pervasive ambiguities and theoretical quandaries besetting Habermas's presentation; looking over the two volumes, the reader occasionally has the impression that the study is the work not so much of a single author but a collective of authors whose views are not always synchronized. Emphases to be found in one section or chapter are sometimes strongly revised if not entirely revoked in another portion of the study; occasionally this imbalance occurs even in the same section or on the same page (as I intend to show). Because of their central role in the study's overall framework I want to concentrate at this point on the key concepts of "communicative action" and "life-world" in an effort to disentangle their meaning and mutual relationship.

Given the crucial weight placed on "communicative action," one might assume that its meaning is relatively clear and unproblematical; this, however, is not the case. One quandary concerns the status of communication (and implicitly of language). Despite recurrent references and attempts at clarification, the study oscillates precariously between a mode of action predicated on a prior, pre-subjective consensus and another view treating consensus as the outcome of divergent individual designs. The oscillation can be restated as the query whether communication signifies a matrix underlying social interaction or else a relatively extrinsic mechanism of social coordination. The quandary seems endemic to Habermas's entire opus. In his earlier publications, "communicative action" tended to denote usually (if not preponderantly) an action orientation proceeding on the basis of conventional or consensually accepted norms and meaning patterns. Thus, in the words of *Knowledge and Human Interests*, "In everyday life-contexts, ordinary-language communication is never isolated from habitual interactions and attendant or intermittent experiential expressions." The view was more poignantly stated in another essay of the same time. "By 'interaction'," Habermas affirmed there, "I understand *communicative action*, symbolic interaction. It is governed by binding *consensual norms* which define reciprocal expectations about behavior and must be understood and recognized by at least two acting subjects. Social norms in this case are enforced through sanctions and their meaning is anchored in ordinary-language communication." These comments did not prevent him from portraying communicative action in another passage (cited before) as a "system of reference" coordinating "interactions between social subjects who know and recognize each other as unique individuals."[19]

The quandary is not entirely resolved in *Theory of Communicative Action* — although the overall tendency is toward the latter meaning. Thus, a passage in the introductory chapter defines communicative action as the kind of "praxis" in which agents rely on "their common life-context, the intersubjectively shared life-world." Similarly, a later section describes communicative action as a consensual mode of interaction, a mode in which "participants pursue their plans consensually on the basis of a commmon situation definition." Noting the limitation of this formulation, however, Habermas adds in the same paragraph, "If a common situation definition must first be negotiated, or if consensual efforts fail in the context of a common definition, then consensus—which normally is the condition for the pursuit of goals—is itself transformed into a goal or objective." In view of the study's pervasive stress on rationality and rationalization, it seems fair to construe consensual interaction more as an achievement than as a premise. This construal is buttressed by Habermas's own distinction between "communicative" and "norm-regulated" action—where the first type denotes a particularly reflexive or rational-discursive form of interaction, while the second type involves behavior in accordance with conventional rules (akin to Weber's notion of "traditional" action). The construal is further underscored by Habermas's comments on consensus or consensual interaction (*Verständigung*). As indicated, consensus in his view does not merely mean a merger of feelings or dispositions or even a factual convergence of opinions, but rather a rationally grounded accord: Communicative processes "aim at a consensus that satisfies the conditions of a rationally motivated assent to the content of an utterance." The same focus on achievement is also evident in the category of "communicative rationality" which serves as a *leitmotiv* throughout the entire study. "The concept of *communicative rationality*," we read (in a passage mentioned earlier), "carries with it connotations which ultimately derive from the central experience of the quietly unifying, consensus-producing function of argumentative speech where participants overcome their initial subjective views and, through the bond of rationally grounded convictions, assure themselves both of the unity of the objective world and the intersubjectivity of their life-context."[20]

The ambiguities surrounding communication have a direct bearing on the status of language in Habermas's framework or on the significance of his "linguistic turn." Appealing to the Humboldtian legacy in ordinary-language philosophy, Habermas at various points portrays language as a concrete presupposition of human interaction which is never fully at the disposal of participants. "Language and culture," he affirms, "are neither identical with the formal world-concepts by means of which participants jointly define their situation, nor are they generally something mundane or 'inner-worldly'; rather, they are constitutive for the life-world itself. They neither coincide with one of the formal worlds to which participants ascribe components of their situation, nor are they part of the objective, social or subjective worlds." In a formulation reminiscent of Gadamer's hermeneutics (which in turn is inspired by Heidegger) the study notes that ordinary language always remains *"in the back"* of participants: "Communicative agents always move *within* the horizon of their life-world which they cannot surpass or transcend." Statements of this kind, however, do not prevent Habermas on other occasions—and sometimes in the same context— from depicting language as a usable instrument, that is, as a "means" of communication or a "mechanism" of action coordination. The same passage pointing to the *"vis a tergo"* character also speaks of language as a "medium" of consensual interaction. The discussion of action theory differentiates communicative action from other types by its reliance on the "linguistic medium in which the world-relations of actors as such are mirrored." Linguistic communication, Habermas adds, is "simply the mechanism of coordination through which the action plans and purposive goals of participants are interactively correlated." The same view is restated in the first theoretical interlude. "For a theory of communicative action," we read there, linguistic communication "seen as mechanism of action coordination becomes the focal point of interest." The stress on coordinating functions— intimately associated with rationalization processes—is bound to cast doubt on Habermas's linguistic turn, by revealing language either as a usable means or else as a property or "competence" of individual speakers (a construal not radically at odds with the traditional philosophy of consciousness).[21]

Another quandary—not unrelated to the status of communication— concerns the distinction between action types, especially between "teleological" and "communicative" action or between "success-orientation" and "consensus-orientation." The quandary seems again endemic to Habermas's approach. Regarding the dichotomy between "labor" and "interaction" (as used in his earlier works), the difficulty of effecting a neat separation has been noted by numerous critics, including Anthony Giddens, who wrote, "All concrete processes of labor, as Habermas emphasizes in his discussion of Marx, and as Marx emphasized so forcibly himself, are social: or in Habermas's terms, involve interaction."[22] Rather than recapitulating Giddens's able critique I want to concentrate here on the special or intrinsic dilemmas of the new study. As it seems to me, not only is instrumental or teleological action regularly social or interactive in character, but communicative action (to the extent that it is a mode of "action") is invariably animated by a "telos" and thus teleological; I shall emphasize the second aspect. *Theory of Communicative Action* repeatedly chides "intentionalist semantics" for reducing communication or semantic understanding to the speaker's intentions. This type of semantics, we read at one point, "does not come to grips with the coordination mechanism of linguistically mediated interaction because it construes communication after the model of teleological action." At the same time, however, Habermas is unable to isolate the communicative category from purposive intent. This is evident already in the adopted terminology: for example, in the opposition between "success-orientation" and "consensus-orientation" — where orientation seems readily interchangeable with intention (or at least closely allied with it). Similarly, the study persistently speaks of the "goal" or "aim" of both illocutionary and perlocutionary acts (and occasionally of the illocutionary "success" of communication). While the "illocutionary aim" of a speaker is said to result from the meaning of the utterance itself, the "perlocutionary aim" is manifest only in effects or consequences of speech. To recall a passage cited earlier, "I label 'communicative' those linguistically mediated interactions in which all participants pursue with their utterances *exclusively* illocutionary aims."[23]

The goal-aspect, moreover, is not only incidental to communicative action but a central ingredient whose status is steadily enhanced in the course of rationalization, that is, with the transition from ordinary exchanges to rational-discursive communication. As Habermas himself admits (and I again repeat his statement), "If a common situational definition must first be negotiated, or if consensual efforts fail in the context of a common definition, then consensus — which normally is the condition for the pursuit of goals — is itself transformed into a goal or objective." In another context, the study is even more forthright by acknowledging the necessary teleological structure of action, including its communicative mode. In an effort to differentiate communicative "action" from communication or rational consensus per se, Habermas observes, "Language is (simply) a medium of communication which serves the task of consensus whereas agents — in interacting with each other and seeking to coordinate their actions — pursue their own distinctive goals. To this extent, the teleological structure is fundamental to *all* types of action"—although these types differ in their specification of contextual conditions. Differently phrased: reciprocal understanding and communicative consensus represent merely a "mechanism of action-coordination"—which does not fully absorb or exhaust the active component of the communicative mode. Regardless of different accents and contextual conditions, action types are said to converge at least on this level: "In all cases the teleological structure of action is presupposed in the sense that actors are presumed to be endowed with the capability of goal-orientation and purposive action, and also with the interest in implementing their action plans."[24]

The prominence of teleology, one might add, casts doubt on the internal coherence of "communicative action" (at least in its rational-reflective mode), that is, on the compatibility between action and communication or between "telos" and consensus. Again, there is a history to this dilemma in Habermas's thought. His early publications, notably *Knowledge and Human Interests*, insisted on the amalgamation of action and communication, presenting both as symbiotic elements of everyday experience. "In everyday life-contexts," he wrote at that time, "ordinary-language communication is never isolated from habitual interactions and attendant or intermittent experiential expressions. . . . Language and action in this case interpret each other reciprocally: this is spelled out in Wittgenstein's notion of 'language games'." As he added, further underscoring this view, "The 'grammar' of ordinary language determines not only internal linguistic relations, but regulates the communicative nexus of sentences, actions, and expressions as a whole, that is, a habitual social life-praxis." The "Postscript" to the same study (mentioned earlier) introduced a sharp conceptual distinction between everyday exchanges and rational-discursive communication, a distinction centering on the respective role of action. The claim to "objectivity" associated with science, the essay stated, is based on the consistent "virtualization of the pressure of action and decision which renders possible the discursive testing of hypothetical validity claims and the accumulation of valid knowledge." Rephrasing the distinction in terms of the dichotomy between "discourses" (or "praxis of inquiry") and "life-praxis," the Postscript elaborated, "In everyday life-praxis, we gain and exchange action-related experiences; statements made for the purpose of communicating experiences are themselves actions." In contrast, "given their communicative structure discourses are divorced from the constraints of action; nor do they provide room for processes of *generating* informations. Rather, discourses are immune from action and free from experience."[25]

The segregation of discourses from ordinary life-praxis has never been revoked in Habermas's subsequent writings. Given the stress on rationality in his recent work, the notion of "communicative action" thus appears fraught with profound tensions, if not entirely paradoxical: in the course of social rationalization, communication is bound to be progressively purged of its active components or concrete action contexts; in any event, the distance between consensus and active "telos" is liable to widen. In *Theory of Communicative Action* Habermas seeks to circumvent, or at least to mollify, this conclusion through recourse to speech-act theory and especially through reliance on the concept of a "formal" or "universal pragmatics" of speech. As indicated, the first interlude associates rational communication or consensus not only with a purely semantic understanding of utterances, but also with the pragmatic acceptance of validity claims and the practical implementation of the consequences of speech; in this manner, despite recognition of the gulf between communication and communicative "action," the interlude seeks to effect a reconciliation or partial reunion of reason and life-praxis. A closer inspection of the argument, however, cannot fail to reveal the imbalance of the merger: that is, the relative accentuation of cognitive understanding over practical implementation (or of theory over practice). The distinctive mark of a "formal-pragmatic" approach, Habermas asserts, resides in its focus on the question "what it *means* to *understand* a communicatively employed sentence or utterance." In addition to a narrowly semantic grasp of terms, such understanding, in his view, includes various other types of "knowledge": "We understand a speech act if we know what renders it acceptable. . . . A hearer understands the meaning of an utterance if—apart from its grammatical correctness and contextual premises—he knows the essential conditions through which he can be motivated by a speaker to take an affirmative stance." Yet, knowing clearly is not the same thing as doing; nor is cognitive understanding synonymous with will-formation or social action. As Agnes Heller observed pointedly (and correctly) in one context, "The assumption that consensus can be achieved in a process of enlightenment is in fact no answer: the *will* to achieve consensus is the problem in question." From Habermas's own perspective, communicative rationality, she added, seems to involve "a choice, a value-choice." While, seen as a cognitive endowment or competence, reason is simply a "rationality in-itself," "to transform it into a rationality for-itself we have to choose communicative rationality as a value."[26]

The quandaries besetting communicative action are matched, if not exceeded, by those surrounding the "life-world" concept. I shall bypass or downplay difficulties of a terminological kind — some of which have surfaced already in previous discussions. Thus, it is at least awkward or confusing to encounter "culture" as a synonym for language and background assumptions in general, and subsequently as a label for one of the subcomponents of the life-world. The same might be said about the term "society," which in some instances designates the fabric of social interactions as a whole, and in others a particular subdivision dealing with normative integration. More important are ambiguities affecting the status of the life-world itself. On repeated occasions the life-world is depicted as an arena of purposive meanings and symbols animating individual agents or speakers. As mentioned, *Legitimation Crisis* contrasted systemic steering mechanisms with the life-world seen as institutional matrix "in which speaking and acting subjects are socially integrated." The formulation is picked up in the second interlude, where the "life-world of a social group" is identified with society as "construed from the participant perspective of acting subjects." The same view also underlies the appeal to Schutzian phenomenology — especially the portrayal of "situations" as experiential patterns "concentrically ordered" around individual agents for whom a given circumstance is "always the center of their life-world." With a slight change of accent (but again with reference to Schutz), the study at another point associates the category with a "subject-writ-large," claiming that "members of a collectivity" typically rely on it "in the first person plural." Statements of this kind are clearly at odds with passages stressing pre-conscious and pre-subjective background conditions — unless subjective meanings are supposed to operate as "*vis a tergo*" behind social subjects (which is barely intelligible). The two opposing appoaches can be termed, respectively, the "weak view" and the "strong view" of the life-world — with the first drawing its inspiration chiefly from Schutzian (and Husserlian) phenomenology and the second tracing its roots to Gadamer (and Heidegger); while in the former the life-world appears as a network of potential or embryonic subjects, the latter breaks more resolutely with traditional subject-object (and ego-alter) polarities. By combining the two ap-

proaches, the study seeks to incorporate advantages intrinsic to both—
but at the price of diminished coherence. The need to separate the
two views has been recognized by numerous observers, including a
philosopher as congenial to Habermas as Karl-Otto Apel. Assessing
recent trends in philosophy, Apel in one instance differentiated "Heidegger's more radical 'analysis of Dasein' " from Husserl's "phenomenology of the life-world," noting the comparatively greater proximity
of phenomenology to traditional problems of "transcendental
constitution."[27]

In *Theory of Communicative Action*, the incoherence of the mixed perspective surfaces in numerous forms and contexts; one has to do with
the availability of the life-world for sociological analysis. On repeated
occasions the study insists on its strictly non-available or non-objec-
tifiable character. Elaborating on the notion of background assumptions
Habermas states that communicative agents cannot objectify or face
frontally "the horizon of their own life-world": "As interpreters they
are with their speech acts part of the life-world, but they cannot refer
to 'something in the life-world' in the same manner in which we refer
to facts, norms or experiences. . . . Differently put: participants cannot
distantiate language and culture in a way akin to their treatment of
the totality of facts, norms or experiences about which communication
is possible." The concluding section of the study reiterates this ("strong")
view of the life-world by presenting the latter as a kind of background
pre-understanding "which is at no one's arbitrary disposal." Given
these and several other statements to the same effect, the reader is
bound to be surprised by the study's tendency toward progressive
objectification, that is, the transformation of the life-world into a pliant
target of sociological inquiry. This transformation occurs in several
stages. The initial, relatively subtle shift involves the bracketing of the
life-world concept in favor of the notion of everyday interaction or
"everyday practice," a notion amenable to narrative description and
especially to the portrayal of processes of social reproduction. In quick
succession, this shift is then found to yield a whole host of sociological
categories and distinctions no longer recalcitrant to empirical research:
first, the differentiation between three "structural components" of the
life-world (culture, society, and personality), and subsequently the segregation between symbolic and material modes of reproduction or
between "system" and "life-world." Clearly, the introduction of these
categories would serve little purpose if it were not possible to pinpoint

their substantive content and respective boundaries. In the case of the three structural components, Habermas indicates their close affinity to existing sociological subdisciplines: namely, sociology of knowledge, institutional analysis, and social psychology. The second and more basic distinction is presented as the opposition between "inner" and "outer" dimensions, or else as the contrast between divergent "sub-systems"—in the sense that, in the course of modernization, the life-world is "steadily reduced to one subsystem among others." At one point, the study even speaks of the "everyday practice of the life-world" as a "clearly demarcated object domain."[28]

The transformation of the life-world sketched is problematical not only because of its objectivist bent, but also in terms of its claimed sociological results. As previously mentioned, the "components" of the life-world in Habermas's account correspond to the three formal "world-concepts" of rational discourse—concepts which in turn can be correlated with "subject-object" and "ego-alter" distinctions; treated as "inner" and "outer" domains even the system—life-world bifur-cation can be traced back to the same set of categories. To the extent that this is the case, however, the life-world ceases to function as polar counterpoint to the formal "worlds," being reduced instead to their simple anticipation. As can readily be seen, the contrast between "weak" and "strong" views surfaces here again, with wide-ranging effects on the study's arguments. Basically, Habermas in this instance exploits the advantages implicit in the weak conception of the life-world—but at the cost of tautology or definitional circularity: culture, society, and personality can be presented as "structural components" because the life-world has been defined from the beginning as a matrix composed of embryonic subjects (and objects). The dilemmas besetting this approach are not only definitional, however, but carry over into other topical areas, including the theory of social development. Por-trayed as "structural components," subject-object and ego-alter re-lations are treated as invariant features of social life—a perspective compressing social "change" into the teleological unfolding of a timeless potential.[29] More important at this point are the developmental im-plications for the life-world itself; once modernization is seen as pro-gressive rationalization of background assumptions through discursive thematization, the life-world is bound to be not only weakened but steadily eclipsed and finally absorbed by world-concepts. Consistently pursued, this process would render nugatory a central pillar of the entire study, thus depriving communicative action of its social moorings. As it happens, however, other arguments of the study tend to cast doubt both on this outcome and the invariance of structural components.

The ambivalent status of the life-world, from a developmental perspective, emerges chiefly in Habermas's discussion of primitive or "archaic" societies. The case is instructive because of the exemplary character ascribed to these societies—the fact that (as the study says) they are "virtually synonymous with the life-world matrix." Given the theoretical prominence of structural distinctions, one would expect them to operate at least incipiently in pre-civilized or "tribal" settings; this, however, is not the case. Pointing to the centrality of lineage and family relations and the prevalence of "mythical world-views," Habermas notes the amorphous blending of culture, personality, and social integration and the virtual absence of rational world-concepts: mythical orientations, he states, "obliterate the categorial distinctions between objective, social and subjective worlds." The same situation obtains regarding the opposition between symbolic and material reproduction. As Habermas observes, primitive world-views do not yet differentiate between society and its "natural environment"; nor do they support a strict dichotomy between instrumental-teleological and communicative action or between systemic imperatives and consensual agreement: "Systemic mechanisms are not yet divorced from institutions promoting social integration"—to the point that "social and systemic integration actually converge." If this is correct, however, how can the study subsequently segregate "system" from "life-world," reducing the latter to a mode of symbolic reproduction—given the absence of this distinction in archaic societies whose life-world is nonetheless presented as prototypical (and as "closest to furnishing an empirical warrant for the life-world concept as such")? Differently phrased: how can the life-world be depicted as an "inner" domain made up of symbolic subcomponents—given the relatively modern character of the inner-outer division and of the subcomponents themselves?[30] At a minimum, Habermas's account at this point conveys a sense of anachronism: the impression that, projected onto an amorphous canvas, recent sociological categories are surreptitiously endowed with structural invariance.

III

Having scrutinized the two concepts of Habermas's study, I want to allude briefly to some broader (and perhaps more worrisome) implications or corollaries. First, to stay with the life-world theme, it seems fair to underscore its generally precarious status in the confines of *Theory of Communicative Action*. In the concluding passages of the study, Habermas reiterates its cognitive unavailability—the fact that life-world patterns are "at no one's disposal." The "horizon knowledge" underlying everyday praxis, he observes, has the character of taken-for-granted assumptions; "but it does not satisfy the criterion of a *knowledge* which is intrinsically related to validity claims and thus can be critically assessed." Although not an isolated instance, this comment seems odd or out of place in a study whose centerpiece is discursive rationality and a theory of communication anchored in reviewable validity claims. In the same context, reflecting on general philosophical underpinnings, Habermas is content to claim for his overall approach at best a "felicitous coherence of different theoretical fragments" and even to regard coherence as "the only criterion of judgment" on this level—a view which is hardly congruent with the strong doctrine of discursive truth (and rightness) championed elsewhere in the study. At another point, Habermas exempts the "totality of a life-form" or life-world from the application of specific rationality standards, stating, "Life-forms and life stories are judged implicitly by criteria of normalcy which do not permit approximation to ideal yardsticks; perhaps we should speak instead only of a balance between mutually complementary life-elements." This assertion—one should note, however—occurs at the end (as a kind of afterthought) in a section devoted to the differentiation between mythical and modern world-views where modernity is singled out precisely for its superior rationality. As it seems to me, life-world arguments cannot simply be juxtaposed to, or amalgamated with, the defense of rationalization—without incurring the risk of incoherence (which is not the same as fragmentary coherence). Differently put: rationality criteria cannot simultaneously be bracketed in favor of "normalcy" and extolled as pacemakers of processes in which earlier life-forms are "categorially devalued."[31] Far from effecting a judicious "balance," one might say, rationality in Habermas's overall presentation tends to jeopardize or erode the life-world (and vice versa).

The same presentation—and this may be more crucial still—places in jeopardy also the role of communicative action and thus the "normative foundations" of critical social theory. Habermas's vindication of rationalization and modern rationality is predicated basically on the saving virtues of communicative consensus—virtues he seeks to guard jealously against the encroachment of systemic imperatives. On closer inspection, however, this vindication is deeply problematical because, in Habermas's own account, rationalization and consensus are by no means readily compatible. In a previous context I pointed to the tension between the active and consensual components within the concept of "communicative action," indicating how, with growing rational reflexivity, the former are increasingly ejected or purged from the consensual ideal. Looking at things from the other side of the coin, a similar purge can be shown to affect consensus itself. According to *Theory of Communicative Action*, modernization involves the steady separation or "uncoupling" of system from life-world, that is, the growing autonomy of systemic social domains (chiefly the economy and the state) governed by success-orientation and standards of rational efficiency. Simultaneously, modernization is said to denote the increasing differentiation of the symbolic life-world itself, that is, the progressive division between its "structural components" and between the three dimensions of the objective, social, and subjective worlds. Translated into "subject-object" and "ego-alter" categories, social development in this sense signifies the growing segregation of the subject from the object world—and actually the relentless subjugation of "nature" by man—and also the segregation of ego from alter or of personal "identity" from social "solidarity." Against this background it is entirely unclear how and why ego (or individual agents) should seek consensus rather than success in any and all areas of behavior, or try to curb teleological-strategic impulses. Contrary to Habermas's claims, the "colonization of the life-world" is not simply a deplorable but avoidable hazard, but a necessary consequence of his own premises and conception of rationalization.

Repeatedly *Theory of Communicative Action* sounds a somber note on the prospects of communicative consensus. Thus, at one point the study speaks of the *"irresistible momentum"* of instrumental-functional subsystems which is "simultaneously the cause of the colonization of the life-world and of the segmentation between science, ethics, and art." As in the discussion of the life-world, however, these and similar comments do not affect the general thrust of the argument; in fact, the same passage ascribes possible "pathological" consequences "neither to the secularization of world-views nor to the structural differentiation of society *per se*." Pressed on the immunity of the life-world from (irresistible) strategic imperatives, Habermas occasionally retreats to an "innatist" position: the thesis that symbolic domains of the life-world are somehow "by nature" ("*von Haus aus*") consensually constituted or pregnant with communicative "order." Despite its time-honored status, however, the thesis seems anomalous in a study which otherwise strongly opposes "foundational" or ontological presuppositions. Once instrumentalism is given free rein against nature (as it is in these volumes), what "natural" barriers could plausibly safeguard the integrity of human or social bonds? Actually, faced with the progressive "anomie" in modern societies, Habermas seems in principle reduced to the same kind of counterfactual plea he ascribes at one point to Durkheim: namely, that there simply ought to be some "oughts." Moreover, even assuming the presence of "oughts" in rationalized settings, Habermas persistently emphasizes the purely "formal" or procedural character of modern norms—a character compatible with any kind of substantive content including success-orientation (or the manipulation of procedures for strategic ends). Occasionally, it is true, the instrumental implications of pure formalism and legalism are acknowledged in the study—for instance, in the query how social identity is supposed to be preserved once social bonds have "evaporated into a merely procedural consensus on the basis of communicative ethics"—but again without noticeable effect on the rationalization model.[32]

The elusiveness of consensus can be traced, at least in part (I believe), to a curious gap in Habermas's presentation: his nonchalance regarding intersubjectivity or its treatment largely as a non-issue. Given the processes sketched of rationalization and modernization, however, intersubjectivity or social "solidarity" can by no means be taken for granted. Due precisely to the growing differentiation of life-world components and formal world-concepts, the status of the "social world" (so-called) is bound to be precarious. Once ego, as Habermas postulates, is increasingly segregated from objects—to the point of even acquiring, through reflexivity, an "extramundane" position toward phenomena—how can one subject maintain a straightforward relation to another (extramundane) subject without reducing the latter somehow to a mundane occurrence? Differently put: how can ego's steady internalization fail to produce the distantiation and externalization of alter? As is well known, the issue has been discussed at length in phenomenological literature—from Husserl's *Cartesian Meditations* to Sartre's analysis of "the Look" in *Being and Nothingness*. Without necessarily endorsing the cogency of the phenomenologists' arguments, one certainly cannot deny the seriousness of their endeavor to come to terms with the problem. Given the centrality of interaction in Habermas's framework, the topic would seem to have merited an equally serious or extensive treatment. At one point the study chides Husserl for not "resolving" the intersubjectivity issue, and Schutz for bypassing its significance—but without offering an alternative approach (beyond a problematic restatement of Mead's self-society correlation). Basically, Habermas seems to regard the issue as settled due to his turn to language; yet, in view of the dilemmas besetting this "turn"—the portrayal of language as a "mechanism" of action projects—the remedy is hardly adequate or persuasive.[33]

As it seems to me, the quandaries or weaknesses mentioned are ultimately linked with an important feature of Habermas's opus, a feature striking because of his guiding ambition: the persistent influence of the "philosophy of consciousness" (or subjectivity), and more generally of the legacy of metaphysics. The influence is evident in the pervasive emphasis on "basic dispositions" or "attitudes" ("*Grundeinstellungen*")—which can only be dispositions of consciousness. Thus, the differentiation between formal world-concepts is associated by Habermas with a corresponding distinction between "attitudes towards worlds"—chiefly: the "objectifying" attitude toward facts, the ethical attitude toward social norms, and the reflective attitude toward self (and language)—all of which are said to depend on "changes in perspective or attitudes which we perform." The same emphasis recurs in the discussion of action types and of speech-act theory. While the contrast between success-orientation and consensus-orientation is traced to the respective "attitude assumed by actors," the classification of speech acts is founded on the "basic attitudes" of individual speakers—with constative, regulative, and expressive speech acts being matched by objectifying, normative, and expressive attitudes or dispositions. Further repercussions of traditional philosophy surface in "inner-outer" dichotomies and in the crucial role assigned to "worldviews." On various occasions, the "objective" and "social" domains are jointly juxtaposed to the "subjective" sphere under the labels of "outer" and "inner" worlds (or perspectives), while "world-views" are singled out for their contribution to "identify-formation" and their ability to "furnish individuals with a core of basic concepts and assumptions."[34] As it happens, of course, most of these notions or categories have come under serious attack in recent decades. Thus, speech-act theory has been denounced for its subjectivist leanings, just as "world-views" for their ideological overtones. On a broader scale, traditional subject-object (and ego-alter) polarities have been challenged by a host of phenomenological, structuralist, and "post-structuralist" writings—writings stressing the porousness of consciousness and the necessary interpenetration of subject and world. Habermas may not personally wish to venture in these directions, preferring instead the *terra firma* of time-honored maxims. But why should "critical theory" (of all outlooks) be hardened into a barrier against innovation and against a critical rethinking of the metaphysical tradition?[35]

There is a corollary to traditional categories (bound to be noticed by students of political theory): the disappearance of politics or political praxis in Habermas's recent work. His early publications, as is well known, were still strongly preoccupied with political praxis and its progressive disintegration under the impact of social-empirical and instrumental-technical imperatives. In an intriguing and challenging passage, *Theory and Practice* bemoaned the medieval substitution of the "social" domain for the Greek "polis" and the redefinition of man as "social" rather than "political animal"—changes which were viewed as harbingers of an impending erosion and decay. *Theory of Communicative Action* bears few if any traces of this original concern. Taking his bearings from Durkheim, Mead, and other sociological "classics," Habermas in the study reveals himself squarely as a "sociologist" (*cum* moralist) or a theorist of the social domain—while relegating politics to the status of a specialized subdiscipline or subsystem.[36] As indicated, in the course of modernization both the economy and the "polity" (or state) are claimed to be progressively transformed into functional-systemic structures governed by success-orientation and standards of technical efficiency, a trend submerging politics inexorably in bureaucratic controls. At the same time, politics has no clear place within the communicative life-world—an arena devoted to symbolic reproduction and differentiated into the subcomponents of culture, society (or social solidarity), and personality (or socialization). At this point the

Habermasian dualism of "labor" and "interaction" (or of system and life-world) exacts its price: by exorcising political praxis seen as an activity which is neither external nor internal, neither purely instrumental-technical nor communicative-consensual in character. Wedged between the alternatives of material and symbolic processes or between "outer" and "inner" worlds, politics as a concrete-transformative endeavor thus appears doomed to insignificance, if not extinction.

Politics, moreover, is not the only casualty of Habermasian categories and dichotomies. Coupled with the "inner-outer" distinction, the process of rationalization is liable to tarnish the emancipatory aspiration (that is, the core) of critical theory. In portraying the image of an "idealized" or fully rationalized life-world, Habermas projects a condition of life in which all "natural" limitations as well as limitations of "otherness" are finally extirpated. "Universal discourse," we read, "points to an idealized life-world" reproduced entirely through rational "mechanisms of consensus"; in this setting the "natural growth" ("Naturwüchsigkeit") of social traditions is dissolved by reason in the same way as are religious traditions by "modern natural science, formalized jurisprudence, and autonomous art."[37] Joined with the study's endorsement of science and technology, this attack on nature reveals ultimately (as Adorno and Horkheimer insisted) an impulse of control and domination—an impulse starkly at odds with the proclaimed goal of freedom from domination. Simultaneously, in the domains of social integration and personality, modernization yields an increasing formalism and abstractness of social bonds and identity structures, a formalism purged entirely of historical or substantive content. Yet, removal of content also means the elimination of all forms of "otherness" and concrete human "difference." Against this background, "universal discourse" signifies basically a retreat to a formal level of identity on which all non-identical properties are erased and "others" can no longer really happen to ego. Differently put: communicative interaction in an idealized setting bears no longer any trace of a real human encounter involving love and hate, joy and pain. Contrary to the professed "decentering" of the *cogito*, *Theory of Communicative Action* thus conjures up the specter of solipsism.

In contradistinction to formalized discourses, the contours of a communicative-political praxis akin to human encounter have been outlined by several writers, including Agnes Heller. Adopting a narrowly rationalist approach, she observes, Habermas is led to conclude that "reflexive theory cannot be applied to strategic activities, that force and discourse cannot be conceived together." Actually, however, social or political struggle "cannot be described—at least not in all its forms—as merely strategic activity and . . . the models of force and of discourse could be interconnected." As Heller continues, "Human beings do not accept social theories (philosophies) from the standpoint fo their group-interests, but from the standpoint of their lives as a whole, from their systems of needs. 'Readiness' for rational argumentation about values and theories presupposes the involvement of the human being as a whole, as a needing, wanting, feeling being." Moreover, "if we accept the plurality of ways of life, we have to accept the plurality of theories as well."[38] In a more philosophical vein, the ontological dimensions of communication or communicative praxis have been highlighted by Heidegger. Commenting on one of Hölderlin's later poems, Heidegger distinguishes communication (Gespräch) sharply from "language use" or the mere exchange of "performative utterances." Participants in communicative interaction, he notes, do not properly initiate, conduct, or perform the communicative process; instead, they become partners in a reciprocal endeavor only by virtue of language and its recollective and disclosing potency. What genuine communication yields, Heidegger adds, is not simply a uniform rational consensus, but rather a substantive mode of mutual recognition—including recognition of "difference" (which is not synonymous with non-rational particularity): Communicative differentiation is "not separation, but a form of emancipation which creates between speakers that open space in which uniqueness can occur" as well as the "harmony" of differences.[39]

Notes

Introduction

1. Martin Heidegger, *Letter on Humanism*, in David F. Krell, ed., *Martin Heidegger: Basic Writings* (New York: Harper and Row, 1977), p. 193 (translation slightly altered).

2. For examples of the extensive analytical literature on action see Alvin I. Goldman, *A Theory of Human Action* (Princeton: Princeton University Press, 1970); Robert Binkley, Richard Bronaugh, Ausonio Marras, eds., *Agent, Action, and Reason* (Toronto: University of Toronto Press, 1971); Arthur C. Danto, *Analytical Philosophy of Action* (Cambridge: Cambridge University Press, 1973); Stephan Körner, ed., *Practical Reason* (New Haven: Yale University Press, 1974); Lawrence H. Davis, *Theory of Action* (Englewood Cliffs, NJ: Prentice-Hall, 1979). For examples of Continental literature compare Oswald Schwemmer, *Philosophie der Praxis* (Frankfurt-Main: Suhrkamp, 1971); Manfred Riedel, ed., *Rehabilitierung der praktischen Philosophie*, 2 vols. (Freiburg: Romach, 1972 and 1974); Rüdiger Bubner, *Handlung, Sprache und Vernunft* (Frankfurt-Main: Suhrkamp, 1976); Pierre Bourdieu, *Outline of a Theory of Practice*, trans. Richard Nice (Cambridge: Cambridge University Press, 1977).

3. Many of the above trends are discussed in detail in Richard J. Bernstein, *Praxis and Action: Contemporary Philosophies of Human Activity* (Philadelphia: University of Pennsylvania Press, 1971). Compare also his *The Restructuring of Social and Political Theory* (New York: Harcourt Brace Jovanovich, 1976) and *Beyond Objectivism and Relativism: Science, Hermeneutics and Praxis* (Philadelphia: University of Pennsylvania Press, 1983).

4. See Heidegger, *Letter on Humanism*, also "The Origin of the Work of Art" and "The Question Concerning Technology," in Krell, *Martin Heidegger: Basic Writings*, pp. 181, 193, 293–294. For the German versions see Heidegger, *Über den Humanismus* (Frankfurt-Main: Klostermann, 1949), p. 5; "Der Ursprung des Kunstwerkes," in *Holzwege* (Frankfurt-Main: Klostermann, 1950), pp. 50–51, 63; "Die Frage nach der Technik," in *Vorträge und Aufsätze*, vol. I (3rd ed.; Pfullingen: Neske, 1967), p. 11. For additional comments on "creative action" (*Schaffen*) compare Heidegger, *Schellings Abhandlung über das Wesen der menschlichen Freiheit (1809)*, ed. Hildegard Feick (Tübingen: Niemeyer, 1971), pp. 157–158, 163, 193.

5. Maurice Merleau-Ponty, *The Visible and the Invisible*, ed. Claude Lefort, trans. Alphonso Lingis (Evanston: Northwestern University Press, 1968), pp. 201, 221; Michel Foucault, *The Archaeology of Knowledge*, trans. A. M. Sheridan Smith (New York: Pantheon Books, 1972), p. 55, and *Language*

Counter-Memory, Practice: Selected Essays and Interviews, ed. Donald F. Bouchard, trans. Bouchard and Sherry Simon (Oxford: Blackwell, 1977), p. 176 (translation slightly altered). As Foucault adds in the latter study (p. 173), "Physics concerns causes, but events, which arise as its effects, no longer belong to it. Let us imagine a stitched causality: as bodies collide, mingle, and suffer, they create events on their surfaces, events that are without thickness, mixture, or passion; for this reason, they can no longer be causes. They form among themselves another kind of succession whose links derive from a quasi-physics of incorporeals." Compare also Gilles Deleuze's comment in the same volume (p. 206): "Who speaks and acts? It is always a multiplicity, even within the person who speaks and acts. All of us are 'groupuscules'."

6. These statements actually are made by Deleuze in a conversation with Foucault; but they also seem to reflect the latter's views. See *Language, Counter-Memory, Practice*, pp. 205-206. See also Heidegger, *Letter on Humanism* in Krell, *Martin Heidegger: Basic Writings*, pp. 236, 239; *Über den Humanismus*, pp. 42, 45.

7. Heidegger, *Letter on Humanism*, pp. 196, 236; *Über den Humanismus*, pp. 7, 42; Foucault, *Language, Counter-Memory, Practice*, p. 185. For a similar move beyond Hegelian (and Sartrean) dialectics of thesis-antithesis-synthesis in the direction of a discontinuous "hyperdialectic" see Merleau-Ponty, *The Visible and the Invisible*, pp. 94-95.

8. Michael Oakeshott, *Experience and Its Modes* (Cambridge: Cambridge University Press, 1933), p. 347; *On Human Conduct* (Oxford: Clarendon Press, 1975), pp. 3 (note 1), 11. Questioning Plato's claim of unconditioned "episteme," the latter study continues (p. 27), "Distracted by his exclusive concern with the engagement of theoretical understanding and with the manifest shortcomings of this platform of understanding [operative in the cave], the intelligibility of the cave-dwellers' world seems to him at once so complete . . . and so minimal that he is disposed to write it off as nescience. This, I think, is a mistake. It is a conditional understanding of the world, valuable so far as it goes, and indispensable in the engagements of practical life, but not fully in command of itself because it is unaware of its conditionality."

9. Hannah Arendt, *Between Past and Future: Six Exercises in Political Thought* (New York: Meridian Books, 1963), pp. 13-14, 31. As she adds (pp. 35-36), "Against the alleged abstractions of philosophy and its concept of man as an *animal rationale*, Kierkegaard wants to assert concrete and suffering men; Marx confirms that man's humanity consists of his productive and active force, which in its most elementary aspect he calls labor-power; and Nietzsche insists on life's productivity, on man's will and will-to-power. . . . The very assertion of one side of the opposites—*fides* against *intellectus*, practice against theory, sensuous, perishable life against permanent, unchanging, suprasensuous truth—necessarily brings to light the repudiated opposite and shows that both have meaning and significance only in this opposition." Compare also the quasi-Heideggerian comments on "thinking" in Arendt, *The Life of the Mind*, vol. I: *Thinking* (New York: Harcourt Brace Jovanovich, 1977), pp. 8, 13-15, 57-62, 121-122, 211-212 (on "metaphysical fallacies" and the need to "dismantle metaphysics").

10. Merleau-Ponty, *Phenomenology of Perception*, trans. Colin Smith (London: Routledge & Kegan Paul, 1962), pp. 328-329, 346-347; Foucault, *Language, Counter-Memory, Practice*, p. 231.

11. See Arendt, *Rahel Varnhagen: The Life of a Jewess* (London: Leo Baeck Institute, 1957), p. xi; also Oakeshott, *Rationalism in Politics, and Other Essays* (New York: Basic Books, 1962), p. 125.

12. See Arendt, *The Human Condition: A Study of the Central Dilemmas Facing Modern Man* (Garden City, NY: Anchor Books, 1959), pp. 71-223; Oakeshott, *On Human Conduct*, pp. 108-118.

13. "Letting-be" (a Heideggerian term) designates not indifference but an agonal reciprocal engagement. In *The Human Condition* (p. 218) Arendt sharply segregates the "unworldly" intimacy of "love" from public friendship—in my view somewhat too neatly. On this score I tend to side with Cicero when he writes, "For it is love (*amor*), the thing that gives us our word for

friendship (*amicitia*), that provides the first impulse toward mutual regard." See Cicero, *On Old Age and On Friendship*, trans. Frank O. Copley (Ann Arbor: University of Michigan Press, 1967), p. 58.

14. Arendt, *Crises of the Republic* (New York: Harcourt Brace Jovanovich, 1969), p. 107. As she adds, perhaps too optimistically (pp. 107–108), "The United States of America is among the few countries where a proper separation of freedom and sovereignty is at least theoretically possible insofar as the very foundations of the American republic would not be threatened by it. Foreign treaties, according to the Constitution, are part and parcel of the law of the land, and—as Justice James Wilson remarked in 1793—'to the Constitution of the United States the term sovereignty is totally unknown.' " A more eloquent denunciation of the State— long before its effects were evident in two world wars—can be found in Nietzsche's writings. As we read in his *Zarathustra*, "State is the name of the coldest of all cold monsters. . . . Only where the State ends, there begins the human being who is not superfluous: there begins the song of necessity, the unique and inimitable tune." See *The Portable Nietzsche*, ed. Walter Kaufmann (New York: Viking Press, 1968), pp. 160, 163.

15. In Heidegger's words, "As existing transcendence abounding in possibilities man is a *being of distance*. Only through an original farness—rooted in his transcendence vis-à-vis all ontic phenomena—does he acquire a genuine nearness to things" and to fellow humans. See "Vom Wesen des Grundes" in Heidegger, *Wegmarken* (Frankfurt-Main: Klostermann, 1967), p. 71. The linkage of friendship and unfamiliarity is also supported in Nietzsche's *Zarathustra*: "I teach you not the neighbor, but the friend. The friend should be the festival of the earth to you and an anticipation of the overman. . . . Let the future and the farthest be for you the cause of your today: in your friend you shall love the overman as your cause." See *The Portable Nieztsche*, pp. 173–174.

16. See Alasdair MacIntyre, *After Virtue: A Study in Moral Theory* (Notre Dame: University of Notre Dame Press, 1981), especially pp. 103–113. The study (p. 108) speaks of "Nietzsche's prophetic irrationalism," a phrase in which I find particularly the last term objectionable. For a critical rejoinder compare Richard J. Bernstein, "Nietzsche or Aristotle? Reflections on Alasdair MacIntyre's *After Virtue*," *Soundings*, vol. 67 (Spring 1984), pp. 6–29.

17. The stress on freedom conflicts, of course, with Heidegger's involvement with the Nazi regime in 1933—especially if the latter is seen as a deliberate, long-range commitment. On the premises of experiential praxis, his involvement *might* be ascribed (in part) to an unwillingness to categorize a regime prior to having any concrete experience with it. The same premises, to be sure, do not sanction persistence in a grievous mistake—which may account for the relative brevity (ten months) of his official involvement.

18. Arendt, *Between Past and Future*, p. 14. As she added (pp. 25–26), "Our tradition of political thought began when Plato discovered that it is somehow inherent in the philosophical experience to turn away from the common world of human affairs; it ended when nothing was left of this experience but the opposition of thinking and acting, which deprived thought of reality and action of sense, makes both meaningless. . . . The end of a tradition does not necessarily mean that traditional concepts have lost their power over the minds of men. On the contrary, it sometimes seems that this power of well-worn notions and categories becomes more tyrannical as the tradition loses its living force and as the memory of its beginning recedes; it may even reveal its full coercive force only after its end has come and men no longer even rebel against it."

Chapter 1

1. Compare, for example, Robert A. Dahl, "Political Theory," *World Politics*, vol. 11 (1958), pp. 89–102; Peter Laslett, "Introduction" to *Philosophy, Politics and Society*, 1st ser. (New York: MacMillan,

1956), p. VII; Alfred Cobban, "The Decline of Political Theory," *Political Science Quarterly*, vol. 68 (1953), pp. 321–337. For more recent assessments of the state of political theory see, for example, John G. Gunnell, "In Search of the Political Object: Beyond Methodology and Transcendentalism," and Richard Ashcraft, "One Step Backward, Two Steps Forward: Reflections upon Contemporary Political Theory," in John S. Nelson, ed., *What Should Political Theory Be Now?* (Albany: State University of New York Press, 1983), pp. 25–52 and 515–548.

2. Ludwig Wittgenstein, *Tractatus Logico-Philosophicus* (Frankfurt-Main: Suhrkamp, 1969), Nos. 6.52 and 6.53. Compare also Lord Russell's comments, written two decades later: "There remains . . . a vast field, traditionally included in philosophy, where scientific methods are inadequate. This field includes ultimate questions of value; science alone, for example, cannot prove that it is bad to enjoy the infliction of cruelty. Whatever can be known, can be known by means of science; but things which are legitimately matters of feeling lie outside its province." See Bertrand Russell, *A History of Western Philosophy* (New York: Simon and Schuster, 1945), p. 834.

3. H. Stuart Hughes, *Consciousness and Society: The Reorientation of European Social Thought, 1890–1930* (New York: Random House, 1958), pp. 401, 405. Although noting important exceptions, Dante Germino concurs in principle when he writes that "it is still true to say that over this period a harmful division of labor tended to prevail between those thinkers who collectively worked to keep alive the flame of theoretical criticism of man and society. The wholeness of great political theory, combining as it does normative and empirical considerations, was lost; thus, a philosopher like Bergson failed to draw out sufficiently the implications of his teaching for an ordered society, while a thinker like Mosca, who brilliantly described the power realities that lay behind the ideological rhetoric of society, dealt inadequately with the basic questions of philosophical anthropology." See his *Beyond Ideology: The Revival of Political Theory* (New York: Harper and Row, 1967), p. 90.

4. Martin Heidegger, *What Is Philosophy?*, trans. with introduction by William Kluback and Jean T. Wilde (New Haven: College and University Press, n.d.), pp. 64–65. (In this and in subsequent citations, the translation has been slightly altered for purposes of clarity.)

5. *What Is Philosophy?*, pp. 20–23. As Heidegger emphasizes, the embroilment must not simply be confused with a psychological or emotional stance (pp. 24–27): If "we point to the possibility that whatever philosophy deals with concerns us humans in our nature and touches or affects us, then it might be (and is worth considering) that this 'affection' has nothing whatever to do with what usually is called the domain of feelings or emotions, that is, with the irrational." For a critique of the spectator's stance compare also Richard Rorty, *Philosophy and the Mirror of Nature* (Princeton: Princeton University Press, 1979); also his *Consequences of Pragmatism* (Minneapolis: University of Minnesota Press, 1982).

6. Heidegger, *What Is Philosophy?*, pp. 28–39. See also Edmund Husserl, *The Crisis of European Sciences and Transcendental Phenomenology*, trans. with introduction by David Carr (Evanston: Northwestern University Press, 1970), pp. 273–276.

7. Heidegger, *What Is Philosophy?*, pp. 46–53, 58–59. (The reference is to Aristotle's *Metaphysics* Z 1, 1028 b 2.)

8. *What Is Philosophy?*, pp. 54–57. (The reference is to *Metaphysics* A 2, 982 b 9.)

9. *What Is Philosophy?*, pp. 58–63, 84–87.

10. *What Is Philosophy?*, pp. 56–61; Heidegger, *Identität und Differenz* (Pfullingen: Neske, 1957), p. 45. Compare also this comment: "Metaphysics only knows the clearing of Being either as the advent of presence in the 'idea' or critically as the perception of categorial representation on the basis of subjectivity. This means: the truth of Being as clearing itself remains hidden

from metaphysics." See Heidegger, *Über den Humanismus* (Frankfurt-Main: Klostermann, 1949), p. 20.

11. *What Is Philosophy?*, pp. 66-73.

12. *Identität und Differenz*, pp. 53, 56-57. Compare also this statement (p. 53): *"Being* means always and everywhere: Being of *being(s)*, a phrase containing a *genitivus obiectivus; being(s)* means always and everywhere: being(s) of *Being*, where the phrase contains a *genitivus subiectivus*. . . . It is clear only that Being of being(s) and being(s) of Being involve in every case a difference."

13. *What Is Philosophy?*, pp. 76-85. For a fuller discussion of philosophical reflection see Heidegger, *What Is Called Thinking?*, trans. Fred D. Wieck and J. Glenn Gray (New York: Harper and Row, 1968).

14. Maurice Merleau-Ponty, *In Praise of Philosophy*, trans. with preface by John Wild and James M. Edie (Evanston: Northwestern University Press, 1963), pp. 33-34.

15. *In Praise of Philosophy*, pp. 4-5, 60. See also Merleau-Ponty, *Phenomenology of Perception*, trans. Colin Smith (London: Routledge & Kegan Paul, 1962), p. xx; *The Visible and the Invisible*, trans. Alphonso Lingis (Evanston: Northwestern University Press, 1968), p. 155.

16. *In Praise of Philosophy*, pp. 30-31.

17. *In Praise of Philosophy*, pp. 33-38.

18. *In Praise of Philosophy*, pp. 38, 58, 61, 63-64.

19. Leo Strauss, *What Is Political Philosophy?* (Glencoe, Il.: Free Press, 1959), pp. 10-11.

20. *What Is Political Philosophy?*, pp. 11, 39. Regarding Platonism compare Eugene F. Miller's comment: "Strauss is an admirer of Farabi's technique and, we must suspect, a 'true Platonist' in the use he makes of historical exposition." See his "Leo Strauss: The Recovery of Political Philosophy," in Anthony de Crespigny and Kenneth Minogue, eds., *Contemporary Political Philosophies* (New York: Dodd, Mead, 1975), p. 68. Strauss has acknowledged some influence of Husserl's writings on his thought in "Philosophy as Rigorous Science and Political Philosophy," *Interpretation*, vol. 2 (1971), pp. 1-9; also in "A Giving of Accounts," *The College* (St. John's College, Annapolis, MD, April 1970), pp. 1-5.

21. *What Is Political Philosophy?*, pp. 10, 12, 14, 16.

22. *What Is Political Philosophy?*, pp. 17-18, 22, 23, 26-27.

23. *What Is Political Philosophy?*, pp. 27, 34. Compare also Strauss, *Natural Right and History* (Chicago: University of Chicago Press, 1953), pp. 126-164; "Philosophy as Rigorous Science and Political Philosophy," p. 1.

24. *What Is Political Philosophy?*, pp. 29, 32, 35, 92-94, 99. Compare also Strauss, *The City and Man* (Chicago: University of Chicago Press, 1964), p. 138; *On Tyranny*, rev. ed. (Ithaca: Cornell University Press, 1963), pp. 102-103; Strauss and Joseph Cropsey, eds., *History of Political Philosophy* (2nd ed.; Chicago: University of Chicago Press, 1972), p. 52.

25. *What Is Political Philosophy?*, pp. 93-94. As Strauss adds, however (p. 94), "This deeper meaning of 'political philosophy' tallies with its ordinary meaning, for in both cases 'political philosophy' culminates in praise of the philosophic life."

26. *What Is Political Philosophy?*, pp. 126-127, 221-222. Compare also *Natural Right and History*, pp. 82-93, 207-212; Miller, "Leo Strauss," pp. 81-83.

27. *What Is Political Philosophy?*, pp. 27–28.

28. *What Is Political Philosophy?*, pp. 115–116; *The City and Man*, p. 11. Regarding Strauss's attitude toward the classics compare Miller's comment: "What Strauss says in his own name about the nature of political philosophy coincides with the view he attributes to the classics. He is often critical of modern viewpoints, but says little about possible defects in classical political philosophy. . . . Allowing for the fact that there are important differences among the various statements of classical political philosophy, we may say that Strauss is inclined toward the classical solution." See "Leo Strauss," p. 79.

29. See Merleau-Ponty, *In Praise of Philosophy*, p. 36; also Eric Voegelin, "The Gospel and Culture," in *Jesus and Man's Hope* (Pittsburgh: Pittsburgh Theological Seminary, 1971), vol. 2, p. 74.

30. See Strauss, *What Is Political Philosophy?*, p. 28; also Paul Ricoeur, *The Symbolism of Evil*, trans. Emerson Buchanan (New York: Harper and Row, 1967), p. 306 (translation slightly altered). One should note that, in the above account, I use the term "practice" broadly to denote human activity in general, and not necessarily in the analytical sense of conventional or "rule-governed" behavior; regarding "praxis" as a synonym for political action see especially chapter 2.

31. Merleau-Ponty, "The Philosopher and Sociology," in *Signs*, trans. Richard C. McCleary (Evanston: Northwestern University Press, 1964), pp. 98, 101–102. Compare also Horkheimer's statements on this issue, contained in his inaugural lecture of 1931 as director of the Frankfurt Institute, entitled "The Present State of Social Philosophy and the Tasks of an Institute for Social Research": "The chaotic specialization of knowledge cannot be overcome through quick (theoretical) syntheses of specialized research findings; nor is an impartial empiricism to be achieved by trying to eradicate the theoretical element. Rather, the problems of empirical research and theoretical synthesis can only be tackled by a philosophy which, concerned with the general or 'essential,' provides the respective research areas with stimulating impulses, while itself remaining open enough to be impressed and modified by the progress of concrete studies." See Max Horkheimer, "Die gegenwärtige Lage der Sozialphilosophie und die Aufgaben eines Instituts für Sozialforschung," in *Frankfurter Universitätsreden*, vol. 37 (Frankfurt-Main: Englert and Schlosser, 1931), p. 11.

32. See Heidegger, "Überwindung der Metaphysik," in *Vorträge und Aufsätze* (3rd ed.; Pfullingen: Neske, 1967), vol. I, p. 72; also Voegelin, "Equivalences of Experience and Symbolization in History," in *Order and History*, vol. IV (Baton Rouge: Louisiana University Press, 1974), p. 23. In "The Philosopher and Sociology," Merleau-Ponty notes in a similar vein (p. 109), "The concept of history in its most profound sense does not shut the thinking subject up in a point of space and time; he can seem to be thus contained only to a way of thinking which is itself capable of going outside all time and place in order to see him in his time and place." The relationship between hermeneutics and "historicism" is discussed at some length in Hans-Georg Gadamer, *Truth and Method* (New York: Seabury, 1975), pp. 460–491; also in Hwa Yol Jung, *The Crisis of Political Understanding* (Pittsburgh: Duquesne University Press, 1979), pp. 145–161. Compare also Jung's essay "Leo Strauss' Conception of Political Philosophy: A Critique," *The Review of Politics*, vol. 29 (1967), pp. 492–517. For a fuller discussion of Jung's book see my review "Life-World and Politics," in *Research in Phenomenology*, vol. 11 (1981), pp. 256–263.

33. See Strauss, *What Is Political Philosophy?*, p. 10; also Michael Oakeshott, *Rationalism in Politics, and Other Essays* (New York: Basic Books, 1962), pp. 115, 117, 120, 123–125.

34. See Merleau-Ponty, *In Praise of Philosophy*, pp. 59–60; Heidegger, *Über den Humanismus*, p. 42. In Heidegger's words (p. 45), as a recollection of Being, *"Andenken"* is "a mode of doing (or participatory involvement)—but a doing which simultaneously transcends all (immediate or instrumental) action."

35. The "friend-foe" distinction was developed mainly by Carl Schmitt in *The Concept of the Political*, trans. George Schwab (New Brunswick, NJ: Rutgers University Press, 1976). The English translation contains a review of the study by Strauss, pp. 81-105. Regarding friendship, Strauss in the discussed lead essay criticized the view "held in certain circles that the basic task of political or social science is to understand the most concrete human relationship, and that relationship is called the 'I-Thou-We' relation"—a critique based on the argument that the latter relation merely supplements the Cartesian "ego"; see *What Is Political Philosophy?*, p. 28.

36. See Oakeshott, *Rationalism in Politics*, pp. 124, 169, 177. For a fuller discussion of "sympathy" compare Max Scheler, *Wesen und Formen der Sympathie* (3rd ed.; Bonn: Cohen Verlag, 1926).

37. See Aristotle, *Nichomachean Ethics*, book VIII, chapter 3 (Baltimore: Penguin Books, 1955), p. 233. See also Rorty, *Philosophy and the Mirror of Nature*, pp. 315-319, 372, 389—394; Richard Bernstein, "Philosophy in the Conversation of Mankind," *Review of Metaphysics*, vol. 33 (1980), pp. 772-774. For the notion of a "recollective ethics" see my *Twilight of Subjectivity: Contributions to a Post-Individualist Theory of Politics* (Amherst: University of Massachusetts Press, 1981), pp. 250-254.

38. As Heidegger writes, to a God conceived as *causa sui* "man can neither pray nor sacrifice. In front of the *causa sui* man can neither reverently bend his knee, nor can he make music and dance. Therefore, a god-less thinking which abandons the God of philosophy or God as *causa sui*, may perhaps be closer to God as God." See *Identität und Differenz*, pp. 64-65. Similarly, Merleau-Ponty's *In Praise of Philosophy* contains these comments (pp. 46-47): "A sensitive and open thought should not fail to guess that there is an affirmative meaning and even a presence of the spirit in this philosophical negativity. Indeed Maritain finally comes to justify the continuous criticism of idols as essential to Christianity. . . . The philosopher will only ask himself if the natural and rational concept of God as necessary being is not inevitably that of the Emperor of the world, if without this concept the Christian God would not cease to be the author of the world, and if the criticism we are now suggesting is not the philosophy which presses to the limit that criticism of false gods which Christianity has introduced into our history?"

Chapter 2

1. Max Weber, *Economy and Society*, ed. Guenther Roth and Claus Wittich (New York: Bedminster Press, 1968), vol. 1, p. 4. To be sure, Weber was aware of the difficulties inherent in his dichotomy. As he notes (pp. 4-5, 7), "The line between meaningful action and merely reactive behavior to which no subjective meaning is attached, cannot be sharply drawn empirically. A considerable part of all sociologically relevant behavior, especially purely traditional behavior, is marginal between the two. In the case of some psychophysical processes, meaningful, i.e., subjectively understandable, action is not to be found at all, in others it is discernible only to the psychologist. . . . [P]rocesses or conditions, whether they are animate or inanimate, human or non-human, are in the present sense devoid of meaning insofar as they cannot be related to an intended purpose. That is to say they are devoid of meaning if they cannot be related to action in the role of means or ends but constitute only the stimulus, the favoring or hindering circumstances."

2. Richard J. Bernstein, *Praxis and Action: Contemporary Philosophies of Human Activity* (Philadelphia: University of Pennsylvania Press, 1971), pp. x, 50-55, 110-118, 140-148, 184-187, 260-278. I bypass here the attempt, in recent analytical philosophy, to overcome dualism by treating intention as a cause of action—mainly because the attempt does not seem to me to move beyond the categories of intentionality and causality. Regarding Hegel's thought, Bernstein's summary is perceptive and eloquent (p. 34): "Philosophy's sole task is to comprehend the actual; it is the actual 'apprehended in thoughts.' But what is the actual? Our discussion of *Geist* provides the answer, for actuality is *Geist* actively realizing itself in the world. . . . *Geist* as

activity itself is *praxis*. *Theoria*, in its purest form, as philosophy, is nothing but the articulation of the rationality ingredient in *praxis*."

3. Hans-Georg Gadamer, *Truth and Method* (New York: Seabury Press, 1975), pp. 307, 310. (In these and subsequent citations I have slightly altered the translation for purposes of clarity.) As he adds (p. 301), Hegel's perspective "is not affected by the objection that it leaves no room for the experience of the Other and of the otherness of history. Rather, the life of the mind (in his sense) consists in recognizing oneself in otherness." Turning against existentialist attacks, he emphasizes (p. 307), "We shall be able to detach the notion of historical hermeneutics from the hybrid consequences of speculative idealism only if, refusing to be satisfied with irrationalist reductions or simplifications, we preserve the truth of Hegel's thought. Our task is to conceive effective-historical consciousness in such a manner that the immediacy and superiority of the text (or event) does not dissolve into a mere reflective ingredient in the consciousness of effects—that is, to conceive a reality which limits the omnipotence of reflection."

4. *Truth and Method*, pp. 310–312. As he adds (p. 311), "To me, however, he still seems dominated by the one-sidedness he criticizes; for he projects the idealized world of exact scientific inquiry into the original experience of the world, in that he makes perception, as something external and directed toward mere physical appearances, the basis for all further experience." Husserl's chief work in this area is *Experience and Judgment: Investigations in a Genealogy of Logic*, trans. James S. Churchill and Karl Ameriks (Evanston: Northwestern University Press, 1973).

5. *Truth and Method*, pp. 314–316.

6. *Truth and Method*, pp. 316–317.

7. *Truth and Method*, pp. 317–318.

8. *Truth and Method*, pp. 318–319. Gadamer's critique of Hegel, however, is subdued and somewhat ambivalent. As he observes in another context, "There is, of course, a temptation to try to avoid the self-apotheosis of thought implied in Hegel's idea of truth by denying it outright and by opposing to it, with Heidegger, the temporality and finitude of human existence, or by contradicting it as Adorno does when he asserts that the whole is not truth but falsehood. Still it can be asked whether this does justice to Hegel. . . . The all-encompassing synthesis which Hegel's speculative idealism claims to accomplish contains rather an unresolved tension—one which is reflected in the way the meaning of the word 'dialectic' shifts in Hegel." See Gadamer, *Hegel's Dialectic: Five Hermeneutical Studies*, trans. P. Christopher Smith (New Haven: Yale University Press, 1976), p. 110. For Gadamer's strong allegiance to the Hegelian legacy see also his essay "Hegel's Philosophy and Its Aftereffects until Today" and his Hegel-Price speech of 1979, "The Heritage of Hegel," both in *Reason in the Age of Science*, trans. Frederick G. Lawrence (Cambridge, MA: MIT Press, 1981), pp. 21–37, 38–68.

9. *Truth and Method*, pp. 319–320. As he adds (p. 320), in such experience "all dogmatism, which proceeds from the soaring desires of the human heart, reaches an absolute barrier. Experience teaches us to recognize reality."

10. Martin Heidegger, "The Nature of Language" (1957–1958), in *On the Way to Language*, trans. Peter D. Hertz (New York: Harper and Row, 1971), pp. 57, 73–74 (translation slightly altered). Heidegger draws on the connection in German between "*erfahren*" and "*er-fahren*."

11. Heidegger, *Hegel's Concept of Experience* (New York: Harper and Row, 1970), pp. 125–127. (In these and subsequent citations I have slightly altered the translation for purposes of clarity.) The German original, "Hegels Begriff der Erfahrung" (1942–1943), appeared first in Heidegger, *Holzwege* (Frankfurt-Main: Klostermann, 1950), pp. 105–192.

12. *Hegel's Concept of Experience*, pp. 113–114, 116, 118–120.

13. *Hegel's Concept of Experience*, pp. 119–121, 131–132. Somewhat later (p. 135) Hegel's philosophy is described as a manifestation of "onto-theology." In his essay "Hegel and Heidegger" Gadamer unduly underplays (in my view) their difference in ontological matters. Commenting on Heidegger's turn to ontology, he asks, "Does he not thereby necessarily move into a renewed proximity to Hegel—who explicitly carried the dialectic of mind beyond the forms of subjective spirit, beyond consciousness and self-consciousness?"—adding that, in any case, Heidegger's "historical self-consciousness is no less all-inclusive than Hegel's philosophy of the absolute." These comments do not prevent him from observing later, "But Heidegger's thought reflects specifically on the nature of language. Thus, in opposition to the Greek *logos*-philosophy which sustained Hegel's methodical self-consciousness he nurtures a counter-thought. His critique of dialectics takes aim at the fact that the 'speculative' or 'positive-rational'—wherever it is construed as (metaphysical) presence—remains tied to an absolute agency of apperception, be this *nous, intellectus agens,* or reason." See Gadamer, *Hegel's Dialectic*, pp. 104, 110, 115.

14. *Hegel's Concept of Experience*, pp. 128–130. Compare also Michael Gillespie, *Hegel, Heidegger and the Ground of History* (Chicago: University of Chicago Press, 1984).

15. Gadamer, *Reason in the Age of Science*, pp. 87, 89–90 (translation slightly altered; since Gadamer himself uses "praxis" I have restored this term in lieu of "practice"). Regarding the pattern in which praxis is embedded, one may note that Heidegger accentuates the ontological and Gadamer a more concrete-mundane context. Comparatively speaking, Gadamer also puts more emphasis on the aspect of prudential judgment or *phronesis* (p. 92): "Since the knowledge or thinking which guides action is essentially shaped by the concrete situations in which we have to choose what is feasible—and no learned and mastered technique can spare us the task of deliberation and decision—practical philosophy oriented toward this practical knowledge is neither theoretical science (in the style of mathematics) nor expert know-how (in the sense of a competent mastery of operational procedures or *poiesis*), but rather a science of a special kind: one which must arise out of praxis and, with all the typical generalizations it brings to light, must be related back to praxis." For a more detailed discussion of the linkage between hermeneutics and praxis in Gadamer's work see Richard J. Bernstein, "From Hermeneutics to Praxis," *Review of Metaphysics*, vol. 35 (1982), pp. 823–845.

16. Michael Oakeshott, *Experience and Its Modes* (Cambridge: Cambridge University Press, 1933), pp. 3–4, 6.

17. *Experience and Its Modes*, pp. 9, 13–14, 16, 23–24. The critique of induction seemed to be directed chiefly against "logical atomism," as is suggested by statements like these (p. 13): "In sensation (thus conceived) there can be nothing more than a bare 'this is', in which the 'this' is utterly indeterminate, without name or character, and the 'is' is limited to merely 'here' and 'now'. That there can be as much as this, is perhaps doubtful; but certainly there can be no more. . . . Sensation, because what is given in it is singular, unrelated and indeterminate, a mere 'this', implies the absence of any continuous or unified experiencing agent."

18. Among the more suggestive observations in the early study I want to pick out these: "Practice is the exercise of the will; practical thought is volition; practical experience is the world *sub specie voluntatis.*" Yet, "volition implies neither mere caprice, nor the exercise of an isolated faculty; it is a form of experience. . . . The realization of the idea in volition is believed to consist in its being translated from a world of mere ideas into an external world of things. To 'put into practice' is to transform an idea into an action. But, whether or not this is what we feel ourselves to be accomplishing in volition, it is certainly not what actually takes place. . . . Volition and action are experience; and in experience there is never the realization of a mere idea in an external world, but always the coordination and completion of a given world of ideas." See *Experience and Its Modes*, pp. 258–259.

19. Oakeshott, "Political Education," in *Rationalism in Politics, and Other Essays* (New York: Basic Books, 1962), pp. 112–115.

20. "Political Education," pp. 116, 118–120, 123–124. The aspect that desires and ideas are not simply negated but transcended and preserved in the broader fabric is evident in the statement (p. 123), "In politics, the only concrete manner of activity detectable is one in which empiricism and the ends to be pursued are recognized as dependent, alike for their existence and their operation, upon a traditional manner of behavior."

21. "Rationalism in Politics," pp. 7–8, 10–11. As defined in the essay (p. 11), rationalism meant "the assertion that what I have called practical knowledge is not knowledge at all, the assertion that, properly speaking, there is no knowledge which is not technical knowledge."

22. Oakeshott, *On Human Conduct* (Oxford: Clarendon Press, 1975), pp. 38–39, 51, 53–55, 60, 62. The middle portion of the study was devoted to a detailed discussion of the "civil condition" and especially to the differentiation between "enterprise association" and "civil association" or *polis*. In line with earlier writings, the study preserved the conception of "philosophy as experience," as is evident in a statement like this (p. 3, note 1): "My use of 'theorizing' as a transitive verb is not an inadvertence; it is the recognition of the enterprise as one of learning to understand; that is, as a transitive engagement." Despite an undeniable influence of ordinary-language philosophy, *On Human Conduct* still paid tribute to Hegel's teachings, especially his *Philosophy of Right* (pp. 257–263).

23. Hannah Arendt, *The Human Condition: A Study of the Central Dilemmas Facing Modern Man* (Garden City, NY: Anchor Books, 1959), pp. 9, 38, 41, 74, 99, 115. In terms of philosophical presuppositions the chief difference between Oakeshott and Arendt resided in the latter's indebtedness to (Jaspers's) existentialism and her relative distance from ontology, particularly Hegelian ontology. Her later writings, it is true, show a slow and cautious turn toward Hei-deggerian ontology—but a turn which did not lessen her dissatisfaction with Hegel. See Arendt, *The Life of the Mind*, 2 vols. (New York: Harcourt Brace Jovanovich, 1977–1978), where we read, for example, with reference to Hegel (vol. I, pp. 89–90, 96) that "large portions of his work can be read as a running polemic against common sense, especially the Preface to the *Phenomenology of Mind*," that his significance "lies in the fact that he, perhaps more than any other philosopher, testifies to the intramural warfare between philosophy and common sense," that with him "the philosopher becomes the organ of the Absolute Spirit, and the philosopher is Hegel himself," and the like.

24. *The Human Condition*, pp. 9–10, 119, 156–157, 159–160. As she added (p. 158), "The fact that man is capable of action means that the unexpected can be expected from him, that he is able to perform what is infinitely improbable. . . . If action as beginning corresponds to the fact of birth, if it is the actualization of the human condition of natality, then speech corresponds to the fact of distinctness and is the actualization of the human condition of plurality, that is, of living as a distinct and unique being among equals."

25. *The Human Condition*, pp. 163–164, 169.

26. *The Human Condition*, pp. 209–211, 216, 219–220.

27. Jürgen Habermas, *Theorie des kommunikativen Handelns* (Frankfurt-Main: Suhrkamp, 1981), vol. I, pp. 377–378, 382–383; translated by Thomas McCarthy under the title *The Theory of Communicative Action*, vol. 1: *Reason and the Rationalization of Society* (Boston: Beacon Press, 1984; hereafter cited as *Reason*), pp. 279–280, 283–284. One of the main tenets of the study is the dominant role of "instrumental rationality" in Weber's thought. In Habermas's words (pp. 207–208; *Reason*, pp. 143–144), "Weber analyzes the process of disenchantment in the history of religion—the necessary internal condition for the emergence of Occidental rationalism—by relying on a complex but largely opaque concept of rationality; at the same time, his analysis of social rationalization as trademark of modernity is guided by a truncated notion of instrumental rationality, a notion he shares on the one hand with Marx and on the other with Horkheimer and Adorno." Regarding the "official" construal, the study appeals primarily

to Wolfgang Schluchter, *Die Entwicklung des okzidentalen Rationalismus* (Tübingen: Mohr, 1979); translated by Guenther Roth under the title *The Rise of Western Rationalism* (Berkeley: University of California Press, 1981).

28. *Theorie des kommunikativen Handelns*, vol. 1, pp. 126–128, 137–138, 141–142; *Reason*, pp. 85–86, 91–92, 94–95. In contrast with reactive behavior and purely logical or mental "operations," Habermas defines actions (p. 144; *Reason*, p. 96) as "only such symbolic performances through which the actor . . . enters into a relationship to at least one surrounding world (including always the objective world). From these performances I distinguish bodily movements and operations which are incidentally performed in actions and which only indirectly . . . can attain the autonomy of actions." For a fuller discussion of "communicative action" see the appendix.

29. Arendt, *The Life of the Mind*, vol. II, p. 58. As she adds, however, this conception does not really "explain action, the subject matter of Aristotelian ethics, for action is not merely execution of the commands of reason; it is itself a reasonable activity, though an activity not of 'theoretical reason' but of what in the treatise *On the Soul* is called '*nous praktikos*', practical reason. In the ethical treatises it is called *phronesis*" (p. 59).

30. See Gadamer, *Truth and Method*, p. 250; Oakeshott, *On Human Conduct*, pp. 57–58. Elaborating further on the rule-governed character of practices, the latter study observes (pp. 67–68) that "rules, duties, and their like (moral principles and dogmas) are, then, passages of stringency in a moral practice. But they should not be thought of as strands of some exceptionally tough material woven into the otherwise somewhat flimsy fabric of moral association. . . . Rather, they are to be recognized as densities obtruded by the tensions of a spoken language of moral intercourse, nodal points at which a practice turns upon itself in a vortiginous movement and becomes steadier in ceasing to be adventurous. They may help to keep a practice in shape, but they do not give it its shape." Like Oakeshott, Gadamer attenuates his accent on tradition— by noting, for example (p. 250), "The fact is that tradition is always an element of freedom and of history itself. Even the most genuine and solid tradition does not persist naturally because of the inertia of existing conditions; it needs to be affirmed, embraced, cultivated." Heidegger's more ontological formulation offers even less support to a mere "traditionalism."

31. Oakeshott, *On Human Conduct*, p. 63; Arendt, *The Human Condition*, pp. 158–159.

32. Oakeshott, *On Human Conduct*, pp. 54, 59; Arendt, *The Human Condition*, pp. 25, 169. Countering the notion of ideal discourse, Oakeshott comments (pp. 63, 69–70), "The conditions which compose a moral practice are not theorems or precepts about human conduct, nor do they constitute anything so specific as a 'shared system of values'; they compose a vernacular language of colloquial intercourse. . . . The invitation to justify need not be accepted; the belief that an action is somehow morally incomplete unless it is supported by a 'justification' is a superstition. But if it is accepted, it may be responded to only in a persuasive argument which refers to the regularian quality of conduct, an argument designed to 'vindicate'. . . . Thus, to justify an action (that is, to invoke rules and rule-like principles as reasons for having chosen actions) is to embark upon a casuistical enterprise of distinctions, exceptions and obliquities related to rules in which the vitality of a spoken language of moral intercourse is impaired and its integrity compromised." Habermas, it is true, recognizes the influence of the "life-world" defined as a "background of implicit knowledge which enters into cooperative processes of interpretation *a tergo*" and of which we become aware only through the "intervention of objective problems which unsettle our natural world-view." See *Theorie des kommunikativen Handelns*, vol. 1, pp. 449–450; *Reason*, pp. 335–336.

33. Michael Theunissen, *Der Andere: Studien zur Sozialontologie der Gegenwart* (Berlin: de Gruyter, 1965), pp. 317–318, 321; translated by Christopher Macann under the title *The Other: Studies in the Social Ontology of Husserl, Heidegger, Sartre, and Buber* (Cambridge, MA: MIT Press, 1984), pp. 331–332, 336. The reference is to Martin Buber, *Schriften über das dialogische Prinzip* (Heidelberg: Schneider, 1954), pp. 15, 78. One may recall in this context that Nietzsche's Zarathustra, as

the teacher of "overcoming," is also the teacher or "advocate of suffering"; see Walter Kaufmann, ed., *The Portable Nietzsche* (New York: Viking Press, 1968), p. 328.

34. See Heidegger, *Hegel's Concept of Experience*, pp. 146–147; Arendt, *The Human Condition*, p. 210; Gadamer, *Reason in the Age of Science*, p. 87.

Chapter 3

1. Compare, for example, George E. G. Catlin, *The Science and Method of Politics* (New York: Knopf, 1927); Charles E. Merriam, *Political Power* (New York: McGraw-Hill, 1934); Harold D. Lasswell and Abraham Kaplan, *Power and Society, a Framework for Political Inquiry* (New Haven: Yale University Press, 1950); Robert A. Dahl, *Modern Political Analysis* (Englewood Cliffs, NJ: Prentice-Hall, 1963).

2. Steven Lukes, *Power: A Radical View* (London: Macmillan, 1974), pp. 27–28. For Weber's definition see Max Weber, *Economy and Society*, ed. Guenther Roth and Claus Wittich (New York: Bedminster Press, 1968), vol. 1, p. 53.

3. For a perceptive study by a political theorist pointing to the relevance of Foucault's work (without specifically concentrating on power) see Michael J. Shapiro, *Language and Political Understanding: The Politics of Discursive Practices* (New Haven: Yale University Press, 1981), especially chapter 5; also my review of that book, "Language and Praxis," in *Human Studies*, vol. 5 (1982), pp. 249–259.

4. "Afterword," in Michel Foucault, *Power/Knowledge: Selected Interviews and Other Writings 1972–1977*, ed. Colin Gordon (New York: Pantheon Books, 1980), pp. 234–235, 237. As Gordon correctly remarks (p. 234), "Within the horizon of contemporary political theory it is difficult indeed to entertain the possibility of any basic change in our conceptualization of power. Outstanding issues in this area are treated as matters of nuance, of the synthesis and harmonization of alternative approaches, the equitable administration of complementary insights."

5. Alan Sheridan, *Michel Foucault: The Will to Truth* (London: Tavistock Publications, 1980), pp. 139, 183; Hubert L. Dreyfus and Paul Rabinow, *Michel Foucault: Beyond Structuralism and Hermeneutics* (Chicago: University of Chicago Press, 1982), pp. 114, 185; Nancy Fraser, "Foucault on Modern Power: Empirical Insights and Normative Confusions," *Praxis International*, vol. 1 (1981), p. 272. Compare also Mark Philip, "Foucault on Power: A Problem in Radical Translation?" *Political Theory*, vol. 11 (1983), pp. 29–52; Charles Taylor, "Foucault on Freedom and Truth," *Political Theory*, vol. 12 (1984), pp. 152–183.

6. As Merleau-Ponty writes at one point, "Whatever one's philosophical or even theological position, a society is not the temple of value-idols that figure on the front of its monuments or in its constitutional scrolls; the value of a society is the value it places upon man's relation to man." See *Humanism and Terror*, trans. John O'Neill (Boston: Beacon Press, 1969), p. xiv. Compare also Agnes Heller, *Das Alltagsleben* (Frankfurt-Main: Suhrkamp, 1975).

7. Lectures held at Stanford University in October 1979; cited in Dreyfus and Rabinow, *Michel Foucault*, p. 138.

8. "Truth and Power," in Foucault, *Power/Knowledge*, pp. 115–116. The French versions of *Madness and Civilization* and *The Birth of the Clinic* were first published in 1961 and 1963, respectively.

9. "Truth and Power" and "The History of Sexuality," in Foucault, *Power/Knowledge*, pp. 118, 183–184. Juxtaposing to repression the "productive aspect of power," the first interview added (p. 119), "In defining the effects of power as repression, one adopts a purely juridical conception

of such power, one identifies power with a law which says no; power is taken above all as carrying the force of a prohibition. Now I believe that this is a wholly negative, narrow, skeletal conception of power, one which has been curiously widespread. If power were never anything but repressive, if it never did anything but to say no, do you really think one would be brought to obey it?. . . . It needs to be considered as a productive network which runs through the whole social body much more than as a negative instance whose function is repression. In *Discipline and Punish* what I wanted to show was how, from the seventeenth and eighteenth centuries onwards, there was a veritable technological take-off in the productivity of power." The first French versions of *Discipline and Punish* and *The History of Sexuality* were published in 1975 and 1976, respectively.

10. "Two Lectures," in Foucault, *Power/Knowledge*, p. 94.

11. *Power/Knowledge*, pp. 88–89.

12. *Power/Knowledge*, pp. 89, 95.

13. *Power/Knowledge*, pp. 89–92, 95. As Foucault adds (p. 92), "It is obvious that all my work in recent years has been couched in the schema of struggle-repression, and it is this . . . which I have now been forced to reconsider, both because it is still insufficiently elaborated at a whole number of points, and because I believe that these two notions of repression and war must themselves be considerably modified if not ultimately abandoned."

14. *Power/Knowledge*, pp. 95–96, 104–105.

15. *Power/Knowledge*, pp. 106–107.

16. *Power/Knowledge*, pp. 96, 102.

17. *Power/Knowledge*, pp. 97–98. Countering the traditional "pluralist" stress on individual or group designs, Foucault added (p. 98) that "individuals are the vehicles of power, not its points of application. . . . In fact, it is already one of the prime effects of power that certain bodies, certain gestures, certain discourses, certain desires, come to be identified and constituted as individuals. The individual, that is, is not the vis-à-vis of power; it is, I believe, one of its prime effects." As he observes at another point, "What I want to show is how power relations can materially penetrate the body in depth, without depending even on the mediation of the subject's own representations. If power takes hold on the body, this is not through its having first to be interiorized in people's consciousnesses. There is a network or circuit of bio-power, or somato-power, which acts as the formative matrix of sexuality itself as the historical and cultural phenomenon within which we seem at once to recognize and lose ourselves. . . . In general terms, I believe that power is not built up out of 'wills' (individual or collective), nor is it derivable from interests. Power is constructed and functions on the basis of particular powers, myriad effects of power. It is this complex domain that must be studied." See "The History of Sexuality," in *Power/Knowledge*, pp. 186, 188.

18. "Two Lectures," *Power/Knowledge*, pp. 99–101.

19. *Power/Knowledge*, p. 108.

20. Both this danger and the fact-value dilemma are stressed in Nancy Fraser's essay cited in note 5. The objectivism of positivist science, one might add, is completely unable to overcome the subject-object dualism—which runs counter to Foucault's central ambition. As he observes at one point, his endeavor "has nothing at all to do with a disqualification of the speculative dimension which opposes to it, in the name of some kind of scientism, the rigor of well established knowledges. It is not therefore via an empiricism that the genealogical project unfolds, nor even via a positivism in the ordinary sense of that term. . . . Genealogies are

therefore not positivistic returns to a more careful or exact form of science. They are precisely anti-sciences." See "Two Lectures," *Power/Knowledge*, p. 83.

21. Foucault, "The Subject and Power," in Dreyfus and Rabinow, *Michel Foucault: Beyond Structuralism and Hermeneutics*, pp. 209, 217.

22. "The Subject and Power," pp. 217–219 (translation slightly altered). In distinguishing between the three dimensions, Foucault points to Habermas's similar differentiation between labor, communication, and domination (or between "technical," "practical," and "emancipatory" interests) as outlined in the latter's *Knowledge and Human Interests*, adding (p. 218, note 1), "I do not think that he sees in them three separate domains, but rather three 'transcendentals'." Despite this affinity, subsequent arguments quickly reveal the gulf separating the two authors: while Foucault seeks to preserve the integrity of power relations, Habermas tends to obfuscate this dimension either by submerging it in external control or coercion or by subordinating it to the goal of intersubjective communication governed by standards of rationality and strict reciprocity.

23. Foucault, "The Subject and Power," pp. 219–220. As he adds (p. 220), "Perhaps the equivocal nature of the term *conduct* is one of the best aids for coming to terms with the specificity of power relations. For to 'conduct' (*conduire*) is at the same time to 'lead' others . . . and a way of behaving within a more or less open field of possibilities."

24. "The Subject and Power," p. 220. "In itself," Foucault continues, "the exercise of power is not violence; nor is it a consent which, implicitly, is renewable."

25. "The Subject and Power," p. 221. Compare in this context also Foucault, "Governmentality," trans. R. Braidotti, in *Ideology and Consciousness*, vol. 6 (1979), pp. 5–21.

26. "The Subject and Power," p. 221 (translation slightly altered); for the list of criteria characterizing contemporary modes of resistance see pp. 211–212. To highlight the interplay of power and freedom, Foucault (pp. 221–222) invokes the classical notion of the "agon," a notion extolled by Nietzsche and which transcends both pure enmity and conformity (or consensus): "At the very heart of the power relationship, and constantly provoking it, are the resistance of the will and the intransigence of freedom. Rather than speaking of freedom as an essence, it would be better to speak of an 'agonism'—a relationship which is at the same time reciprocal incitation and struggle; less a direct hostility which paralyzes both sides than a permanent provocation." As he adds (p. 233), responding again to the charge of determinism, "To say that there cannot be a society without power relations is not to say either that those which are established are necessary or, in any case, that power constitutes a fatality at the heart of societies, such that it cannot be undermined. Instead I would say that the analysis, elaboration, and questioning of power relations and the 'agonism' between power relations and the intransitivity of freedom is a permanent political task inherent in all social existence."

27. "The Subject and Power," p. 225.

28. "The Subject and Power," pp. 225–226. As he continues (p. 226), "What makes the domination of a group, or a class, together with the resistance and revolts which that domination comes up against, a central phenomenon in the history of societies is that they manifest in a massive and universalizing form, at the level of the whole social body, the locking together of power relations with relations of strategy and the results proceeding from their interaction."

29. See Hannah Arendt, *The Human Condition: A Study of the Central Dilemmas Facing Modern Man* (Garden City, NY: Anchor Books, 1959), pp. 35–45 (on "the rise of the social"), 84–95 (on "labor and life" and "labor and fertility"), 210–211 (on "sovereignty"), and 286–292 (on "life as the highest good" and "the victory of the *animal laborans*").

30. Lukes, *Power: A Radical View*, pp. 28–31.

31. Jürgen Habermas, "Hannah Arendt's Communications Concept of Power," *Social Research*, vol. 44 (1977), pp. 3–6, 8–9 (translation slightly altered). Regarding the linkage between Weber and functionalism Habermas notes (p. 5), "Talcott Parsons understands by power the general capacity of a social system 'to get things done in the interest of collective goals.' The mobilization of consent produces the power which is transformed into binding decisions through the exploitation of social resources. . . . [In this manner] he repeats at the level of systems theory the same teleological concept of power (i.e., as potential to realize goals) that Weber pursued at the level of action theory." The German version of the essay appeared first in *Merkur*, No. 10 (1976), pp. 946–960.

32. "Hannah Arendt's Communications Concept of Power," pp. 15, 17–18, 21. Habermas objects not only to Arendt's exclusion of strategic coercion, but also to her segregation of politics from social and economic life (pp. 14–15): "Arendt stylizes the image she has of the Greek polis to the essence of politics as such. This is the background to her favored conceptual dichotomies between the public and the private, between state and economy, freedom and welfare, political-practical activity and production—dichotomies which modern bourgeois society and the modern state escape. . . . I only want to indicate the curious perspective Arendt adopts: a state which is relieved of the administrative processing of social problems; a politics which is cleansed of social-economic issues; an institutionalization of public liberty which is independent of the organization of welfare; a radical political democracy which does not disturb or infiltrate the domain of social repression—this path is inconceivable for *any* modern society." For similar criticisms compare Richard J. Bernstein, "Hannah Arendt: The Ambiguities of Theory and Practice," in Terence Ball, ed., *Political Theory and Praxis: New Perspectives* (Minneapolis: University of Minnesota Press, 1977), pp. 141–158; Bhikhu Parekh, "Hannah Arendt's Critique of Marx," in Melvyn A. Hill, ed., *Hannah Arendt: The Recovery of the Public World* (New York: St. Martin's Press, 1979), pp. 67–100.

33. Peter Fuss notices, correctly, in Arendt's work a mingling of an "agonal" with a consensual conception of politics; see his "Hannah Arendt's Conception of Political Community," in Hill, ed., *Hannah Arendt: The Recovery of the Public World*, pp. 171–172. In part, this ambivalence seems to be due to Arendt's indebtedness to Jaspers's theory of existential "communication"; compare in this context my "Kommunikation und Gemeinschaft," in Wolfgang Kuhlmann and Dietrich Böhler, eds., *Kommunikation und Reflexion: Antworten auf Karl-Otto Apel* (Frankfurt-Main: Suhrkamp, 1982), pp. 191–220.

34. Habermas, "Hannah Arendt's Communications Concept of Power," pp. 22–23. Interpreting her notion of "promising" in a quasi-rationalist vein, he claims at the end (p. 24) that Arendt "retreats into the traditional contract theory of natural law." See also Arendt, "Truth and Politics," in Peter Laslett and W. G. Runciman, eds., *Philosophy, Politics, and Society*, 3rd Series (Oxford: Blackwell, 1967), pp. 104–133.

35. Arendt, *The Human Condition*, pp. 155–156, 158, 218. Compare also her comment (p. 19) that, in the Greek view, "the task and potential greatness of mortals lie in their ability to produce things—works and deeds and words—which would deserve to be and, at least to a degree, are at home in everlastingness."

36. *The Human Condition*, pp. 29, 179–180, 210. As she adds (pp. 183, 197–198), "Perhaps nothing in our history has been so short-lived as trust in power, nothing more lasting than the Platonic and Christian distrust of the splendor attending its space of appearance, nothing—finally in the modern age—more common than the conviction that 'power corrupts. . . . The most obvious salvation from the dangers of plurality is monarchy, or one-man-rule, in its many varieties, from outright tyranny of one against all to benevolent despotism and to those forms of democracy in which the many form a collective body so that the people 'is many in one' and constitute themselves as 'monarch.' . . . The greater part of political philosophy since Plato could easily be interpreted as various attempts to find theoretical foundations and practical ways for an escape from politics altogether. The hallmark of all such escapes is the concept

of rule, that is, the notion that men can lawfully and politically live together only when some are entitled to command and the others forced to obey." I am aware of Arendt's ambivalence on this score, evident, for example, in her comment (p. 220), "Sovereignty, which is always spurious if claimed by an isolated single entity, be it the individual entity of the person or the collective entity of a nation, assumes, in the case of many men mutually bound by promises, a certain limited reality." For more detailed elaborations on "power" and "violence" (and also on "strength," "force," and "authority") see Arendt, "On Violence," in *Crises of the Republic* (New York: Harcourt Brace Jovanovich, 1972), pp. 105–198.

37. The aspect of potency is recognized by Arendt when she writes, referring to the term "power," "The word itself, its Greek equivalent *dynamis*, like the Latin *potentia* with its various modern derivatives or the German *Macht* (which derives from *mögen* and *möglich*, not from *machen*), indicates its 'potential' character. Power is always, as we should say, a power potential and not an unchangeable, measurable, and reliable entity like force of strength." See *The Human Condition*, p. 179. In several passages Heidegger presents "Being" itself as an "agon" or contest—but a contest which, pursued in its integrity, does not entail enmity but rather a "loving struggle." See, for example, "The Origin of the Work of Art" and "Letter on Humanism," in David F. Krell, ed., *Martin Heidegger: Basic Writings* (New York: Harper and Row, 1977), pp. 172–173, 181, 216, 237, and for the German versions: "Der Ursprung des Kunstwerks," in Heidegger, *Holzwege* (4th ed.; Frankfurt-Main: Klostermann, 1963), pp. 37–38, 51; *Über den Humanismus* (Frankfurt-Main: Klostermann, 1949), pp. 24, 43.

38. Commenting on Heidegger, Derrida writes in a remarkable essay (unfortunately ignored by too many political theorists), "The thought of Being—which alone can 'let' others 'be' in their truth, thus making room for dialogue and face-to-face encounter—is thus as close as possible to nonviolence. We do not say pure nonpower: like pure violence, pure nonpower is a contradictory concept." See Jacques Derrida, "Violence and Metaphysics," in *Writing and Difference*, trans. Alan Bass (Chicago: University of Chicago Press, 1978), p. 146 (translation slightly altered). For a more detailed discussion of Heidegger's views on power and domination see Hermann Mörchen, *Macht und Herrschaft im Denken von Heidegger und Adorno* (Stuttgart: Klett-Cotta, 1980).

Chapter 4

1. For a brief synopsis of events see David F. Krell, ed., *Martin Heidegger: Basic Writings* (New York: Harper and Row, 1977), pp. 27–28, and the literature cited there; also Krell's "Analysis," in Heidegger, *Nietzsche*, vol. 4: *Nihilism*, trans. Frank A. Capuzzi (New York: Harper and Row, 1982), pp. 263–269. Compare also George Steiner, *Heidegger* (Glasgow: Fontana-Collins, 1978), pp. 19–20, 111–121.

2. Otto Pöggeler, *Philosophie und Politik bei Heidegger* (Freiburg-Munich: Alber, 1972), pp. 109, 111, note 2. In David Krell's words, "Weary of the political divisiveness, economic crises, and general demoralization that plagued postwar Germany, many German academics—Heidegger among them—supported the Nazi Party's call for a German 'resurgence'." *Martin Heidegger: Basic Writings*, p. 27.

3. Hannah Arendt, "Martin Heidegger at Eighty," in Michael Murray, ed., *Heidegger and Modern Philosophy: Critical Essays* (New Haven: Yale University Press, 1978), pp. 301–303. For Max Müller's remarks see Bernard Willms, "Politik als Geniestreich?" in *Martin Heidegger: Fragen an sein Werk; Ein Symposium* (Stuttgart: Reclam, 1977), p. 16.

4. Willms, "Politik als Geniestreich?," p. 17. In a similar vein Krell comments, "It is of course convenient to decide that Heidegger's shortlived but intense involvement in political despotism 'taints' his work: that is the fastest way to rid the shelves of all sorts of difficult authors from

Plato to Nietzsche and to make righteous indignation even more satisfying than it normally is. But neither does it do to close the eyes and stop up the ears to the dismal matter." See *Martin Heidegger: Basic Writings*, p. 28, note 31. Some of these comments seem squarely applicable to Mark Blitz, *Heidegger's Being and Time and the Possibility of Political Philosophy* (Ithaca: Cornell University Press, 1981).

5. François Fédier, "Trois attaques contre Heidegger," *Critique*, No. 234 (1966); see also Beda Alleman, "Martin Heidegger und die Politik," in Otto Pöggeler, ed., *Heidegger: Perspektiven zur Deutung seines Werks* (2nd ed.; Cologne-Berlin: Kiepenheuer and Witsch, 1970), pp. 252, 255. Fédier's and Alleman's views are supported by Krell, who writes, "By the beginning of the new year (1934) Heidegger had recognized the impossibility of the situation and the bankruptcy of his hopes for resurgence. In lectures and seminars he began to criticize at first cautiously and then more stridently the Nazi ideology, of *Blut and Boden* chauvinism that preached a racist origin for even poetry." See *Martin Heidegger: Basic Writings*, pp. 27–28. Compare also Steiner, *Heidegger*, p. 116.

6. Leo Strauss, "Philosophy as Rigorous Science and Political Philosophy," *Interpretation*, vol. 2 (1972), pp. 2, 5.

7. Compare, for example, his comments: "Philosophy is essentially not possession of truth, but quest for the truth. The distinctive trait of the philosopher is that 'he knows nothing'. . . . For moderation is not a virtue of thought. Plato likens philosophy to madness, the very opposite of sobriety or moderation; thought must not be moderate, but fearless, not to say shameless." See Strauss, "What Is Political Philosophy?" in *What Is Political Philosophy? and Other Studies* (Glencoe, IL: Free Press, 1959), pp. 11, 32.

8. See Jacob Klein and Leo Strauss, "A Giving of Accounts," *The College* (St. John's College, Annapolis, MD, April 1970), p. 3; also Strauss, *What Is Political Philosophy?*, p. 27.

9. Jürgen Habermas, *Philosophisch-politische Profile* (Frankfurt-Main: Suhrkamp, 1971), pp. 81–82; translated by Frederick G. Lawrence as *Philosophical-Political Profiles* (Cambridge, MA: MIT Press, 1983), pp. 57–58.

10. Pöggeler, *Philosophie und Politik bei Heidegger*, p. 145, note 12. Pöggeler gives the French original of Heidegger's comments at Thor (citing from "Séminaire tenu au Thor en septembre 1969 par le Professeur Martin Heidegger"). A similar periodization is also used by Herrmann Mörchen in his *Macht und Herrschaft im Denken von Heidegger und Adorno* (Stuttgart: Klett-Cotta, 1980).

11. Pöggeler, *Philosophie und Politik bei Heidegger*, p. 145, note 12.

12. See Beat Sitter, "Zur Möglichkeit dezisionistischer Auslegung von Heideggers ersten Schriften," *Zeitschrift für philosophische Forschung*, vol. 24 (1970), pp. 516–535; Christian Graf von Krockow, *Die Entscheidung: Eine Untersuchung über Ernst Jünger, Carl Schmitt, Martin Heidegger*, Göttinger Abhandlungen zur Soziologie, vol. 3 (Stuttgart: Enke, 1958); Herbert Marcuse, "Beiträge zu einer Phänomenologie des historischen Materialismus," *Philosophische Hefte*, No. 1 (1928), pp. 45–68, trans. as "Contributions to a Phenomenology of Historical Materialism," *Telos*, No. 4 (1969), pp. 5–33. Compare also Gerold Prauss, *Erkennen und Handeln in Heidegger's "Sein u. Zeit"* (Freiburg-Munich: Alber, 1977).

13. See Hannah Arendt, *The Human Condition* (Garden City, NY: Anchor Books, 1959); Alexander Schwan, *Politische Philosophie im Denken Heideggers* (Cologne-Oplanden: Westdeutscher Verlag, 1965). For a similar criticism see also Werner Marx, *Heidegger and the Tradition*, trans. Theodore Kisiel and Murray Greene (Evanston: Northwestern University Press, 1971).

14. Pöggeler, *Philosophie und Politik bei Heidegger*, pp. 44–45; Hans Köchler, *Skepsis und Gesellschaftskritik im Denken Martin Heideggers* (Meisenheim: Anton Hain, 1978).

15. Krockow, *Die Entscheidung*, pp. 2, 76, 123.

16. Schwan, *Politische Philosophie im Denken Heideggers*, pp. 86, 144–145. For a critique of Schwan's approach compare Pöggeler's comments: "To attempt to develop Heidegger's political philosophy on the basis of the 'Art-Work' lectures—without explicitly pinpointing the place of these lectures in the overall opus—this means to accentuate in an excessive way the 'romantic' phase of Heidegger's thought as the decisive one." See *Philosophie und Politik bei Heidegger*, pp. 122–123, note 5. On the other hand, some romantic-Promethean tendencies are indeed evident in Eugen Fink's *Traktat über die Gewalt des Menschen* (Frankfurt-Main: Klostermann, 1974), a study loosely inspired by Heideggerian arguments.

17. Ernst Tugendhat, *Der Wahrheitsbegriff bei Husserl und Heidegger* (Berlin: Walter de Gruyter, 1967), pp. 383, 393.

18. Martin Heidegger, *Sein und Zeit* (11th ed.; Tübingen: Niemeyer, 1967), pp. 296–297, 301 (section 60). For a perceptive and instructive discussion of "resoluteness" and freedom in the context of *Being and Time* see Charles M. Sherover, "Heidegger and Practical Reason," in Ronald Bruzina and Bruce Wilshire, eds., *Phenomenology: Dialogues and Bridges* (Albany: State University of New York Press, 1982), pp. 23–36.

19. Heidegger, *Sein und Zeit*, pp. 298, 300 (section 60).

20. "On the Essence of Truth," in Krell, *Martin Heidegger: Basic Writings*, pp. 125–126. (In these and subsequent citations I have slightly altered the translation for purposes of clarity.) For the German original see "Vom Wesen der Wahrheit" in Heidegger, *Wegmarken* (Frankfurt-Main: Klostermann, 1967), pp. 81–82.

21. "On the Essence of Truth," pp. 127, 130; *Wegmarken*, pp. 83–84, 86.

22. "On the Essence of Truth," pp. 128–130; *Wegmarken*, pp. 84–86.

23. Heidegger, *Vom Wesen der menschlichen Freiheit: Einleitung in die Philosophie* (Gesamtausgabe vol. 31), ed. Hartmut Tietjen (Frankfurt-Main: Klostermann, 1982), pp. 7, 30–33.

24. *Vom Wesen der menschlichen Freiheit*, pp. 22, 24–25, 28–29.

25. *Vom Wesen der menschlichen Freiheit*, pp. 21, 137, 139.

26. *Vom Wesen der menschlichen Freiheit*, pp. 198–199, 209–210, 300–302. As Heidegger adds (p. 303), "To let an encounter with beings happen and to comport oneself to beings in a mode of openness or disclosedness is possible only on the basis of freedom. Thus, *freedom is the condition of possibility of the disclosure of the Being of beings and of the understanding of Being.*"

27. *Vom Wesen der menschlichen Freiheit*, pp. 134–135, 303.

28. Heidegger, *Schellings Abhandlung Über das Wesen der menschlichen Freiheit (1809)*, ed. Hildegard Feick (Tübingen: Niemeyer, 1971), pp. 2, 108.

29. *Schellings Abhandlung*, pp. 13, 118. As Heidegger adds (p. 12), the "need of philosophy" can never be demonstrated so long as we treat it merely as one enterprise among others— that is, "so long as we merely pay lip service to philosophy and do not allow it to transform us so that we might see that philosophy is possible only on the basis of freedom and that its pursuit is an act of utter freedom." For more detailed discussions of the relation between Heidegger and Schelling compare Parvis Emad, "Heidegger on Schelling's Conception of Freedom," *Man and World*, vol. 8 (1975), pp. 152–174; Michael G. Vater, "Heidegger and Schelling: The Finitude of Being," *Idealistic Studies*, vol. 5 (1975), pp. 20–58.

30. *Schellings Abhandlung*, pp. 10-11.

31. *Schellings Abhandlung*, pp. 83, 90-95, 104-105.

32. *Schellings Abhandlung*, pp. 109, 116. According to both Schelling and Heidegger, the focus on "real" freedom seen as the "capacity for good and evil" is a move beyond the confines of idealist philosophy. As Heidegger adds (p. 122), the problem of evil links up with the question of the relation between Being and non-being (or nothingness): more precisely, the question of the "being of non-being"—where non-being is "not simply nothing but rather something stupendous, the most stupendous dimension in the essence of Being."

33. *Schellings Abhandlung*, pp. 129-130, 169-170.

34. *Schellings Abhandlung*, pp. 171-172, 176, 182, 189-190. As Heidegger's commentary makes clear (pp. 177-180, 184-186), capability "for good and evil" does not simply yield, or coincide with, indifference; nor is preference for one over the other merely the result of arbitrary choice or an act of "free will." Rather, such preference has in turn to be seen as conditioned by an ontological "inclination"; differently put: capability (*Vermögen*) is grounded in a steadily nurtured liking or affection (*Mögen*) which is neither arbitrary nor imposed as an external destiny. Thus, inclination adumbrates the reconciliation of freedom and necessity.

35. "The Question Concerning Technology," in Krell, *Martin Heidegger: Basic Writings*, pp. 305-307 (translation slightly altered). For the German version see "Die Frage nach der Technik," in Heidegger, *Vorträge und Aufsätze* (3rd ed.; Pfullingen: Neske, 1967), vol. 1, pp. 24-25.

36. "Building Dwelling Thinking," in Krell, *Martin Heidegger: Basic Writings*, pp. 326-327 (translation slightly altered). For the German version see "Bauen Wohnen Denken," in Heidegger, *Vorträge und Aufsätze*, vol. 2, p. 23.

37. For the notion of an ontological ethics grounded in "ethos" see my *Twilight of Subjectivity: Contributions to a Post-Individualist Theory of Politics* (Amherst: University of Massachusetts Press, 1981), pp. 250-254. For a sustained critique of the category of causality see Heidegger, *Der Satz vom Grund* (Pfullingen: Neske, 1957). Compare also Foucault's comment, "History has long since abandoned its attempts to understand events in terms of cause and effect in the formless unity of some great evolutionary process." See Michel Foucault, "The Discourse on Language," in *The Archaeology of Knowledge*, trans. A. M. Sheridan Smith (New York: Pantheon, 1972), p. 230.

38. Hannah Arendt, *Between Past and Future: Six Exercises in Political Thought* (New York: Meridian Books, 1963), pp. 144-146.

39. *Between Past and Future*, pp. 148-149, 164-165. For a similar attack on "sovereignty" see *The Human Condition*, pp. 210-211; and for a fuller treatment of "willing," Arendt's *The Life of the Mind*, vol. 2: *Willing* (New York: Harcourt Brace Jovanovich, 1978).

40. Maurice Merleau-Ponty, *Phenomenology of Perception*, trans. Colin Smith (London: Routledge & Kegan Paul, 1962), pp. 438, 448; *The Visible and the Invisible*, trans. Alphonso Lingis, ed. Claude Lefort (Evanston, IL: Northwestern University Press, 1968), p. 263. As *Phenomenology of Perception* adds, with reference to alternative modes of being (pp. 438-439, 442), "But either this total choice is never mentioned, since it is the silent upsurge of our being in the world, in which case it is not clear in what sense it could be said to be ours, since this freedom glides over itself and is the equivalent of fate—or else our choice of ourselves is a genuine choice, a conversion involving our whole existence. In this case, however, there is presupposed a previous acquisition which the choice sets out to modify and it founds a new tradition: which leads us to ask whether the perpetual severance in terms of which we initially defined freedom is not simply the negative aspect of our universal commitment to a world. . . . The rationalist's dilemma: either the free act is possible or it is not—either the event originates in me or is

imposed on me from outside, does not apply to our relations with the world and with our past."

Chapter 5

1. For a critique of the notion see, for example, Reiner Schürmann, "Anti-Humanism: Reflections on the Turn towards the Post-Modern Epoch," *Man and World*, vol. 12 (1979), pp. 160-177; and for a defense Mikel Dufrenne, *Pour L'Homme* (Paris: Seuil, 1968). Compare also my *Twilight of Subjectivity: Contributions to a Post-Individualist Theory of Politics* (Amherst: University of Massachusetts Press, 1981), pp. 8-37; Anthony Giddens, *Central Problems in Social Theory* (Berkeley: University of California Press, 1979), pp. 9-48; and my review of Giddens's book under the title "Agency and Structure," *Philosophy of the Social Sciences*, vol. 12 (1982), pp. 427-438.

2. Jean-Paul Sartre, "Existentialism Is a Humanism" (1946), trans. Philip Mairet, in Walter Kaufmann, ed., *Existentialism from Dostoevsky to Sartre* (New York: Meridian Books, 1956), pp. 303, 310. Rejecting ideological surrogates, he observed (p. 310) that "an existentialist will never take man as the end, since man is still to be determined. And we have no right to believe that humanity is something to which we could set up a cult, after the manner of August Comte. The cult of humanity ends in Comtian humanism, shut-in upon itself, and—this must be said—in Fascism. We do not want a humanism like that."

3. Charles C. Lemert, *Sociology and the Twilight of Man: Homocentrism and Discourse in Sociological Theory* (Carbondale, IL: Southern Illinois University Press, 1979), pp. 13, 16, 18-19.

4. Robert C. Tucker, "Introduction," in Tucker, ed., *The Marx-Engels Reader* (New York: W. W. Norton, 1972), p. xxii. A similar emphasis on continuity, despite the recognition of a persistent "process of self-criticism," can be found in Richard J. Bernstein, *Praxis and Action: Contemporary Philosophies of Human Activity* (Philadelphia: University of Pennsylvania Press, 1971), pp. 41 (note 42), 55-57. For some studies emphasizing the early writings compare, for example, Erich Fromm, *Marx's Concept of Man* (New York: Ungar, 1961) and Leszek Kolakowski, *Toward a Marxist Humanism: Essays on the Left Today* (New York: Grove Press, 1968); for an opposing view see Louis Althusser, *For Marx* (New York: Vintage Books, 1970).

5. Marx's misgivings are clearly spelled out in his "Theses on Feuerbach" (written in the spring of 1845), especially in Theses IV-VII. Thus, he writes (VI, VII), "Feuerbach resolves the religious essence into the human essence. But the human essence is no abstraction inherent in each single individual. In its reality it is the ensemble of the social relations. . . . Feuerbach, consequently, does not see that the 'religious sentiment' is itself a *social product*, and that the abstract individual whom he analyzes belongs in reality to a particular form of society." See Tucker, *The Marx-Engels Reader*, p. 109.

6. The article, written in the form of a letter to Arnold Ruge, was published in *Deutsch-Französische Jahrbücher* in 1844; see Tucker, *The Marx-Engels Reader*, pp. 9-10.

7. See "Contribution to the Critique of Hegel's *Philosophy of Right*: Introduction," in Tucker, *The Marx-Engels Reader*, pp. 11-12. Written in 1843, this introduction was published in *Deutsch-Französische Jahrbücher* in the following year. The emphatically humanist outlook is also evident in this later passage in the introduction (p. 18): "To be radical is to grasp things by the root; but for man the root is man himself. . . . The criticism of religion ends with the doctrine that *man is the supreme being for man*."

8. Ibid., p. 22. The conclusion of the introduction returned to the humanist theme, noting (p. 23) that emancipation is "only possible in practice if one adopts the point of view of that theory according to which man is the highest being for man."

9. The term "species-being," designating a generic human nature, was taken over by Marx from Feuerbach—although his writings from the beginning accentuated the term's social and historical connotations. On Marx's use of "species-being" and its progressive replacement by class struggle and proletarian class activity see Bernstein, *Praxis and Action*, pp. 66–69.

10. See "On the Jewish Question," in Tucker, *The Marx-Engels Reader*, pp. 37, 43–45. Written in the fall of 1843, the essay appeared in *Deutsch-Französische Jahrbücher* in 1844.

11. See "Economic and Philosophic Manuscripts of 1844," in Tucker, *The Marx-Engels Reader*, pp. 89–90, 99 (translation slightly altered).

12. Ibid., pp. 57–58, 61–62, 70, 98. As Bernstein comments, "Marx's 'depth' reading of Hegel shows that the *Phenomenology* is not properly a phenomenology of *Geist*, but of *man*. The point here is the way in which Marx transforms the meaning of the activity of *Geist*, of its self-realization in history. This is in reality a concealed way of describing and criticizing the 'development of man as a process.' 'Process' is not a general vague term: it refers to human activity in the form of work." See *Praxis and Action*, p. 40.

13. See *The Holy Family: A Critique of Critical Criticism*, in Tucker, *The Marx-Engels Reader*, pp. 104–105; also *The German Ideology*, in Tucker, *The Marx-Engels Reader*, pp. 113–114, 118, 155. As Marx and Engels added (p. 156), "Only at this stage does self-activity coincide with material life, which corresponds to the development of individuals into complete individuals and the casting-off of all natural limitations."

14. See Bernstein, *Praxis and Action*, p. 58; also *Capital* in Tucker, *The Marx-Engels Reader*, pp. 216–217, 320.

15. See "Traditional and Critical Theory" (1937) and "Postscript" (of same year) in Max Hork-heimer, *Critical Theory: Selected Essays*, trans. Matthew J. O'Connell et al. (New York: Herder and Herder, 1972), p. 244. (In these and subsequent citations the translation is slightly altered for purposes of clarity.)

16. Ibid., pp. 197, 199, 207, 209.

17. Ibid., pp. 204, 210, 216–217, 229, 241, 244–255. Compare also this comment (pp. 198–199): "The real self-knowledge of contemporary man is accomplished not in a mathematical natural science elevated to the status of an eternal 'Logos,' but rather through a critical theory of existing society, a theory animated at every turn by an interest in rational (or reasonable) conditions of life." Regarding the concrete agents of social reconstruction, Horkheimer placed less confidence than Marx in the proletariat's role. "Even the condition of the proletariat," he wrote (pp. 213–214, 241), "offers in the present society no guarantee of correct insight. The proletariat may indeed experience meaninglessness in the form of continuing and increasing wretchedness and injustice in its own life; yet this awareness is prevented from becoming a social force by the differentiation of social structure (promoted from above) and by the conflict between personal and class interests which is transcended only at very special moments. . . . In the general historical upheaval the truth may reside with numerically small groups of people." Concerning the waning of "humanist" leanings in the later Horkheimer (and later Adorno) see Martin Jay, "The Frankfurt School's Critique of Marxist Humanism," *Social Research*, vol. 39 (1972), pp. 285–305.

18. Lemert, *Sociology and the Twilight of Man*, pp. 20–21, 194.

19. Ibid., p. 206.

20. Jürgen Habermas, *Knowledge and Human Interests*, trans. Jeremy J. Shapiro (Boston: Beacon Press, 1971), pp. 3–5. (In this and subsequent citations the translation has been slightly altered for purposes of clarity.)

21. Ibid., pp. 7–9, 13–15, 17, 19. "Phenomenological reflection," Habermas continued (p. 19), "moves in a dimension in which transcendental categories themselves take form. It contains no absolutely fixed point; only the experience of reflection as such can be elucidated in the form of a learning process."

22. Ibid., pp. 10–11, 20–21. I cannot at this point assess the adequacy of Habermas's interpretation of Hegel. My own hunch is that Hegel's concept of identity cannot simply denote the collapse of objects into the subject—although he probably was insufficiently critical of the premise of "subjectivity." For a sensitive recent exegesis, from the perspective of the dialectic of essence and appearance, see Michael Theunissen, *Sein und Schein: Die kritische Funktion der Hegelschen Logik* (Frankfurt-Main: Suhrkamp, 1978).

23. *Knowledge and Human Interests*, pp. 24, 27–28, 30, 32.

24. Ibid., pp. 30, 34–36, 39. Fichte's mediating role was emphasized again in a later context in the discussion of "cognitive interests" and especially of reason's "interest" in the implementation of rationality. According to Habermas, Fichte explicated the linkage between theory and practice (which in Kant's philosophy remained obscure) through the notion of "intellectual intuition" embodying the act of self-production. "As developed by Fichte," he stated (p. 210), "the concept of self-reflection as self-constitutive act has systematic significance for the category of knowledge-constitutive interests."

25. Ibid., pp. 42, 53, 62–63. Regarding the role of subjectivity, Habermas attributed self-production through labor to a "social subject" and critical self-formation to "class subjects." In the latter domain, one may note, the study paid tribute to (early) insights of Hegel, especially to his discussion of the "struggle for recognition" and the dialectic of moral life (*Sittlichkeit*). In subsequent chapters, critical understanding was further subdivided into hermeneutics (guided by a "practical interest") and critique of ideology (guided by an "emancipatory interest").

26. Habermas, *Legitimation Crisis*, trans. Thomas McCarthy (Boston: Beacon Press, 1975), pp. 4–5. (In this and subsequent citations the translation has been slightly altered for purposes of clarity.) In later contexts the study points to "three dimensions" of social evolution, obtained through a subdivision of system integration into economic and political components: namely, "development of productive forces, augmentation of systemic autonomy (political power), and transformation of normative structures" (p. 5).

27. Ibid., pp. 9–10, 14–15.

28. Habermas, *Zur Rekonstruktion des Historischen Materialismus* (Frankfurt-Main: Suhrkamp, 1976), pp. 20, 68, 94–100; also Habermas, *Communication and the Evolution of Society*, trans. Thomas McCarthy (Boston: Beacon Press, 1979), pp. 74, 106.

29. *Zur Rekonstruktion des Historischen Materialismus*, pp. 162–163, 170–173; *Communication and the Evolution of Society*, pp. 147–148, 154–158.

30. Habermas, "On Systematically Distorted Communication," *Inquiry*, vol. 13 (1970), pp. 210–211.

31. Habermas, *Communication and the Evolution of Society*, pp. 42–43, 55, 57. In an earlier context, Habermas labeled expressive speech acts "self-representatives"; he also mentioned as a fourth type "communicatives," acts aiming at the elucidation of the linguistic sense of an utterance; see "Vorbereitende Bemerkungen zu einer Theorie der kommunikativen Kompetenz," in Habermas and Niklas Luhmann, *Theorie der Gesellschaft oder Sozialtechnologie — Was leistet die Systemforschung?* (Frankfurt-Main: Suhrkamp, 1971), pp. 111–114.

32. *Communication and the Evolution of Society*, pp. 1–3, 26, 44, 63–64, 66. For a more detailed review of Habermas's theory of language see my *Language and Politics: Why Does Language Matter*

to Political Philosophy? (Notre Dame: University of Notre Dame Press, 1984), pp. 123-136; and for a discussion of his more recent *Theorie des kommunikativen Handelns* see the appendix.

33. Habermas writes at one point, "Historical materialism does not need to assume a *species-subject* that undergoes evolution. The bearers of evolution are rather societies and the acting subjects integrated into them." See *Zur Rekonstruktion des Historischen Materialismus*, p. 154; *Communication and the Evolution of Society*, p. 140. Compare also "Über das Subjekt der Geschichte," in Habermas, *Kultur und Kritik: Verstreute Aufsätze* (Frankfurt-Main: Suhrkamp, 1973), pp. 389-398; Thomas McCarthy, *The Critical Theory of Jürgen Habermas* (Cambridge, MA: MIT Press, 1978), pp. 121, 127-134; also my review of McCarthy's book under the title "Between Theory and Practice," *Human Studies*, vol. 3 (1980), pp. 175-184.

34. Lemert, *Sociology and the Twilight of Man*, pp. 215, 220-222.

35. Ibid., pp. 218-220, 224-225.

36. In the earlier work, history was described as "the first and as it were the mother of all the sciences of man" and "perhaps as old as human memory." Possibly, Foucault added, "history has no place, in fact, among the human sciences, or beside them: it may well be that it maintains with them all a relation that is strange, undefined, ineffaceable, and more fundamental than any relation of adjacency in a common space would be." See *The Order of Things: An Archaeology of the Human Sciences* (New York: Random House, 1970), p. 367.

37. Michel Foucault, *The Archaeology of Knowledge*, trans. A. M. Sheridan Smith (New York: Pantheon Books, 1972), pp. 6-7.

38. Ibid., pp. 8-9, 12, 204.

39. Ibid., pp. 12-14.

40. Foucault refers with approval to Louis Althusser's thesis of an "epistemological break" between the early (ideological) and the later (scientific) Marx; ibid., p. 5, note 1.

41. Lemert, *Sociology and the Twilight of Man*, pp. 216-217, 225; Foucault, *The Archaeology of Knowledge*, pp. 227, 229 ("The Discourse on Language"). At another point, it is true, Foucault writes (p. 218), "Certainly, as a proposition, the division between true and false is neither arbitrary, nor modifiable, nor institutional, nor violent." One should also note Foucault's more recent turn to "freedom"; see pp. 94-95.

42. Martin Heidegger, *Über den Humanismus* (Frankfurt-Main: Klostermann, 1949), p. 31. See also Foucault, *The Archaeology of Knowledge*, pp. 127, 157, 168, 186, 208 (on "positivity"), 202, 205 (on "positivism"), 203 (on "transcendental narcissism"); and his *Language, Counter-Memory, Practice: Selected Essays and Interviews*, trans. Donald F. Bouchard and Sherry Simon (Oxford: Blackwell, 1977), pp. 33-38 (on "transgression"). For some post-Hegelian reflections on Hegel compare, for example, Hans-Georg Gadamer, "Das Erbe Hegels," in Gadamer and Jürgen Habermas, *Das Erbe Hegels* (Frankfurt-Main: Suhrkamp, 1979), pp. 33-64.

Chapter 6

1. The story of the progressive submergence of politics in the "social realm" during the modern era has been eloquently told by Hannah Arendt in *The Human Condition* (Garden City, NY: Anchor Books, 1959), especially pp. 23-69.

2. On the legacy of practical wisdom, seen against the background of the rise of scientific explanatory models, especially in the American context, see Bernard Crick, *The American Science*

of Politics: Its Origins and Conditions (Berkeley: University of California Press, 1964); on the Aristotelian tradition compare Wilhelm Hennis, *Politik und praktische Philosophie: Eine Studie our Rekonstruktion der politischen Wissenschaft* (Neuwied: Luchterhand, 1963).

3. David Easton, "The New Revolution in Political Science," *American Political Science Review*, vol. 63 (1969), pp. 1051, 1057.

4. David Easton, *A Framework for Political Analysis* (Englewood Cliffs, NJ: Prentice-Hall, 1965), pp. 7, 89. In a larger companion volume published at the same time, "policies" were briefly mentioned in the discussion of "outputs" and defined mainly as "associated statements" indicative of "the more general intentions of the authorities of which any specific binding output might be a partial expression"; see Easton, *A Systems Analysis of Political Life* (New York: Wiley, 1965), p. 358. Regarding the "behavioral creed," compare also Albert Somit and Joseph Tanenhaus, *The Development of Political Science, from Burgess to Behavioralism* (Boston: Allyn and Bacon, 1967), pp. 176–179.

5. Regarding the Committee on Policy and the Citizenship Clearing House see Somit and Tanenhaus, *The Development of Political Science*, pp. 97–99, 195–199. Professional service during World War II is mentioned by Robert A. Dahl as one of the factors contributing to the sway of behavioralism; compare his "The Behavioral Approach in Political Science: Epitaph for a Monument to a Successful Protest," *American Political Science Review*, vol. 55 (1961), pp. 763–772.

6. Karl W. Deutsch, *The Nerves of Government: Models of Political Communication and Control* (New York: Free Press, 1963), p. 76. As Deutsch added (pp. 77–78), "Cybernetics suggests that steering or governing is one of the most interesting and significant processes in the world, and that a study of steering in self-steering machines, in biological organisms, in human minds, and in societies will increase our understanding of problems in all these fields." Regarding structural functionalism, compare especially Gabriel Almond, "A Developmental Approach to Political Systems," *World Politics*, vol. 17 (1965), pp. 183–214.

7. See Raymond A. Bauer and Kenneth J. Gergen, eds., *The Study of Policy Formation* (New York: Free Press, 1968), p. 2; Charles E. Lindblom, *The Policy-Making Process* (Englewood Cliffs, NJ: Prentice-Hall, 1968), p. 4; Yehezkel Dror, *Public Policymaking Reexamined* (San Francisco: Chandler, 1968), p. 35. The neglect of normative questions did not mean the absence of (unexamined) normative preferences or priorities. Thus, as Dror stated with regard to industrialization processes (p. 39), "The goal of industrialization is accepted in some of the developing countries as the dominant value for policy-making; effects on traditional family structure and culture, which are regarded as more expendable, do not have to be heavily considered by the policy-makers in evaluating the industrialization policy."

8. See Thomas R. Dye, *Understanding Public Policy* (2nd ed.; Englewood Cliffs, NJ: Prentice-Hall, 1975), pp. 1–3, 7.

9. Ibid., pp. 4–6.

10. See Yehezkel Dror, "Some Features of a Meta-Model for Policy-Studies," and Robert L. Bish, "The Assumption of Knowledge in Policy Analysis," *Policy Studies Journal*, vol. 3 (Spring 1975), pp. 248–250, 256. In Dror's essay, the clarification of politicians' values was to be effected through "value analysis," that is, through "methodologies designed to structure the judgment field and to explicate value dimensions in a way that permits more conscious, comprehensive and explicit judgment by the legitimate value judges" (p. 250). According to Bish (pp. 256–257), estimation of citizens' values was relatively easy in market analysis through reliance on consumer preferences; but in the public domain "preference revelation is much less specific," with the result that "knowledge of the value of the service to citizen-consumers may never be directly revealed."

11. See Eugene J. Meehan, "What Should Political Scientists Be Doing?" in George J. Graham, Jr., and George W. Carey, eds., *The Post-Behavioral Era: Perspectives on Political Science* (New York: McKay, 1972), pp. 55-56.

12. Ibid., pp. 56-58, 60. To implement his recommendations in the empirical and normative fields, Meehan proposed the development both of an "adequate inventory of existing social conditions" and of an instrumental value or priority system (pp. 62, 65): "An agreed value system, a priority schedule for allocating resources, is also required, and a social technology would have to be developed that could translate normative standards into meaningful social conditions."

13. Ibid., pp. 58-59.

14. Ibid., pp. 61, 70.

15. Meehan, "Philosophy and Policy Studies," *Policy Studies Journal*, vol. 2 (Autumn 1973), pp. 43-44, 47. Philosophy's inadequacy was said to be manifest in both empirical and normative domains (pp. 44-45): "To be honest about it, philosophy has about as much relation to empirical inquiry as Aristotelian science has to modern physics. . . . Yet by reference to the needs of the policy-maker, what philosophers have to offer with respect to normative matters is far more pernicious and misleading than their contributions to empirical affairs."

16. Theodore J. Lowi, "The Politics of Higher Education: Political Science as a Case Study," in *The Post-Behavioral Era*, pp. 29, 32.

17. Ibid., pp. 33, 35.

18. Ibid., pp. 34-35.

19. Lowi, "Decision Making vs. Policy Making: Toward an Antidote for Technocracy," *Public Administrative Review*, vol. 30 (May-June 1970), pp. 318-319. Regarding his own contributions to policy research, most well known is probably his delineation of three main types of public policy—distributive, regulatory, and redistributive—in "American Business, Public Policy, Case Studies, and Political Theory," *World Politics*, vol. 16 (1964), pp. 677-715.

20. Duncan MacRae, Jr., *The Social Function of Social Science* (New Haven: Yale University Press, 1976), p. 5. For some of MacRae's earlier writings see "Scientific Communication, Ethical Argument and Public Policy," *American Political Science Review*, Vol. 65 (1971), pp. 38-50; "Normative Assumptions in the Study of Public Choice," *Public Choice*, vol. 16 (1973), pp. 27-41; "Justice, Normative Discourse, and Sociology," *Contemporary Sociology*, vol. 2 (1973), pp. 129-132; and "Policy Analysis as an Applied Social Science," *Administration and Society*, vol. 6 (1975), pp. 363-388. For a more detailed review of *The Social Function of Social Science* compare my "Knowledge and Commitment: Variations on a Familiar Theme," *Polity*, vol. 12 (1979), pp. 291-302.

21. MacRae, *The Social Function of Social Science*, pp. xi-xii, 52.

22. Ibid., pp. 51, 80, 87, 92-93.

23. "The social function of social science," the conclusion stated (ibid., p. 306), "is thus not simply to serve the interest of any particular class in a given period of history, nor is it to serve the interests of academics themselves. Rather, it is to provide guidance to society, through research, reasoned discourse, and education as to what interests should be served in particular circumstances and as to the means to do so."

24. John Ladd. "Policy Studies and Ethics," *Policy Studies Journal*, vol. 2 (Autumn 1973), pp. 42-43; compare also his "The Ethics of Participation," in J. Roland Pennock and John W.

Chapman, eds., *NOMOS XVI: Participation in Politics* (New York: Lieber-Atherton Press, 1975), pp. 98–125. See also Frank Fischer, *Politics, Values, and Public Policy* (Boulder, CO: Westview Press, 1980).

25. Regarding the theory of cognitive interests, compare Jürgen Habermas, *Knowledge and Human Interests*, trans. Jeremy J. Shapiro (Boston: Beacon Press, 1971); for the turn to "discourse," see "A Postscript to *Knowledge and Human Interests*," *Philosophy of the Social Sciences*, vol. 3 (1975), pp. 157–189. The broader relevance of "critical theory" for public administration is discussed in William N. Dunn and Bahman Fozouni, "Toward a Critical Administrative Theory," in *Administrative and Policy Studies Series*, Vol. 3 (Beverly Hills: Sage Publications, 1976).

26. Habermas, *Toward a Rational Society: Student Protest, Science, and Politics*, trans. Jeremy J. Shapiro (Boston: Beacon Press, 1970), pp. 52–53, 57, 60–61. As he adds (p. 61), "The substance of domination is not dissolved by the power of technical control; to the contrary, the former can simply hide behind the latter. The irrationality of domination, which today has become a collective peril to life, could be mastered only through the development of a political decision-making process tied to the principle of general discussion free from domination."

27. Habermas, "Scientization of Politics and Public Opinion" and "Technology and Science as 'Ideology' " in *Toward a Rational Society*, pp. 62–64, 66, 68, 75, 118–119.

28. Habermas, *Legitimation Crisis*, trans. Thomas McCarthy (Boston: Beacon Press, 1975), pp. 104–105, 107–108.

29. Michael Oakeshott, *On Human Conduct* (Oxford: Clarendon Press, 1975). The study has been reviewed and strongly criticized by Hanna F. Pitkin, Sheldon S. Wolin, and David Spitz in *Political Theory*, vol. 4 (1976), pp. 301–352.

30. *On Human Conduct*, pp. 59, 112, 114, 122, 160, 174.

Chapter 7

1. Richard Rorty, *Philosophy and the Mirror of Nature* (Princeton: Princeton University Press, 1979), pp. 315–316, 318.

2. Ibid., p. 320.

3. Michael Oakeshott, "The Voice of Poetry in the Conversation of Mankind," in *Rationalism in Politics, and Other Essays* (New York: Basic Books, 1962), p. 198. For Rorty's references to Oakeshott see *Philosophy and the Mirror of Nature*, pp. 318, 389.

4. See Oakeshott, "Political Education" and "The Activity of Being an Historian," in *Rationalism in Politics*, pp. 129–130, 150; Rorty, *Philosophy and the Mirror of Nature*, pp. 357, 363.

5. Hans-Georg Gadamer, *Truth and Method* (New York: Seabury Press, 1975), pp. 321, 323–325. (In these and subsequent citations I have altered the translation slightly for purposes of clarity.)

6. Ibid., pp. 331–333, 340, 349.

7. Ibid., pp. 321, 331, 341, 345. In another context Gadamer stresses as an "essential feature of the being of language" its basic "I-lessness," adding, "To that extent, speaking does not belong in the sphere of the 'I' but in that of the 'We'. . . . When one enters into dialogue with another person and then is carried along further by the dialogue, it is no longer the will of the individual person, holding itself back or exposing itself, that is determinative. Rather, the

rule of the subject matter is at issue in dialogue, eliciting statement and counterstatement and in the end playing them into each other." See Gadamer, *Philosophical Hermeneutics*, trans. and ed. David E. Linge (Berkeley: University of California Press, 1976), pp. 65–66.

8. Gadamer, *Truth and Method*, pp. 340–341, 349–351. Compare also his comments: "The consciousness of the individual is not the standard by which the being of language can be measured; indeed, there is no individual consciousness at all in which a spoken language is actually present. How then is language present? Certainly not without individual consciousness, but also not in a mere aggregation of many individuals, with each construed as a particular consciousness." See *Philosophical Hermeneutics*, p. 64.

9. As Gadamer notes with regard to artificial idioms, "Invented systems of artificial communication are never properly languages. For artificial languages, such as secret codes or mathematical symbol systems, have no basis in a community of language and life, but are introduced and applied only as means or tools of communication. This means that they always presuppose a living communication in a (natural) language; as is well known, the convention by means of which an artifical language is introduced necessarily belongs to another language." See *Truth and Method*, pp. 404–405.

10. Ibid., pp. 346, 349, 427–428. Regarding the status of poetry, Hoy remarks that "hermeneutic theory can reconcile the apparent conflict . . . between the immanence of the poetic text and the historicity of interpretation. . . . *Both* poetry and interpretation are essentially historical in character." See David C. Hoy, *The Critical Circle: Literature, History, and Philosophical Hermeneutics* (Berkeley: University of California Press, 1978), p. 99.

11. Martin Heidegger, *Sein und Zeit* (11th ed.; Tübingen: Niemeyer, 1967), par. 35, pp. 168–169. As Heidegger emphasized, the description of chatter was not meant in a "moralizing" sense; above all, genuine understanding or communication was never able to extricate itself completely from the pre-understandings or prejudgments of everyday life. *Being and Time* also spoke of the "derivative mode" of propositions or propositional assertions—a notion which reverberates in Gadamer's discussion of scientific inquiry; ibid., par. 33, p. 153.

12. Heidegger, *Unterwegs zur Sprache* (Pfullingen: Neske, 1959), pp. 31, 100, 151, 169. For an English version see Heidegger, *On the Way to Language*, trans. Peter D. Hertz (New York: Harper and Row, 1971), pp. 13, 52, 66; also *Poetry, Language, Thought*, trans. Albert Hofstadter (New York: Harper and Row, 1971), p. 208. Compare also Ernesto Grassi and Hugo Schmale, eds., *Das Gespräch als Ereignis* (Munich: Fink, 1982) and my *Language and Politics: Why Does Language Matter to Political Philosophy?* (Notre Dame: University of Notre Dame Press, 1984), especially pp. 174–192.

13. Georges Gusdorf, *Speaking (La Parole)*, trans. Paul T. Brockelman (Evanston: Northwestern University Press, 1965), p. 50.

14. Ibid., p. 54.

15. Ibid., pp. 56, 58. Compare also his comment (p. 61), "In contrast to the impersonality of dead third-person language, expression manifests the *I*. Communication is a search for the *you* and the *I* and the *you* tend to join together in the unity of *we*."

16. "For us who speak," Ricoeur wrote, "language is not an object but a mediation. Language is that through which, by means of which, we express ourselves and express things. Speaking is the act by which the speaker overcomes the closure of the universe of signs, in the intention of saying something about something to someone. . . . We actually change levels when we pass from the units of a language to the new unit constituted by the sentence or the utterance. This is no longer the unit of a language (*langue*), but of speech or discourse." See his *The Conflict of Interpretations: Essays in Hermeneutics*, ed. Don Ihde (Evanston: Northwestern University Press,

1974), pp. 84-86. Ricoeur proceeded to list as main traits of "discourse" (pp. 86-88) its character as an "act" or event, involving a "series of choices" productive of "new combinations," dealing with a subject matter or "reference," and addressed to an audience.

17. See Habermas, "Introduction: Some Difficulties in the Attempt to Link Theory and Praxis" (first German version 1971), in his *Theory and Practice*, trans. John Viertel (Boston: Beacon Press, 1973), pp. 18-19 (translation slightly altered). Habermas in this context appealed explicitly to Edmund Husserl's concept of "bracketing," denoting the disengagement of rational reflection from the experiences of the "natural attitude." With respect to hermeneutics, the turn to "discourse" further widened the distance from Gadamer's approach already implicit in the earlier stress on emancipation from tradition. Regarding the charge that hermeneutics remains inextricably tied to traditional "prejudgments," one should in fairness consider Gadamer's comment (one among many to this effect): "Hermeneutical experience also has its consequence: that of strenuous listening. A subject matter does not yield to hermeneutical experience without a special effort—an effort which basically consists in a readiness 'to be negative against oneself.' Someone who is trying to understand a text also has to bracket or distance something: namely, everything that prestructures meaning expectations in the light of personal prejudices, once it is rejected by the sense of the text itself." See *Truth and Method*, p. 422.

18. Habermas, *Legitimation Crisis*, trans. Thomas McCarthy (Boston: Beacon Press, 1975), p. 105. See also "Nachwort (1973)," in *Erkenntnis und Interesse* (Frankfurt-Main: Suhrkamp, 1973), pp. 367-417, especially p. 386; for an English version see "A Postscript to *Knowledge and Human Interests*," *Philosophy of the Social Sciences*, vol. 3 (1975), pp. 157-189. In the same year (1973), Habermas also outlined the logic of "theoretical discourses" relevant chiefly to the validation of factual propositions or cognitive truth claims; see "Wahrheitstheorien," in *Wirklichkeit und Reflexion: Walter Schulz zum 60. Geburtstag* (Pfullingen: Neske, 1973), pp. 211-265.

19. As he pointed out, the ideal speech situation implies "a number of symmetrical relations": "Pure intersubjectivity is determined by a symmetrical relation between I and You (We and You), I and He (We and They)," that is, by a "complete symmetry in the distribution of assertion and dispute, revelation and concealment, prescription and conformity, among the partners of communication." See Habermas, "Towards a Theory of Communicative Competence," *Inquiry*, vol. 13 (1970), p. 371; also "What Is Universal Pragmatics?" in his *Communication and the Evolution of Society*, trans. Thomas McCarthy (Boston: Beacon Press, 1979), pp. 1-68.

20. Michel Foucault, "The Discourse on Language," in his *The Archaeology of Knowledge* (New York: Random House, 1972), pp. 216-218, 221, 223, 226-227.

21. Ibid., pp. 219, 227. The address appeared first under the title *L'ordre du discours* (Paris: Gallimard, 1971). Compare also Mark Poster, ed., "Foucault and Critical Theory: The Uses of Discourse Analysis," *Humanities in Society*, vol. 5, Nos. 3 and 4 (Summer and Fall 1982), pp. 173-295.

22. See Gusdorf, *Speaking (La Parole)*, p. 99; Ricoeur, *The Rule of Metaphor: Multi-Disciplinary Studies of the Creation of Meaning in Language*, trans. Robert Czerny (Toronto: University of Toronto Press, 1977), pp. 257-258, 280. For a more elaborate classification of modes or "regions" of discourse, inspired in part by Ricoeur's phenomenology, compare Bernard P. Dauenhauer, *Silence: The Phenomenon and Its Ontological Significance* (Bloomington: Indiana University Press, 1980), pp. 26-53.

23. Rorty, *Philosophy and the Mirror of Nature*, pp. 367-368, 372-373, 384.

24. Ibid., pp. 353, 360, 378-379. The notion of an ordinary hermeneutics is expressly acknowledged by Rorty when he writes (pp. 320-321) that "hermeneutics is the study of an abnormal discourse from the point of view of some normal discourse—the attempt to make some sense of what is going on at a stage where we are still too unsure about it to describe

it, and thereby to begin an epistemological account of it. The fact that hermeneutics inevitably takes some norm for granted makes it, so far forth, 'Whiggish.' But insofar as it proceeds nonreductively and in the hope of picking up a new angle on things, it can transcend its own Whiggishness."

25. Ibid., pp. 365-366.

26. Oakeshott, "The Voice of Poetry in the Conversation of Mankind," in *Rationalism in Politics*, pp. 197, 200-202. Philosophy is not treated as a distinct voice in this essay, but only as a kind of "kibitzing" behavior (p. 200): "Philosophy, the impulse to study the quality and style of each voice, and to reflect upon the relationship of one voice to another, must be counted a parasitic activity; it springs from the conversation, because this is what the philosopher reflects upon, but it makes no specific contribution to it."

27. "The self appears as activity," Oakeshott writes. "It is not a 'thing' or a 'substance' capable of being active; it is activity. And this activity is primordial; there is nothing antecedent to it. . . . The self is constituted in the activity of making and moving among images." Ibid., pp. 204-205. In this respect his account seems to occupy a position somewhere between Gadamer's ontological and Gusdorf's egological stance.

28. Ibid., pp. 206-210.

29. Ibid., pp. 211-212. While these comments place the practical idiom on the level of Gusdorf's "pragmatic language," the moral endeavor to achieve mutual recognition would seem to require a move toward genuine conversation.

30. Ibid., pp. 213-216.

31. Ibid., pp. 217, 223-224. Oakeshott is careful to differentiate his use of "contemplation" from both epistemological reflection and the metaphysical contemplation of "essences" (deriving from Plato). "For many centuries in the intellectual history of Europe," he notes (pp. 219-220), "contemplation, understood as a purely receptive experience of real entities, occupied the highest place in the hierarchy of human experiences, scientific inquiry being recognized as, at best, preparatory to it, and practical engagements as mere distractions. In recent times, however, not only has it been demoted from this position of supremacy (by a philistine concern with useful knowledge), but it has been called in question by the re-emergence of an understanding of activity which has no place for it. . . . Contemplation, as I understand it, is activity and it is image-making."

32. Ibid., pp. 221, 224, 234-236. Due to the stress on the "contemplative self" and its delight in making and viewing images, Oakeshott's account sometimes is in danger of lapsing into a romantic aestheticism or "aesthetic consciousness" which Gadamer takes pains to overcome; see *Truth and Method*, pp. 73-90.

33. *Truth and Method*, p. 324.

34. Gusdorf, *Speaking (La Parole)*, p. 74.

35. Using Max Weber's terminology, one might say that everyday talk is governed by habit and tradition, and discourse by instrumental and substantive rationality ("instrumental-rational" and "value-rational" standards). For a distinction between "discourse" and "dialogue" or conversation in terms of formal constraints see Eric Gans, *The Origin of Language: A Formal Theory of Representation* (Berkeley: University of California Press, 1981), pp. 197-273.

36. See *Truth and Method*, pp. 325-326; also Gadamer, "Was ist Wahrheit?" in his *Kleine Schriften I: Philosophie, Hermeneutik* (Tübingen: Mohr, 1967), pp. 46-58. In treating the historical tradition

as a purely alien "archaeology," incidentally, Foucault also escapes its continuing effects or claims, thus exemplifying Gadamer's "historical consciousness." Compare also Stephen Toulmin, *The Uses of Argument* (Cambridge: Cambridge University Press, 1964); Paul W. Taylor, *Normative Discourse* (Englewood Cliffs, NJ: Prentice-Hall, 1961); Kurt Baier, *The Moral Point of View* (Ithaca: Cornell University Press, 1958); and Paul Edwards, *The Logic of Moral Discourse* (New York: Free Press, 1955).

37. Gusdorf, *Speaking (La Parole)*, p. 62; Oakeshott, "The Voice of Poetry in the Conversation of Mankind," in *Rationalism in Politics*, pp. 243–247. For a critique of the conception of poetry as "expression" see *Rationalism in Politics*, pp. 228, 230–232. To be sure, the inclusion of the search for truth would require a reconsideration of the status of "philosophy" and the acceptance of a kind of poetic thinking, beyond a mere "kibitzing" function.

38. See Habermas, *Theory and Practice*, p. 25; Rorty, *Philosophy and the Mirror of Nature*, pp. 315, 318; Oakeshott, "Political Education" and "The Voice of Poetry in the Conversation of Mankind," in *Rationalism in Politics*, pp. 125, 129, 241. Rorty's reference is to Oakeshott, *On Human Conduct* (Oxford: Clarendon Press, 1975). In Gusdorf's case, the preference is for "authentic communication" as a means of self-disclosure and as manifestation of the "will to achieve a state of peace among men" beyond "misunderstandings and violence"; see *Speaking (La Parole)*, p. 91.

39. George J. Graham, Jr., "Ethics and Public Policy," *News for Teachers of Political Science*, No. 29 (Spring 1981), pp. 1, 8–9. Compare also his "The Role of the Humanities in Public Policy Evaluation," *Soundings*, vol. 64 (1981), pp. 150–169.

40. "The principle of 'publicity'," Habermas notes, "which initially—in the hands of cultivated, enlightened, art-loving individuals and through the medium of the bourgeois press—had played a clearly critical role vis-à-vis the secrecy of absolutism and been implanted in the procedures of constitutional government, now tends to be remolded for demonstrative and manipulative ends. Despite its technical potential for emancipation, the ever more densely strung network of electronic mass media today is organized in such a manner that it controls the loyalty of a depoliticized population, rather than serving to make social and political controls in turn subject to a decentralized, effectively structured and uninhibited discursive formation of will and judgment." See *Theory and Practice*, p. 4. With regard to American politics Graham writes, "Most Americans are politically inactive, thus indicating low political interest. The statistics on level of political interest and information possessed by the public give one pause in confronting the task of introducing the contributions of the humanities" (for example, ethical considerations) in this domain; see "Ethics and Public Policy," p. 8.

41. Habermas distinguishes three main aspects or functions of parties and organized groups: theoretical analysis of the overall social situation; internal education or enlightenment of group members; and finally, strategic-pragmatic pursuit of group goals. See *Theory and Practice*, pp. 27, 32–33.

42. In Habermas's words, "To oversimplify somewhat: After the bold fiction of the dependence of all politically significant decision-making processes on legally guaranteed, discursive deliberations among the citizenry was shattered in the nineteenth century by restrictive conditions of the mode of production, a polarization of forces has resulted." See *Theory and Practice*, p. 26.

43. See Duncan MacRae, Jr., *The Social Function of Social Science* (New Haven: Yale University Press, 1976). For a primary emphasis on Toulmin's work compare William Dunn, *Public Policy Analysis: An Introduction* (Englewood Cliffs, NJ: Prentice-Hall, 1981); and for an approach combining insights gleaned from Toulmin, Habermas, and Paul Taylor, Frank Fischer, *Politics, Values, and Public Policy: The Problem of Methodology* (Boulder, CO: Westview Press, 1980).

44. Drawing on Charles Péguy's terminology, Maurice Merleau-Ponty distinguished between a "historical *period*, in which political man is content to administer a regime or an established

284

Notes to Pages 222-227

law," and an "*epoch*, or one of those moments where the traditional ground of a nation or society crumbles and where, for better or worse, man himself must reconstruct human relations"; see *Humanism and Terror, An Essay on the Communist Problem*, trans. John O'Neil (Boston: Beacon Press, 1969), p. xvii. Rorty at one juncture comes close to making the same distinction; see his *Philosophy and the Mirror of Nature*, p. 322.

45. As Graham writes, "Though Supreme Court decisions have long been studied as central to the history of American thought, we have only recently become fully aware of the significance of how non-constitutional political conversation affects judicial decisions. *Amicus curiae* briefs, for example, introduce ethical arguments and sociological facts that go beyond considerations of the issues raised by the adversaries in a case." See "Ethics and Public Policy," p. 8. For Oakeshott's comments see "The Voice of Poetry in the Conversation of Mankind," in *Rationalism in Politics*, p. 202, note 1; his observations are akin to the conception of "natality" and of the linkage of action and speech developed by Hannah Arendt, *The Human Condition* (Chicago: University of Chicago Press, 1958).

46. Aristotle, *Nicomachean Ethics*, Book VIII, chapter 3; Oakeshott, "The Voice of Poetry in the Conversation of Mankind," in *Rationalism in Politics*, pp. 243-244.

Appendix

1. Jürgen Habermas, *Theorie des kommunikativen Handelns*, 2 vols. (Frankfurt-Main: Suhrkamp, 1981); hereafter cited as *Theorie*. The English translation of the first volume has appeared under the title *The Theory of Communicative Action*, vol. 1: *Reason and the Rationalization of Society*, trans. Thomas McCarthy (Boston: Beacon Press, 1984), hereafter cited as *Reason*. The present essay was written prior to the publication of the English volume; I have compared my translation with McCarthy's, but have not always adapted mine to his.

2. *Theorie*, vol. 1, pp. 367-452, vol. 2, pp. 171-293. In his translation McCarthy renders *Zwischenbetrachtungen* as "intermediate reflections"; see *Reason*, p. 273.

3. Habermas, *Knowledge and Human Interests*, trans. Jeremy J. Shapiro (Boston: Beacon Press, 1971), p. 137 (translation slightly altered).

4. Habermas, "Nachwort (1973)" to *Erkenntnis und Interesse* (Frankfurt-Main: Suhrkamp, 1973), p. 397; for an English version see "A Postscript to *Knowledge and Human Interests*," *Philosophy of the Social Sciences*, vol. 3 (1975), p. 181. Compare also the sections on "knowledge and interest" and "action and discourse" in the "Introduction" (1971) to *Theory and Practice*, trans. John Viertel (Boston: Beacon Press, 1973), pp. 7-10, 16-19. The distinction between life-praxis and discourses (or between the "a priori of experience" and the "a priori of argumentation") was further fleshed out in Habermas, "Wahrheitstheorien," in Helmut Fahrenbach, ed.. *Wirklichkeit und Reflexion: Walter Schulz zum 60. Geburtstag* (Pfullingen: Neske, 1973), pp. 211-265.

5. Compare, for example, Habermas, "Towards a Theory of Communicative Competence," *Inquiry*, vol. 13 (1970), pp. 360-375; also the essays "What Is Universal Pragmatics?" and "Moral Development and Ego Identity," in Habermas, *Communication and the Evolution of Society*, trans. Thomas McCarthy (Boston: Beacon Press, 1979), pp. 1-68, 69-94.

6. *Theorie*, vol. 1, pp. 28, 30; *Reason*, pp. 10-11. I prefer to translate *Verständigung* as "consensus" (or consensual interaction) rather than "understanding," since the latter can be unilateral, whereas *Verständigung* is always reciprocal.

7. *Theorie*, vol. 1, pp. 37, 44; *Reason*, pp. 17, 22. As a fourth arena of communication amenable to discursive validation (by means of "explicative discourse") the study mentions linguistic

"comprehensibility" or the correctness of symbolic expressions. Reformulating the same basic perspective, a later passage states (*Theorie*, vol. 1, p. 114; *Reason*, p. 75), "The concept of communicative rationality refers, on the one hand, to different forms of the discursive redemption of validity claims (in this sense Wellmer speaks of 'discursive rationality'); on the other hand, it points to different 'world' relations into which communicative agents enter by raising validity claims for their utterances."

8. *Theorie*, vol. 1, pp. 126-127, 129-130; *Reason*, pp. 85, 87-88.

9. *Theorie*, vol. 1, pp. 127-128, 132, 137, 140; *Reason*, pp. 85-86, 88-91, 93. The "dramaturgical' approach has been articulated chiefly by Goffman and some spokesmen of phenomenological interactionism.

10. *Theorie*, vol. 1, pp. 128, 141-143, 147-148;*Reason*, pp. 86, 94-96, 98-99.

11. *Theorie*, vol. 1, pp. 385-387, 389-390, 396; *Reason*, pp. 285-287, 289-290, 295. The distinction is further elaborated in these terms (*Theorie*, vol. 1, p. 394; *Reason*, p. 293): "Perlocutionary effects, like the results of teleological actions in general, can be described as mundane states of affairs produced by intervention in the world. By contrast, illocutionary effects are reached on the level of interpersonal relations in which participants achieve a consensus about something in the world; these effects are thus not '*innerworldly*' but extra-mundane."

12. *Theorie*, vol. 1, pp. 398-401, 406, 410, 412-414; *Reason*, pp. 296-298, 305, 307-309. Habermas rounds out his scheme of speech acts (*Theorie*, vol. 1, p. 436; *Reason*, p. 326) by adding "communicative acts" (dealing with the organization of discourse) and "operative acts" (reflecting the internal logic or syntax of speech). Introducing the new category of "conversation," he also links speech acts with corresponding action types (*Theorie*, vol. 1, pp. 437-439; *Reason*, pp. 327-329): namely, constatives with conversation, regulatives with norm-regulated action, expressives with dramaturgical action, and perlocutionary acts with teleological-strategic action.

13. *Theorie*, vol. 1, pp. 449, 451; *Reason*, pp. 335-336. Habermas also depicts the life-world as "a continent that remains hidden so long as the theorist analyzes speech acts from the perspective of the speaker who, in his utterance, places himself in relation to something in the objective, social and subjective world" (*Theorie*, vol. 1, p. 452; *Reason*, p. 337).

14. Habermas, *Legitimation Crisis*, trans. Thomas McCarthy (Boston: Beacon Press, 1975), pp. 4-5.

15. *Theorie*, vol. 1, pp. 32, 106-108; *Reason*, pp. 13, 69-71. For the distinction between "world" and "life-world" compare also pp. 123-124 (*Reason*, p. 82), where Habermas places the accent on the different attitude—non-reflective versus reflective—which members assume toward the cultural tradition: "In the *one* case the shared cultural tradition of a community is constitutive for the life-world which members encounter as a pre-interpreted context; the shared life-world forms here the background for communicative action.... In the *other* case particular ingredients of the cultural tradition are specifically thematized; now members must adopt a reflective attitude toward cultural meaning patterns which otherwise render possible their efforts of interpretation."

16. *Theorie*, vol. 2, pp. 179, 187-189, 192.

17. *Theorie*, vol. 2, pp. 208-209, 218. In this context (pp. 210-212) Habermas chides Schutz, Durkheim, and Mead for a one-sided focus on *one* component of the life-world: Schutz on culture, Durkheim on society, and Mead on socialization.

18. *Theorie*, vol. 2, pp. 226-228, 273, 293.

19. *Knowledge and Human Interests*, pp. 137, 167; "Technology and Science as 'Ideology'," in Habermas, *Toward a Rational Society*, trans. Jeremy J. Shapiro (Boston: Beacon Press, 1970), p. 91.

20. *Theorie*, vol. 1, pp. 28, 32, 386-387; vol. 2, pp. 193-194; *Reason*, pp. 10, 13, 287. Compare also the comment (*Theorie*, vol. 1, p. 410; *Reason*, p. 305), "As communicative action we describe all those interactions in which participants coordinate their individual action plans without reservations on the basis of a communicatively achieved consensus. . . . Communicative action embraces only those speech acts with which a speaker raises reviewable validity claims." What these and similar statements leave open is whether achieved consensus yields a common or joint action plan or only the pursuit of divergent goals on the basis of a reciprocal acknowledgment of differences.

21. *Theorie*, vol. 1, pp. 141, 143, 148, 370; vol. 2, pp. 190-192; *Reason*, pp. 94, 99, 274. Even when presenting language as precondition of interaction Habermas oscillates between an "ontological" and a "transcendental" construal (where the latter specifies a foundational or a priori "condition of possibility"). Thus, after noting the "non-surpassable" character of language and the life-world, he adds (*Theorie*, vol. 2, p. 192), "The structures of the life-world determine the forms of possible intersubjective consensus. . . . The life-world is, so to speak, the transcendental plane on which speaker and hearer encounter each other."

22. Anthony Giddens, "Labour and Interaction," in his *Profiles and Critiques in Social Theory* (London: Macmillan, 1982), p. 108.

23. *Theorie*, vol. 1, pp. 371, 390, 394, 396; *Reason*, pp. 274, 290, 293, 295.

24. *Theorie*, vol. 1, pp. 150-151; vol. 2, pp. 193-194; *Reason*, p. 101.

25. *Knowledge and Human Interests*, pp. 167-168, 172; "Nachwort (1973)" to *Erkenntnis und Interesse*, pp. 386, 397. Habermas acknowledged only an indirect linkage between discourses and life-praxis: argumentation or the praxis of inquiry could proceed only within the boundaries of a given experiential domain. Compare also *Theory and Practice*, p. 18.

26. Agnes Heller, "Habermas and Marxism," in John B. Thompson and David Held, eds., *Habermas: Critical Debates* (Cambridge, MA: MIT Press, 1982), pp. 25, 29; *Theorie*, vol. 1, pp. 400-401; *Reason*, pp. 297-298. For an argument that Habermas's general framework tends to resolve the theory-practice issue in favor of theory see my "Between Theory and Practice," *Human Studies*, vol. 3 (1980), pp. 175-184.

27. Karl-Otto Apel, *Transformation der Philosophie* (Frankfurt-Main: Suhrkamp, 1973), vol. 1, pp. 38-39; Habermas, *Legitimation Crisis*, pp. 4-5; *Theorie*, vol. 2, pp. 179, 187-188, 200. In a more critical fashion Alexandre Métraux pointed to a certain half-heartedness in the phenomenological approach: "Although taking as its point of departure quite correctly the 'world of the natural attitude', Husserl's account continues to be permeated by a dualist conception of the relationship between subject and world which finds no warrant in everyday experience." See his preface to Aron Gurwitsch, *Die mitmenschlichen Begegnungen in der Milieuwelt* (Berlin and New York: de Gruyter, 1977), p. xx. For a defense of the "strong view" of the life-world, against Habermas's own half-heartedness, see Ulf Matthiesen, *Das Dickicht der Lebenswelt und die Theorie des kommunikativen Handelns* (Munich: Fink, 1983); also Dieter Misgeld, "Communication and Societal Rationalization: A Review Essay of Jürgen Habermas's *Theorie des kommunikativen Handelns*," *Canadian Journal of Sociology*, vol. 8 (1983), pp. 433-453, especially pp. 438-439.

28. *Theorie*, vol. 2, pp. 192, 210-212, 223, 229, 561, 589.

29. For a general critique of Habermas's view of social development see my *Twilight of Subjectivity: Contributions to a Post-Individualist Theory of Politics* (Amherst: University of Massachusetts Press,

1981), pp. 179–207; also Michael Schmid, "Habermas's Theory of Social Evolution," in *Habermas: Critical Debates*, pp. 162–180.

30. *Theorie*, vol. 2, pp. 233–234, 237–238, 244. The dilemma carries over into sociological and anthropological methodology. Though admitting the problem, Habermas fails to draw broader theoretical conclusions from it. Due to the coincidence of archaic society with the "socio-cultural life-world," he claims (pp. 245–246), anthropology has tended to be a "hermeneutical science *par excellence*." Simultaneously recognizes, however, that the overlapping of systemic and social integration renders social processes at that stage "not only transparent but also in many ways opaque." The latter aspect, in his view, accounts for the incursion of depth psychology and linguistic structuralism into anthropology.

31. *Theorie*, vol. 1, pp. 104, 112; vol. 2, pp. 588–589; *Reason*, pp. 68, 72. Habermas's oscillation in these matters recurs also in his discussion of "world-views" and of the meaning-context issue. "Through their holistic character," he writes (*Theorie*, vol. 1, pp. 92–93; *Reason*, p. 58), "world-views, it is true, are removed from the domain in which truth criteria can meaningfully be applied; even the choice of criteria determining the truth status of utterances may depend on the fundamental context of a world-view. This does not mean, however, that the idea of truth itself should be construed in a particularist sense: whichever language system we choose, we always rely intuitively on the premise that truth is a universal validity claim." Appealing to Searle's speech-act theory, Habermas notes at another point (*Theorie*, vol. 1, p. 450; *Reason*, pp. 335–336), "Once we begin to alter relatively deep-seated and trivial background conditions, we notice that apparently context-invariant validity conditions change their meaning and thus are by no means absolute." To which he adds, "Actually the knowledge of the validity conditions of a speech act must not depend *completely* on contingent background assumptions—for otherwise formal pragmatics would lose its subject matter." To use Giddens's phrase, these instances are good examples of "wanting to have one's cake and eat it too." See *Profiles and Critiques in Social Theory*, p. 108.

32. *Theorie*, vol. 2, pp. 165, 178–179, 488, 536, 541. As in the case of other key issues, Habermas is profoundly ambivalent regarding the formalization and "juridification" of ethics. In modern societies, he notes (vol. 2, p. 166), traditional life-forms "have lost their totalizing and exclusive sway, having been subordinated to the universalism of law and ethics; but as concrete life-forms they obey a standard other than universalization." Concerning juridification the study (vol. 2, pp. 541–542) finds the central ailment of contemporary welfare society in the use of the law as a functional "medium" rather than an "institution" adapted to life-world processes (a diagnosis of disarming simplicity).

33. *Theorie*, vol. 1, pp. 106–107; vol. 2, pp. 15–30, 65–68, 147–163 (on Mead), 192, 197–198; *Reason*, pp. 69–70. Compare Habermas's somewhat bland observation (*Theorie*, vol. 2, p. 279): "After the paradigm change brought about by the theory of communication the formal properties of possible intersubjective consensus can take the place of the (Kantian) conditions of possibility of objective experience." The restatement of Mead's approach is problematical not only because of implicit idealist or quasi-idealist premises but because, in Habermas's own account, the process of rationalization is liable to render increasingly tenuous the self-society correlation (or the mediation between personal identity and social solidarity). In his introduction McCarthy is more sanguine on this issue (*Reason*, pp. xx–xxi)—an assessment I cannot fully share. For a detailed discussion of intersubjectivity, especially in the context of phenomenological literature, see my *Twilight of Subjectivity*, pp. 38–115; also Michael Theunissen, *The Other: Studies in the Social Ontology of Husserl, Heidegger, Sartre, and Buber* (Cambridge, MA: MIT Press, 1984).

34. *Theorie*, vol. 1, pp. 75, 80–81, 83, 100, 376, 386, 415; *Reason*, pp. 45, 49, 51, 64, 278, 286, 309. Indebtedness to the "philosophy of consciousness" is equally clear in the portrayal of art as subjective "expression"—a portrayal which ignores both Heidegger's and Gadamer's arguments to the contrary; see Hans-Georg Gadamer, *Truth and Method* (New York: Seabury Press, 1975), pp. 39–90, and Heidegger, "The Origin of the Work of Art," in *Poetry, Language, Thought*, trans. Albert Hofstadter (New York: Harper and Row, 1971), pp. 17–87.

35. A pioneering venture, of course, was Heidegger's notion of "being-in-the-world" as developed in *Being and Time* (of 1927), trans. John Macquarrie and Edward Robinson (London: SCM Press, 1962). Compare also Heidegger, "The Age of the World View," trans. Marjorie Grene, in W. V. Spanos, ed., *Martin Heidegger and the Question of Literature* (Bloomington: Indiana University Press, 1979), pp. 1-15; Jacques Derrida, "Signature Event Context," *Glyph*, vol. 1 (Baltimore: Johns Hopkins University Press, 1977), pp. 182-197. *Theory of Communicative Action* repeatedly singles out Heidegger and post-structuralist writers as "bêtes noirs" for their critique of rationalization; e.g., vol. 2, pp. 165, 222.

36. As Habermas asserts in the opening section (*Theorie*, vol. 1, pp. 18, 20; *Reason*, pp. 3, 5), among the social sciences, and especially in contrast with political science and political economy, "it is sociology which in its conceptual structure is closest to the problematic of rationality. . . . Alone among social-scientific disciplines sociology has maintained attention to the questions of society as a whole." Compare also *Theory and Practice*, pp. 47-48.

37. *Theorie*, vol. 2, pp. 219, 221. In this and other passages Habermas uncritically accepts the positivist thesis of enlightenment leading from theology over metaphysics to positive science— an endorsement warranting the charge of the incipient positivism of his framework. See, for example, Giddens, *Profiles and Critiques in Social Theory*, p. 97.

38. Heller, "Habermas and Marxism," in *Habermas: Critical Debates*, pp. 27, 31. Compare also her comments (pp. 23, 36), "Marx's theory had one advantage, as well as a certain grandeur which disappears in Habermas's interpretation: Marx grasped human progress as suffering. He conceives of the fate of the individual human being together with the development of production and of institutions. . . . Even in a world of organized discourse, our main needs will be those we once attributed to God: creation and love."

39. Martin Heidegger, *Hölderlins Hymne "Andenken"* (*Gesamtausgabe*, vol. 52), ed. Curd Ochwadt (Frankfurt-Main: Klostermann, 1982), pp. 157, 161, 165. For a detailed elaboration of the concept "world" in its various meanings see Heidegger, *Die Grundbegriffe der Metaphysik: Welt-Endlichkeit-Einsamkeit* (*Gesamtausgabe*, vol. 29/30), ed. F.-W. von Herrmann (Frankfurt-Main: Klostermann, 1983).

Index

291

Index